Introduction to Information Processing

Second Edition

Introduction to Information Processing

Second Edition

Donald D. Spencer

Educational Consultant

CHARLES E. MERRILL PUBLISHING COMPANY
A Bell & Howell Company
Columbus   Toronto   London   Sydney

Published by
Charles E. Merrill Publishing Company
A Bell & Howell Company
Columbus, Ohio 43216

This book was set in Times Roman.

The production editors were Michael Robbins and Sharon Thomason.

The cover was prepared by Will Chenoweth.

Photo by Larry Hamill.

Library of Congress Catalog Card Number: 76-47185
International Standard Book Number: 0-675-08520-9
Printed in the United States of America
6 7 8 9 10/80 79 78

Preface

This book is designed to be used as a text in introductory data processing and/or computer science courses at the college level. It provides a comprehensive view of the components of a modern information processing system and the part each element plays in the processing of data. Since the emphasis is on business, the techniques and examples in each chapter are related to business operations and procedures.

To use the book, however, no prior knowledge of business methods or data processing is required. A basic knowledge of arithmetic is sufficient for understanding the information offered in this introductory text.

The book's approach avoids exhaustive treatment of subject matter and, instead, discusses the salient points of each topic in a brief and easy-to-understand manner. The material presented is broad enough to satisfy the reader planning to specialize in the information processing field, as well as the reader who wants only an introduction to basic concepts.

This revised edition preserves the same basic concepts of its predecessor, with the addition of new developments in the field. The chapter on Boolean Algebra has been deleted from this edition. Many chapters have been condensed or expanded to reflect the current trend in information processing. Twelve new chapters have been added to this edition.

The book is divided into nine parts. Each chapter is self-contained to provide flexibility in the selection of topics to be discussed.

Part One discusses different methods of data processing, especially electronic data processing, and some typical uses of computer systems in medicine, education, government, law enforcement, engineering, transportation, and business. A historical survey of calculating machines is presented to acquaint the student with many of the early devices used to perform data processing functions so that the student can better appreciate the modern digital computer by having some knowledge of how it evolved.

Part Two introduces the punched card and the unit record machines used to process data in punched card systems. Although newer computers, such as the IBM System/360 Model 20, IBM System/3, and IBM System/32 have replaced most of the electromechanical data processing systems technologically, there are still many thousands of businesses which use unit record equipment. Because of their importance in such systems, one chapter is devoted to discussing card handling equipment such as the keypunch, sorter, and accounting machine.

A student new to information processing concepts should have some familiarity with how data is processed by a computer. Part Three introduces the reader to number systems (binary, octal, and hexadecimal) and computer arithmetic. One chapter explains just how data is represented on media suitable for entry into an information processing system. The *metric system* of weights and measures became the law of the land with President Ford's signing of the Metric Conversion Act of 1975. Soon, all Americans will have to use the metric system. Chapter 5 discusses the effect the metric changeover will have on information processing. All examples in this book use both the metric and English units.

Part Four deals with the functional units that comprise an information processing system. The central processing unit is described in some detail, along with its role as the control element of any information processing system. Devices used to input data to computers and accept data from computers are described at the functional level. New devices such as intelligent terminals and point-of-sale terminals are covered. A variety of internal and auxiliary computer storage devices and concepts are also presented. The last chapter in this part provides the vital statistics about several modern computer systems commonly used to solve business problems—IBM System/370, IBM System/360, IBM System/32, IBM System/3, Univac 1100, Univac 9700, NCR Century 200, and others. Minicomputers, including the IBM 5100, microcomputers, and their relation to solving business problems are also discussed.

Part Five is concerned with computer programming fundamentals. The reader is introduced to the steps used in solving problems with a computer. One chapter is devoted to flowcharting business problems for computer solution. Chapter 13 introduces the reader to programming languages: machine language, assembly language, and higher-level programming languages. The discussion on languages covers the important aspects of languages as well as how to choose a language for a specific application.

Part Six includes detailed discussions of the most popular higher-level programming languages: BASIC, FORTRAN, COBOL, PL/I, RPG, and APL. After reading any of these chapters, the student will understand the capabilities and features of the language.

Information processing systems of the 1970s and 1980s will involve using complex networks of equipment and sophisticated software systems. Discussed in Part Seven are the concepts of time-sharing systems, real-time systems, teleprocessing networks, multiprocessing systems, multiprogramming systems, batch processing systems, operating systems, and structured programming. Several business examples and the concept of system flowcharting are presented in one chapter.

Part Eight covers the management aspects of information processing. Information processing center management and the problems management faces when using information processing systems are explained.

In Part Nine, the effect of computers on society is covered. Also presented is a discussion of what might happen in the information processing field during the next two decades.

For ease in study, all chapters have a summary and a list of key terms. Review questions are included throughout the book to help the reader identify the important concepts in each chapter.

This edition includes a Student Manual. The objectives and the basic format of the Manual will remain similar. The Instructor's Manual includes behavioral objectives for each chapter, teaching suggestions, answers to questions and problems contained in the Student's Manual, and a collection of viewgraph masters coordinated with material in the text.

Although designed as a textbook, this book can be used equally well for self-study by interested readers. All terms used in the book, plus many others, are included in a comprehensive glossary.

New features to this edition are:

1. A new chapter on information processing and the metric system. The metric system of measurement is used throughout the text, supplemented with English units.

2. The inclusion of new input-output units, such as intelligent terminals and point-of-sale terminals.

3. The inclusion of new memory devices and concepts, such as floppy disks and virtual memory.

4. The latest computer systems, including the IBM System/32 and IBM 5100 Portable computer. Minicomputers and microcomputers are discussed. Minicomputer business systems are introduced.

5. The inclusion of the important aspects of comparing programming languages with one another and how to choose a programming language.

6. Separate chapters are included on the following higher-level programming languages: BASIC, FORTRAN, COBOL, PL/I, RPG, and APL. Business applications are emphasized in each chapter.

7. A new chapter on systems design and functions of the systems analyst.

8. A new chapter on how the computer has affected and is affecting the management of a company.

9. A new chapter on organization and management of the information processing center.

10. A new chapter on the effect of the computer on modern society.

11. A new chapter on hardware and software trends and a look at what the computer might be doing for society in the year 2001.

12. The inclusion of new terms in the glossary.

13. An expanded description of the operating system and computer output micro-film (COM).

The pedagogical goal throughout the book is to keep the material as understandable as possible. The reader will find many cartoons, illustrations, photographs, and practical problems. Hopefully, these will help make the subject matter interesting and alive. Toward these goals, then, I welcome the student to a world of reward and accomplishment in his or her encounter with this wonderful tool—the computer.

I wish to thank Infosystems (Hitchock Publishing Company) for allowing me to reproduce several of the cartoons in the book. Most of the cartoons, however, were drawn by Don Robison, who has helped immensely in making this a more pleasing book. I wish to thank the many computer manufacturers, computer users, and schools who supplied me with the numerous photographs that make the text more meaningful. Finally, a deep appreciation of thanks is due my wife Rae for her typing skill in the preparation of the manuscript.

Ormond Beach, Florida   *Donald D. Spencer*
1976

Contents

six   **Programming Languages**   **349**

☐ 14   **BASIC**   350

☐ 15   **FORTRAN**   376

Introduction to Information Processing

Second Edition

to my mother

one

Functions
and
History

1

Data Processing Functions

Courtesy of American Telephone and Telegraph Company

Computers are having a profound effect on today's society. Our lives are being influenced by these machines and are, in many ways, dependent upon them. Since the development of the electronic computer in 1946, the computer has risen from a military research device to a modern day "human helper." The computer exercises such an important and widespread influence on our society that it is essential that every well-educated person know something about the potential benefits and dangers of its use.

☐ What Does the Computer Do?

Here are only a few ways computers are being put to work. There are several thousand different applications for computers, and new applications are being developed almost every day.

In Airline Transportation

Airline traffic is one of the fastest growing segments of modern transportation. To meet the increasing demand for efficient passenger reservations systems, aircraft flight scheduling, supply and spare parts inventory control, crew scheduling, airline administration, freight control, and countless other tasks, the airlines have turned to the computer. Only with the computer can airlines keep up with rapidly changing day-to-day operations.

An airline's most important commodity is its passenger seat. An unsold seat is a complete loss, for it can never be recouped. With a computerized reservation system, the airline can provide for optimal use of seats up to the moment of a plane's departure. Using a computer-controlled reservation system enables the airline agents to "talk" directly with a central computer system. Each agent is equipped with a desk-size console (see Figure 1–1) that includes buttons, a keyboard, and a display screen. Able to communicate instantaneously with the central computer system, the agent, in seconds, may reserve flight space or complete any particular action requested by the customer.

In addition to handling passenger seat reservations, computer systems process information on flight scheduling, cargo loading, meal planning,

(Courtesy of Sanders Associates, Inc.)

Figure
1–1
An agent at an airline reservation counter enters and receives information on flight availability through a computer display terminal. Such a unit allows the agent to be in continuous direct contact with a central computer system which maintains flight schedules, passenger lists, and other passenger information.

crew availability, aircraft maintenance scheduling, and many other tasks of an experimental nature. One experimental automatic ticket vendor system is being developed by American Airlines at Chicago's O'Hare International Airport. This system allows a person to obtain airline tickets in less than a minute. Figure 1–2 illustrates a passenger retrieving her special magnetically encoded credit card and taking her ticket after indicating that she wants first-class accommodations round-trip, Chicago–Los Angeles, on the next available American flight. This passenger-operated Ticket Vendor machine is linked to an IBM System/360 computer which confirms the reservation, checks credit, and verifies that the card has not been reported lost or stolen.

In Law Enforcement

Crime rates are rising in virtually every part of the country. Law enforcement agencies are finding many practical uses for computers to help them fight crime.

Chicago pioneered computer crime fighting in 1962 by putting the license numbers of stolen cars in computer storage. Now the license numbers can be checked out and identified in seconds. Chicago police use the sys-

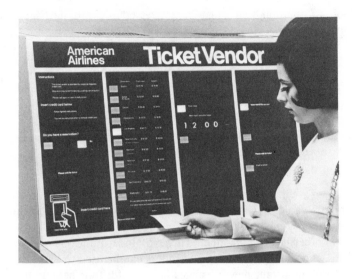

(Courtesy of American Airlines)

Figure 1–2 A computer-controlled Ticket Vendor allows passengers to obtain a ticket in less than a minute. Shown here is a passenger retrieving her special magnetically encoded credit card and taking her ticket after indicating the destination, departure time, and type of accommodations she wanted.

tem to warn them if a suspect is dangerous, is driving a stolen car, or is wanted for any crime ranging from murder to parking in front of a fire hydrant.

In New York City, police use a computer to find a set of matching fingerprints from files of tens of thousands. A computer is helping collect a backlog of traffic and parking fines from San Francisco motorists. In California, a computer keeps track of all weapon sales and stolen property; while in Florida, a computer system is increasing inter-agency cooperation throughout the state. St. Louis' 900,000 vehicle license plate numbers are stored in a computer file for immediate access. Similar systems are being implemented in many other cities and states.

Computers are also used very effectively in crime mapping. For example, trends in the incidence of crime can be analyzed from computer-plotted maps that illustrate movements from one locality to another.

In Medicine

Medicine is facing the problem of information overload similar to that being faced by many professions today. Doctors, nurses, and hospital administrators are not capable of effectively handling the large amount of information that must be processed in both medical research and patient care.

In recent years, the computer has begun to aid the medical profession. What exactly does this mean? Will a computer—instead of a doctor—diagnose your illness? Is it possible that computers will replace the family physician? The answer to these questions, at this point in time, must be "no"; for, however remarkable it may be, the computer is merely a machine. Nevertheless, computers can *help* a doctor to diagnose a disease. In medicine, a computer is simply another tool—like a microscope or a stethoscope—that can help a doctor do a better job.

There are many reasons for wanting to use computers in medicine. Computers can help to make more medical care available, in the face of an apparently inevitable decrease in the number of trained doctors, nurses, and other health personnel. Through modern information storage, indexing, and retrieval systems, computers can be used to keep doctors abreast of the important new advances in the field, thus helping to improve the quality of medical care. In a similar way, computers are also likely to help extend the frontiers of medicine and perhaps help medical research conquer some of today's diseases.

Today, the largest use of computers in the hospital is in the hospital administration areas—patient billing, accounts receivable, inventory control, payroll, and bed accounting. More and more, however, medical personnel will use these machines for patient-care functions. They will be used to:

Study heart disease, cancer, and many other diseases
Train doctors and health personnel
Free the doctors and nurses to spend more time with patients
Help speed processing of hospital patients' laboratory tests
Analyze brain waves to help investigators learn more about fatigue, stress, and mental illness
Monitor pulse, temperature, blood pressure, and other vital clinical facts about critically ill patients
Provide immediate information to aid diagnosis and treatment of accidental-poisoning victims
Provide early warning profiles of mentally ill patients.

Hospitals throughout the country are developing centralized data processing systems which bring hospital administrative, technical, and medical departments into direct and instant contact with a patient's hospital record. With such a system, computer input stations, such as the one shown in Figure 1–3, are located at key spots throughout the hospital. From admission to discharge, key information may be entered continually upon a patient's record. At the same time, doctors can instantly receive information on a patient's medical history and check the results

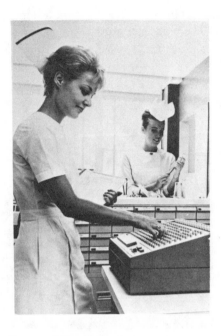

(Courtesy of IBM Corporation)

Figure 1–3 A centralized hospital computer system can receive and send information on patients, drugs, room availability, and clinic appointments from terminals throughout the hospital. Shown here is a nurse entering a drug order on a patient.

of laboratory tests. Nurses can be advised of what drugs a doctor has ordered for a patient from the hospital pharmacy and when they should be administered. The system also provides excellent control over billing for doctors, nurses, drugs, and other hospital services. The result is better and more economical service to patients.

In Education

Computers have invaded the schools—not only universities and colleges, but also secondary and elementary schools. These machines are used not only as a source of instruction, but also, in some cases, as an aid to the teacher in his teaching assignment. Machines will never replace teachers; but, when coupled with keyboard-display devices and well-developed learning programs, computers may enable the student to learn more quickly and with greater understanding than ever before. Figure 1–4 illustrates a third grade student performing drill and practice in mathematics at a typewriter-like terminal connected to a computer. Taking turns with her classmates, the student identifies herself each day by pecking out her number and name on the machine. Searching its memory, the computer locates her file, reviews her performance, and picks up with the day's practice problems. After the work is done, the computer grades the assignment. The computer works with many students—all at the same time.

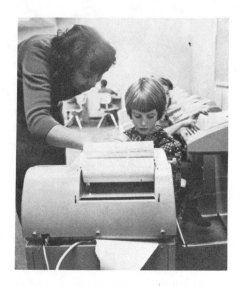

(Courtesy of Hewlett-Packard)

**Figure
1–4**   An elementary school student communicating with a computer. Using this system, the student works her way through an arithmetic drill at a typewriter-like terminal. Such a system can speed the rate of learning and frees the teacher to explain new concepts.

In 1973, about 2 000 high schools offered some form of computer education. By 1980, over half of our 27 000 high schools may very well be teaching students how to use computers to solve many algebra, geometry, science, chemistry, and business problems.

Today, practically every college and university uses computers for educational administration, student use, or educational research. More and more college students are using computers in the non-scientific and non-business disciplines. In years to come, every college student, regardless of his major, will take at least one course in using and appreciating computers.

As Control Systems

Computers are used in many control applications: industrial process control, numerical tool control, military command and control, air-traffic control, missile and spacecraft guidance, and traffic-light control.

In controlling a process, like that in a paper plant, steel mill, or oil refinery, the computer reads measuring and sampling instruments, checks the

*"We acquired all the data, programmed it, analyzed it,
used it to control production and marketing, then went
broke paying for the computer."*

readings for conformity to preset limits, relays corrections to adjusting devices, and prints out a continuous record of instrument readings.

When numerical control of machine tools was introduced in the mid-1950s, a new era in manufacturing began. Numerical control offered economy—a way to produce short runs of complex parts profitably—and it made the entire manufacturing operation much easier and more flexible. Numerical control guides a machine through a complete cycle by means of coded instructions. Thus, once the work is placed in position on the machine, a coded program controls, for example, the selection of the tools, feed rate, spindle speed, coolant setting, and the direction and distance of movements, until the piece of work is completed. Figure 1–5 shows a high-speed, precision drilling machine that is controlled by a computer-prepared control tape.

The United States military uses hundreds of computers in defense command and control systems. These systems keep track of hostile military forces and equipment and are constantly on the alert to detect and monitor enemy movements.

Similarly, many large airports use computer-based systems to track local airport air traffic. The Atlanta airport was one of the first major airports to install such an air-traffic control system. This system used computers, as well as radar and display equipment, to enable air traffic controllers to direct airplanes into the quickest airport takeoff and landing patterns.

The computer plays a similar role in spacecraft guidance. When a missile leaves the launch pad at Cape Kennedy, Florida, or most other launching sites, it is continuously controlled and watched by radar and computers.

(Photo courtesy of Collins Radio Company)

Figure Numerically controlled drilling machine that operates from instructions
1–5 produced by a computer.

If the missile runs into trouble, a computer command can cause the missile to be destroyed before any damage occurs on the ground. The computer can send signals to the missile to cause it to change course, separate stages, or perform some new function. Our nation's past space accomplishments, such as the Apollo moon landings (Figure 1–6), would not have been possible without computers.

Computers are used to control traffic on the ground too. By sensing the movement of vehicles and regulating traffic lights, the optimal flow of traffic can be maintained.

In Fine Arts

Most computers are used to perform some straightforward application such as payroll computation, inventory processing, insurance calculations, etc. But there is a lighter side to the computer's role of late, a side that is a far cry from the popular view of the computer. The computer is used to assist man in generating music, producing art, composing poetry, making movies, designing sculpture, designing textile fabrics, and making television commercials and programs.

The first substantial piece of music produced by computer was finished in 1957, by composers Lejaren Hiller and Leonard Isaacson at the University of Illinois. Their music was called the *Illiac Suite for String Quartet.*

a

b

(Courtesy of NASA)

Figure 1–6 Our space program is highly dependent upon computer assistance. Shown in (a) above is an Apollo spacecraft being tested prior to manned thermal-vacuum testing. The techniques shown in (b) are monitoring and controlling operations on the third day of the Apollo 8 lunar orbit mission. Seen on the television monitor is a picture of the earth being telecast from the Apollo 8 spacecraft 176,000 miles away.

Since this time, many composers have used the computer in the production of scores, as well as in the generation of other sounds.

"All right—just one more game—then I've got to get back to work."

The field of computer-generated moving pictures is often called *computer animation*. Animated movies are commonly made by copying a single frame at a time—a time-consuming and expensive process. Using photo-optic equipment under the control of a computer can be a more economical method to generate films. Bell Telephone Laboratories have even developed a special programming "movie language," called BE-FLIX (Bell Flicks), to simplify making computer-produced animated films.

A number of people have used the computer to write poetry. Quite often the computer-generated poems are sheer nonsense; however, occasionally, poems of some quality are generated. The following poem was generated by computer.*

Noiseless Roots

little	flowers	cooly	breathe	pastoral	woods	
pastoral	woods	mold	patiently	white	blossoms	
the	road	wanders	from	the	little	valley
fires	turn	away	the	road		

Computer art dates back to the mid-1950s. Since then artists, engineers, doctors, poets, businessmen, architects, philosophers, and composers have been using the computer to produce pictures. Students enjoy seeing

---

* Reprinted with permission from "Computers and Automation," August, 1968, copyright 1968 by and published by Berkeley Enterprises, Inc., 815 Washington St., Newtonville, Mass. 02160. Poem appeared in *Poetry by Computer* by Dr. Giuseppe M. Ferrero diRoccaferrera.

a computer draw pictures of Snoopy and Peanuts. Engineers use the computer to draw pictures of airplanes, wiring diagrams, and other works of a scientific nature. The computer also reproduces X-ray images, body organs, and other medical pictures for research doctors. Businessmen use the computer to draw graphs, PERT charts, and statistical diagrams; while architects find the computer helpful in drawing floor layouts, buildings, and perspectives. Most of the previously mentioned drawings have a practical value. However, artists are using the computer to create a form of *computer art*. Computer drawings can be made using a digital plotter, a display screen, or a printing device. Figure 1–7 is a picture drawn by a computer-controlled digital plotter.

Computers aid sculptors in the design and building of complex sculptures, and are even used to help produce television commercials and

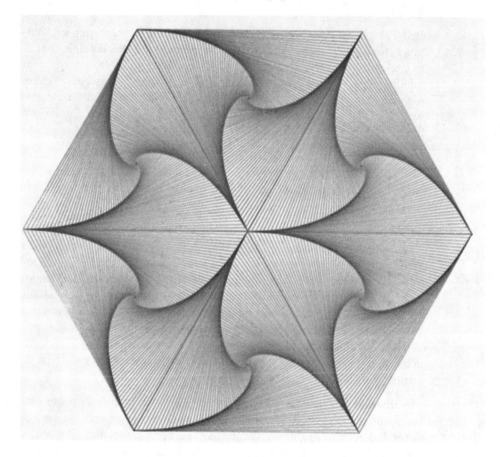

(Courtesy of California Computer Products, Inc.)

Figure 1–7   Computer Art: A computer, programmed to draw, guided the ink pen of a digital plotter that produced this drawing.

programs. For example, computers put together the CBS "Hee Haw" show. Each program is composed of up to 200 segments on one particular theme. The computer pieces these segments together to form the show.

In Printing and Publishing

The computer and related electronic equipment have penetrated the printing and publishing industries. Today, even the smallest newspapers use the computer in production. Newspapers, books, and other publications are prepared for printing by first producing a paper tape from the computer. This tape is then used to operate an automatic typesetting device. A 400-page book of 45 lines per page can be processed in about three and one-half hours, a job that otherwise would take a printer about a month.

Bell Telephone Laboratories uses a type and image generating and setting system where copy is formed on the screen of a display unit similar to a television screen. The letters and images are formed from a series of rapidly appearing and disappearing segments called "patches." These segments are put together like a jigsaw puzzle so that when a time exposure of the screen is taken, the desired letters or images are captured on film.

Shown in Figure 1–8 are the letter "r" and the musical flat sign made up of such patches. Because only a few instructions are needed to describe each patch, letters and images of high quality can be formed rapidly.

In Government

The federal government is the largest user of computers. The United States Bureau of the Census was the first group to use the computer for data processing. Today, when the national population is over 200 million, a census could not be taken without the aid of computers. All 50 states use computers to process tax, payroll, and personnel data. Many states have expanded the use of the computer to cover such diverse applications as planning new highways, analyzing laws, controlling new school locations, designing public work projects, and determining teacher requirements.

The Internal Revenue Service has turned to the computer for a faster and more complete method of checking and controlling income tax collections. Tax returns are forwarded to the appropriate regional IRS center where the information from each return is coded on punched cards. The cards are then read into a computer system which checks the mathematical accuracy of the returns and makes preliminary calculations on tax deductions and exemptions. Returns with mistakes are fed into a computer which prints out notices for corrections to the individuals or busi-

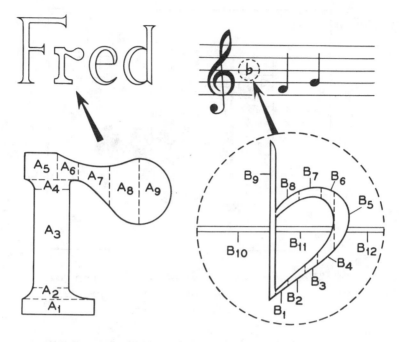

(Courtesy of Bell Telephone Laboratories)

**Figure
1–8**   Type and images can be formed on the screen of a computer-controlled display screen. The letters or images can then be captured on film by taking a time exposure of the screen. Shown here are the letter "r" and the musical flat sign being composed of many segments, called "patches." The size and shape of the patches vary with each typeface.

nesses involved. Correct returns are recorded on magnetic tape (one reel of tape holds about 20,000 individual returns) and forwarded to the IRS National Center in Martinsburg, West Virginia. A record of every taxpayer in the country is available in this center. At a rate of about one per minute, the computer system checks each return against all reports of payments to that individual or business from all sources. If the return is not within certain predetermined guidelines, the computer "flags" it for further checking by IRS tax personnel. The computer has helped the IRS increase collections and has reduced tax evasion and delinquencies.

The Weather Bureau uses computers for forecasting weather, generating computer-printed maps, plotting the course of hurricanes, and communicating with weather satellites such as Tyros and Nimbus. The National Aeronautics and Space Administration (NASA) also uses computers to perform operations in space. Without computers, development, test, preflight checkout, launch, control, guidance, navigation, re-entry, recovery, and evaluation of space vehicles would not be possible.

"Your plans seem perfect, Mr. Wilson—spray your
roses now, put the lime on next week and the
fertilizer next month."

The Department of Defense uses computers to tie together Navy, Army, Marine, and Air Force systems as well as to link other agencies such as the National Security Agency, Civil Defense, and the State Department. The Atomic Energy Commission uses hundreds of computers to solve complex scientific problems relating to atomic and nuclear energy. With computers, AEC scientists are able to discover and measure phenomena and to solve problems that were beyond exploration a few years ago.

In Business

It is not surprising that soon after the great potential of the computer became clear, American business became the largest single area of application. Computers are used to control stacks of raw materials and finished products, bill customers, calculate employee pay and taxes, analyze who is buying the company products, and perform hundreds of other administrative functions. Over half of the computers now in use were installed by business to control and reduce administrative paper work and cost.

Banks are large users of computers. Loan accounting, customer account updating, deposits and withdrawals, check processing, and daily report preparation are but a few of the computer applications in banking. Automatic check processing is perhaps the most frequent use of these machines, primarily because most money transactions within a bank are completed by the use of checks. In 1959, the American Banking Association adopted a special magnetic ink character system to be imprinted on checks. Using this system, check identification could be read by either bank personnel or special reading equipment connected to computers. This equipment can process checks at speeds of more than 2,500 per minute.

Banks have also developed systems which are used for updating of customer accounts. Figure 1–9 shows a bank teller updating a customer's passbook after a transaction. Such a system prints the transaction in the passbook and automatically adds or subtracts the transaction amount from the computer record of the customer's account.

Other banking systems use computers to provide 24-hour banking service to their customers. In a New York City suburb, checking account customers at a local bank are able to make purchases at local stores by using a special plastic banking card. The card is inserted into a reading device at the store, registers an automatic credit to the merchants' account at the bank, and affixes an automatic debit to the customer's account.

Display systems that depict computerized information instantly on television-like screens are used by many banks, insurance companies, and

(Courtesy of IBM Corporation)

Figure 1–9   A bank computer terminal deposits and withdraws money and then enters interest on the passbook, while updating the master record of the account kept in computer storage.

other businesses. One such system is used by Wall Street brokerage firms. With this system, brokerage personnel can call up and display financial data, make additions, changes, or deletions, and send the information back to the computer—all in a matter of seconds. The system computes a master file of all transactions that have taken place, permitting supervisors to summarize vital information instantly. Figure 1–10 shows a broker entering information into the system.

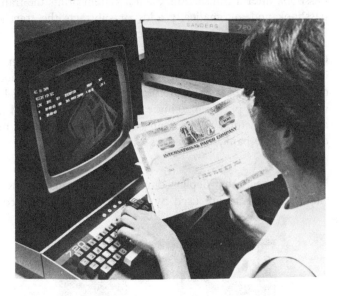

(Courtesy of Sanders Associates, Inc.)

**Figure
1–10**   Using the above keyboard/display device, brokerage personnel can enter security and cash transactions directly into a computer system. This system displays an up-to-the-second cash and security position.

In retail business, the computer is rapidly changing the internal financial operating and control system of the modern department store. Sales are automatically used to update accounts, while the computer provides employee pay and commission data, updates inventories, and provides store management with important statistical data. The computer may also be used to determine instantly the credit status and history of a customer. This information may be needed prior to approving large purchases or for checking on delinquent accounts. The computer's storage file also contains a list of stolen, lost, and discontinued credit cards. The computer can check the account number within seconds and advise the clerk whether the card is acceptable.

Another form of credit card where automatic checking is often used is the gasoline credit card. Computer-controlled credit centers are located throughout the country for use by gasoline station managers (see Figure 1–11). To use the system, the manager places a toll-free telephone call to the nearest center giving the oil company name, station number, credit card number, and purchase amount. The manager is informed whether the card is "good" or "bad" in about 20 seconds after receipt of the call.

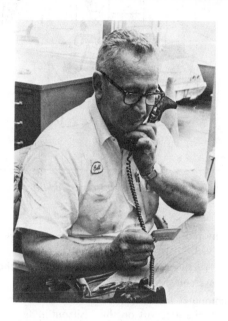

(Courtesy of Sperry Rand Corporation's Univac Division)

**Figure
1–11**   A gasoline station manager can determine if a credit card is "good" by calling a nearby credit center. The manager places a telephone call to the center giving the oil company name, station number, credit card number, and purchase amount. The center, using a computer system, determines whether the card is valid in about 20 seconds after receipt of the call.

Since 1954, when the General Electric Company installed the first computer (Univac I) for data processing activities, business leaders have depended upon the computer to help them improve services and products. Today, it would be difficult to imagine a large business conducting everyday operations without the aid of computers.

☐ Review Questions

1. What are some of the ways in which the computer is being used?
2. What are some of the ways in which the computer is affecting today's society? Do you think computers present any threat to our society? Explain your views.

*"It's the boss—we forgot to run his horoscope
this morning."*

3. Discuss any recent articles or news items you have read where computers were involved.

4. Bring to class five samples of data you can find that were produced by a computer system.

5. Visit a computer installation in your school or in a local business establishment. Write a report on this visit outlining what type of information the computer provides.

6. Present any ideas you may have about where or how a computer might be used. Example: How could a computer be used in a church or social organization?

7. What are some reasons why a business would use a computer or other business data processing equipment?

Data Processing—What Is It?

Because of the rapid growth of society, man's need for information has increased greatly. Clerical tasks have multiplied. More reports are required. It seemed, before computers, that every organization—whether business, social, industrial, or governmental—would eventually be overwhelmed by paperwork. This deluge of paperwork has come to be called *data processing.*

In the comparatively new vocabulary of data processing, *data* and *information* are used more or less interchangeably. If a distinction is necessary, "data" are generally defined as the raw figures and facts to which meaning may or may not have been ascribed. "Information," on the other hand, is the knowledge that grows out of data when they have been processed. One of the chief goals of data processing is to convert raw data into useful information.

Data processing is nothing new. Whenever information is gathered or disseminated, we can say it is "handled" or "processed." When the department store manager keeps track of his stock so that he knows when and what to reorder, his records are *data* and he is *processing* them. Likewise, when he calculates an employee's weekly paycheck on the basis of the number of hours worked, he is processing data. Data processing, then, is a term which encompasses any collection of facts, manipulation of information to get other facts, or output of information. This collecting, processing, and distributing facts and figures is done toward some desired result. The equipment and procedures by which that result is achieved form a *data processing system.*

Review Questions

8. Give a brief definition of the following terms:
    (a) data
    (b) information
    (c) data processing
    (d) data processing system.
9. Give a concrete example of data; of information.

Methods of Processing Data

Data processing can be performed by machines, by pencil and paper, or by man and machines working together (see Figure 1–12). The procedures, however, remain basically the same.

Manual data processing techniques are used to a certain degree in every business; they are still the predominant method of processing data in smaller businesses. It is possible to complete by hand all the operations in the data processing cycle, from the preparation of the original documents to the final reports, by using such standard tools as pens, pencils, journals, ledgers, files, trays, folders, and other manual devices.

Mechanical data processing involves the use of typewriters, adding machines, credit card imprinters, accounting machines, check writers, calculating machines, and cash registers. A basically manual data processing system may be mechanized in varying degrees by using mechanical devices. For example, a typewriter might be used to record input data or an adding machine might be used to accumulate data.

Although mechanical devices generally require manual aid, many of them include mechanisms that enable them to simultaneously produce punched paper or magnetic tape while performing a primary function. These by-

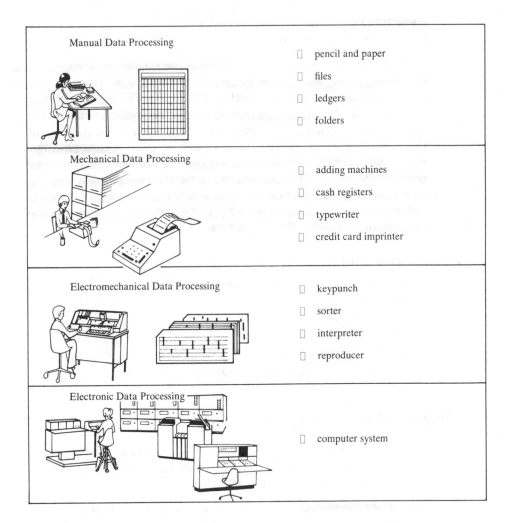

Manual Data Processing

☐ pencil and paper

☐ files

☐ ledgers

☐ folders

Mechanical Data Processing

☐ adding machines

☐ cash registers

☐ typewriter

☐ credit card imprinter

Electromechanical Data Processing

☐ keypunch

☐ sorter

☐ interpreter

☐ reproducer

Electronic Data Processing

☐ computer system

**Figure
1–12**   Methods of processing data.

products then serve as input to computer equipment. For example, sales transactions that are recorded on a cash register may also be recorded on punched paper tape which may then be used as input to a computer system.

Electromechanical data processing is distinctly different from either manual or mechanical data processing. This type of data processing requires data to be in a machine-readable form, usually punched cards. Because punched card equipment is automatic, it eliminates much of the human effort that is required in the processing of data by manual or mechanical means. Punched card machines perform six data processing operations

"Oh, it's really Smadby back there giving me
the answers. I just didn't want other businessmen
to think I'm not in step with the times."

automatically: sorting, comparing, recording, calculating, summarizing, and reporting.

Electromechanical data processing equipment is often called *unit record equipment*. It involves the use of the following eight punched card devices: Keypunch, Verifier, Sorter, Collator, Interpreter, Calculator, Reproducer, and Accounting Machine. Detailed discussion of electromechanical data processing techniques and equipment will appear in Chapter 4.

Electronic data processing (EDP) involves processing by computer. A computer is used for the same reason that any other machine is used, because it does certain jobs better than a human being. In particular, it can process data much faster and more accurately.

Like electromechanical data processing equipment, electronic data processing also requires that the data be in a machine readable form—holes punched in paper tape or cards, magnetized spots on magnetic tapes or disks, magnetic ink characters, etc. The data are then manipulated or processed by the computer and results are presented in the form of printed reports, magnetic tape recordings, punched cards, visual displays, etc.

Unlike electromechanical processing equipment, processing in an electronic computer is accomplished by the movement of electrical impulses through the computer's circuitry rather than by the movement of mechanical parts. By using preprepared computer instructions, thousands of operations can be completed in a second.

☐ Review Questions

10. What are the four main methods of processing data? Describe each.
11. What are the principal advantages of electronic data processing over the other methods?

☐ Summary

The digital computer is a device that is having a dramatic effect on today's society. Computers are aiding mankind in solving many of today's complex problems.

In transportation, computers are used to aid in reserving passenger seats, scheduling services, controlling transportation vehicles, performing administrative functions, handling baggage, running supply and spare parts inventory control, and performing other similar functions.

Police enforcement officers and lawyers use computers to help them control crime. Information retrieval from crime data banks can provide law enforcement personnel with immediate data (fingerprints, stolen vehicles, criminal records, etc.) to aid them in apprehending criminals.

Doctors and hospital personnel are faced with handling vast amounts of information related to medical research and patient care. Computers are used in most hospitals to perform administrative functions, such as patient accounting, payroll, bed accounting, and inventory control. Within the next decade it will be commonplace for medical personnel to use computers in tasks such as monitoring patients, taking patient histories, diagnosing patient illness, expediting medical research, improving medical education, analyzing EKG, and performing laboratory tests.

Computers have invaded the schools—not only colleges and universities, but also secondary and elementary schools. Computers are used to control industrial processes, to automatically control machine tools, to control traffic lights, to monitor and control air traffic, to guide missiles and spacecraft to foreign planets, and to control many military systems.

Not only businessmen and scientists use computers. Artists, musicians, and writers are using computers to produce drawings, music, and poetry for a variety of purposes.

Printing and publishing firms use computers to set type for newspapers, magazines, and books. The federal government, the largest user of computers, uses these machines to help collect taxes, forecast the weather, plan highways, control projects, analyze laws, and perform in many more capacities.

Even though the computer is used in thousands of different applications, the largest single application area is business. Computers are used in businesses, large and small, to perform such task as payroll, customer billing, inventory control, order processing, accounting, account updating, check processing, and daily report preparation.

This chapter introduces the definitions for *data processing, data,* and *information.* Data processing can be performed by machines, by pencil and paper, or by man and machines working together. The four techniques used to process data are *manual data processing, mechanical data processing, electromechanical data processing,* and *electronic data processing.* Of course, the remainder of this book is about electronic data processing (EDP), which involves processing data by a computer.

Key Terms

computer application   manual data processing
data   mechanical data processing
information   electromechanical data processing
data processing   electronic data processing

*"Well, you won't catch me wearing one of those
computer-designed bathing suits."*

2

History of
Data Processing Tools

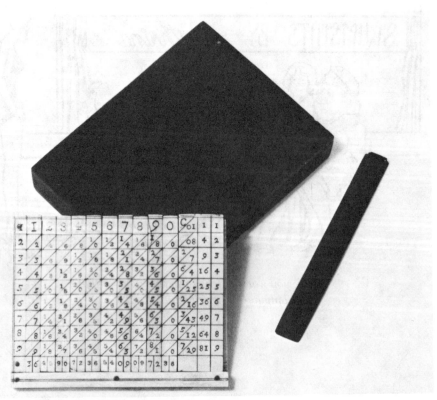

Courtesy of IBM Corporation

☐ Primitive Calculations

When people first began to use numbers, they knew only one way to work with them—counting. Man counted the number of sheep in the flock, the number of animals he saw during a hunt, or the number of spears he owned. Man used stones, sticks, shells, knots in a rope, notches on a stick, or marks in the sand to represent numbers.

The absence or rarity of suitable writing material led to the use of the fingers as a way of representing numbers. From finger notation there developed an extensive use of finger computation.

In fact, students attending Roman schools were taught to perform multiplication and division on their fingers. A student was required to learn the multiplication table only up through 5 × 5. To determine the product of larger numbers, he would use his fingers. To illustrate this method of multiplication, consider finding the product of 6 × 8. First, raise one finger on one hand to represent the number over five (that is, six) and three fingers on another hand to represent six, seven, and eight. The

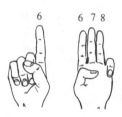

product is obtained by adding the number of fingers raised (1 + 3 = 4) and then multiplying the number of fingers not raised (4 × 2 = 8). The first computation gives the value of the ten's position, while the second computation gives the value of the unit's position. Thus, 6 × 8 = 48.

As society became more complicated, man had to develop fairly elaborate calculations involving subtraction, multiplication, and division that could not be done by finger computation only. It is easy to imagine how impractical it would be to use finger computations in performing the many thousands of business computations that are done each hour by American businesses.

One of the earliest types of devices used to facilitate computations was the *abacus*. This reckoning board was particularly an instrument of the merchants and tradesmen, and it could be applied universally, regardless of differences in languages and number systems. Four types of these devices were the Roman *abacus*, the Chinese *swanpan*, the Japanese *soroban*, and the Russian *schoty*. Structurally, all four consisted of balls in movable rows or beads on movable rods.

The Roman *abacus* was a metal plate on which units, fives, tens, and so on were represented by balls which could be moved in grooves, as shown in Figure 2–1. The Chinese *swanpan* (see Figure 2–2) had a horizontal bar across a frame separating five beads strung on the rod in the lower

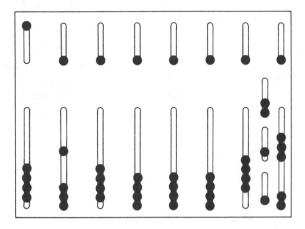

Figure 2–1   Ancient bronze abacus used by the Romans.

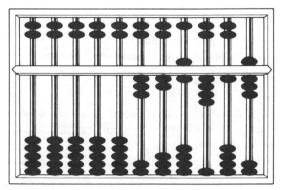

Figure 2–2   Chinese *swanpan* with the number 326 418 represented.

compartment and two beads in the upper compartment. Each of the upper beads represented a value five times as large as each of the lower beads. Whenever five units of the lower column were reached, they were replaced by one of the upper. All operations could be performed by sliding the beads up and down. The Japanese *soroban* (see Figure 2–3) was quite similar to the Chinese device, except there were only one upper bead and four lower beads strung on each rod. The number 326 418 is represented on both of the devices shown in Figures 2–2 and 2–3.

In Russia, a type of abacus known as the *schoty* (Figure 2–4) is still in use.

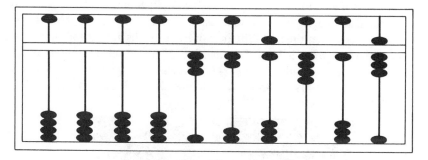

Figure 2–3 The number 326 418 represented on the Japanese *soroban*.

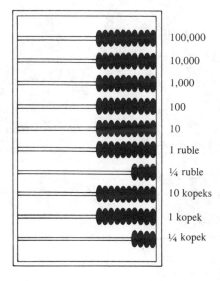

Figure 2–4 Russian schoty.

The interesting picture shown in Figure 2–5 is from a book that was well-known about 400 years ago. The book was first printed in 1503, and it shows two styles of computing at that time—the counters and the numerals. The number on the counting board at the right is 1 241. The one at the left represents the attempted division of 1 234 by 97.

The seventeenth century brought a great step forward in computational work. In 1617, John Napier, a Scottish politician, magician, and nobleman, turned to mathematics for amusement and relaxation. Napier's Bones, an ingenious device for multiplying, dividing, and extracting roots, was used for many years. The "bones" are made from slips of bone, wood, metal, or cardboard. Each of them are divided by cross lines into nine little squares. In the top square one of the digits is engraved, and the results of multiplying it by 2, 3, 4, 5, 6, 7, 8, and 9 are respectively entered in the eight lower squares. Where the result is a number of two digits, the ten-digit is written above and to the left of the unit-digit and separated from it by a diagonal line. Figure 2–6a represents nine such bones side by side; Figure 2–6b shows the seventh bone. Suppose we wish to multiply 2 985 by 7. The process as effected by the use of these

Figure 2–5   Abacist vs algorismist. (From Gregor Reisch: *Margarita Philosophica;* Strassbourg, 1504).

bones is as follows. The bones headed 2, 9, 8, and 5 are used and placed side by side as shown in Figure 2–6c. The result of multiplying 2 985 by 7 may be written thus:

$$
\begin{array}{r}
2985 \\
7 \\
\hline
35 \\
56 \\
63 \\
14 \\
\hline
20895
\end{array}
$$

Now, in the seventh line in Figure 2–6c, the upper and lower rows of figures are respectively 1653 and 4365. Moreover, these are arranged by the diagonals so that roughly the 4 is under the 6, the 3 under the 5, and the 6 under the 3; thus

$$
\begin{array}{cccc}
1 & 6 & 5 & 3 \\
& 4 & 3 & 6 & 5
\end{array}
$$

The addition of these two numbers gives the required result.

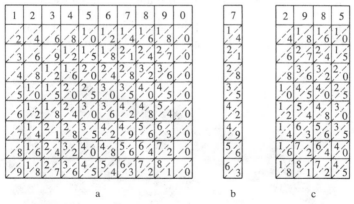

a   b   c

Figure 2–6   Napier's bones.

☐ Review Questions

1. Name several old devices used by man to help him calculate.
2. What is an abacus? How does it differ from a slide rule?
3. John Napier invented logarithms and a calculating device called _____ _____ _____. Explain how this device could be used to multiply two numbers.

☐ Mechanical Calculators

Not until modern times has man had both the need for using more advanced calculators and the knowledge required to build them.

The first practical calculating machine was built in 1642 by a 19-year-old Frenchman, Blaise Pascal. Pascal was a mathematical wizard. Before he was out of short pants, he created many theorems identical with those to be found in the first book of Euclid. He did this entirely without reference to books. Pascal went on to become one of France's greatest mathematicians and philosophers.

Pascal built his calculator when he tired of adding long columns of figures while working in his father's tax collection office in Rouen. His machine was based on the concept of gear-driven counter wheels which was used in almost every mechanical calculator for the following three hundred years. This calculator was a simple device about the size of a shoe box (see Figure 2–7); however it established three principles important to the development of later calculators: that a "carry" could be accomplished automatically, that subtraction could be accomplished by reversing the turning of the dials, and that multiplication could be performed by repeated addition. Pascal's machines (several of them were built) worked very well, but could only perform addition or subtraction.

The first calculator which could also multiply and divide was invented by Gottfried Wilhelm Leibnitz (1646–1716) in Germany and was first

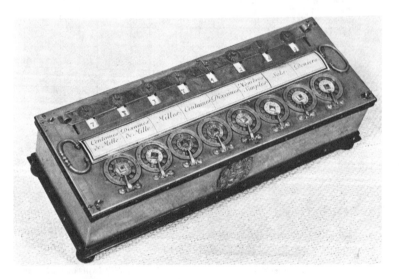

(Courtesy of IBM Corporation)

Figure 2–7   Pascal's calculating machine.

built in 1671. The key elements in Leibnitz's machine were the "stepped cylinders"—in effect, long gears with nine teeth, each a different length. Smaller gears were set above them, each representing a digit of the multiplicand and placed so as to be engaged by a corresponding number of the long gears' teeth. Each complete turn of the set of long gears therefore registered the multiplicand once; the multiplier was expressed by the number of times the long gears were turned. Although the calculator worked, it was very unreliable and awkward to use.

In 1786, J. H. Muller, a German, invented a calculating machine called a "difference engine." Muller did not actually build the machine; however, a similar one was built around 30 years later by Charles Babbage. Babbage, a man before his time, attempted to develop the largest *Difference Engine* anyone might ever want (see Figure 2–8) which was accurate to 20 digits and produced printed output.

The idea for a Difference Engine that would compute mathematical tables, such as logarithms, was conceived by Babbage in 1812. After twenty years of labor, financial difficulties compelled him to stop work on this machine. The concept was brilliant; however the assembly of the machine required parts with unheard-of precision. In 1832, Babbage lost interest in the Difference Engine and began working on his new machine.

In 1833, Babbage conceived the *Analytical Engine* and worked on it with his own money until he died. This machine, like the Difference En-

(Courtesy of IBM Corporation)

Figure 2–8   A difference engine conceived by Charles Babbage in 1812.

gine, was never built. However, Babbage's ideas are of the greatest interest today, because the Analytical Engine, as conceived, would have contained all the basic parts of a modern general-purpose digital computer: control, arithmetic unit, memory, input, and output. Babbage proposed using two types of punched cards to control the operation of his machine. He would use *operation cards* to control the action of the arithmetic unit and to specify the kind of operation to be performed and *variable cards* to control the transfer of numbers (data) to and from the store. As designed, the memory was to hold 50 000 digits (one thousand 50-digit numbers) and the arithmetic unit was to add or subtract in one second and multiply two 50-digit numbers in about one minute.

The concept of Babbage's Analytical Engine was brilliant, but the engineering problems were overwhelming. Moreover, it was Babbage's fate to live in an age that did not yet value man's time at its true worth. At his death in 1871, Babbage was remembered chiefly as an elderly eccentric; but his concepts in mathematics and precision mechanics are recognized today as forerunners of achievements in contemporary science. Poor Babbage! He was born 100 years too soon. Today, we can appreciate the magnitude of his achievements and the depth of his insight into calculating machines.

A description of Babbage's machines would not be complete without some mention of Lady Ada Augusta, Countess of Lovelace. She was familiar with Babbage's work and helped to document and clarify some of his efforts. She had considerable mathematical talent and developed several programs for performing mathematical calculations on the Analytical Engine.

In 1854, twenty years after the principles of Babbage's Difference Engine were published in the Edinburgh Review, a Swedish printer named George Scheutz constructed a model of Babbage's machine. A year later, this machine won a gold medal in Paris where it was exhibited with drawings made by Charles Babbage and his son.

During the eighteenth century, many attempts were made to improve the reliability of the machines invented by Pascal and Leibniz, but the engineering production techniques of this period could not produce precision instruments. The first machine to perform basic arithmetic operations well enough for commercial use was the *Arithmometer,* built by Charles Zavier Thomas in 1820. Only about 1 500 Thomas machines were actually constructed, since the commercial use of mechanical calculators was not widespread until the last two decades of the nineteenth century.

In 1850, D. D. Parmalee developed a key-driven adding machine that could add a single column of numbers at a time. This machine was not very reliable and was never manufactured commercially.

In 1875, Frank Stephen Baldwin invented the first practical reversible four-process calculator in the United States. Baldwin patented a variant of the Leibniz wheel—a wheel with a variable number of protruding teeth—in 1875. W. T. Odhner, a Russian, designed a similar machine in 1878. His calculator used the "Odhner wheel" developed by Baldwin and made possible the more compact machines that are available today. A large number of Odhner-type machines have since been made in many countries.

The first commercially practical adding-listing machine was invented in 1884, by William Seward Burroughs, who was granted a patent on it in 1888. Burroughs, himself a bookkeeper, was born in Rochester, New York in 1857, and his dream was to develop a machine that would add long columns of figures *accurately*. In 1884, he succeeded in developing a key-set adding-printing machine with a crank. Burroughs formed a company (later to become Burroughs Corporation) to produce this adding machine. Burrough's machine incorporated most of the features found in modern adding machines. With the introduction of this machine, mechanized accounting—first initiated by Blaise Pascal—had become a reality.

Dorr Felt, in 1885, designed an experimental multiple-order key-driven calculating machine. The machine was built from a wooden macaroni box and employed keys made from meat skewers, key guides made from staples, and rubber bands used for springs. In 1887, Felt formed a partnership with Robert Tarrant (Felt and Tarrant Manufacturing Company, now the Victor Comptometer Corporation) to produce the *Comptometer*. This calculating machine was so successful that no other comparable machine was placed on the market in competition until 1902.

In 1887, Leon Bollee of France designed the first machine to perform multiplication successfully by a direct method instead of by repeated addition. The device had a multiplying piece consisting of a series of tongued plates representing in relief the ordinary multiplication table up to nine times. The *Millionaire,* a popular commercial calculating machine based on principles developed by Bollee, was manufactured in Switzerland. E. Steiger of Germany held the patents and released the machine in 1889. The machine required only one turn of the handle for each figure of the multiplier and included a feature that allowed an automatic shift to the next position.

Finally, in 1911, Jay R. Monroe, using earlier designs of Frank Baldwin, developed the first keyboard rotary machine to attain commercial success.

Review Questions

4. An early mechanism for adding and subtracting using geared wheels was developed by the Frenchman _____.

5. In 1834, Charles Babbage designed a machine that contained all the parts of a modern digital computer. What was the name of this machine?
6. Line up the developments in column 2 to match the correct name in column 1.

1	2
(1) Gottfried Leibnitz	(a) Comptometer
(2) Leon Bollee	(b) Difference Engine
(3) Charles Babbage	(c) adding machine
(4) Charles Zavier Thomas	(d) "stepped cylinders"
(5) William Burroughs	(e) Millionaire
(6) Dorr Felt	(f) Arithmometer

☐ Punched Cards

Perforated paper cards were first used in the weaving industry. As early as 1725, perforated paper was employed in the operation of a loom designed by Basile Bouchon. Basically, the loom worked in this manner: lines of holes were punched into a roll of paper in accordance with the design to be woven. When this "coded" paper was pressed against a row of needles, those which lined up with the holes remained in place; the others moved forward. The loom's action, as controlled by these selected needles, formed the pattern of the fabric. Bouchon's loom was the simplest kind of drawloom, using only a single row of needles. But it was the beginning.

Improvements soon appeared which made possible drawlooms with several rows of needles, these activated not by a roll of paper, but by narrow perforated or punched cards strung together in a long belt.

In 1728, French inventor M. Falcon designed a loom that operated with punched cards to make various pattern-weaving operations automatic. This technique was later adopted for use in the first successful machine to operate from punched cards. In 1741, a watchmaker named Jacques de Vaucanson built an automatic loom for weaving figured silks.

In 1801, Joseph Marie Jacquard invented an automatic textile loom which revolutionized the weaving industry. His loom used an endless chain of punched cards that rotated past the needles of the loom. Charles Babbage, in the design of his Analytical Engine, borrowed the punched card principles from Jacquard's loom. What Bouchon, Falcon, and Jacquard did with their punched paper and cards was, in essence, to provide an effective means of communicating with the loom. The language was limited to just two "words": *hole* and *no hole*. The same binary, or two-based, system is all but universal in today's machine communication. Jacquard was unable to gain public acceptance for his automatic machine; and, in the city of Lyons, he was physically attacked and his machine destroyed. Sometime later, he rebuilt his machine with Napoleon's support. Lyon's prosperity in the mid-1800s was attributed largely to the success of Jacquard's automatic loom. Around 11,000 Jacquard looms were operating in France during this period.

It was not until about twenty years after Babbage's death that the use of punched cards was applied to data processing. In 1887, the first system of punched-card tabulating machines was developed by Herman Hollerith in response to an immediate need (see Figure 2–9). Because the population of the United States had grown so fast in the latter half of the nineteenth century, it was estimated that the results of the 1890 census could not be processed within ten years, thus resulting in an overlap with the taking of the next census. To shorten this time, Hollerith built a set of machines to reduce the processing time required to obtain the 1890 census.

(Courtesy of IBM Corporation)

Figure 2–9   Hollerith Tabulating Machine, 1890.

The 1890 census data was placed on cards by means of holes cut with a hand-operated punch. The cards were individually positioned over mercury-filled cups. Rows of telescoping pins descending on the card's surface dropped through the holes into mercury, thus completing electrical circuits and causing pointers on appropriate counting dials to move one position. This machine allowed personnel to tabulate cards at a rate of

50 to 75 a minute and allowed the 1890 census of 62 million people to be completed in one-third the time needed for completion of the 1880 census of 50 million people.

In 1896, Dr. Hollerith organized the Tabulating Machine Company (TMC) to promote the commercial use of his machines. Before 1900, his machines were used in many different applications, including insurance actuarial work, railroad car accounting, and sales analysis. His machines were used in the 1900 census; however, in 1910, even though he had developed a more automatic card handling machine, he was unable to reach an agreement with the Census Bureau on use of the improved machine. When Hollerith's company became too large for individual control, he sold it. It later became one of the parents of International Business Machines Corporation.

In 1907, James Powers, one of the Census Bureau machine shop experts, developed a punched card system that was used in the 1910 census. The Power's machine had 240 keys corresponding to different items on the census questionnaire and operated somewhat in the manner of a typewriter or adding machine. All the necessary keys for punching a given card were set before any of the holes were actually punched. This machine increased the accuracy of punching and the speed with which it was done. The success of this machine in the 1910 census encouraged Powers to form the Powers Tabulating Machine Company in 1911. For many years this was the principal competitor of the Hollerith Company. Through a series of mergers, this company first became part of the Remington Rand organization and, more recently, the Sperry Rand Corporation's Univac Division.

☐ Review Questions

7. What was the source of Herman Hollerith's idea for the punched card?
8. Punched cards, developed by Herman Hollerith, were first used in what application?
9. What contribution did James Powers make to data processing?
10. How was information communicated in the punched cards used in early automatic textile looms?

☐ Electromechanical Computing Machines

All of the early calculators were mechanical devices using gears, levers, pulleys, etc. Most of these early machines were unreliable, bulky, heavy, and slow. It was inevitable that smaller, lighter, faster, and more reliable machines would be developed.

Several early electromechanical machines were built at Bell Telephone Laboratories. Started in 1938, these special-purpose relay computers were based initially on the work of Dr. George R. Stibitz. The first relay computer was called the *complex calculator* and is believed to have been the first computer to employ binary components. This machine, put into operation in 1940, was capable of performing arithmetic operations on two complex numbers. Moreover, it could be remotely controlled. Other models were built, primarily to solve military problems. Model II and III machines were built for the National Defense Research Council and were placed in operation in 1943 and 1944. Later, Model V was built for the National Advisory Committee on Aeronautics at Langley Field, Virginia, and for the Ballistic Research Laboratory at Aberdeen, Maryland. This machine contained 9 000 relays and 50 pieces of Teletype equipment, weighed 10 tons, and occupied 92.9 m² (1000 square feet) of floor space. Model VI, the last of the family, was built for Bell Laboratories' own use. It had many improvements, including magnetic tape storage units.

Another early electromechanical machine was the Automatic Sequence Controlled Calculator (Mark I), conceived in 1937 by Howard H. Aiken of Harvard University, and constructed by his staff and the International Business Machines Corporation. The ASCC (Figure 2–10) was completed in 1944, when it was formally presented to Harvard University by T. J. Watson, IBM's president. The development of this machine was the first major advancement since Babbage's work.

(Courtesy of IBM Corporation)

Figure 2–10 Automatic Sequence Controlled Calculator (Harvard Mark I). Developed by Professor Howard Aiken of Harvard University and IBM in 1944. It was the first automatic calculator.

The ASCC was 15.55 m (51 feet) long and 2.44 m (8 feet) high, contained 760 000 parts, used 926 km (500 miles) of wires, and weighed about 5 tons. The ASCC used a program to guide it through a long series of calculations. It could add, subtract, multiply, divide, calculate trigonometric functions, and perform other complicated calculations. A 23-digit addition or subtraction took $\frac{3}{10}$ second, a 23-digit multiplication operation took $5\frac{7}{10}$ seconds, and a division operation took $15\frac{3}{10}$ seconds.

The ASCC was in operation for more than fifteen years. Compared with modern machines, it was slow and had a very limited storage capacity. Nevertheless, it was the world's first automatic machine to be completed.

In the eight years following the completion of the ASCC, research in the Harvard Computation Laboratory resulted in the construction of three new large-scale machines. Mark II, a relay computer, was completed in 1948. Mark III, an electronic machine completed in 1950, became the first computer to use magnetic drums for the storage of information. Mark IV, one of the first computers to employ magnetic core storage, was completed in 1952.

Review Questions

11. A partly electronic, partly mechanical computer developed at Harvard University was known as _____.
12. Who developed the ASCC (Harvard Mark I)? In what years?
13. What were some of the disadvantages of the early electromechanical calculators?

Electronic Machines

In 1934, Dr. John V. Atanasoff, a professor of physics at Iowa State College (now Iowa State University), modified an IBM punched card machine to perform calculations mechanically. Five years later, he built a prototype of an electronic digital computer, called the ABC (Atanasoff-Berry Computer). His assistant on this computing machine was Clifford Berry. The ABC, which had a "memory" consisting of 45 vacuum tubes, was assembled in 1942. In 1946, the Electronic Numerical Integrator And Calculator (ENIAC) went into operation at the Moore School of Electrical Engineering of the University of Pennsylvania. This specialized computer was built to compute firing and ballistic tables to help guide army artillerymen in aiming their guns.

*"I don't know his exact age, but he speaks of having
programmed an IBM 650 computer."*

ENIAC, invented by two researchers at the University of Pennsylvania
—Dr. John W. Mauchly and J. Presper Eckert—occupied a space of
139.95 m² (1500 square feet), weighed about 30 tons, contained about
19 000 vacuum tubes, and required 130 kw of power (see Figure 2–11).
The computing elements consisted of many components linked by about
a million hand-soldered connections. The input-output system consisted
of modified IBM card readers and punches. ENIAC had a limited storage
capacity for only 20 ten-digit numbers. (It took 12 vacuum tubes to
store one decimal digit). ENIAC could perform 5 000 additions or 300
multiplications per second. ENIAC, by today's standards, is relatively
slow; however, in 1946, the only other machine that could even compete
was the ASCC relay calculator that could perform 10 additions per
second. Needless to say, ENIAC made all relay calculators obsolete.

ENIAC could perform several operations simultaneously—a capability
that has only recently become possible with the advent of modern digital
computer systems. It could perform several additions, a multiplication
and a square root in parallel, as well as solve several independent
problems at the same time. It was a fascinating machine that could have
been built many years earlier had there been a need for such a machine.
Even though there are many amusing stories about ENIAC (stories
claiming that all the lights in West Philadelphia would dim when the
ENIAC was turned on or that three or more tubes would always burn
out when it was started), it was a machine that was so successful that it

(Courtesy of the Moore School of Electrical Engineering, University of Pennsylvania)

**Figure
2–11**   ENIAC (1946).

marked the end of the pioneer stage of automatic computer development. ENIAC was retired from service in 1955, after nine years of operation. ENIAC was shortly followed by a wide variety of other machines.

The Selective Sequence Electronic Calculator (or SSEC) went into operation at IBM New York World Headquarters in 1947 and was used through 1952. This machine was 100 times faster than the ASCC. The SSEC was not completely an electronic machine, since it contained 23 000 relays, about 13 000 tubes, and an external punched tape. About the same time, IBM built a machine that could multiply six-digit numbers by counting electronic pulses. This machine, which was simply a tabulating machine connected to some vacuum tubes in a "black box," was identified as the IBM 603 electronic multiplier.

In 1948, IBM introduced a general-purpose electronic digital computer called the IBM 604. More than 4 000 of these machines were built until production was stopped in 1960. The IBM 604 contains an electronic arithmetic and storage unit with over 1 400 vacuum tubes and a separate card-handling machine. All input-output was performed on punched cards.

The Card Programmed Calculator, or CPC, was produced by IBM in the late 1940s (one version in 1947–48, another in 1948–49). The CPC was basically several IBM devices connected by cables. The arithmetic speed of the CPC was rather slow (even in those days): top speed was 150 operations per *minute*. Up until about 1950, there were about 700 machines in use. Today, a medium-size IBM System/370 computer could do more work in half a day than all 700 CPC's ever did.

General-purpose computers require large amounts of storage. Earlier machines used vacuum tubes for storage elements. Large vacuum tube memories were not economical, prompting developers to perfect the use of acoustic mercury delay lines as storage devices. The Electronic Delay Storage Automatic Calculator (EDSAC) was the first machine to use this form of storage. The EDSAC was designed and constructed at Cambridge University in England by Professor Maurice V. Wilkes and his associates. It was started at the end of 1946, and it performed its first completely automatic calculation in May, 1949.

The government played a very important role in the early days of digital computer development. One governmental department, the National Bureau of Standards (NBS), developed two computers. One computer, called the Standards Eastern Automatic Computer, or SEAC, was started in June, 1948, and put into operation in May, 1950. It was built as a stored-program computer with a design based upon that of EDSAC. The SEAC is a binary machine containing some 750 vacuum tubes. The original installation consisted mainly of the control and computing circuitry, a memory providing for the storage of 512 words, and a keyboard for direct input and a printer for direct output. The SEAC was built primarily to help the Air Force solve massive logistics problems. It was also used in the design of the first H-bomb and in solving innumerable problems for many governmental agencies. After 14 years of use, the SEAC was retired and holds the record as the first internally programmed digital computer in the United States.

The other NBS computer, originally called the Zephyr, was the Standards Western Automatic Computer. The SWAC was very fast compared to the machines of the same vintage, though limited in the scope of its applications by having a very small memory.

The Whirlwind I computer was built in the late 1940s and early 1950s by personnel at the Massachusetts Institute of Technology. Put into operation in March, 1951, it was probably the first computer designed with eventual *real-time* applications in mind. The development of Whirlwind I was sponsored by the Office of Naval Research and the United States Air Force. Whirlwind I was a stored-program computer, with instructions stored in the internal memory of the computer. It contained some 5 000 vacuum tubes. It could perform over 300 000 additions and

60 000 multiplications per second. Whirlwind I was a reliable machine and many of the ideas embodied in this machine exist in most modern computers. The most important was magnetic core memory—used as internal memory on almost all modern computers.

In 1951, UNIVAC I, the first business data processing system, was delivered to the United States Bureau of Census. UNIVAC I (Universal Automatic Computer) was developed by J. Presper Eckert and Dr. John Mauchly. It was a machine containing some 5 000 vacuum tubes. Internal storage which provided for 1 000 twelve-decimal-digit words was composed of 100 mercury delay lines. Input-output equipment consisted of an electric typewriter and several magnetic tape units. Forty-eight UNIVAC I machines were built. During the early 1950s, it was the best large-scale machine in use for data processing applications. UNIVAC I received a large amount of publicity in 1952, when it correctly predicted the victory of Dwight D. Eisenhower in the presidential election using incomplete early returns. Not long after UNIVAC I was operational, *automatic programming* techniques were developed to help man better use these machines. These techniques have since become programming languages that are used extensively in solving problems on modern computers. The first UNIVAC I (serial 1) completed its last tabulation for the Bureau of Census 12½ years after it went into operation. The UNIVAC I is shown in Figure 2–12.

(Courtesy of Department of the Air Force)

Figure 2–12   UNIVAC I, the first commercial data processing system.

At the University of Pennsylvania, even before ENIAC was completed, the Moore School and the Ordnance Department had agreed upon an improved model. This model, called the Electronic Discrete Variable Automatic Computer (EDVAC), was smaller, more versatile, and more flexible than ENIAC. The construction of this machine was started in 1946; however, due to many delays, it was not completed until 1952. EDVAC was designed to be a true stored-program binary machine using binary numbers for both instructions and data. It occupied 13 m² (140 square feet) and contained about 5 900 vacuum tubes. It could perform an addition in 864 microseconds and a multiplication in 2.9 milliseconds. Important features of EDVAC have been used in many other machines.

The design of the IAS Computer (Institute for Advanced Study Computer) was started shortly after ENIAC was completed, but construction was not completed until June, 1952. The machine was developed under the direction of Professor John von Neumann. The IAS computer was a stored-program machine, the instructions being stored in the Cathode Ray Tube (CRT) memory. It contained 2 300 vacuum tubes and could perform an addition in 62 microseconds, a multiplication in 720 to 990 microseconds, and a division in 1 100 microseconds. Input-output equipment consisted of punched card units, paper tape units, and a magnetic drum (added later to the machine). Many machines have been patterned after the IAS computer, among them the ILLIAC (University of Illinois), the JOHNIAC (Rand Corporation), MANIAC (Los Alamos), ORDVAC (University of Illinois), and the WEIZAC (Weizman Institute in Israel).

Shortly after the Korean War started, IBM announced its Defense Calculator, a large-scale scientific computer designed specifically to perform calculations of all kinds. This machine used parallel binary arithmetic and contained a Williams tube memory. The Defense Calculator, a machine much faster than the Univac I, was renamed the IBM 701. The first machine was delivered in early 1953. The IBM 701 used 33 instructions and could perform over 16 000 additions per second. It used a CRT memory patterned after the Williams tube store. Auxiliary storage was provided by 8 192 and 16 384-word magnetic drums and magnetic tape units. Input to the 701 was via punched cards. Output could be punched on cards or printed on a 150 line per minute printer. Only nineteen of these computers were completed.

The IBM 650 was the most popular computer in the late 1950s. Development on this machine began in 1949. The first machine was installed in 1954. Since then over 1 000 machines have been placed in service. The 650 (see Figure 2–13) consists of three units: a punched card input-output unit, a console unit, and a power unit.

(Courtesy of IBM Corporation)

Figure 2–13   IBM 650 computer system.

The IBM 702 was IBM's first large-scale computer designed for business purposes. The first machine was constructed in 1955. The 702 weighs 11 tons and contains approximately 5 000 vacuum tubes. Its arithmetic and logic unit alone contains 2 500 vacuum tubes. The 702 could perform over 43 000 additions per second.

The 702, like other first generation computers, when compared with modern machines looks something like an electronic tin lizzie. It required tons of air conditioning to keep the room cool. The 702 printer could produce reports at a rate of 150 lines per minute; but, in 1973, printers with the capability of producing 2 000 lines per minute were available. In 1955, the cost of performing 100 000 computations on the IBM 702 was $1.38. In 1973, the cost for performing the same number of computations was about two cents.

Although this model was an improvement over then-existing computers, only a few 702 computers were delivered. As soon as IBM announced a newer, more powerful machine—the IBM 705—the 702 was withdrawn from the market. The 702 was actually an obsolete machine before it was delivered.

In 1954, IBM announced the replacement for the IBM 702 as the 705. It was about a year later when the competition—Remington Rand—

announced the replacement for the Univac I. Early 705 computers used a Cathode Ray Tube memory; however, later models were constructed with faster and more reliable magnetic core memories. IBM delivered the first 705 by the end of 1955. Univac II, the 705's competitor, was a water-cooled machine that weighed 15 tons and used some 500 vacuum tubes that fit into a 14 foot by 10 foot cabinet. Remington Rand delivered the first of 29 Univac IIs in 1957, two years after the first IBM 705 was delivered.

The IBM 704, IBM's first large scale machine for the scientific community, was introduced in 1956. The 704 had 91 instructions, could add in 24 microseconds, and could perform either a multiplication or division in 240 microseconds.

IBM machines to follow were the 709, 7090, and 7094. The 709 used the same core memory as the 704 and was only slightly faster. The major improvement over the 704 was a new input-output system that permitted reading from tape or cards, provided print-out on tape or printer, and allowed computation to proceed simultaneously. This was made possible by sharing the core memory between the computer and input-output data channels. The IBM 7090, first delivered in 1959, was a transistorized system compatible with the 709. It was, however, about five times faster than the 709, and used more advanced magnetic tape units. The 7094 was similar to the 7090 except it contained a faster core memory.

During the 1960s, dozens of companies began to manufacture high-speed computers. All of these machines were much faster and more reliable than the early computers. Most of the machines made during the late 1950s and early 1960s belonged to the second generation of computers. These machines were much smaller, required less power, and produced much less heat. The use of transistors as basic components of internal computer circuits was the main reason for this improvement.

The third generation of computers appeared in 1964 when IBM announced the System/360. Most computers made during the late 1960s and 1970s employed microminiature circuits for the computer's internal circuitry. Third generation machines are smaller, more reliable and faster than earlier machines. Along with third generation computers, newer and faster equipment has been introduced for storage and handling of input and output.

At present there are about two dozen American manufacturers of computers. Many of these manufacturers, however, specialize in making small computers, called *minicomputers*. Minicomputers will be discussed in chapter 11.

☐ Review Questions

14. Give the names of two early all-electronic digital computers.

15. What is the basic difference between the Harvard Mark I and the ENIAC?

16. What is the name of the first commercial data processing machines?

17. Modern computers are _____ and _____ than the early computers.
    (a) larger, stronger
    (b) faster, larger
    (c) faster, smaller
    (d) slower, smaller

18. Make a table of all the computers named in this chapter showing the dates of first operation, naming the developer, and detailing addition or multiplication speeds.

□ Summary

The development of tools to aid man in calculating began with early man. Man first used sticks, stones, shells, notches on a stick, marks in the sand, or knots in a rope to aid him in counting. Later, fingers were used to perform simple computations.

One of the earliest calculating devices created by man was the abacus. This ancient calculating instrument has been used for the past 2 000 years and, even today, is widely used in oriental countries.

In the seventeenth century, John Napier developed an ingenious device for multiplying and dividing. The device, called "Napier's Bones," was used for many years.

It was not until 1642 that the first practical calculating machine was built. It was developed by a 19-year-old Frenchman named Pascal. Pascal's calculator was limited to performing only addition and subtraction operations. About 30 years later, a German mathematician named Leibnitz developed a similar machine that could also multiply and divide.

Probably the most outstanding work done in the field of mechanical calculation was accomplished by Charles Babbage. This English mathematician designed a machine in 1833, called the *Analytical Engine,* which was the forerunner of the modern digital computer. Babbage's machine was never built due to engineering problems; however, this device laid the foundation for machines to follow.

In the nineteenth century, several key-driven machines were developed, including the first commercially practical adding machine invented in 1884 by William Burroughs.

It was not until about 20 years after Charles Babbage's death that the use of punched cards was applied to data processing. Cards had been used earlier to control patterns in textile looms. In 1887, Herman Hollerith, an employee of the Census Bureau, used punched card equipment to process the 1890 census. In 1907, James Powers developed a punched card system to process the 1910 census. The machines developed by Hollerith and Powers were improved and used for many years to follow. These machines were forerunners of the electromechanical data processing systems in use today.

The development of the computer, like other calculating devices, took many years. Charles Babbage planted the seed in 1833. In 1938, George Stibitz at Bell Telephone Laboratories built several electromechanical computers.

In the years 1937–44, Howard Aiken of Harvard University led a group of engineers in the design of the Automatic Sequence Controlled Calculator (also called the Mark 1). This large machine used a program to guide it through a long series of calculations. It could perform an addition operation in $\frac{3}{10}$ of a second. The Mark I was used for more than 15 years. Compared with modern computers, it was slow and had a very limited storage capacity, Nevertheless, it was the first *electromechanical computer*.

In 1942 the ABC, designed by Dr. John V. Atanasoff, went into operation. In 1946, at the University of Pennsylvania, the ENIAC went into operation, computing firing and ballistic tables for army artillery guns.

"Do you think there might be something wrong with the traffic control computer?"

In the late 1940s, several electronic machines were developed to perform computations. However, it was not until 1951 that computers were thought to be anything other than scientific computing instruments. At this time the Univac I machines were built, and during the early 1950s they were used extensively for data processing applications. Shortly after the Korean War, IBM (International Business Machines Corp.) began to manufacture machines for business users. Early IBM machines included the 650, 701, 702, 704, 705, 7090, and 7094.

Thus, by the mid 1960s, computers had already assumed an important role in U.S. society, leading the way toward their almost universal application in major business and governmental areas today.

Key Terms

abacus	EDSAC
Analytical Engine	vacuum tube
punched card	transistor
ENIAC	ABC

two

Punched Card
Data
Processing

3

Punched Card Systems

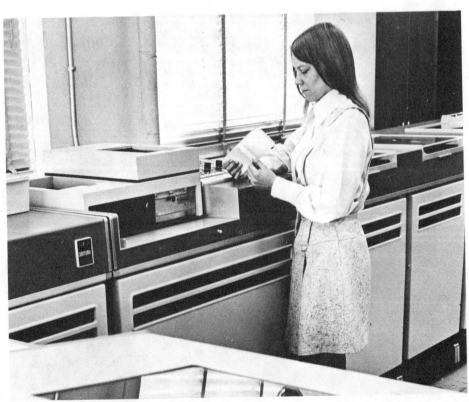

(Courtesy of National Cash Register Company)

Punched cards are the most popular medium for entering data into the computer. There are two types of punched cards currently in use: the standard 80-column card and the smaller 96-column card used with the IBM System/3 computer.

In this chapter we will describe these two types of cards as well as the keypunch and the verifier, which are machines used for preparing punched cards. We will then discuss the machines used to arrange the data and, finally, those machines that process the data.

☐ The Card

The punched card is familiar to almost everyone because of the frequency with which it appears in such forms as utility bills, payroll checks, money orders, magazine subscription notices, insurance premium notices, and security meeting notices. The standard card measures 18.7 cm × 8.3 cm (7⅜ inches by 3¼ inches) and it has 80 columns. The card is cut from a durable paper stock that provides strength and long life. Most of the newer cards have round corners.

Examine the card in Figure 3–1. It is divided into 80 vertical *card columns*. A scale at the top and bottom of the card designates each of the columns. Only a single digit, letter, or symbol may be recorded in each of the 80 columns. Horizontally, each card column is divided into twelve *card rows*. These twelve rows are the designated areas in which a punch may be placed. Rows 0 to 9 are usually printed on the card. The top two rows, the eleventh and twelfth rows, normally are not printed on the card.* Punches in either of these two positions are called *zone punches*.

Punches in the 1 through 9 locations are referred to as *digit punches*. A zero position may be either a zone punch or a digit punch. It is a digit punch when no other punch is recorded on the column. It is a zone

---

* The twelfth row is called the *Y position;* the eleventh row is the *X position.*

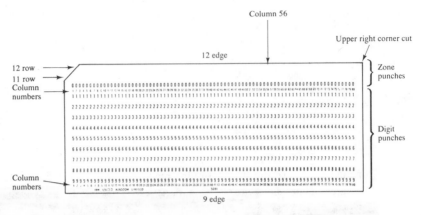

Figure 3–1   Standard 80-column card.

punch if a digit punch is recorded below it. The top edge of the card is referred to as the "12 edge," and the bottom edge is called the "9 edge." Cards are fed through the data processing machines either 12 edge or 9 edge first.

Cards may be made from any color stock and any information can be printed on the card. A further method of visually identifying a type of card is the corner cut. By using a certain color and by cutting a specific corner off the card, one can identify cards of the same type. For example, a payroll card could be red with a right corner cut, an inventory card yellow with a left corner cut, and a billing card blue with no corner cut. Data processing equipment has only the ability to read the information punched into cards—they cannot read the card by its color or corner cut.

☐ Review Questions

1. How many columns are there in a standard punched card? How many rows? *80 ~ 12 Row*
2. How are the top and bottom edges in the card identified? *Top—12 Edge Bot —9 Edge*
3. Can the number 78 be punched in one card column? Explain. *No*
4. Does the color of the card or corner cuts affect the reading of a punched card? *No*
5. What is the purpose of card corner cuts and color stripping? *Identify cards of same type.*

☐ Numeric Code

Numeric information is recorded on a card by punching a single hole in a card column. This hole is punched in the numbered row that is the same number as the digit that is to be recorded. For example, if the number 4 371 is recorded in card columns 1 to 4, the card will be punched as follows:

Card column 1 will contain a punched hole in row 4.
Card column 2 will contain a punched hole in row 3.
Card column 3 will contain a punched hole in row 7.
Card column 4 will contain a punched hole in row 1.
(See Figure 3–2).

The card illustrated in Figure 3–3 shows the digits 0 through 9 printed in each vertical column. This card also shows the digits 0 through 9 punched in card column 1 through 10. The interpretation of each punched hole is printed at the top of the card.

More than one digit cannot be punched in the same column. If a number has seven digits, then seven card columns must be used to properly represent the number.

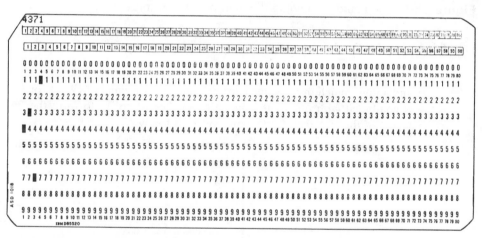

Figure 3–2   Punched card containing the number 4,371.

Numbers punched in a card can represent practically anything. For example, the digits 4027 could mean $40.27; it could mean the population of a small town; or it might signify the number of television sets sold by a specific store. It could be an employee's identification number or the code number of a product. The number means nothing until meaning is assigned to it.

☐ Review Questions

6. How many card columns would be needed to record the number 863?

7. Can a multiple-digit number (such as 47) be punched in a single column of a card? Explain.

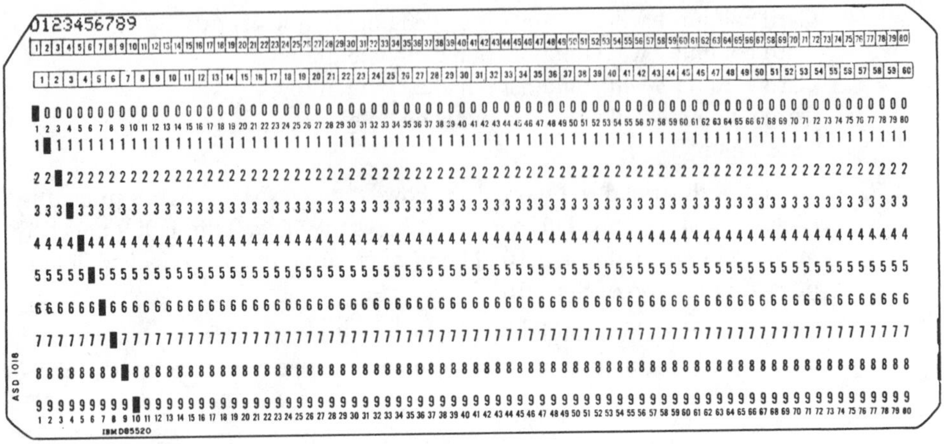

Figure 3–3   Punched card containing the digit punches 0 through 9.

☐ Alphabetic Code

The letters of the alphabet are represented by the combination of a zone and a digit punch in the same card column. A zone punch (12, 11, or 0) is combined with one of the numeric punches (1 to 9) to form the 26 letters of the alphabet. Letters are coded as follows:

Letter	Zone	Number Punch
A		1
B		2
C		3
D	12	4
E	Zone	5
F		6
G		7
H		8
I		9
J		1
K		2
L		3
M	11	4
N	Zone	5
O		6
P		7
Q		8
R		9
S		2
T		3
U	0	4
V	Zone	5
W		6
X		7
Y		8
Z		9

Figure 3–4 shows all of the letters of the alphabet punched in a card. The interpretation of the punches is shown at the top of the card. As with the digits, only one letter can be punched in a single card column. The letter C, for example, is represented by punches in the 12 and 3 rows.

Review Questions

8. How many card columns would be needed to record this address?

VOLUSIA OFFICE SUPPLY
3641 GRANADA AVE MIAMI FLORIDA

Assume one card column is used for spacing between words.

9. Why is it necessary to use two punched holes in a card column to represent an alphabetic character?

10. What letter is represented by punches 0 and 6 in a card column?

11. What is the maximum number of alphabetic characters that can be punched in a single card column?

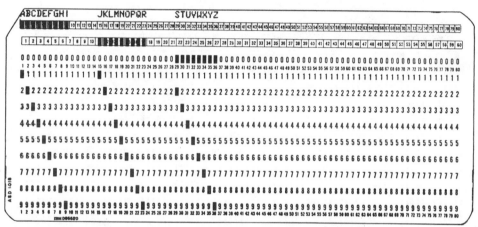

Figure 3–4   Punched card containing the letters of the alphabet.

Special Characters

The special characters are represented by zero, one, two, or three punches in a single card column. Figure 3–5 shows the punches that represent the different special characters. As shown in this illustration, a decimal point consists of a 12, 3, and 8 punch, while a hypen (-) consists of an 11 punch only.

The card shown in Figure 3–6 shows digit, alphabetic, and special character punches.

Review Questions

12. What special character is represented by punches in rows 12, 6, and 8?

13. What punches are used to represent the @ symbol?

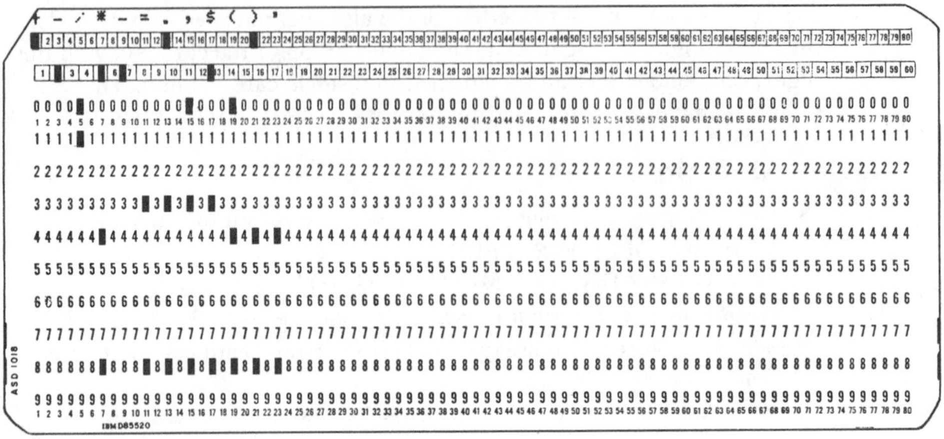

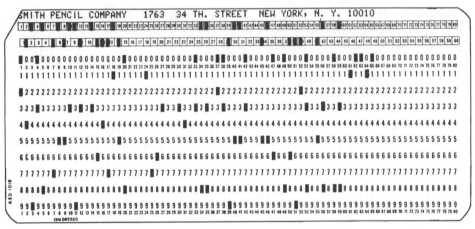

Figure 3–5 Punched card containing special characters.

Figure 3–6 Card containing digit, alphabetic, and special character punches.

☐ Card Fields

Data of a particular type, such as a customer name, invoice number, salesman number, or item amount must be recorded in some predetermined section of the card called a *field*. A field may consist of a single column or a group of consecutive columns and may contain numeric, alphabetic, or alphameric information. Figure 3–7 illustrates a card with six field assignments. From left to right, they are the ITEM CODE field, the ITEM DESCRIPTION field, the UNIT COST field, the UNIT PRICE field, the ON HAND field, and the ON ORDER field.

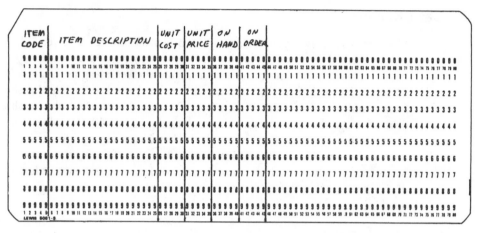

Figure 3–7   Punched card containing six fields.

Alphabetic information is usually punched starting in the left-most column within the field. This is often referred to as *left justification*. Numeric information is recorded with the units position of a number in the right-most column within a field. This is called *right justification*. If the number to be punched in the field is smaller than the number of card columns assigned to the field, zeros are normally placed to the left of the number.

Review Questions

14. What is a field?
15. Define "left justification" and "right justification."
16. True or false? The smallest possible field on a card is two card columns.
17. True or false? A field in card columns 15 to 24 contains 9 columns of data.

Marked Sensed Cards

Mark sensed cards allow users to enter data directly into a computer system without any form of intermediate data representation. Carefully controlled pencil marks are used to identify data to mark sense readers. The readers sense the presence or absence of pencil marks. The computer must then correlate these marks with preprogrammed data to determine their significance. The mark sensed card is one of the most economical forms of automatically entering data into a computer.

Review Questions

18. What are mark sensed cards? How are they used?

☐ Card Reading

Most card reading machines contain a brush or brushes that read the holes punched in a card. As the card passes through the machine, it passes between a reading brush and a metal roller carrying an electrical current (Figure 3–8). The card acts as an insulator keeping the brush from contacting the roller. When a hole in the card is reached, the brush drops through the card, thus making electrical contact with the roller. An electrical impulse then flows through the brush and can be directed by control panel wiring or by machine circuits to perform a specific function. Many card reading machines contain 80 brushes, one for each column of the card, so that the entire card may be read as it passes through the machine.

☐ 96-Column Card

In 1969, IBM introduced a new 96-column card (three rows of 32 columns) for use with the System/3 computer, which was designed for small businesses. This card is considerably smaller in size than the standard 80-column card, yet it can contain more information. Figure 3–9 illustrates this card, which is approximately the same length as the common credit card, but is wider by one-half inch.

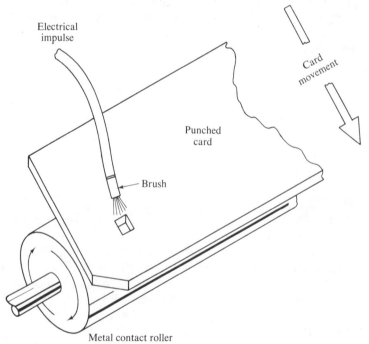

Figure 3–8   Schematic of punched card reading.

The 96-column card is divided into two sections: the upper section is reserved for printed information; the lower section is designed for punching. The punch area is divided into three horizontal tiers, each containing 32 card columns. Any of the digits or letters of the alphabet or one of 28 special characters can be represented in a card column. A column is broken down into two zone positions (A and B) and four digit positions (8, 4, 2, and 1). The digits and alphabetic characters are represented by the following punches:

Letter	Zone (A, B)	Digit (8, 4, 2, 1)
A		1
B		2
C		1 and 2
D	AB	4
E	Zone	1 and 4
F		2 and 4
G		1, 2, and 4
H		8
I		1 and 8
J		1
K		2
L		1 and 2
M	B	4
N	Zone	1 and 4
O		2 and 4
P		1, 2, and 4
Q		8
R		1 and 8
S		2
T		1 and 2
U		4
V	A	1 and 4
W	Zone	2 and 4
X		1, 2, and 4
Y		8
Z		1 and 8
0		· · · [no digit punch]
1		1
2		2
3		1 and 2
4		4
5		1 and 4
6		2 and 4
7		1, 2, and 4
8		8
9		1 and 8

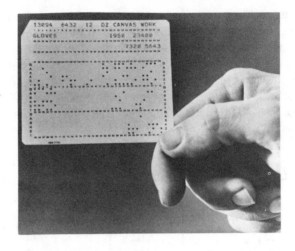

(Courtesy of IBM Corporation)

Figure   96-column card.
3–9

Special characters are represented by a combination of punches in the digit and zone portions of the card column.

Data punched in a 96-column card can be interpreted at the top of the card. The 96 printing positions correspond to the 96 punching positions.

⬜ Microfilm Card

Microfilm cards have areas reserved for a frame of microfilm. Figure 3–10 illustrates a card with punched information on the left side of the

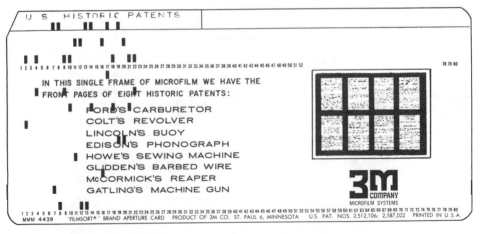

Figure   Microfilm card.
3–10

card and a microfilm on the right side of the card. In this example, the front pages of eight historic patents are represented on the microfilm. Microfilm cards are used primarily in computer-controlled microfilm information retrieval and storage systems.

☐ Keypunch

The *keypunch,* shown in Figure 3–11, is the most common device for recording information from source documents into punched cards. It may be used to punch numerical, alphabetic, and special-character information. To begin punching, the keypunch operator places blank cards in the hopper of the machine and sits at a typewriter-like keyboard. The card hopper holds approximately 500 cards. The cards are inserted face forward with the 12 edge up. At the touch of the REL (release) button, cards are fed down to the *card bed* and move across it from right to left. As the card moves, it passes under the punching and reading stations. Punching is done by hitting the keys of the keyboard. As each key is depressed, the proper code is punched and printed in the column under the punching station. Then, the card moves to the left, advancing one column at a time. When the card reaches the left end of the card bed, it is placed in the stacker; at the same time, a new card is taken from the hopper

(Courtesy of IBM Corporation)

Figure   IBM 29 keypunch.
3–11

and placed at the right-hand end of the card bed. After keypunching is complete, the newly punched card is automatically placed in the stacker on the left of the machine.

Keypunches are available with more than one type of keyboard. One keyboard is used for recording numeric data only. Figure 3–12 illustrates the combination keyboard which is used for punching alphabetic, numeric, and special-character information in a card. Observe the keys in the outlined area in Figure 3–12. These keys are used for punching both letters and numbers. For example, the K key will punch both K and the number 5. The letter is punched by merely depressing the indicated key; the number is punched by depressing the NUMERIC key along with the indicated key. Using the keypunch keyboard is similar to typing on a typewriter and operators can become proficient with only a small amount of training and practice.

The keypunch includes several features which aid in punching cards. Basically, the features consist of a skip key, a duplicate key, a program card, and a special key for inserting zeros in the unused columns of a numeric field.

(Courtesy of IBM Corporation)

**Figure
3–12**   Keyboard of an IBM 29 keypunch machine.

A *skip key* is provided to move quickly from one punching field to another. It is similar to a tabulator bar on a typewriter. The key is used in conjunction with a program card. The *program card* automatically provides for skipping, duplicating, and shifting. Each of these operations is designated by a specific code punched in a program card which automatically controls the punching operation column by column. A separate program card must be prepared for each job. For example, one program card must be prepared for punching information in cards for payroll, another for punching information for student registration.

A program card is illustrated in Figure 3–13. This card is prepared for each different punching application and can be used repeatedly. Proper punching in this program card controls the automatic operations for the corresponding columns of the cards being punched. Each punch in the program card governs a specific function:

Punches	Function
0	*Automatic Duplication*—A punch in the 0 position in the first column of a field automatically starts duplication, which is then continued by the 12s punched in the remaining columns of the field.
1	*Alphabetic Punching*—A punch in the 1 position shifts the keypunch keyboard to the alphabetic position so that alphabetic characters will be punched in the field.
11	*Automatic Skip*—A 11 punch in the first column of any field automatically starts a skip, which is then continued by the 12s punched in the remaining columns of the field.
12	*Field Definition*—A 12 punch must be recorded in every column except the first of every field to be automatically skipped, duplicated, or manually punched.
blank (no punch)	A blank column on the program card indicates the beginning of a field in which numeric data are to be punched on the keypunch by the operator.

The IBM 29 keypunch allows for following two separate programs punched in one program card. The keypunch operator can switch from one program to the other by merely depressing either the PROG ONE or PROG TWO keys (reference Figure 3–12). One program is punched at the top of the program card while the other is punched near the middle of the card (rows 4, 5, 6, and 7 instead of rows 12, 11, 0, and 1).

Cards can be duplicated on the keypunch. Pressing a duplicate key (DUP) on the keyboard causes a sensing device to read the punches in the card at the reading station and punches this information into the card at the reading station and punches this information into the card at the punching station (see Figure 3–11 for locations of the reading and punch-

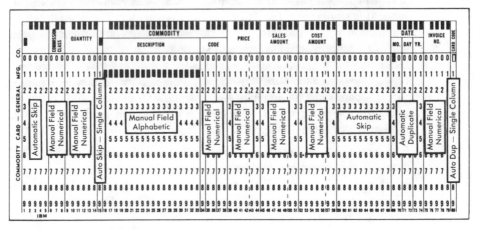

(Courtesy of IBM Corporation)

**Figure
3–13**   Program card.

ing stations). After a card has been duplicated, accuracy can be determined by a "sight check" of the cards. This is accomplished by placing the duplicated card in front of the original card and holding them both up to the light to insure that daylight appears in all punched columns.

With program control, zeros punched to the left of the first significant digit in a numeric field determined by 12s in the program card are automatically suppressed in normal printing (00036 is printed 36). The IBM 29 keypunch is equipped with a special key (the LEFT ZERO key) which, when depressed, will automatically determine the number of zeros needed and will cause the extra zeros to be punched. The LEFT ZERO key works in conjunction with a program card placed in the machine.

☐ **Verifier**

It is very important that cards be punched correctly or all subsequent processing will be in error. Thus, after cards are punched they are immediately checked for correctness. This can be done with a machine that looks like a keypunch, called a *verifier* (Figure 3–14). The main difference between these machines is that the verifier is equipped with a sensing device to read holes rather than with a punching mechanism to punch holes.

In order to verify a set of cards, the operator places the card deck in the hopper of the verifier and proceeds as if he were punching on the keypunch (he uses the source documents that were used during key-

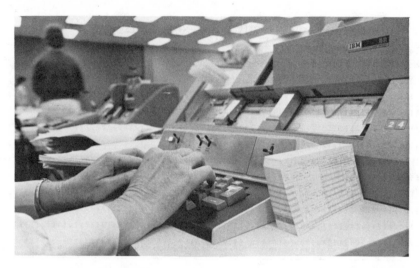

(Courtesy of Delta Air Lines, Inc.)

Figure 3–14   Operator checking the correctness of punched cards with an IBM 59 verifier.

punching). When a key is pushed on the verifier, the result must agree with the code already punched on the card. If the punched card agrees with what the operator "punches," a notch is cut at the end between rows 0 and 1 (Figure 3–15). This is called the OK notch. If the card is incorrect, a notch is cut in the card over the column containing an error (Figure 3–16). When an error is detected, a red error light goes on. The light goes

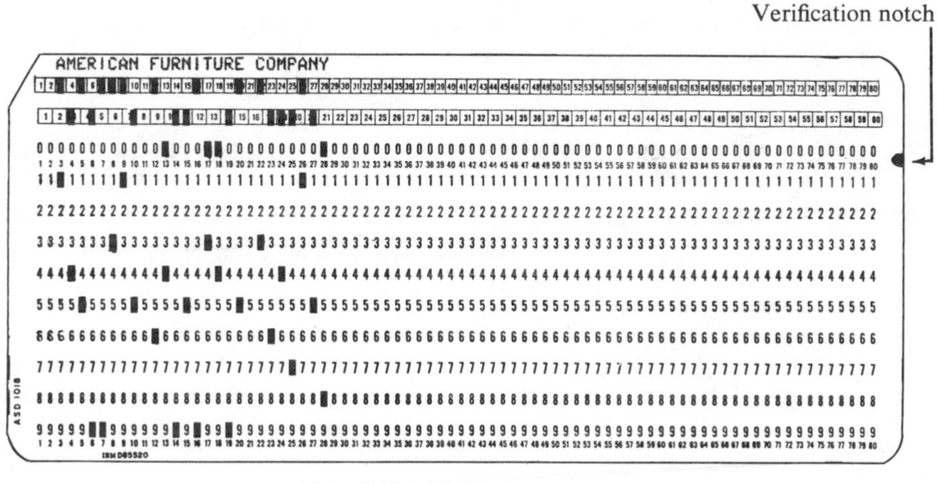

Verification notch

Figure 3–15   A verified card.

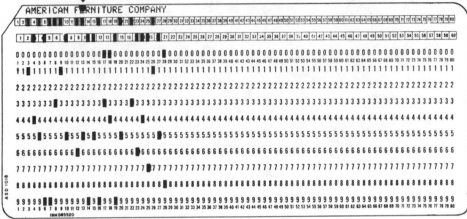

Figure   An error-notched card.
3–16

off if the second attempt at verification is correct; if not, it goes off when the third attempt is made.

☐ Review Questions

19. What is the keypunch used for?

20. What is a verifier?

21. What are the functions of the reading and punching stations on a keypunch?

22. Which key on the keypunch is similar to the tabulator bar on a typewriter?

23. What punch in the program card starts skipping? Duplicating? Alphabetic shifting?

24. What is the purpose of the 12 zone punch in a program card?

25. How are correctly punched cards identified by a verifier?

☐ Punched Card Equipment

In addition to the keypunch and the verifier for preparing punched cards, there are several card machines that together provide data processing capabilities without the use of a computer. Today, due to the availability of low-cost, small-scale computer systems, it is more common to see punched card equipment used as part of a computer system. There are six types of card equipment (also called *unit record equipment*): sorters, collators, interpreters, calculators, accounting machines, and reproducers.

After the cards have been punched, they can be sorted into the desired sequence on the punched card *sorter*. While the sorter can be used to arrange a single file of cards, many operations require that two files be processed together. The machine used to merge and match two punched card files is the punched card *collator*. The collator is capable of performing four operations: (1) combining two card files into one complete file, (2) matching two files of cards while selecting any unmatched cards from the file, (3) selecting specific cards from a file, and (4) checking the sequence of cards in a file.

A special machine is available to read punches in cards and to print the characters on the face of the card to facilitate ease of reading. This machine, the punched card *interpreter,* is used to interpret the cards which have not been interpreted on the keypunch machine.

Another machine is used to calculate data which have been punched into cards. This machine, the punched card *calculator,* can add, subtract, multiply, and divide data and punch the answer into the same card or another card.

The machine used to prepare printed documents from punched cards is the *accounting machine*. It can print a line from each card, or it can summarize the data from several cards into one printed line.

The final punched card machine to be discussed is the *reproducer.* This machine has the ability to punch data into cards at a speed of 100 cards per minute from data which have been previously punched, from pencil marks on the cards, or from data accumulated on the accounting machine.

Each of these punched card machines is a separate system with an input device, output device, and some sort of control. The keypunch, verifier, and sorter are controlled by operators. The remaining machines are controlled by a *wired board or control panel* which can be wired (programmed) to specify the exact operation to be performed. For example, the accounting machine can print a management inventory report, as directed by one control panel, and print payroll checks, as directed by another control panel.

The punched card machines are victims of the times. They have been generally replaced by small-scale computer systems. Machines such as the IBM System/3, IBM System/32, minicomputer based business systems, and other small-scale computer systems have reduced the popularity of the punched card equipment.

☐ Review Questions

26. Identify six punched card machines.
27. Briefly describe the functions of the punched card machines presented in this chapter.
28. Why is the use of punched card equipment diminishing in popularity?

☐ Summary

Although punched cards date back to the late 1800s, they have remained popular throughout the years. They are a convenient and inexpensive means of storing information suitable for entry into a data processing system.

The most commonly used punched card has 80 columns and 12 rows. Information is represented on the card by the presence or absence of coded punches. Numeric information is recorded on a card by punching

a single hole in the card column. Letters of the alphabet are represented by two holes punched in a column. Special characters are represented by one, two, or three punches in a column.

The card code discussed in this chapter is the principle code used with data processing equipment today. Information represented by this punched code is accepted by most card handling equipment.

Information may be represented on cards in a form other than coded punches. Mark sensed cards allow information to be represented in the form of pencil marks. Mark sense card readers are used to detect the presence or absence of pencil marks on the card. Microfilm cards are another form of information storage which have areas reserved for a frame of microfilm.

Punched card machines were the most popular means of handling large amounts of data before the computer. There are eight different punched card machines, and each has a special purpose. The keypunch and verifier are used to prepare cards for processing; the sorter and collator arrange the data; and the interpreter, calculator, accounting machine, and reproducer process the data. The punched card machines are victims of the times and have been replaced by low-cost computer systems.

Key Terms

card column

card row

zone punch

digit punch

twelve edge

nine edge

field

left justification

keypunch

verifier

sorter

interpreter

right justification

numeric punch

alphabetic punch

mark sensed card

80-column card

96-column card

microfilm card

collator

accounting machine

calculator

reproducer

three

Number and Data Representation

4

Number Systems and Computer Arithmetic

Courtesy of IBM Corporation

It is quite possible to understand data processing techniques and equipment without knowing the detail operations that take place inside the machines. Nevertheless, understanding the basic workings of these machines brings an increased appreciation for them.

One basic rule that computer programmers learn early is "If anything can go wrong, it will." Programming any large problem for a computer is an exacting task that leaves much room for making mistakes. In short, very few programs of any size ever work the first time they are run on a computer. The programmer usually examines the program, step-by-step until it is free from errors. Often during this process, the programmer uses intermediate results from the computer to aid in his error-correcting process. In many cases, these intermediate results are printed in hexadecimal or octal number bases. Therefore, it is advisable that the programmer have a working knowledge of the different number bases that are used with computers.

In this chapter, we will discuss the number systems and arithmetic that are used with computers.

□ A Short History of Number Systems

The concept of number and the process of counting developed so long before the time of recorded history that the manner of this development is largely conjecture. It is not difficult, though, to imagine how it probably came about. A primitive tribe had to know how many members it had and how many enemies it opposed, while a shepherd found it necessary to know whether his flock of sheep was decreasing in size. Probably the earliest way of keeping a count was by some simple tally method, employing the principle of one-to-one correspondence. Using sticks, stones, fingers, notches in woods and knots in a string, a man was able to keep count of his sheep or any other possessions.

When it became necessary to make more extensive counts, the counting process had to be systematized. By arranging the numbers into convenient basic groups, early man introduced the concept of *number bases*.

There is evidence that three and four served as primitive number bases. Today, some South American tribes count by hands, base five. Base 12 was used in prehistoric times, chiefly in relation to measurements. The American Indian and Mayan tribes used a base 20 number system. The ancient Babylonians used a number system based on 60. This system is still used when measuring time and angles in minutes and seconds.

The number system that modern man is most familiar with has a *base* or *radix* of 10. This system undoubtedly resulted from finger counting. This system appeared first in India about A.D. 500. Over the years, the decimal notation spread throughout Europe.

The decimal system has the ten symbols 0, 1, 2, 3, 4, 5, 6, 7, 8, and 9. From elementary school on, students are taught to compute primarily with the decimal system. However, the computer does not use this number base for calculating. The computer uses a number system of radix two. This system has only two digits, 0 and 1.

The number system in base two is called the *binary system*. It was not until 1945, when John von Neumann outlined the stored-program concept for digital computers, that the binary system was to be made the common language for all future computers. The binary system is used within the computer for the following reasons.

1. To simplify the arithmetic circuitry of the computer.
2. To provide a simple way to store information and instructions.
3. To provide reliability.

Two other number systems are used when working with computers: hexadecimal and octal. These number systems are used primarily as a means of representing binary numbers. The hexadecimal system, base 16, uses the following digits: 0, 1, 2, 3, 4, 5, 6, 7, 8, 9, A, B, C, D, E, and F. The octal system, base eight, uses the digits 0, 1, 2, 3, 4, 5, 6, and 7. Both of these number systems offer a shorthand method of representing binary numbers. For example, the binary number 1111000000011-11001110110 can be represented in hexadecimal as F01E76, and in octal as 74017166. Both of these numbers are considerably shorter than the long binary number.

Every number system has three concepts in common: (1) a base or radix, (2) digit value, and (3) positional notation. The base is the number of different digits used in that system. Each digit of a specified number system has a distinct value. Each number position carries a specific weight depending on the base of the system. For example, the decimal number 3,417 can be described as shown on page 105.

As seen in this example, each digit position has a value equal to the product of the digit appearing in the position and a corresponding power of ten.

$$3 \quad 4 \quad 1 \quad 7$$

$$7 \times 10^0 = 7 \times 1 \quad = \quad 7$$
$$1 \times 10^1 = 1 \times 10 \quad = \quad 10$$
$$4 \times 10^2 = 4 \times 100 \quad = \quad 400$$
$$3 \times 10^3 = 3 \times 1000 = \underline{3000}$$
$$3417$$

Let us now briefly examine the binary, hexadecimal, and octal number systems. Table 4–1 illustrates the first few numbers in each of these num-

Table 4–1   Decimal, binary, hexadecimal and octal notation.

Decimal	Binary	Hexadecimal	Octal
0	00000	0	0
1	00001	1	1
2	00010	2	2
3	00011	3	3
4	00100	4	4
5	00101	5	5
6	00110	6	6
7	00111	7	7
8	01000	8	10
9	01001	9	11
10	01010	A	12
11	01011	B	13
12	01100	C	14
13	01101	D	15
14	01110	E	16
15	01111	F	17
16	10000	10	20
17	10001	11	21
18	10010	12	22
19	10011	13	23
20	10100	14	24
21	10101	15	25
22	10110	16	26
23	10111	17	27
24	11000	18	30
25	11001	19	31
26	11010	1A	32
27	11011	1B	33
.	.	.	.
.	.	.	.
.	.	.	.

ber systems. Numbers on the same row of this table are equivalent—
that is,

$$14(\text{decimal}) = 1110(\text{binary}) = E(\text{hexadecimal}) = 16(\text{octal})$$

□ Binary Number System

The binary number system is based on 2, rather than 10, so that numbers
are expressed in powers of 2. A short table of powers of 2 follows:

$2^0 = 1$	$2^7 = 128$
$2^1 = 2$	$2^8 = 256$
$2^2 = 4$	$2^9 = 512$
$2^3 = 8$	$2^{10} = 1024$
$2^4 = 16$	$2^{11} = 2048$
$2^5 = 32$	$2^{12} = 4096$
$2^6 = 64$	$2^{13} = 8192$

The value of a binary number in base 10 is determined by multiplying
the value of each digit (0 or 1) by the corresponding power of two and
summing all the products. The presence of a one in a digit position of a
binary number indicates that the corresponding power of two is used in
determining the value of the number. A zero in a digit position indicates
that the corresponding power of two is absent from the number. For
example, the binary number

100111 may be expressed as

$$\begin{aligned}
100111 &= (1 \times 2^5) + (0 \times 2^4) + (0 \times 2^3) + (1 \times 2^2) \\
&\quad + (1 \times 2^1) + (1 \times 2^0) \\
&= (1 \times 32) + (0 \times 16) + (0 \times 8) + (1 \times 4) \\
&\quad + (1 \times 2) + (1 \times 1) \\
&= 32 + 0 + 0 + 4 + 2 + 1 \\
&= 39
\end{aligned}$$

The binary number 100111 is equivalent to the decimal number 39.

To avoid confusion when several systems of notation are employed, it is
customary to enclose each number in parentheses and to write the base
as a subscript, in decimal notation. Thus, the previous example could
be written as

$$(100111)_2 = (39)_{10}$$

Binary fractions are handled in the same way by assigning negative powers of 2 to the right of the binary point in ascending sequence. A short
table of the negative powers of 2 follows:

$$2^{-1} = \tfrac{1}{2} = .5 \qquad\qquad 2^{-5} = \tfrac{1}{64} = .03125$$
$$2^{-2} = \tfrac{1}{4} = .25 \qquad\qquad 2^{-6} = \tfrac{1}{128} = .015625$$
$$2^{-3} = \tfrac{1}{8} = .125 \qquad\qquad 2^{-7} = \tfrac{1}{256} = .0078125$$
$$2^{-4} = \tfrac{1}{16} = .0625$$

The binary fraction 0.1101 means

$$.1101 = (1 \times 2^{-1}) + (1 \times 2^{-2}) + (0 \times 2^{-3}) + (1 \times 2^{-4})$$
$$= \tfrac{1}{2} + \tfrac{1}{4} + 0 + \tfrac{1}{16} = \tfrac{13}{16}$$

or

$$= .5 + .25 + 0 + .0625 = .8125$$

Thus,

$$(.1101)_2 = \tfrac{13}{16} = (.8125)_{10}$$

As was the case with the binary number, an expansion of the binary fraction yields an equivalent decimal fraction.

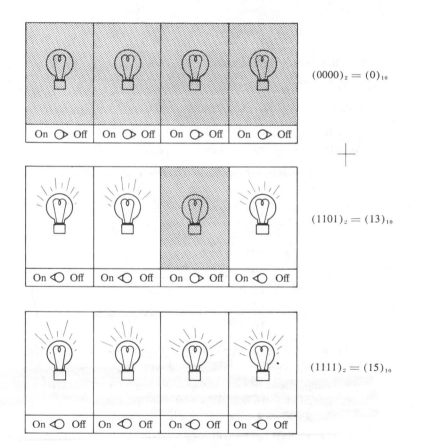

$(0000)_2 = (0)_{10}$

$+$

$(1101)_2 = (13)_{10}$

$(1111)_2 = (15)_{10}$

Figure 4–1   Binary lights representing decimal data.

Figure 4–1 illustrates how a binary device can be used to represent the decimal values from 0 to 15.

☐ Hexadecimal Number System

The hexadecimal number system is based on a radix of 16 and uses the following 16 digits: 0, 1, 2, 3, 4, 5, 6, 7, 8, 9, A, B, C, D, E, and F. The decimal value of a hexadecimal number is determined by multiplying the value of each digit by the corresponding power of 16 and summing all the products. For example, the equivalent decimal value of the hexadecimal number 83.5 may be determined in the following manner.

$$
\begin{array}{llll}
8 & 3 & . & 5 \\
\end{array}
$$

$$5 \times 16^{-1} = 5 \times \tfrac{1}{16} = .3125$$
$$3 \times 16^{0} = 3 \times 1 = 3.$$
$$8 \times 16^{1} = 8 \times 16 = 128.$$
$$\overline{131.3125}$$

Thus, the hexadecimal number 83.5 is equivalent to the decimal number 131.3125 and is written as

$$(83.5)_{16} = (131.3125)_{10}$$

It may be useful to refer to the following table for powers of 16 when converting hexadecimal numbers to decimal numbers.

Powers of Sixteen	Decimal Equivalent
16^4	65536
16^3	4096
16^2	256
16^1	16
16^0	1
16^{-1}	0.0625
16^{-2}	0.003906
16^{-3}	0.00024414

The hexadecimal number system provides a shortcut method of representing binary numbers. To convert a binary number to hexadecimal notation, divide the binary number into groups of four digits, starting from the binary point, and replace each group with the corresponding hexadecimal symbol. For example, the binary number

$$
\begin{array}{rcccccc}
1101111100011010.0011 & = & 1101 & 1111 & 0001 & 1010 & . & 0011 \\
& = & D & F & 1 & A & . & 3
\end{array}
$$

Thus,

$$(1101111100011010.011)_2 = (DF1A.3)_{16}$$

For reference, the binary groupings for each of the hexadecimal digits is as follows:

Binary Grouping	Hexadecimal Symbol
0000	0
0001	1
0010	2
0011	3
0100	4
0101	5
0110	6
0111	7
1000	8
1001	9
1010	A
1011	B
1100	C
1101	D
1110	E
1111	F

Similarly, to convert a hexadecimal number into binary, substitute the corresponding group of four binary digits for each hexadecimal digit. For example,

$$(2A67.2F)_{16} = 2 \quad A \quad 6 \quad 7 \quad . \quad 2 \quad F$$
$$= 0010 \ 1010 \ 0110 \ 0111 \ . \ 0010 \ 1111$$
$$= (10101001100111.00101111)_2$$

As shown in the previous example, leading zeros are discarded.

□ Octal Number System

An octal number system is a number system whose base is 8 and which uses the digits 0, 1, 2, 3, 4, 5, 6, and 7. Let us take the number $(143)_8$ and convert it into decimal.

$$(1 \quad 4 \quad 3)_8$$

$$3 \times 8^0 = 3 \times 1 = 3$$
$$4 \times 8^1 = 4 \times 8 = 32$$
$$1 \times 8^2 = 1 \times 64 = 64$$
$$(99)_{10}$$

Note that the conversion is done exactly as was done with binary and hexadecimal numbers, except that powers of eight were used. The following table may be useful for such conversions.

Powers of Eight	Decimal Equivalent
8^7	2097152
8^6	262144
8^5	32768
8^4	4096
8^3	512
8^2	64
8^1	8
8^0	1
8^{-1}	0.125
8^{-2}	0.015625
8^{-3}	0.001953125
8^{-4}	0.000244140625

Similar to the hexadecimal number system, the octal number system has special characteristics that make it especially useful in many situations involving binary numbers. Since three binary digits may be grouped and represented as one octal digit, many binary numbers may be represented by using octal notation. This representation is extremely useful when working with the operator's console of many computers and when printing the contents of a computer's memory. The following octal digits are used to represent the groupings of three binary digits.

Binary Grouping	Octal Digit
000	0
001	1
010	2
011	3
100	4
101	5
110	6
111	7

As was done with hexadecimal numbers, grouping of a binary number starts from the binary point and goes outwards in both directions. For example,

$$(111010000001.110)_2 = 111 \ 010 \ 000 \ 001 \cdot 110$$
$$= 7 \quad 2 \quad 0 \quad 1 \cdot 6$$

Thus,

$$(111010000001.110)_2 = (7201.6)_8$$

Again, the writing and reading of binary numbers has been simplified in this case by using octal notation.

An octal number is converted to binary by using the opposite procedure. For example,

$$(263.4)_8 = 2 \quad 6 \quad 3 \quad . \quad 4$$
$$= 010 \quad 110 \quad 011 \quad . \quad 100$$
$$= (10110011.100)_2$$

☐ Review Questions

1. What is meant by the *base* or *radix* of a number system?
2. Match the following number system names (column 1) with their appropriate base (column 2).

1	2
(a) Decimal	(1) Base 16
(b) Binary	(2) Base 2
(c) Hexadecimal	(3) Base 8
(d) Octal	(4) Base 10

3. Express the positional values of the following decimal numbers.
   (a) $(3,264)_{10}$
   (b) $(48.9)_{10}$
   (c) $(1763.402)_{10}$
4. What is the decimal value of the following binary numbers?
   (a) $(111010)_2$
   (b) $(.1110111)_2$
   (c) $(1010.0011)_2$
5. What is the decimal value that is indicated by the following binary device?

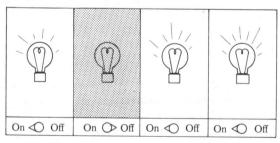

| On ◁○ Off | On ○▷ Off | On ◁○ Off | On ◁○ Off |

6. Expand the hexadecimal number $(2F.A6)_{16}$ into positional notation.
7. Express the hexadecimal number $(84.E)_{16}$ as a decimal value.
8. Show the binary equivalents of the following hexadecimal numbers.
   (a) $(29)_{16}$
   (b) $(42C)_{16}$
   (c) $(63.4F)_{16}$
   (d) $(163A7.2E7)_{16}$

9. Convert the following binary numbers to hexadecimal.
   (a) $(11110010)_2$
   (b) $(101100001110)_2$
   (c) $(.11010010)_2$
   (d) $(1011000000000011.01100111)_2$
10. Express $(237.4)_8$ as a decimal number.
11. Show the binary equivalents of the following octal numbers.
    (a) $(36)_8$
    (b) $(147)_8$
    (c) $(4.7)_8$
    (d) $(621.33)_8$
12. Convert the following binary numbers to octal.
    (a) $(110000111)_2$
    (b) $(101111000001)_2$
    (c) $(111111.011)_2$
    (d) $(111000001.011110)_2$

☐ Computer Arithmetic

A further understanding of number systems can be gained by studying arithmetic operations in different bases. Although all arithmetic can be performed by counting, we are more familiar with the labor-saving operations of addition, subtraction, multiplication, and division. All of these operations can be carried out in binary, octal, or hexadecimal, as well as in the decimal system.

Most people are familiar with performing arithmetic operations in decimal notation and the decimal addition and multiplication tables (shown in Table 4–2) are taught in elementary school. Arithmetic operations in other number systems can be performed by means of similar tables.

Binary Arithmetic

Since there are only two numbers in the binary system, 0 and 1, arithmetic operations are rather simple. Binary numbers are added in the same manner as decimal numbers, although binary arithmetic is easier. There are only four possible combinations resulting from the addition of two binary digits.

$$0 + 0 = 0$$
$$0 + 1 = 1$$
$$1 + 0 = 1$$
$$1 + 1 = 0 \text{ and carry 1 to the next column}$$

Thus, these four combinations are all that are needed to add in the binary number system. These combinations may be summarized even more briefly as shown in Table 4–3.

**Table
4–2**   Decimal addition and multiplication tables.

Decimal Addition Table										
+	0	1	2	3	4	5	6	7	8	9
0	0	1	2	3	4	5	6	7	8	9
1	1	2	3	4	5	6	7	8	9	10
2	2	3	4	5	6	7	8	9	10	11
3	3	4	5	6	7	8	9	10	11	12
4	4	5	6	7	8	9	10	11	12	13
5	5	6	7	8	9	10	11	12	13	14
6	6	7	8	9	10	11	12	13	14	15
7	7	8	9	10	11	12	13	14	15	16
8	8	9	10	11	12	13	14	15	16	17
9	9	10	11	12	13	14	15	16	17	18

Decimal Multiplication Table										
×	0	1	2	3	4	5	6	7	8	9
0	0	0	0	0	0	0	0	0	0	0
1	0	1	2	3	4	5	6	7	8	9
2	0	2	4	6	8	10	12	14	16	18
3	0	3	6	9	12	15	18	21	24	27
4	0	4	8	12	16	20	24	28	32	36
5	0	5	10	15	20	25	30	35	40	45
6	0	6	12	18	24	30	36	42	48	54
7	0	7	14	21	28	35	42	49	56	63
8	0	8	16	24	32	40	48	56	64	72
9	0	9	18	27	36	45	54	63	72	81

**Table
4–3**   Binary addition table.

+	0	1
0	0	1
1	1	10

Examples

Addend	1011	1011	1011	1011	1011
Augend	100	100	100	100	100
Sum		1	11	111	1111

		1↰	1		1↰	1
Addend	1101	1101	1101	1101	1101	1101
Augend	1001	1001	1001	1001	1001	1001
Sum		0	10	110	0110	10110

		1↰	1	
Addend	.101	.101	.101	.101
Augend	.001	.001	.001	.001
Sum			0	10	.110

The rules for subtraction are the same in the binary system as in the decimal system. The subtraction of each column of two binary numbers results in a difference digit, which is either 0 or 1. As for addition, there are four rules for subtraction.

$$1 - 1 = 0$$
$$1 - 0 = 1$$
$$0 - 1 = 1 \quad \text{with a borrow from the next column of the minuend}$$
$$0 - 0 = 0$$

As shown above, "borrowing" is necessary whenever a digit in the subtrahend is larger than a digit in the minuend. A borrow will cause a 1 in the minuend to become 0 and a 0 to become 1. In the latter case, the succeeding 0s in the minuend are changed to 1s until a 1 can be changed to a 0. For example, 0001 from 10000 will cause a borrow and make the remaining minuend equal to 0111.

Examples

		01	01	01	0	0
Minuend	10100	10100	10100	10100	10100	10100
Subtrahend	1001	1001	1001	1001	1001	1001
Difference		1	11	011	1011	01011

					01	01	01
Minuend	100011	100011	100011	100011	100011	100011	100011
Subtrahend	11001	11001	11001	11001	11001	11001	11001
Difference		0	10	010	1010	01010	001010

In most computers, binary subtraction is not accomplished as explained. Instead computers performed subtraction by complementing the subtrahend and adding the complement. This method is discussed later in the chapter.

The binary multiplication table (Table 4–4) is easy to remember. There are no carries in binary multiplication. The four possible products of multiplying two binary numbers are:

$$0 \times 0 = 0$$
$$0 \times 1 = 0$$
$$1 \times 0 = 0$$
$$1 \times 1 = 1$$

Table 4–4 Binary multiplication table.

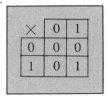

×	0	1
0	0	0
1	0	1

Examples

Multiplicand	101	101	101	101
Multiplier	111	111	111	111
		101	101	101
(partial products)			101	101
				101
Product				100011

Multiplicand	110101	110101	110101	110101
Multiplier	101	101	101	101
		110101	110101	110101
(partial products)			000000	000000
				110101
Product				100001001

As shown in the previous examples, the multiplicand is copied whenever the multiplier digit is 1, and not when it is 0. The partial products are added according to binary addition rules.

Binary division is a series of repeated subtractions, just as binary multiplication is a series of repeated additions. The following procedure is used.

(1) Subtract the divisor from the dividend a number of times.

(2) If subtraction is possible, put a 1 in the quotient and subtract the divisor from the corresponding digits of the dividend.

(3) If subtraction is not possible, place a 0 in the quotient.

(4) Bring down the next digit from the dividend to add to the remaining digits.

(5) Proceed in a manner similar to long division in the decimal notation.

Examples

```
                        011   Quotient
         Divisor    110/10110   Dividend
                        000
                        ────
                        1011
                         110
                        ────
                        1010
                         110
                        ────
                         100   (remainder)
```

$$
\begin{array}{r}
111 \quad \text{Quotient} \\
\text{Divisor} \quad 10\overline{)1110} \quad \text{Dividend} \\
\underline{10} \\
11 \\
\underline{10} \\
10 \\
\underline{10} \quad \text{(no remainder)}
\end{array}
$$

Here, the quotient represents the number of times the divisor was subtracted from the dividend.

Octal Arithmetic

Adding decimal numbers is a process that is learned by using or memorizing the decimal addition table. It is equally simple to add in octal by using Table 4–5.

Table 4–5   Octal addition table.

+	0	1	2	3	4	5	6	7
0	0	1	2	3	4	5	6	7
1	1	2	3	4	5	6	7	10
2	2	3	4	5	6	7	10	11
3	3	4	5	6	7	10	11	12
4	4	5	6	7	10	11	12	13
5	5	6	7	10	11	12	13	14
6	6	7	10	11	12	13	14	15
7	7	10	11	12	13	14	15	16

Octal addition, which uses only the digits 0 through 7, closely resembles decimal addition, with the exception of the absence of 8s and 9s. Moreover, octal addition is performed just like decimal addition, except that the next digit after 7 is a 0 with a carry (instead of an 8). For example, $7 + 1 = 10, 7 + 2 = 11, 7 + 3 = 12$, etc.

Examples

Addend	23	23	23
Augend	41	41	41
Sum		4	64

		1↰		
Addend	127	127	127	127
Augend	42	42	42	42
Sum		1	71	171

		1↰	1̂1	1̂1	1
Addend	1777	1777	1777	1777	1777
Augend	777	777	777	777	777
Sum		6	76	776	2776

Octal subtraction is performed just like decimal or binary subtraction, by using the "borrowing" technique. In octal subtraction, whenever the subtrahend is larger than the minuend, a 1 is borrowed from the next column.

Examples

	.62	62	62
Minuend	.62	62	62
Subtrahend	41	41	41
Difference		1	21

	124	124	124
Minuend	124	124	124
Subtrahend	63	63	63
Difference		1	41

Octal multiplication is equivalent to repeated octal addition.
For example,

$$4_8 \times 5_8 = 5_8 + 5_8 + 5_8 + 5_8 = 24$$

Octal multiplication is performed in the same way multiplication is performed in all other number bases, including decimal and binary.
For example,

	13
Multiplicand	327
Multiplier	4
Product	1534

Table 4–6 includes a table of multiplying digits in octal.

Examples

	23	23	23
Multiplicand	23	23	23
Multiplier	57	57	57
		205	205
			137
Product			1575

Multiplicand	326	326	326	326
Multiplier	235	235	235	235
		2056	2056	2056
			1202	1202
				654
Product				101476

Table 4–6   Octal multiplication table.

×	0	1	2	3	4	5	6	7
0	0	0	0	0	0	0	0	0
1	0	1	2	3	4	5	6	7
2	0	2	4	6	10	12	14	16
3	0	3	6	11	14	17	22	25
4	0	4	10	14	20	24	30	34
5	0	5	12	17	24	31	36	43
6	0	6	14	22	30	36	44	52
7	0	7	16	25	34	43	52	61

Octal division reverses the process of octal multiplication and is carried out by the same procedure used in decimal division or binary division (as described earlier in this chapter).

Example

	502	Quotient
Divisor	123/64202	Dividend
	637	
	302	
	000	
	302	
	246	
	34	(remainder)

Multiplying the quotient by the divisor and adding the remainder provides a check of the answer. For the previous problem, the check calculation is the following:

$$502$$
$$\times 123$$
$$\overline{1706}$$
$$1204$$
$$\underline{502}$$
$$\overline{64146}$$
$$\underline{+\ 34}$$
$$\overline{64202}$$

Hexadecimal Arithmetic

The hexadecimal system uses the numbers 0, 1, 2, 3, 4, 5, 6, 7, 8, 9, A, B, C, D, E, and F. Calculating with letter symbols may, at first, seem unusual, but the hexadecimal system is not very different from either the decimal, binary, or octal systems. The basic rules of arithmetic are the same. The hexadecimal addition and multiplication tables are shown in Tables 4–7 and 4–8. The tables for the binary and octal system are both easy to remember; however, the hexadecimal tables each contain 256 values (16 $\times$ 16). Using the tables in this book as a reference when performing hexadecimal arithmetic thus seems a more practical method of computing with hexadecimal numbers than attempting to memorize such large tables.

Table 4–7 Hexadecimal addition table.

+	1	2	3	4	5	6	7	8	9	A	B	C	D	E	F
1	02	03	04	05	06	07	08	09	0A	0B	0C	0D	0E	0F	10
2	03	04	05	06	07	08	09	0A	0B	0C	0D	0E	0F	10	11
3	04	05	06	07	08	09	0A	0B	0C	0D	0E	0F	10	11	12
4	05	06	07	08	09	0A	0B	0C	0D	0E	0F	10	11	12	13
5	06	07	08	09	0A	0B	0C	0D	0E	0F	10	11	12	13	14
6	07	08	09	0A	0B	0C	0D	0E	0F	10	11	12	13	14	15
7	08	09	0A	0B	0C	0D	0E	0F	10	11	12	13	14	15	16
8	09	0A	0B	0C	0D	0E	0F	10	11	12	13	14	15	16	17
9	0A	0B	0C	0D	0E	0F	10	11	12	13	14	15	16	17	18
A	0B	0C	0D	0E	0F	10	11	12	13	14	15	16	17	18	19
B	0C	0D	0E	0F	10	11	12	13	14	15	16	17	18	19	1A
C	0D	0E	0F	10	11	12	13	14	15	16	17	18	19	1A	1B
D	0E	0F	10	11	12	13	14	15	16	17	18	19	1A	1B	1C
E	0F	10	11	12	13	14	15	16	17	18	19	1A	1B	1C	1D
F	10	11	12	13	14	15	16	17	18	19	1A	1B	1C	1D	1E

Table 4–8   Hexadecimal multiplication table.

×	1	2	3	4	5	6	7	8	9	A	B	C	D	E	F
1	1	02	3	4	5	6	7	8	9	A	B	C	D	E	F
2	2	04	06	08	0A	0C	0E	10	12	14	16	18	1A	1C	1E
3	3	06	09	0C	0F	12	15	18	1B	1E	21	24	27	2A	2D
4	4	08	0C	10	14	18	1C	20	24	28	2C	30	34	38	3C
5	5	0A	0F	14	19	1E	23	28	2D	32	37	3C	41	46	4B
6	6	0C	12	18	1E	24	2A	30	36	3C	42	48	4E	54	5A
7	7	0E	15	1C	23	2A	31	38	3F	46	4D	54	5B	62	69
8	8	10	18	20	28	30	38	40	48	50	58	60	68	70	78
9	9	12	1B	24	2D	36	3F	48	51	5A	63	6C	75	7E	87
A	A	14	1E	28	32	3C	46	50	5A	64	6E	78	82	8C	96
B	B	16	21	2C	37	42	4D	58	63	6E	79	84	8F	9A	A5
C	C	18	24	30	3C	48	54	60	6C	78	84	90	9C	A8	B4
D	D	1A	27	34	41	4E	5B	68	75	82	8F	9C	A9	B6	C3
E	E	1C	2A	38	46	54	62	70	7E	8C	9A	A8	B6	C4	D2
F	F	1E	2D	3C	4B	5A	69	78	87	96	A5	B4	C3	D2	E1

Examples

Addition:

Addend	3B2	3B2	3B2	3B2
Augend	41C	41C	41C	41C
Sum		E	CE	7CE

		1↶	1	1↶	1
Addend	A27	A27	A27	A27	A27
Augend	C3B	C3B	C3B	C3B	C3B
Sum		2	62	662	1662

Hexadecimal subtraction uses the same principle of "borrowing" as decimal, binary, or octal subtraction. In the hexadecimal system, a "borrow" of one means a "borrow" of 16.

Examples

Subtraction:

Minuend	6E	6E	6E
Subtrahend	29	29	29
Difference		5	45

Minuend	AC3	AC3	AC3	AC3
Subtrahend	604	604	604	604
Difference		F	BF	4BF

The rules for hexadecimal multiplication are the same as those used in decimal, binary, and octal; however, because of the added symbols and a common unfamiliarity with working with such symbols, it is suggested that Table 4–7 be used frequently when working problems.

Examples

Multiplication:

Multiplicand	15	15
Multiplier	8	8
Product		A8

Multiplicand	432	432	432
Multiplier	6A	6A	6A
		29F4	29F4
			192C
Product			1BCB4

Hexadecimal division follows the rules of decimal division.

Examples

Division:

```
                      7C49   Quotient
    Divisor      E/6CBFE   Dividend
                   62
                  ───
                   AB
                   A8
                  ───
                    3F
                    38
                   ───
                    7E
                    7E
                   ───
                        (no remainder)
```

```
                    29F.D6   Quotient
    Divisor      BC/1ED61.28   Dividend
                  178
                 ───
                  756
                  69C
                 ───
                  BA1
                  B04
                 ───
                   9D2
                   98C
                  ───
                   468
                   468
                  ───
                        (no remainder)
```

☐ **Review Exercises** Due Monday 3-5-79

13. Perform the following additions in binary.
    (a) 11001   (b) 100011   (c) 1010
          101   10010   1000
       _____   _____   1001
                                    _____

14. Perform the following additions in hexadecimal.
    (a) 84   (b) C23   (c) 642
        61   8A   A10
       ____   ____   3D1
                                 ____

15. Perform the following additions in octal.
    (a) 14   (b) 246   (c) 261
        63   573   140
       ____   ____   710
                                 ____

16. Perform the following subtractions in the number systems indicated.
    (a) Binary
          1110   110110
           100   1001
         _____   _____

    (b) Hexadecimal
          D6   FA
          47   63
         ____   ____

    (c) Octal
          54   1063
          27   712
         ____   ____

17. Perform the multiplications in the noted number systems.
    (a) Binary
          1101   10010
           111   101
         _____   _____

    (b) Hexadecimal
          53   76B
          27   2A4
         ____   ____

    (c) Octal
          74   564
          32   137
         ____   ____

18. Perform the following divisions in the indicated number systems.
    (a) Binary
        $1100/\overline{100100}$
    (b) Hexadecimal
        $23/\overline{A63F}$
    (c) Octal
        $283/\overline{34612}$

Binary Arithmetic Using Complements

As initially surprising as this may seem, it is nevertheless a fact that, in most computers, all four arithmetic functions are performed by binary addition. This simplifies the computer circuitry, since subtraction can then make use of the addition circuitry. Multiplication is basically addition, and division involves subtraction.

To subtract by adding requires a technique known as *complementation*. In the decimal system, a number may have a *nines* or *tens complement*. The corresponding binary number complements are the *ones* and *twos complements*.

The *nines complement* is found by simply subtracting the number from nine while the *tens complement* is found by subtracting the number from ten. For example, the nines complement of six is three and the tens complement of two is eight.

One method of subtracting by adding complements is called the *End Around Carry* method. This method requires that the *nines complement* be taken of each digit of the subtrahend. The minuend is then added to this complemented subtrahend and if a carry is generated from the left-most digit (called the *MSD* or *most significant digit*) the carry is added to sum for the final answer.

Example

Minuend	842	842	
Subtrahend	−365 =	+634	(nines complement of 365)
Difference	477		

$$\begin{array}{r} 476 \\ (\text{carry}) \quad \to 1 \\ \hline 477 \end{array}$$

If a larger number is subtracted from a smaller number by using the nines complement, no carry will be generated. The answer will be wrong for this case and therefore the nines complement of the answer must be taken. The result of this last complementation should be assigned a negative sign.

Example

Minuend	152	152	
Subtrahend	−290 =	+709	(nines complement of 290)
Difference	−138	861	

(no carry)

The nines complement of 861 is 138; therefore, the answer here is −138.

The *ones complement* of a number is found by subtracting each "bit" (binary digit) of the number from 1. For example:

Minuend	111	
Subtrahend	-101	(five)
Difference	010	(ones complement of five)

This representation of a negative binary number may also be obtained by substituting 1s for 0s and 0s for 1s.

The value zero can be represented in ones complement notation in two ways:

000.....00	Positive Zero
111.....11	Negative Zero

The rules regarding the use of these two forms of zero for computation vary with computers.

The *twos complement* of a number is found by subtracting each bit of the number from 1 and adding 1. For example:

Minuend	111	
Subtrahend	-101	(five)
Difference	010	
	$+\ \ 1$	
	011	(twos complement of five)

It is observed from the above example that the twos complement of a number may be formed by adding 1 to the ones complement representation of the number.

In complementary form, the most significant bit represents the sign. A negative number will have a 1 in the sign position, while a 0 in the sign position designates a positive number. This is illustrated in Table 4–9 by following the binary representation of the decimal numbers 0 through 7 and -0 through -7.

If numbers are represented in ones complement notation, both positive and negative numbers may be added using the normal rules for addition, provided the carry out of the most significant position is added to the least significant position (end-around-carry). Subtraction is performed by the addition of the ones complement of the subtrahend.

Two examples of binary subtraction using ones complement notation will now be given. In the first example, 16 is subtracted from 25 as follows:

Minuend	11001	(25)
Subtrahend	-10000	(direct subtraction of 16)
Difference	1001	(9)

Addend	11001	(25)
Augend	+01111	(ones complement of 16)
Sum	101000	
	1	(end-around-carry)
	1001	(remainder = 9)

Table 4–9   Complementary form of the numbers in the range $-7 \leq x \leq 7$.

Signed Binary Number	Signed Decimal Number	Ones Complement Binary Number	Twos Complement Binary Number
+111	+7	00....00111	00....00111
+110	+6	00......110	00....00110
+101	+5	00....00101	00....00101
+100	+4	00....00100	00....00100
+011	+3	00....00011	00....00011
+010	+2	00....00010	00....00010
+001	+1	00....00001	00....00001
+000	+0	00....00000	00....00000
−000	−0	11....11111	—
−001	−1	11....11110	11....11111
−010	−2	11....11101	11....11110
−011	−3	11....11100	11....11101
−100	−4	11....11011	11....11100
−101	−5	11....11010	11....11011
−110	−6	11....11001	11.....1010
−111	−7	11....11000	11.....1001

In the first example, there is no end-around-carry involved in the direct subtraction method; but, in adding the complement of the subtrahend, an end-around-carry must be performed to obtain the correct result.

In the second example, using larger numbers, 129 is subtracted from 256 as follows:

Addend	100000000	(256)
Augend	+101111110	(ones complement of 129)
Sum	1001111110	
	1	(end-around-carry)
	1111111	(127)

As with ones complement notation, if numbers are represented in twos complement notation, positive and negative numbers may be added using the normal rules for addition. Subtraction is performed by the addition of the twos complement of the number to be subtracted.

To illustrate twos complement arithmetic, six-bit numbers are used. Negative eight in twos complement form appears as

$$
\begin{array}{lll}
 & 001000 & \text{(binary } +8) \\
\text{Addend} & 110111 & \text{(ones complement of } +8) \\
\text{Augend} & +\qquad 1 & \\
\hline
\text{Sum} & 111000 & \text{(twos complement of } -8)
\end{array}
$$

Similarly for negative three,

$$
\begin{array}{lll}
 & 000011 & \text{(binary } +3) \\
\text{Addend} & 111100 & \text{(ones complement of } +3) \\
\text{Augend} & +\qquad 1 & \\
\hline
\text{Sum} & 111101 & \text{(twos complement of } -3)
\end{array}
$$

As shown in these examples, the first bit is a sign indicator. Positive numbers begin with zero, whereas negative numbers begin with one.

Examples (twos Complement Arithmetic)

Addition:

$$
\begin{array}{rcl}
15 & = & 001111 \\
+(-\ 3) & = & +111101 \\
\hline
12 & = & 001100
\end{array}
$$

Note: In twos complement arithmetic the last carry is ignored.

$$
\begin{array}{rcl}
14 & = & 001110 \\
+(-19) & = & +101101 \\
\hline
-\ 5 & = & 111011
\end{array}
$$

Proof of the last sum is obtained by complementing the result,

$$
\begin{array}{ll}
111011 & \text{(sum)} \\
000100 & \text{(ones complement of sum)} \\
+\qquad 1 & \\
\hline
000101 & \text{(twos complement)}
\end{array}
$$

and the magnitude of the result is seen to be 5.

Subtraction:

$$
\begin{array}{rcll}
15 & = & 001111 & \\
-8 & = & +111000 & \text{(twos complement of 8)} \\
\hline
7 & = & 000111 &
\end{array}
$$

$$
\begin{array}{rcll}
15 & = & 001111 & \\
-(-3) & = & +000011 & \text{(twos complement of } -3) \\
\hline
18 & = & 010010 &
\end{array}
$$

$$
\begin{array}{rcl}
-3 & = & 111101 \\
-(-5) & = & +000010 \quad \text{(twos complement of } -5) \\
\hline
2 & = & 000010
\end{array}
$$

☐ Review Exercises

19. What is the nines complement of 6907?
20. What is the tens complement of 325?
21. What is the ones complement of 1001011010?
22. What is the twos complement of 011100101?
23. Perform the following binary subtractions using regular subtraction and then ones complement subtraction.

(a) 1001 (b) 100101 (c) 100010
 − 11   1000   1010

O.K., smarty, here's one for you. The cube root of 9 265 432 176 times the fourth root of 10 643 987 243 610 723 003 plus. . . .

☐ Summary

This chapter introduces the number systems most often encountered when working with computers. The binary system (base 2) is the basic operating language of all computers, while the octal (base 8) and hexadecimal (base 16) number systems are used primarily as easy methods of representing binary numbers.

Converting numbers from one base to another is an activity that data processors encounter frequently. Included in this chapter are the procedures used to convert from one base to another.

A further understanding of number systems is gained by studying arithmetic operations in the different bases. Shown in this chapter are the methods for performing addition, subtraction, multiplication, and division in binary, octal, and hexadecimal. Binary complement arithmetic is also covered.

Key Terms

number base	octal number system
positional notation	complement
radix	most significant digit
binary number system	end-around-carry
hexadecimal number system	

5

Information Processing and the Metric System

Courtesy of National Airlines

The *metric system* of weights and measures became the law of the land with President Ford's signing of the Metric Conversion Act of 1975. Very soon all Americans will have to use the metric system. All information processing systems that handle measurement-sensitive data will be affected to some degree. Since all future information processing systems will be required to handle both the metric and the English (inch, foot, yard, rod, mile, gallon, pint, quart, barrel, etc.) units for many years, every systems designer, information processing manager, and programmer should become familiar with the modern metric system. This chapter identifies the impact of metric conversion on information processing.

☐ What Is The Metric System?

The *metric system* is a decimal system of weights and measures, employing *kilometers, liters, grams,* and other such units. This system is in widespread general use throughout the world*, except notably in the United States where it is used for scientific measurements, but not for everyday purposes.

The metric system currently being used in most of the world is called the *SI.* It is the system that the United States has adopted and is a refinement of older versions of the metric system.

You are already using the metric system more frequently than you probably realize. In international athletic competition, such as swimming and field and track events, measurements of length are referred to by sports reporters in *meters* rather than in yards or feet. Our astronauts, from the surface of the moon, excitedly told a worldwide audience how far their rocket had landed from a lunar hill—in *meters.* If your automobile is imported or even if it is domestic with a metric-designed motor, the end wrenches or socket wrenches that you need if you want to work on your car are metric rather than customary. You already know about 35-*millimeter* film and cigarettes that are 100 *millimeters* long, or even 1 *millimeter* longer than that. You read and

---

* Ninety-two percent of the world population is using the metric system.

hear that air pollution is measured in micrograms per cubic *meter*. You see weights expressed in *grams* on more and more packaged items at the grocery store. And the trend is toward even greater use of the metric system.

In science, the metric system has been in extensive use for many years, although not to the exclusion of the customary system. But today, as the problems in science become more complex, educators throughout the world are seeking to simplify computing and teaching by using the metric system in terms of everyday measurements.

☐ Why Is The Metric System Being Increasingly Used?

The metric system's use is increasing throughout the world for two principal reasons: It is a *simple* system, and it is a *decimal* system.

It is simple because each physical quantity, such as length or weight, has its own unit of measurement (*meter* and *kilogram*), and no unit is used to express more than one quantity. By contrast, the customary system has several units of length (inch, foot, yard, mile) or weight (ounce, pound, ton, etc.); *pound* can mean either force (as in pounds required to break a rope) or weight (as in a pound of sugar); an *ounce* can mean either volume (as the number of ounces in a quart) or weight (as the number of ounces in a pound). It is easier to learn to use the metric system rather than the customary system to solve problems that involve computation. This is because metric units bear a decimal relationship to one another, as opposed to the nondecimal mixed numbers and fractions that characterize relationships among our customary units.

The U. S. monetary system has been based on decimals (factors of ten) since the founding of our country; that is, the dime equals one-tenth of a dollar and the cent equals one-hundredth of a dollar. By contrast, our customary measurement system involves units that are not decimally related to one another and thus requires the use of common fractions. Consider the measurement of length. In the metric system, a centimeter is one-hundredth of a meter; a millimeter is one-thousandth of a meter; and a kilometer is one thousand meters. In the customary system, an inch is one thirty-sixth of a yard; a foot is one-third of a yard, and a mile is 1 760 yards. Centimeters are divided into millimeters, each of which is 1/10 centimeter. But inches are divided into halves, quarters, eights, and so forth. Therefore, computations using the decimal steps of the metric system are much simpler than those using the nondecimal mixed numbers and fractions common in our customary system.

SI Measurement Concepts

SI (for *Systeme International d'Unites*) is the international system of units of measurement, identified as SI in all languages. It is the *modernized metric system*—a high refinement of the original metric system first proposed in 1670 and improved upon many times since then.

SI is by far the most superior system of measurement and calculation yet derived. It is logical in concept. It is extremely convenient to use. It provides greater speed in operation. It is the easiest system to teach and the simplest system to learn. Its metric predecessors are already used throughout the world.

The SI system consists of

- seven basic units,
- two supplementary units,
- derived units, some of which have special names while others carry the units of the original units which are combined.

In addition to these "official" members of the system, certain additional operational techniques are included in the total system:

- a structured system of decimal multiples and submultiples expressed as word prefixes, and
- a collection of general recommendations regarding symbols and abbreviations for units.

Altogether, these official and closely related parts form an integrated system which provides immeasureably simpler measurement and calculating techniques.

Seven Basic SI Units

The following base units serve as the fundamental module of the modern metric measurement system.

Quantity	Unit	SI Symbol
Length	meter	m
Mass	kilogram	kg
Time	second	s
Electric current	ampere	A
Temperature	kelvin	K
Light intensity	candela	cd
Molecular substance	mole	mol

For everyday use, most of us will have to learn only three metric units and how to work with them.

These units are the *meter* (to measure length), the *kilogram* (to measure weight) and the degree *Celsius* (to measure temperature).

A fourth SI unit you will use every day is the *second* (to measure time). But that is nothing new—you are already using the second and its multiples in exactly the right way!

The remaining three units (ampere, candela, and mole) are mainly used in scientific applications.

See the table at the bottom of page 662 for the most common relationships for measuring length (meter), weight or mass (gram), and capacity (cubic meter or liter).

☐ Two Supplementary SI Units

Two supplementary units included in SI, the *radian* and *steradian,* are used for measuring plane and solid angles.

Quantity	Unit	SI Symbol
Plane angle	radian	rad(. . .^{r})
Solid angle	steradian	sr

These units are referred to as supplementary units because the International Conference on Weights and Measures has yet to agree on how to incorporate the units into the measurement system.

☐ Derived SI Units

The derived units are the common and, in some cases, more sophisticated units that we use in everyday measurement. Each derived unit is developed by combining the base units in accordance with various techniques of mathematics and physics. Most readers will be able to obtain sufficient information from the following tabulation to meet their calculation needs.

Quantity	Unit	SI Symbol*	Formula
Area	Square meter	—	m^2
Volume	Cubic meter	—	m^3
Density	Kilogram per cubic meter	—	kg/m^3
Velocity	Meter per second	—	m/s
Acceleration	Meter per second squared	—	m/s^2
Angular velocity	Radian per second	—	rad/s
Angular acceleration	Radian per second squared	—	rad/s^2
Force	Newton	N	$kg\text{-}m/s^2$
Pressure	Pascal	Pa	N/m^2
Work, energy, quantity of heat	Joule	J	$N\text{-}m$
Power	Watt	W	J/s
Magnetic flux	Webar	Wb	$V\text{-}s$
Inductance	Henry	H	$V\text{-}s/A$
Magnetic flux density	Tesla	T	Wb/m^2
Magnetic field strength	Ampere per meter	—	A/m
Luminous flux	Lumen	lm	$cd\text{-}sr$
Luminance	Candela per square meter	—	cd/m^2
Illumination	Lux	lx	lm/m^2
Entropy	Joule per kelvin	—	J/K
Specific heat	Joule per kilogram kelvin	—	$J/kg\text{-}K$
Thermal conductivity	Watt per meter kelvin	—	$W/m\text{-}K$
Radiant intensity	Watt per steradian	—	W/sr
Activity (of a radioactive source)	1 per second	—	(disintegration)/s
Wave number	1 per meter	—	(wave)/m
Kinemetic viscosity	Square meter per second	—	m^2/s
Dynamic viscosity	Newton second per square meter	—	$N\text{-}s/m^2$
Frequency	Hertz	Hz	(cycle)/s
Electric charge	Coulomb	C	$A\text{-}s$
Voltage, electromotive force	Volt	V	W/A

* A dash indicates that no SI symbol has been assigned.

Quantity	Unit	SI Symbol*	Formula
Electric field strength	Volt per meter	—	V/m
Electric resistance	Ohm	Ω	V/A
Conductance	Siemens	S	A/V
Electric capacitance	Farad	F	A-s/V

☐ Prefixes

A convenient shorthand method of indicating multiples and submultiples of ten is the method of powers, where the *superscript* or *index* number indicates the number of times that the *base* number is multiplied by itself. In general

$$x \times x \times x = x^3$$

and

$$10 \times 10 \times 10 = 1000$$

Most people working in the information processing field have been exposed to at least a few of the prefixes which represent powers of ten. You have used millisecond, microsecond, nanosecond, and perhaps even picosecond to represent the speeds of computer circuitry, instruction operating speeds, and information transfer speeds. The following prefixes are based on increasing and decreasing powers of 10 and provide the flexibility for measuring various ranges of parameters.

Power of Ten	Value	Prefix	SI Symbol
10^{-18}	0.000 000 000 000 000 001	atto	a
10^{-15}	0.000 000 000 000 001	femto	f
10^{-12}	0.000 000 000 001	pico	p
10^{-9}	0.000 000 001	nano	n
10^{-6}	0.000 001	micro	μ
10^{-3}	0.001	milli	m
10^{-2}	0.01	centi	c
10^{-1}	0.1	deci	d
10^{0}	1.0		
10^{1}	10.	deka	da
10^{2}	100.	hecto	h
10^{3}	1000.	kilo	k
10^{6}	1 000 000.	mega	M
10^{9}	1 000 000 000.	giga	G
10^{12}	1 000 000 000 000.	tera	T

* A dash indicates that no SI symbol has been assigned.

☐ Some Rules for Using SI Units

There are a few recommended practices for using SI units, and you should become familiar with them.

1. When writing a decimal number smaller than 1, always precede the decimal point with a zero:

   0.047 *instead of* .047

2. In most European countries, a comma is used as a decimal indicator instead of a period, thus

   1,264 *instead of* 1.264

   It is possible that in the future, the United States may use the comma as a decimal marker.

3. There are no periods used at the end of abbreviations or between letters of compound abbreviations:

   mm, *not* m.m.

4. There is no *s* added for plurals: the symbol or abbreviation is the same for both singular and plural:

   1 cm   20 cm   0.05 cm

5. Only SI units are abbreviated. All other units are spelled out:

   14 kg *but* 26 pounds

6. Multiplication can be indicated by uniting the units, with no space, no hyphen, and no other symbol:

   $4\,g \times 20\,cm = 80\,gcm$ *or* 80 g·cm

7. Division may be indicated by three methods:

   $\dfrac{cm}{s}$ cm/s   cm·s^{-1}

8. Numerical powers are preferable to word prefixes. Write 40 m² *rather than* 25 sq m.

9. Third powers of ten are preferred:

$$264 \times 10^3 \text{ instead of } 2.64 \times 10^5 \text{ or } 0.264 \times 10^6$$

10. Always leave a space between numerals and symbols used with them:

$$100 \text{ m}, \textit{not } 100\text{m}$$

11. When writing large numbers, use spaces to separate the groups of three numerals now separated by commas:

$$20\ 000\ 000, \textit{not } 20,000,000$$

12. When expressing an amount like kilometers per hour, use the slash as follows:

$$\text{kilometers per hour} = \text{km/h}$$

Gee! Only 90?

☐ Review Questions

1. What is the metric system?
2. Briefly explain why it is important that the United States begins a widespread use of the metric system.
3. What is the SI system of measurement?
4. What are the seven basic SI units?
5. What are the two supplementary SI units?
6. What are the SI symbols for force, pressure, power, and frequency?
7. What is the prefix and SI symbol for the numerical value of 0.000 001 or 10^{-6}?

8. Indicate which of the following are recommended practices:
   (a) .023 or 0.023
   (b) 5,50 or 5.50 (five dollars and fifty cents)
   (c) 30 cm or 30 cms
   (d) 200 m or 200m
   (e) 40 000 or 40,000

☐ Three Solved Problems

Problem 1.   What is the area of the floor of a room with the following dimensions?

Length	475 cm
Width	380 cm

Solution.   The area is determined by multiplying the length of the room by its width.

$$475 \times 380 = 180\ 500 \text{ cm}^2$$

Answer.   Total square centimeters divided by number of square centimeters in a square meter (10 000) equals number of square meters; i.e., move decimal point 4 places to left.

$$\frac{180\ 500}{10\ 000} = 18 \text{ m}^2 \text{ (approx.)}$$

Problem 2.   What is the approximate total weight of the contents of a basket that contains the following items:

Meat	2.07 kg
Potatoes	1.47 kg
Tomatoes	1.33 kg
Cereal	650 g

Solution.

$$
\begin{array}{r}
2070 \\
1470 \\
1330 \\
\underline{650} \\
5520
\end{array}
$$

Answer.   Approximately 5.5 kg.

Problem 3.   What is the volume of the following two comparable but not equal mixtures:

Milk	6.5 l
Water	3.5 l
Flavoring	250 ml

Solution.

$$
\begin{array}{r}
6500 \\
3500 \\
\underline{250} \\
10250
\end{array}
\quad
\begin{pmatrix}
\text{multiplied liters by } 100 \\
\text{to convert to milliliters}
\end{pmatrix}
$$

Answer. Approximately 10 l.

☐ Review Questions

9. Obtain a metric measuring device and measure the 17 indicated dimensions in millimeters.

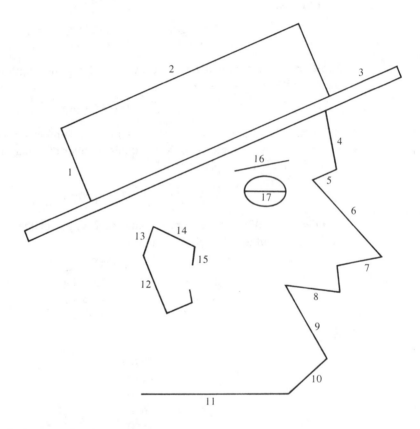

10. What is the floor area of a room that measures 12 m by 14 m?
11. What is the area of a triangle of base 85 mm and height 36 mm? (Area = ½ bh).
12. A hotel bedroom measures 3 m by 3,9 m. What is the perimeter of the room?
13. An office is to accommodate 4 rows of 6 desks each. Each desk is 750 mm wide, and 900 mm is allowed between desks for chairs and clearance. One desk is allowed to touch a wall. How long must the room be?

14. How far will a car go in 8 minutes at an average speed of 65 km/h?
15. A carpenter works a regular 6½ hour day at $6,20 per hour, and 2,2 hours overtime at time and a half. What is his income for the day?

☐ Metrication and Information Processing

The transition to the modern metric measurement system will impact information processing systems in several areas: conversion of historical data; logic of mathematical calculations; definition of data field sizes; numeric precision or accuracy; use of character sets, sizes of continuous forms, and positioning of computer-driven devices, such as digital plotters and machine tools.

Systems that generate measurement-sensitive data for use in statistical analysis, forecasting, etc., face a major discontinuity in their data. It will be difficult to compare the last 10 years' automobile-performance data in gallon per mile with next year's data in liters per kilometer. Cost accounting systems will suddenly generate unit costs per kilogram or cubic meter, while all previous data is in cost per pound or cubic yard.

The typical calculations performed in any information processing system are affected by the inherent change in units and by the elimination of many customary conversion factors. Because the SI system is coherent, most of the traditional conversion factors are no longer needed. The conversion to metric units will impact all systems that perform routine calculations using English units. Computer-assisted design packages and other scientific and engineering information processing systems will be impacted most severely.

Each metric unit is intrinsically more or less precise than the customary unit that it replaces. Centimeters are more precise than inches, and kilometers are more precise than miles; but meters are less precise than feet, and kilograms are less precise than pounds. This difference in accuracy dictates that metric units require more or less digits than do customary units to represent the same range of values. As an overly simple example, representing 0 to 99 miles requires only two digits, while the equivalent range in metric units of 0 to 159 kilometers requires a data field of three digits. Only 62 miles, that is, 99 kilometers, can be represented by two digits.

Similarly, the representation of mass in kilograms requires fewer digits than pounds for various ranges of values. Thus, 100 to 218 pounds requires three digits, while the metric equivalent of 45 to 99 kilograms uses only two digits. Obviously, as we begin to process metric measurement data, the selection of appropriate field sizes will become quite significant.

Similarly, the inherent difference in precision has a major impact on numeric accuracy. If, for example, data are given in cubic inches (in.^{3}) accurate to one decimal place or ± 0.05 inch, the same one-decimal place in cubic centimeters (cm^3) would provide ± 0.05 centimeters or 0.00305 inch, which is more accurate than necessary.

However, if data are in pounds accurate to one decimal place or ± 0.05 pound, then the equivalent one-decimal place in metric kilograms provides accuracy to ± 0.05 kilogram or 0.110 pound, which may be inadequate. The net effect of this difference in precision of each measurement system is an increased system sensitivity to field sizes, both to the right and to the left of the decimal point.

The SI system requires the use of both upper- and lowercase alphabetic characters. These characters are essential in using the system's symbols for each unit. Without this distinction, it is impossible to distinguish between k (kilo) and K (kelvin) or between m (milli) and M (mega).

The requirement for upper- and lowercase characters cannot be met by many existing information processing systems. In addition, symbols for two SI terms, ohm (Ω) and Micro (μ), and for exponential notations are not currently available on any standard U.S. computer system.

To help users cope with SI units, the American National Standards Institute (ANSI) has developed proposed ANSI and ISO (International Standards Organization) standard "representations for SI and other units to be used in systems with limited character sets," which provide an interim solution to the problem.

As the metric system's use has spread worldwide, the development of international standards has also moved to metric units. This has resulted in an international standard for paper sizes (see the following table) that is incompatible with continuous form usage.

Designation	Size (mm)	Size (inches)
A0	841 × 1189	33.11 × 46.81
A1	594 × 841	23.39 × 33.11
A2	420 × 594	16.54 × 23.39
A3	297 × 420	11.69 × 16.54
A4	210 × 297	8.27 × 11.69
A5	148 × 210	5.83 × 8.27
A6	105 × 148	4.13 × 5.83
A7	74 × 105	2.91 × 4.13
A8	52 × 74	2.05 × 2.91
A9	37 × 52	1.46 × 2.05
A10	26 × 37	1.02 × 1.46

The continuous form industry has compounded the problem by developing two standards for continuous form depths as follows:

In the United States		In Europe	
Inch	**mm**	**Inch**	**mm**
11	279.4	12	304.8
8 ½	215.9	8	203.2
7	177.8	6	152.4
5 ½	139.7	4	101.6
3 ½	88.9	3	76.2

Many computer systems are used to drive electrical or mechanical devices that handle measurement data. These devices include digital plotters, graphical displays on cathode-ray tube display units, numerically controlled machine tools, process control systems, and other computer-coupled devices. All these processes use measurement data to position or control an item with some specified accuracy. These systems usually are designed to operate within a specific accuracy, such as 0.001 inch. Often these devices operate incrementally, using decimal inch increments, and not continuously over a given range of values. These systems cannot readily be changed to operate in millimeters or other metric units. An application that uses these devices will have to provide dual metric-inch capabilities over a number of years during the conversion program.

☐ Metric Impact

The degree of impact from metric conversion will vary, depending upon the particular information processing system. Many installations will be affected in only a minor way. Other systems will have to be converted to accept and process both metric and English units data.

Since the United States metric transition will progress in an orderly fashion over the next decade, most systems will have to process both metric and English units data during the overlapping years. Typically, an inventory control system would be required to handle both metric and English unit-sized items. The result is a possible 10 to 30 percent increase in inventories or materials processed by such a system. A similar requirement for dual capabilities will exist in the generation of reports and performing design calculations.

It is clear that the use of the metric system will impact the total information processing industry. To minimize the effect of metrication on an organization's information processing system, the information processing manager and all information processing employees should be exposed to the SI measurement system as well as to specific examples of potential impact on the organization, such as dual inventory of items, purchasing changes, new engineering standards, part numbering changes, and order entry changes.

☐ Review Questions

16. List several areas in the information processing field that will be affected by the transition to the modern metric measurement system.

17. Explain why it is important that information processing personnel become familiar with the SI metric system.

18. Give several examples of how you think your school's information processing system will be affected by the metric system.

☐ Summary

Clearly, metric transition in the United States presents a unique challenge to the information processing industry since it will impact the total industry. Information processing personnel must act now to meet this challenge. The long lead time for systems conversions and redesign combined with the rapid acceleration of the metric transition dictate that people in the information processing field must take action at once to meet the metrication challenge.

Key Terms

metric system	meter
SI units	kilogram
Celsius	second
radian	ampere
steradian	kelvin
superscript	candela
base	mole
	ANSI
	ISO

6

Data Representation

Courtesy of IBM Corporation

⬜ Symbols

Symbols convey information. The symbol itself is not information, but it represents something that is. The printed characters on this page are symbols that convey one meaning to some persons, a different meaning to others, and no meaning at all to those who do not know their significance. Look at the symbols shown in Figure 6–1. Which are meaningful to you?

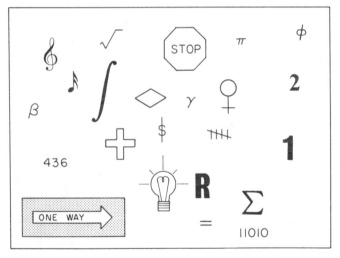

Figure 6–1   Symbols for communication.

Computers are often called *data processors* or *information processors*. What is being processed? Numbers, facts, names, etc.—they are all called *symbols*. What form do these symbols take? Since a computer is a physical device, the symbols it handles must be in some physical form. In the abacus, numbers are represented by the position of numbered beads. In an adding machine, numbers are represented by the position of geared wheels. In each case, we assign a number to a bead or to a gear; then we represent that particular number by positioning the beads

119

or gears. We can also represent numbers by using electric lights. In chapter four (Figure 4–1) we illustrated how four lights could be turned on and off to represent numbers. In principle, this technique is used to represent numbers in a digital computer. Computers are built from components which have only two states—*on* or *off,* for example. Some examples of such components are shown in Figure 6–2. A switch can be either on or off, the magnetic field in a magnetic core can be in either one direction or the other, and electric current through a transistor can be arranged to be either on or off. Such elements are used in electronic digital computers.

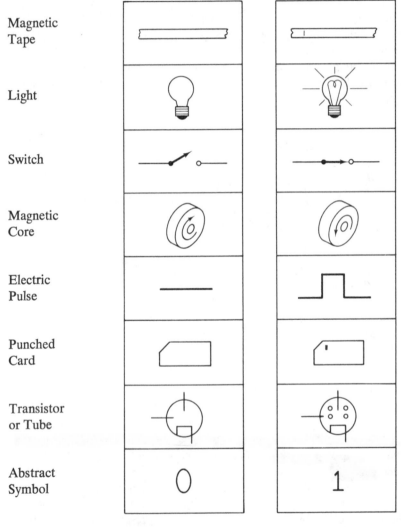

Magnetic Tape

Light

Switch

Magnetic Core

Electric Pulse

Punched Card

Transistor or Tube

Abstract Symbol

Figure 6–2   Binary indicators.

In chapter three, we discussed the punched card. A punch in the card could be used to represent a one. A no-punch represented a zero. Symbols to be used with computer systems are called *computer codes*. These codes can be punched in cards or paper tape, recorded as spots on magnetic tape, represented by magnetic ink characters, sent as communication-network signals, and so forth. These computer codes provide a way for humans and machines to communicate with one another.

Where Does Data Originate?

Data originates in many different forms. In a department store, it could take the form of cash register receipts, customer purchases, inventory status, bills, business expenses, employee payroll, or business forecasts. In a bank, it could take the form of customer deposits and withdrawals.

In a utility company, customer payments, bills, available facilities, and new customer names are forms of data. In a military command and control center, data could take the form of detected hostile aircraft, missile positions, or telemetry signals from a remote radar site. Data can originate in all activities—from everyday business to exploration on the moon. A function of data processing is to capture this data and process it into useful information.

Computer Codes

Computer code provides a method of representing data so that it can be interpreted by machines. A selected code relates data to a fixed number of binary indications (zero bits and one bits). One computer code, called BCD (*Binary Coded Decimal*) is a six-bit code that represents all upper-case letters of the alphabet, the 10 numerical digits, and several special characters (comma, plus sign, period, dollar sign, parentheses, etc.)

Using the symbols of this code, shown in Table 6–1, we can construct symbols for strings of these characters and thus form symbols for arbitrary numbers of English words. For example, the number 843 is represented as 001000 000100 000011, and the word DATA is represented

Table 6–1   Six-bit alphanumeric characters.

Alphanumeric Character	Computer Code	Alphanumeric Character	Computer Code
0	000000	↑	100000
1	000001	J	100001
2	000010	K	100010
3	000011	L	100011
4	000100	M	100100
5	000101	N	100101
6	000110	O	100110
7	000111	P	100111
8	001000	Q	101000
9	001001	R	101001
[	001010	—	101010
#	001011	$	101011
@	001100	*	101100
:	001101	)	101101
>	001110	;	101110
?	001111	,	101111
(space)	010000	+	110000
A	010001	/	110001
B	010010	S	110010
C	010011	T	110011
D	010100	U	110100
E	010101	V	110101
F	010110	W	110110
G	010111	X	110111
H	011000	Y	111000
I	011001	Z	111001
&	011010	←	111010
.	011011	,	111011
]	011100	%	111100
(	011101	=	111101
<	011110	"	111110
\	011111	!	111111

by 010100 010001 110011 010001. Because the code includes symbols representing commas, spaces, and periods; we can easily construct symbols representing sentences, paragraphs, or even complete books. Figure 6–3 shows the title of this book written in computer code.

I	N	T	R	O
011001	100101	110011	101001	100110
D	U	C	T	I
010100	110100	010011	110011	011001
O	N	Space	T	O
100110	100101	010000	110011	100110
Space	I	N	F	O
010000	011001	100101	010110	100110
R	M	A	T	I
101001	100100	010001	110011	011001
O	N	Space	P	R
100110	100101	010000	100111	101001
O	C	E	S	S
100110	010011	010101	110010	110010
I	N	G		
011001	100101	010111		

**Figure
6–3**   Title of this book written in six-bit BCD computer code.

The six-bit BCD code permits representation of 64 different characters. Other codes have been developed that provide for the representation of more characters. EBCDIC (Extended Binary Coded Decimal Interchange Code) is an eight-bit code that can represent 256 characters, including both uppercase and lowercase alphabetic characters, a wide range of special characters, and several control characters meaningful to certain computer equipment. At present, many code combinations have no assigned meanings; they are reserved for future assignments. Table 6–2 shows the characters available in EBCDIC.

Another code, called ASCII (American Standard Code for Information Interchange), is a seven-bit computer code that is used primarily for data communication. This code allows computers produced by different manufacturers to be used together in a data processing communication system (teleprocessing network).

☐ Review Questions

1. Give some examples of symbols. Explain what each represents.
2. List the items of data that a bank needs in order to keep a customer's savings and checking account records.
3. Discuss some coding system used to represent data in the computer.

Table 6–2   EBCDIC character representation.

EBCDIC Character	Computer Code	EBCDIC Character	Computer Code	EBCDIC Character	Computer Code
NUL	0000 0000	SM	0010 1010		0101 0100
SOH	0000 0001	CU2	0010 1011		0101 0101
STX	0000 0010		0010 1100		0101 0110
ETX	0000 0011	ENQ	0010 1101		0101 0111
PF	0000 0100	ACK	0010 1110		0101 1000
HT	0000 0101	BEL	0010 1111		0101 1001
LC	0000 0110		0011 0000	!]	0101 1010
DEL	0000 0111		0011 0001	$	0101 1011
	0000 1000	SYN	0011 0010	*	0101 1100
RLF	0000 1001		0011 0011	)	0101 1101
SMM	0000 1010	PN	0011 0100	;	0101 1110
VT	0000 1011	RS	0011 0101	¬	0101 1111
FF	0000 1100	UC	0011 0110	—	0110 0000
CR	0000 1101	EOT	0011 0111	/	0110 0001
SO	0000 1110		0011 1000		0110 0010
SI	0000 1111		0011 1001		0110 0011
DLE	0001 0000		0011 1010		0110 0100
DC1	0001 0001	CU3	0011 1011		0110 0101
DC2	0001 0010	DC4	0011 1100		0110 0110
TM	0001 0011	NAK	0011 1101		0110 0111
RES	0001 0100		0011 1110		0110 1000
NL	0001 0101	SUB	0011 1111		0110 1001
BS	0001 0110	SP	0100 0000		0110 1010
IL	0001 0111		0100 0001	,	0110 1011
CAN	0001 1000		0100 0010	%	0110 1100
EM	0001 1001		0100 0011	—	0110 1101
CC	0001 1010		0100 0100	>	0110 1110
CU1	0001 1011		0100 0101	?	0110 1111
IFS	0001 1100		0100 0110		0111 0000
IGS	0001 1101		0100 0111		0111 0001
IRS	0001 1110		0100 1000		0111 0010
IUS	0001 1111		0100 1001		0111 0011
DS	0010 0000	¢[	0100 1010		0111 0100
SOS	0010 0001	.	0100 1011		0111 0101
FS	0010 0010	<	0100 1100		0111 0110
	0010 0011	(	0100 1101		0111 0111
BYP	0010 0100	+	0100 1110		0111 1000
LF	0010 0101	|	0100 1111		0111 1001
ETB	0010 0110	&	0101 0000	:	0111 1010
ESC	0010 0111		0101 0001	#	0111 1011
	0010 1000		0101 0010	@	0111 1100
	0010 1001		0101 0011	'	0111 1101
=	0111 1110	z	1010 1001	N	1101 0101

Table   continued
6–2

EBCDIC Character	Computer Code	EBCDIC Character	Computer Code	EBCDIC Character	Computer Code
"	0111 1111		1010 1010	O	1101 0110
	1000 0000		1010 1011	P	1101 0111
a	1000 0001		1010 1100	Q	1101 1000
b	1000 0010		1010 1101	R	1101 1001
c	1000 0011		1010 1110		1101 1010
d	1000 0100		1010 1111		1101 1011
e	1000 0101		1011 0000		1101 1100
f	1000 0110		1011 0001		1101 1101
g	1000 0111		1011 0010		1101 1110
h	1000 1000		1011 0011		1101 1111
i	1000 1001		1011 0100		1110 0000
	1000 1010		1011 0101		1110 0001
	1000 1011		1011 0110	S	1110 0010
	1000 1100		1011 0111	T	1110 0011
	1000 1101		1011 1000	U	1110 0100
	1000 1110		1011 1001	V	1110 0101
	1000 1111		1011 1010	W	1110 0110
	1001 0000		1011 1011	X	1110 0111
j	1001 0001		1011 1100	Y	1110 1000
k	1001 0010		1011 1101	Z	1110 1001
l	1001 0011		1011 1110		1110 1010
m	1001 0100		1011 1111		1110 1011
n	1001 0101		1100 0000		1110 1100
o	1001 0110	A	1100 0001		1110 1101
p	1001 0111	B	1100 0010		1110 1110
q	1001 1000	C	1100 0011		1110 1111
r	1001 1001	D	1100 0100	0	1111 0000
	1001 1010	E	1100 0101	1	1111 0001
	1001 1011	F	1100 0110	2	1111 0010
	1001 1100	G	1100 0111	3	1111 0011
	1001 1101	H	1100 1000	4	1111 0100
	1001 1110	I	1100 1001	5	1111 0101
	1001 1111		1100 1010	6	1111 0110
	1010 0000		1100 1011	7	1111 0111
−	1010 0001	⌐	1100 1100	8	1111 1000
s	1010 0010		1100 1101	9	1111 1001
t	1010 0011	⊔	1100 1110	≠	1111 1010
u	1010 0100		1100 1111		1111 1011
v	1010 0101		1101 0000		1111 1100
w	1010 0110	J	1101 0001		1111 1101
x	1010 0111	K	1101 0010		1111 1110
y	1010 1000	L	1101 0011	EO	1111 1111
		M	1101 0100		

4. Represent your name in six-bit BCD code; in eight-bit EBCDIC code.

5. Interpret the caption for the following cartoon using the code in Table 6–1.

010111	011001	110101	010101	010000
011001	110011	010000	010001	010000
010111	100110	100110	010100	111011
110010	110110	011001	010110	110011
010000	100010	011001	010011	100010

Data Representation

Some of the methods used to represent data were mentioned at the beginning of this chapter. The position of a punched hole on a card, paper tape, or paper tag can be used to represent both alphabetic and numerical characters. Magnetic devices—such as magnetic tapes, cards, disks, cores, and drums—can represent data in one of two ways: either by the direction of magnetization on the surface or by the presence or absence of magnetized spots. Printed characters on paper documents are another familiar means of data representation. These characters are machine readable if imprinted with magnetic ink or recorded in specially designed characters.

In chapter four, computer number systems—including the binary system—were explained. Earlier in this chapter, codes using binary digit patterns were discussed. Let us now look at how various code patterns are represented on data recording media.

Punched Cards

Punched cards and punched card codes were discussed in chapter three. The card was one of the earliest and is still perhaps the most common media for introducing data into data pocessing equipment. In chapter four, we discussed the way many businesses use cards with unit record machines. Cards are also used quite extensively with electronic data processing equipment.

The most serious drawback in using punched cards as an input-output medium for computers has been the relatively slow speed of the card reading and punching equipment as compared to the internal speed of the computer itself. For example, a typical card reader can read cards at a rate of 800 cards per minute. If all the cards to be read were punched in all 80 columns, the effective reading rate would be 64,000 characters per minute. But the computer can transfer 80-character records internally at a rate of over two million characters per minute, which is over 30 times faster than the maximum character rate from the card reader.

☐ Punched Paper Tape

Punched paper tape serves much the same purpose as punched cards. It can be used either as an input or an output medium for a data processing system. Originally developed for transmitting telegraph messages over land wires or between ships at sea, paper tape is now produced as a by-product of many document-preparing machines. Paper tape punches are often attached to electric typewriters, desk calculators, cash registers, adding machines, teletypewriters, or accounting machines, so that paper tape records can be produced at the same time other operations are being performed. Combining document preparation with the creation of a machine-readable medium can eliminate a separate keypunching operation and hence reduce the costs of preparing data for entry into a computer system.

Paper tape is available in several different widths; however, for use with data processing equipment, the one-inch size is most often used. Paper tape is handled in short strips of only a few feet long or in reels of up to several hundred feet. Information is recorded as holes punched across the width of the tape. Figure 6–4 shows the code used with eight-channel

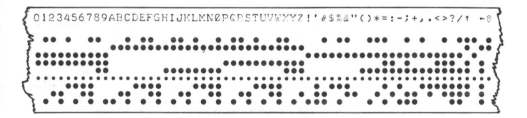

Figure Paper tape code.
6–4

tape. Data is punched and read as holes located in eight parallel *channels* running horizontally along the length of the tape. One column of eight possible punching positions across the width of the tape is used to code numeric, alphabetic, and special characters and functions. Figure 6–5 shows the title of this book punched in paper tape.

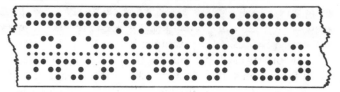

Figure 6–5   Coding on paper tape.

Punched paper tape has certain advantages over punched cards as a medium of input to a computer. The most important is that punched paper tape records are not limited in length and can be as long or as short as desired. With punched cards, on the other hand, the entire card must be read even if only one or two columns are needed to record the data. Extra cards must be used if the data takes up more than 80 or 96 columns. Also, punched tape can sometimes be produced more quickly and less expensively than punched cards. Both the tapes and the tape-producing equipment require less space than punched cards and card-producing equipment.

Punched paper tape also has disadvantages as a computer input medium. Once data are punched into paper tape, it is difficult to correct errors. While certain correction procedures permit data punched into the tape to be ignored automatically, such an approach is not equivalent to the capability of deleting the data completely before they enter the system. Also, after data have been recorded in punched paper tape, they cannot be manipulated. Consequently, data are often hand-sorted before being punched into the tape.

☐ Review Questions

6. Name some of the media used for presenting input to electronic data processing systems.
7. Briefly discuss the primary differences between punched cards and punched paper tape media.
8. Using the paper tape code shown in Figure 6–4, translate the message coded in the following segment of paper tape.

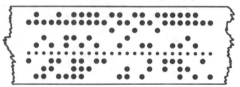

☐ Magnetic Tape

Magnetic tape is a principal input-output recording medium for computer systems. Magnetic tape provides a rapid way of entering data into the computer system and an equally fast method of recording processed data from the system. Information is recorded on magnetic tape as magnetized spots called *bits*. The recording can be retained indefinitely, or the information can be automatically erased and the tape reused many times.

Magnetic tape is wound on individual reels or inserted in cartridges or cassettes. Tape on the individual reels is typically 1.27 cm (½ inch) wide and 731.52 m (2 400 feet) long. A full reel of tape weighs about 1.8 kg (4 pounds) and can contain information equivalent to that recorded on 400 000 punched cards (see Figure 6–6).

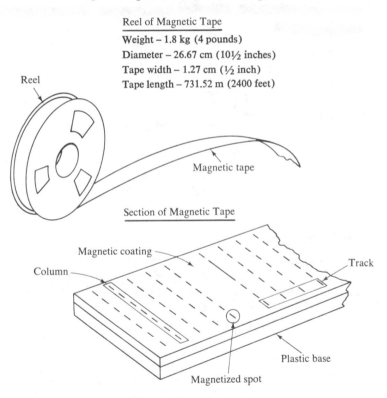

Reel of Magnetic Tape

Weight – 1.8 kg (4 pounds)
Diameter – 26.67 cm (10½ inches)
Tape width – 1.27 cm (½ inch)
Tape length – 731.52 m (2400 feet)

Reel

Magnetic tape

Section of Magnetic Tape

Magnetic coating

Column

Track

Plastic base

Magnetized spot

**Figure
6–6**
Magnetic tape characteristics.

Data is recorded on *tracks* that run the length of the tape. The spacing between the rows or *channels* is generally controlled during the recording or writing operation. Spacing can vary between 200, 556, 800, or 1,600 characters per inch (2.54 cm).

Figure 6–7 shows one type of coding on magnetic tape. It is a six-bit BCD coding with a seventh bit for a check bit. The short vertical lines on the tape represent spots or positions on the tape that are magnetized.

0 1 2 3 4 5 6 7 8 9   A B C D E F G H I J K L M N O P Q R S T U V W X Y Z   & . □ - S *   . ' - # @ b

Figure 6–7   Coding on seven-track magnetic tape (in even parity).

Figure 6–8 illustrates the type of coding used with a nine-track tape. Eight of the nine bit positions are used in the character code. The ninth bit, called a *check bit* or *parity bit,* is used to check on the accuracy of tape operations.

0 1 2 3 4 5 6 7 8 9   A B C M N O X Y Z   & $ * — / %

Figure 6–8   Coding on nine-track magnetic tape.

☐ Review Questions

9. Name some of the characteristics of magnetic tape that make it a desirable data recording medium for data processing systems.

10. Identify the six-bit code in the following segment of magnetic tape (use code shown in Figure 6–7).

11. Represent your name in six-bit code (use code shown in Figure 6–7).

Your Name

12.

The caption for the above cartoon is coded on the following strip of tape. Can you decipher the message?

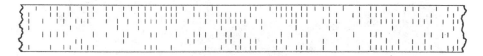

☐ Magnetic Ink Characters

The *magnetic ink character* set which MICR (Magnetic Ink Character Recognition) machines can read comprises the 10 numerals and four special symbols used in check processing: the *dash,* used in account numbers; the *amount symbol,* which indicates the beginning of the amount field; the *ABA transit routing symbol,* which indicates the beginning of the numerical code of the drawee bank; and the *on-us symbol,* which is put on a check only by the drawee bank and marks off a field used for internal accounting codes.

The MICR characters are printed on paper with a magnetic ink. The ink looks like a normal black ink, but it contains a very finely ground magnetic material and a binder to make the magnetic particles adhere to the paper. Figure 6–9 shows the 10 magnetic character numerals and how they appear when printed on a check.

The printing of magnetic ink characters on paper documents, such as checks, is done by a printing machine. Another machine, called a MICR reader, reads the printed information from the paper documents, converts it to a computer-acceptable code, and enters it into the data processing system. The significant aspect of this procedure is that mag-

Figure 6–9   Magnetic ink characters and their use on a check.

netic ink characters do not have to be copied or punched on another special input form.

☐ Optically Readable Characters

Optical scanners are used in data processing systems to recognize characters printed on documents. One of the simplest optically readable characters is the pencil mark used to indicate answers on survey forms, test sheets, questionnaires, or special forms. Figure 6–10 shows a typical form of this type. The person using the form responds to questions by making marks in specific areas of the form with an ordinary pencil. These optical marks can be read by an *optical mark page reader*.

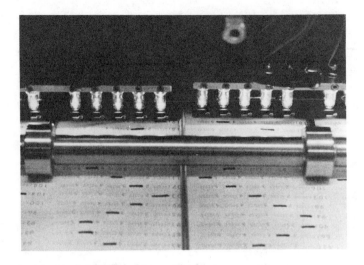

(Courtesy of IBM Corporation)

Figure   Form with optical marks as it passes under the reading mechanism of
6–10   an optical reader.

There is another type of printed character that can be read by an *optical character recognition* (OCR) *reader*. The characters have a slightly irregular typeface, as shown in Figure 6–11. They consist of the 26 letters of the alphabet, the 10 digits, and several special characters. These characters are often printed on utility bills, insurance premium

ABCDEFG
HIJKLMN
OPQRSTU
VWXYZ , ∎
$ / ✳ — 123
4567890

Figure   OCR characters.
6–11

notices, credit cards, sales invoices, and so forth. Figure 6–12 shows a utility bill printed with OCR characters.

Enter Partial Payment Below	MUNICIPAL WATER WORKS

Figure 6–12   Utility bill printed with OCR characters.

Some OCR devices can also read handwritten data. The numbers and letters, however, must be written clearly and precisely. Figure 6–13 shows a form with handwritten characters.

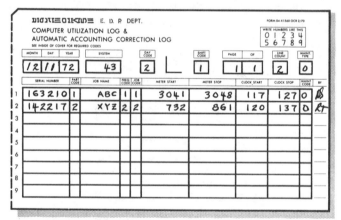

Figure 6–13   Form with handwritten data.

☐ Review Questions

13. What is the primary advantage of recording data in the form of magnetic ink readable characters?

14. Distinguish between optically readable characters and magnetic ink characters.

15. What is meant by the two acronyms OCR and MICR?

16. Describe some common business situations in which OCR capabilities might be used.

17. Why is MICR not used in industries other than banking?

"My dad is a banker."

☐ Summary

This chapter examined some of the basic considerations involved in coding information for processing purposes. First, a computer code is simply a means of representing data. The data to be coded originates in many forms—cash register receipts, bills, business expenses, customer purchases, payroll time cards, etc. A function of data processing is to capture this data and process it into useful information.

Computer codes discussed in this chapter include the BCD (Binary Coded Decimal) code, the EBCDIC code, the ASCII code, punched card code, paper tape code, magnetic tape code, magnetic ink character set (MICR), and optically readable characters (OCR).

Key Terms

symbols	bits
computer code	track
binary coded decimal	parity bit
EBCDIC	magnetic ink character
ASCII	optical scanner
paper tape	optical mark page reader
channel	optical character recognition
magnetic tape	MICR

four

Electronic
Data
Processing

7

Electronic Data Processing

Courtesy of Sperry Rand Corporation's Univac Division

As discussed in chapter six, punched card data processing is accomplished by mechanically passing cards through a variety of unit record machines. The speed of the processing is limited by the speed with which these cards can be moved. On the other hand, in an electronic data processing system, the medium is an electrical impulse moving through electronic circuits. As a result, the speed of processing data is much greater.

With unit record equipment, each machine serves its own independent function, and communication among machines is accomplished by physically transporting the punched cards from machine to machine. In electronic data processing systems, various pieces of equipment are linked together so that there is a free and continuous exchange between machines, permitting each to perform its special function even while other machines in the system are performing theirs—perhaps with all machines using the same data.

Electronic data processing equipment provides storage for holding data, access to that data, and control of them while they are in the computer's memory. It also provides facilities for performing arithmetic and logical operations on the data. Using stored data, it can make simple decisions and select alternate courses of action based on those decisions. The heart of an electronic data processing system is the *computer*.

☐ Basic Types of Computers

There are two general types of computers: digital and analog. A *digital computer* counts, using strings of digits to represent numbers. An *analog computer* measures, representing numbers by physical magnitudes, such as voltage, temperature, current, and pressure. (Figure 7–1.)

The *analog computer*, as its name implies, processes work by analogy. It takes a continuous input, performs a processing function, and transforms this information to a continuous measurable output form. A familiar example is the speedometer on the dashboard of an automobile. The rotations of the car wheels are transferred through a flexible cable

Digital Computer

☐ Processes information
by counting.

☐ Two types—general-purpose
and special-purpose.

Analog Computer

☐ Processes information
by measuring.

Hybrid Computer

☐ Combines the best
features of both
analog and digital
computers.

(Courtesy of Electronic Associates, Inc.)

Figure   Types of computers.
7–1

"It was formerly owned by a little old lady corporation president who never did more than 25 million volume a year with it."

to the internal governor device under the dashboard. This device then interprets the car's rate of speed in terms of a miles-per-hour dial reading. Like the speedometer, the analog computer can perform only that function for which it is programmed, with no decision path alternation. This computer is generally not as accurate as the digital computer. The main advantage of analog computers is their efficiency in certain continuous-type calculations. They are used almost exclusively in real-time simulation systems and scientific laboratory work. For business applications, however, analog computers are generally not used.

The computer that we will be concerned with in this book is the digital computer which performs calculations by counting. The analog computer was discussed only to differentiate between the two. The digital computer is the most versatile machine in the electronic computer family. There are two main types of digital computers: special-purpose and general-purpose. The *special-purpose computer* is designed for a specific application. It may incorporate many of the features of a general-purpose computer, but its applicability to a particular problem is a function of design rather than of program. For example, a special-purpose computer could be designed to process flight information in an air traffic control system. It would compute destination, departure time, route, payload, etc. It could not, however, be used for other applications. Special-purpose machines have been used in military weapon systems, highway toll collection systems, airline reservation systems, and bank check-processing systems.

General-purpose computers are versatile in that they may be used in many different applications. Classification of general-purpose machines is determined by the power and speed of the equipment, measured in terms of the machine's data handling and storage capacities, the variety of input-output possibilities, and the internal computer speed required to perform certain operations. The general-purpose digital computer lends itself to solving a variety of problems or applications by simply changing the instructions within the computer's memory. This computer is capable of performing a long sequence of programmed operations without human intervention.

Although both analog and digital computers have been extensively used and widely accepted in both industry and business, another type of computer has been designed that combines the best features of both of these machines. The *hybrid computer system* has both analog and digital characteristics. It combines the advantages of both the systems into a working system. The hybrid computer provides greater precision than can be attained with analog computers, and has greater control and speed than is possible with digital computers.

☐ Review Questions

1. What are some advantages of using an electronic data processing system over a unit record system?
2. What are the two general types of computers?
3. What are some disadvantages of analog computers?
4. What is the difference between an analog computer and a digital computer?
5. A digital computer performs its computations by _____.
6. What is the difference between general-purpose and special-purpose computers?
7. What is a hybrid computer system?

☐ Basic Components of All Computers

Although computers differ widely in their particulars, they are all organized similarly and are composed of five major components, as shown in Figure 7–2. The components are:

(1) An *arithmetic unit* in which numbers can be added, subtracted, multiplied, divided, and compared.

(2) A *storage unit* in which computer instructions, data, and intermediate calculations are stored.

(3) An *input unit* which accepts the necessary input data and instructions.

(4) An *output unit* which provides the computed results in a usable form.

(5) A *control unit* which directs the operation of the other four units.

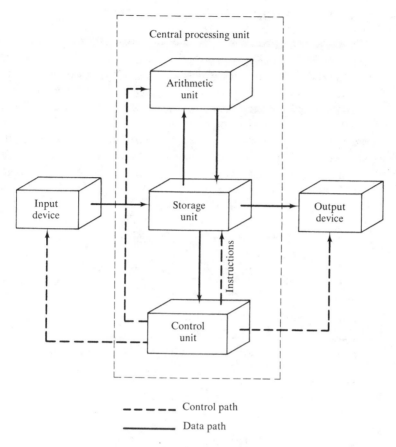

Control path

Data path

**Figure
7–2**   The five basic parts of an electronic digital computer.

The arithmetic unit performs operations such as addition and multiplication at a very high speed. The storage unit holds the instructions for
calculating, the data to be processed, and the intermediate results of calculations. Since the instructions are in the memory, it is possible for the
computer to modify the instructions themselves during the calculation
process. The control unit directs the flow of information and calculations
and supervises the overall operation of the computer. The control functions are shown as dotted lines in Figure 7–2. The input and output units
are devices for getting information and instructions into and out of the
computer.

☐ Review Questions

8. List the five basic components of all computers.
9. Briefly describe the basic function of each component mentioned in
   Question 8.

☐ **Central Processing Unit**

The *central processing unit* (CPU) of an electronic data processing system consists of the three elements shown in Figure 7–2 labeled "storage unit," "arithmetic unit," and "control unit." The CPU is the heart of the electronic data processing system. The storage unit of the CPU is often called the *internal storage, primary storage,* or *main memory.* In addition to this internal storage, most computer systems include additional forms of storage, called *secondary storage* or *auxiliary storage.* This auxiliary storage is used primarily to supplement the internal storage of the CPU. Figure 7–3 illustrates the association between the internal storage of the CPU and the auxiliary storage.

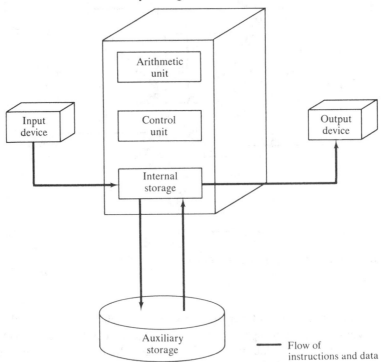

Figure 7–3   Relation between the CPU and auxiliary storage.

Let us now briefly discuss the three main components of the CPU—arithmetic unit, storage unit, and control unit.

Arithmetic Unit

The arithmetic unit performs additions, subtractions, multiplications, and divisions on numerical data as directed by the control unit. The unit usually includes a small amount of storage to hold both of the *operands* (the numbers which are to be added, subtracted, etc.) which are to

be acted upon and the partial answers that are generated during calculation. Another function of the arithmetic unit is to compare two numbers
and determine whether the numbers are equal or if one is larger than
the other. It can also compare alphabetic information, such as names,
or determine whether one name is the same as or different than another.

Consider the following problem. Assume that the personnel director of
the International Oil Company uses the company's electronic data
processing system to find an employee to send to Germany. The employee must be married, be under 35, speak German, and must not own
his own home. Figure 7–4 shows the selection process that the computer

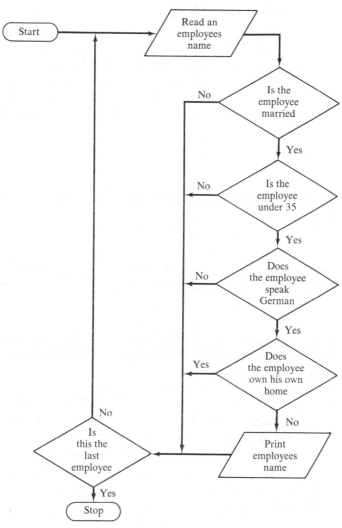

Figure   Decision process for example.

7–4

would use in searching for an employee with these specific qualifications. The computer would obtain the marital status, age, languages spoken, and home-owning status of an employee and compare this information with the conditions that are specified. If the comparison indicates that the employee is a non-home-owning, married, German-speaking person under 35, then the employee's name is printed. The computer then repeats the procedure for all other employees. Any employee's failure on one of the tests immediately causes the computer to cease further comparisons of the data on that particular employee. Instead, the computer automatically proceeds to the next employee. At the end of the processing cycle, the printed report contains only the names of those employees meeting the four tests. All comparisons in this example are made in the arithmetic unit which acts as the decision-making unit of the computer.

The arithmetic unit performs all arithmetic operations by addition. It subtracts by using complement arithmetic, which is a form of addition. Multiplication is accomplished by a series of additions, and division is accomplished by a series of subtractions or complemented additions. The arithmetic units of most computers perform all arithmetic operations using binary numbers.

Storage Unit

The storage unit or internal storage of the CPU is its memory. This is where instructions and data are located while they are being used or processed. While the CPU is solving a problem, the program instructions and data might continually pass back and forth between the arithmetic unit, the control unit, and the storage unit.

The internal storage of most computers is *magnetic core*. This storage media, along with other forms of storage will be discussed in Chapter 9.

Control Unit

The control section performs the most vital function in the CPU. All program steps are interpreted here and instructions are issued to carry out the required operations. This section directs the overall functioning of the other units of the computer and controls the data flow between them during the process of solving a problem. When the computer is operating under program control, the control unit brings in data, as required, from the input devices and controls the routing of results to the required output devices.

The control section is composed of many miles of wire. Figure 7–5 shows a technician connecting the maze of wires that are used to control an IBM System/360 Model 75 computer.

Registers

The CPU contains several *registers,* which are devices that are capable of receiving information, holding it, and then transferring it as directed

(Courtesy of IBM Corporation)

Figure 7–5   A technician connecting a maze of wires used to control a System/360 Model 75 computer.

to some controlling circuitry. Some types of registers, along with their functions, are:

(1) *Accumulator*—holds the results of a calculation

(2) *Address register*—holds the address or designation of a storage location or device

(3) *Instruction register*—holds the instruction currently being interpreted or executed

(4) *Storage register*—holds data taken from or being sent to storage

(5) *Index register*—maintains a count whose contents may be increased or decreased

(6) *General register*—holds several types of data

Information placed in registers may be shifted to the right or left within the register or, in some cases, may be transferred between two registers. A register may temporarily hold information while other parts of the CPU analyze the data. Logical operations (such as *and* or *or*) and arithmetic operations (such as multiply or divide) can be performed on information in registers. The value of a single character, a bit (binary digit), or a combination of bits may be checked or set in registers. Contents of the more important registers of the CPU, particularly those used in normal processing and data flow, are displayed on the computer console.

Machine Cycles

All computer operations are performed in fixed intervals of time, measured by regular pulses emitted from the CPU's electronic clock at extremely high frequencies (several million per second). A machine cycle is measured as a fixed number of pulses. In most second generation computers, the memory cycle time was measured in microseconds; however, many of the newer machines have memory cycle times in the nanosecond range. A *microsecond* is one millionth (1/1 000 000) of a second; a nanosecond is one billionth (1/1 000 000 000) of a second.

Within a machine cycle, the CPU can perform a specific machine operation. Several machine operations are combined to execute an instruction. In many CPUs, most of the instructions can be executed in two machine cycles; however, instructions such as multiply, divide, and shift often take three or more cycles. A CPU performs an addition operation by executing two successive machine cycles: instruction cycle and execution cycle. During the instruction cycle, the CPU takes the instruction from the program in internal storage, places the instruction in the instruction register, and decodes the instruction which informs the CPU of what it must do. Then, it places the data address in the register and brings the data to be processed into the data register. At this point, the CPU knows what it is to do and has the data to be processed in the registers. During the execution cycle, the CPU adds the data to the contents of the accumulator, thus completing the addition operation. The sum is found in the accumulator at the termination of instruction execution.

Word Length

Fixed and *variable word length* describe the unit of data that can be addressed and processed by the CPU. In a fixed-word-length computer, information is addressed and processed in words containing a fixed number of positions. The word size varies with the computer; however, word sizes consisting of 12, 16, 24, 32, and 36 bits are most common. In many computers, the word size represents the smallest unit of information that can be addressed for processing in the CPU. However, in computers such as the IBM System/360 it is possible to work with bytes (8-bits), half-words ($\frac{1}{2}$ standard word), and double-words (two standard words). Registers, accumulators, storage, and input-output data channels are primarily designed to accommodate the fixed word.

In a variable-word length computer, information is processed serially as single characters. Information may be of any practical length within the capacity of the available storage. For example, in a variable-word length computer the addition of 14263207 and 421632910 is performed character-by-character starting at the right: 0 + 7, then 1 + 0, then 9 + 2 carry 1, then 2 + 3 + 1, then 3 + 6, etc., until the sum is computed. This is exactly how this operation would be performed with pencil and paper.

Input-Output Channels

The process of transferring information into and out of internal computer storage is called an input-output operation. Input-output (I-O) operations are performed by I-O channels which connect the input and output devices with the CPU. The I-O channel acts like a small subsystem of the CPU and allows input-ouput communications to occur independently of computing. The I-O channel relieves the CPU of the task of communicating directly with input-output devices. On most computers there are two types of I-O channels: the selector channel and the multiplexor channel.

A *selector channel* is used to transmit information to or from one input or output device at a time. This channel is often used when very high-speed I-O devices are connected to a computer.

A *multiplexor channel* permits the simultaneous operation of several input and output devices. This channel allows both low-speed I-O devices and high-speed I-O devices to be operating simultaneously. Reading, writing, and computing can take place simultaneously when the multiplexor channel is used. Using selector channels, this can only occur when two or more channels are used.

In some computer systems, the I-O data channels are called "input-output systems" or "input-output processors." A data channel is more than wires connecting I-O devices to the computer. It is constructed with electronic circuitry and is capable of responding to its own commands. It may be built physically into the CPU or it may be a separate unit.

*"This one says he failed to read the instructions
enclosed with the machine . . ."*

☐ Input and Output Devices

Input devices are machines that can read previously recorded data from punched cards, punched paper tape, magnetic tape, along with magnetic ink characters, printed characters, and other forms of coding. Output devices are machines that report information from computer storage, in a form that can be understood by human beings or in a form suitable for use as input for another computer system. Common output devices are printers, typewriters, card punches, paper tape punches, magnetic tape units, display devices, digital plotters, and other units.

Input and output units are an integral part of a computer system and operate under the control of the CPU as directed by the computer program. Figure 7–6 illustrates a computer system that includes a CPU and several input-output devices. The input-output devices are used to get information and data into and out of the CPU.

(Courtesy of Sperry Rand Corporation's Univac Division)

Figure 7–6   A Univac 418 III computer system consisting of a CPU and several input-output devices.

☐ Review Questions

10. The central processing unit is composed of what three units?
11. What are the major arithmetic operations that a computer can perform?
12. What is the purpose of the storage unit of a computer?
13. What is meant by "internal storage"?
14. In what way is auxiliary storage different from internal storage?
15. What are the basic functions of the control unit?
16. What is a register?
17. How many microseconds are there in four seconds?
18. How many nanoseconds are there in three microseconds?
19. Which is the shortest period of time: 0.6 microseconds or 800 nanoseconds?
20. What type of computer would be more suitable for solving a real-time traffic control application—fixed-word-length machine or variable-word-length machine?

21. What is the purpose of input and output devices?
22. Name several input devices; output devices.

The Stored Program

Control is the process of directing the operation of the computer system, either manually or automatically. *Manual control* is performed by a human operator pressing buttons and switches on a computer control panel. Once a computer program or instructions are placed in the storage unit of the computer, and the computer is manually started by the operator, the computer will operate automatically under *program control.* The instructions that guide the operation of the computer are called a *stored program.* Without a program, a computer is merely an inert mass of metal, wire, and plastic. With a program, it comes to life and slavishly follows its instructions. For this reason, the program is as essential as the computer itself; for, without it, no work could be performed.

A different program is written for each new problem to be solved. The program is punched into cards or recorded on some other input media and placed in the computer's storage. Computer programs are often referred to as *software.* The computer and other data processing machines are called *hardware.* We will look more closely at programs and how they are developed in later chapters.

Computer Console

A computer console, such as the one shown in Figure 7–7, is used to initiate the execution of the stored program and to monitor the computer system after the computer is under program control. The console is used by a human operator to start and stop the computer as well as to load instructions and data into the computer's storage. The console is equipped with switches, lights, and buttons for entering information into the system and for inspecting information already stored in the computer.

The control console can be housed as part of the CPU, as is the case with the IBM System/360 console; or it may be a separate unit. Figure 7–8 shows a console as a separate unit. Shown in this console is a built-in typewriter. With it, the operator can enter instructions and data into the computer. Computer error messages can also be typed on this type of console. Still another type of console is shown in Figure 7–9. This console uses two Cathode Ray Tube displays and a keyboard. The operator enters information into the computer via the keyboard. The operating status of the computer is then shown on the displays.

(Courtesy of IBM Corporation)

**Figure
7–7**   Control console for the IBM System/360 computer.

(Courtesy of Walter Reed Army Medical Center)

**Figure
7–8**   Computer console with typewriter input-output device.

(Courtesy of Control Data Corporation)

Figure Computer console with two CRT displays and a keyboard input
7–9   device.

☐ Parallel and Serial Operation

Computers are classified as either *serial* or *parallel* depending on the method the computer uses to perform arithmetic. Essentially, all arithmetic is performed by addition.

In a *serial computer,* numbers to be added are considered one position at a time (the units position, tens position, hundreds, and so on), in the same way that addition is done with paper and pencil. Whenever a carry is developed, it is retained temporarily and then added to the sum of the next higher-order position.

The time required for serial operation depends on the number of digits in the factors to be added. Serial addition is shown below.

	Step 1	**Step 2**	**Step 3**	**Step 4**
Addend	6146	6146	6146	6146
Augend	2246	2246	2246	2246
Carry	1	1		
Sum	2	92	392	8392

In a *parallel computer,* addition is performed on complete data words. The words are combined in one operation, including carries. Any two data words, regardless of the magnitude of the numbers contained in the words, can be added in the same amount of time. The following example illustrates parallel addition.

Addend	56346914
Augend	10003102
Carry	11
Sum	66350016

☐ Review Questions

23. What is meant by "control"? "manual control"? program control"?
24. What is a stored program?
25. What is meant by the term "software"? the term "hardware"?
26. Discuss the role of the computer console in the processing of data.
27. What are the functions of the lights and switches on the computer's control panel?
28. What is the difference between serial and parallel arithmetic?

☐ Computer Generations

The *first generation* of digital computers was built using *vacuum tube* logic circuitry. Because of this, many of the early machines were so large that they completely filled one or more rooms. The first electronic computer (ENIAC) contained almost 19,000 vacuum tubes, weighed about 30 tons, and filled an area of more than 139.35 m² (1 500 square feet). Many of these first generation computers worked at speeds measured in thousandths of a second (milliseconds).

The *second generation* of computers used a device developed by Bell Telephone Laboratories in 1948—the *transistor.* The transistor is an electronic device that performs the same function in second generation computers that the vacuum tube performed in first generator computers. The transistor is smaller, generates almost no heat, is less expensive, and requires much less power than a vacuum tube. The use of transistors in computers greatly increased their reliability, since these components are relatively trouble-free and nondeteriorating compared to vacuum tubes. Transistors replaced tubes in most military computers in 1956, and in most commercial computers in 1959. The speed of second generation machines was measured in microseconds, a factor 1,000 times faster than the speed of first generation machines. Figure 7–10 shows rows of transistor circuit cards.

(Courtesy of Systems Engineering Laboratories)

**Figure
7–10**   Transistor circuit cards used in second generation computers.

The *third generation* computers were made using microminiature components: integrated circuits, solid-logic technology, thin-film, and tunnel diodes. These components are much smaller, faster, and more reliable than either vacuum tubes or transistors. The speed of third generation machines is measured in nanoseconds. Figure 7–11 shows a thimble that contains about 50,000 microminiature circuits, used in IBM System/360 computers—a third generation computer.

Figure 7–12 compares the three generations of circuitry. An array of vacuum tubes is shown compared with a transistor circuit board and a microminiature circuit.

Computers of the future may use circuitry much smaller than that used in modern computers. Figure 7–13 shows a *large scale integration* circuit

(Courtesy of IBM Corporation)

Figure 7–11   Microminiature circuits used in third generation computers.

that contains, on a single slice of silicon 3.81 cm (1½ inches) in diameter, the equivalent of 16 000 electronic devices: 6 000 or more transistors, 6 000 resistors, and 4 000 diodes, interconnected to perform a specific electronic function.

(Courtesy of IBM Corporation)

Figure 7–12   Three generations of computer circuitry. Vacuum tubes (rear), transistors, (right center), and microminiature circuits (foreground).

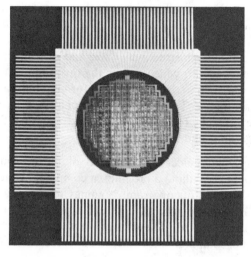

(Courtesy of Texas Instruments Incorporated)

Figure 7–13 A large scale integrated circuit that contains the equivalent of 16 000 electronic devices interconnected to perform a specific electronic function. The circuit is mounted on a single slice of silicon, 3.81 cm (1½ inches) in diameter.

☐ Review Questions

29. Compare computers of the first three generations. Name the type of circuitry used in each.

30. List several reasons why transistors are an improvement over vacuum tubes? why microminiature circuits are an improvement over transistors?

31. The fourth generation of computers will probably be introduced sometime around the mid-1970s. Check out a magazine article or book from your school library and read about the type of circuitry that might be used in these future computers.

☐ Summary

The heart of an electronic data processing system is the computer. Discussed in this chapter are the two general types of computers: *digital* and *analog*. A digital computer counts, using strings of digits to represent numbers. An analog computer measures, representing numbers by physical magnitudes, such as temperature, voltage, current, and pressure. Another type of computer used in both business and industry is called a *hybrid* computer. A hybrid computer system combines digital and analog computers into one working system.

Although computers differ widely in their particulars, they are all organized similarly and are composed of five major components: an *arithmetic unit* in which numbers can be added, multiplied, etc.; a *storage unit* in which computer instructions, data, and intermediate calculations are stored; a *control unit* which directs the operation of the other units; and *input* and *output units* which provide for communications with external devices and media. Three of the functional units grouped together are called the *central processing unit*. These units are the arithmetic unit, the storage unit, and the control unit.

Instructions that guide the operation of the computer are called the *stored program*. Without a program, a computer cannot perform even the simplest task. With a program, it comes to life and performs the task specified by the program. A different program is written for each new problem to be solved. These computer programs are called *software,* whereas the computer and other data processing machines are called *hardware.*

The computer console is used by a human operator to start and stop the computer, as well as to enter programs and data into the computer's storage. It may be an integral part of the CPU or it may be housed in a separate unit.

The first computers (ENIAC, Univac I, IBM 650, etc.) were said to belong to the *first generation* of computers. They all used vacuum tube circuitry and were rather slow and unreliable. The *second generation* of computers used transistors instead of vacuum tubes and, besides their increased speed and reliability, they did not require air-conditioned computer rooms. The *third generation* of computers were made from microminiature components, such as integrated circuits, and solid-logic technology. These components are much smaller, faster, and more reliable than either transistors or vacuum tubes. The speed of third generation machines is measured in nanoseconds.

Key Terms

electronic data processing	magnetic core
digital computer	fixed word length
analog computer	variable word length
hybrid computer	input-output channel
special-purpose computer	selector channel
general-purpose computer	multiplexor channel
arithmetic unit	manual control
storage unit	program control
control unit	stored program
input unit	software
output unit	hardware
central processing unit (CPU)	computer console

internal storage
auxiliary storage
register
operand
machine cycle
millisecond
microsecond

parallel computer
serial computer
first generation computer
second generation computer
third generation computer
large scale integration (LSI)
nanosecond

8

Input-Output Devices

Courtesy of Control Data Corporation

☐ General

Input and output devices are the means by which the computer communicates with the outside world. Input units transfer data to the computer and output units receive data from it. These units are often called *peripheral units*. When input or output units are connected directly to the computer, they are considered to be *on-line*. When they operate independently of the computer, they are called *off-line*.

The off-line concept involves separating the slow input-output equipment from the central processing unit by intermediate storage: magnetic tape or disk pack. This separation maximizes the usage of the central processing unit, since it allows input-output operations to occur at a higher rate.

A large computer system may involve many different types of off-line equipment: punched cards-to-magnetic tape, paper tape-to-magnetic tape, keyboard-to-magnetic tape, keyboard-to-disk pack, magnetic tape-to-printed form, magnetic tape-to-digital plotted form, magnetic tape-to-microfilm, and printed document-to-paper tape. The most common off-line input conversion is from punched cards to magnetic tape. As a consequence, magnetic tape-to-printed form is the most used output conversion. In both cases, the information transfer is accomplished by physically transferring magnetic tape from one system to the other.

From the early stages of computer development, input and output equipment have acted as restraining factors on the high speed of the computer. Since most of the data which a computer uses or produces must go through input-output equipment, it is understandable that there is much concern over the speed of these input-output devices. The relatively slow speed of devices such as card readers and paper tape readers is the reason many computer systems use magnetic tape and removable magnetic disks as the primary method of communicating with the computer. Data is then recorded on magnetic tape or magnetic disk prior to its use on the computer. This can be accomplished by using off-line data preparation equipment or even a small off-line computer system dedicated to this purpose. Likewise, computer output can be recorded on magnetic tape or disk packs and later transcribed to printed or other forms by off-line equipment.

Input-output devices operate under the control of the computer as directed by a stored computer program. For example, an instruction to read a card would cause the card reader to read a card and transmit the information to computer storage. An instruction to print a message would cause one or more lines of print to be output on a printing device such as the typewriter or line printer. Thus, instructions in the program select the required device, direct it to read or write, and indicate the location in computer storage where data will be inserted or retrieved.

Typical input devices are punched card readers, paper tape readers, typewriters, MICR readers, optical character and mark readers, magnetic tape units, removable disk units, microfilm readers, data communication equipment, and CRT keyboard and light pen. There are also special-purpose input units such as special keyboards, analog-to-digital conversion units, special operator control panels, etc. Typical output devices are card punches, paper tape punches, typewriters, line printers, cathode ray tube display devices, magnetic tape units, removable disk units, digital plotters, and data communication equipment. Special-purpose output units include devices such as large board displays, special control and display panels, and digital-to-analog conversion equipment. Table 8–1 lists in a condensed form several input and output devices and their operating speeds.

Two input-output devices which are also used extensively as auxiliary storage devices are the magnetic tape unit and magnetic disks. These devices are discussed in chapter nine.

"Another way you can save wear and tear on your equipment is to get a more modern entry system."

Table 8–1 Input-output devices.

Input or Output	Device Name	Medium Used	Operating Speed Range
Input Devices	Card reader	punched card	200–2 000 cards per minute
	Paper tape reader	paper tape	350–1 000 characters per second
	Typewriter	keyboard	10–200 characters per second
	MICR reader	paper	2 500 documents per minute
	Optical character reader	paper	1 000 documents per minute
	Magnetic tape unit	magnetic tape	30 000–500 000 characters per second
	Magnetic disk unit	magnetic disk	100 000–3 000 000 characters per second
Output Devices	Card punch	punched card	100–500 cards per minute
	Paper tape punch	paper tape	20–150 characters per minute
	Typewriter	paper	10–200 characters per second
	CRT display	display	250–10 000 characters per second
	Line printer	paper	300–2 500 lines per minute
	Digital plotter	paper	7–10 cm per second
	Magnetic tape unit	magnetic tape	30 000–500 000 characters per second
	Magnetic disk unit	magnetic disk	100 000–3 000 000 characters per second
	Microfilm output unit	microfilm	125 000 characters per second

☐ Punched Card Readers and Punches

The card reader (Figure 8–1) is one of the most common devices used in small to medium-size computer systems. It is designed to recognize holes punched in a card and transmit this information (in electronic form) to the computer. After a card is read, it is placed into a stacker for removal by an operator. There are two types of card-reading units in general use: the brush-type reader and the "brushless" or photoelectric cell reader.

(Courtesy of IBM Corporation)

Figure 8–1   Card reader used with IBM System/370 computers.

In the *brush-type reader,* cards are mechanically moved from a card hopper, through the card feed unit, and under reading brushes. The reading brushes electrically sense the presence or absence of holes in each column of the card. This electric sensing converts the information of the card to electrical impulses that can be utilized by the card reader circuitry and stored as data. After the cards are read, they are moved from the card feed unit and placed in the card stacker, still in the same sequence in which they were fed into the reader (Figure 8–2).

The *photoelectric card reader* performs the same functions as the brush-type reader—the difference is in the method of sensing the holes. Photoelectric cells are activated by the presence of light, one cell for each column of the card. As the punched card is passed over a light source in the card reader, light passing through the punched holes activates the appropriate photoelectric cells.

Card punching is the reverse process of reading, since it converts the electrical impulses sent from the computer into holes punched into cards.

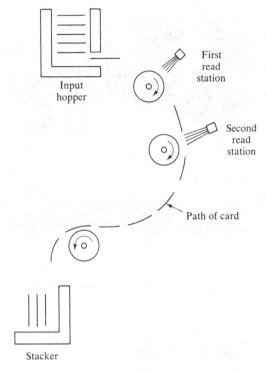

Stacker

Figure 8–2   Reading a punched card with a brush-type reader.

The *card punch* automatically moves blank cards, one at a time, from the card hopper, under a punching mechanism that punches data received from computer storage (Figure 8–3). After the card is punched, it is moved to a checking station where the data are read and checked with the information received at the punching station. The card is then moved to the stacker. A card punch is shown in Figure 8–4.

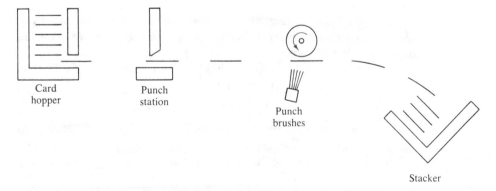

Figure 8–3   Punching mechanism of the card punch.

(Courtesy of Control Data Corporation)

Figure 8–4   Top view of a card punch. The card input hopper is shown on the right, the output stacker on the left.

☐ Paper Tape Readers and Punches

A paper tape reader provides input to a computer by reading prepunched data from paper tape. It also provides output from a computer by punching output information in the same medium. The *paper tape reader* works much like the card reader. It moves the tape past a reading unit where the presence or absence of holes in the tape is sensed and converted to electronic impulses acceptable to the computer. Paper tape readers are characterized by their reading methods: mechanical readers detect the presence of holes by mechanical means, while photoelectric readers detect holes by light-sensitive elements.

Mechanical readers operate by passing the surface of the tape over heads consisting of pins or brushes which open or close contacts as the heads are passed over holes. One disadvantage of mechanical readers is that they cause wear on the tape, limiting paper-tape life to several hundred passes. However, using a special metal-coated tape, called *Mylar,* reduces the wear problem to insignificance.

Photoelectric readers are more reliable than mechanical readers since they have no mechanical sensors to wear out or jam. They can also read information at a rate 5 to 20 times faster than mechanical readers.

A *paper tape punch* is used to generate paper tape output. Information is punched in blank tape as the tape moves through a punching mechanism which punches round holes. Tape punches, being entirely mechanical in nature, are subject to physical restrictions that are similar to mechanical readers.

Paper tape readers and punches are often combined into one input-output unit—a paper tape reader-punch. Figure 8–5 shows one model in which the upper portion is a paper tape punch and the lower portion is a paper tape reader.

(Courtesy of Systems Engineering Laboratories)

Figure 8–5   Paper tape reader-punch unit. The paper tape punch is in the upper portion and the reader is in the lower portion.

☐ Review Questions

1. What is a peripheral unit?
2. Distinguish between on-line and off-line equipment.
3. List five input and three output devices.
4. What is the function of a card reader? a card punch?
5. Explain the difference between the reading mechanism in the brush-type and photoelectric card readers.
6. Which can be accomplished faster—card reading or card punching? Explain why.
7. Briefly explain how information represented on paper tape can be read into a computer's storage.
8. Name two input-output devices that are also used in auxiliary storage devices.

☐ Printing Devices

Printing devices provide permanent and readable records of information from the computer. The printing device receives information in electronic form which activates printing elements in the printer, thus causing information to be printed. There are two main printing devices used with computers: the typewriter and the line printer.

The *typewriter,* which may be used as a keyboard input device as well as an output printing device, provides a method for printing limited amounts of information. This device can print up to 200 characters per second. Typewriters, such as the one shown in Figure 8–6, are com-

(Courtesy of IBM Corporation)

Figure 8–6   A typewriter that is controlled by a computer. It provides keyboard input to a computer and printed output from a computer.

monly used as control devices in medium and large computer systems and as primary I-O devices in many small computer systems. Often minicomputer systems use a typewriter-like device, called a teletypewriter, as the primary method of getting information into or out of the computer. Included as part of the teletypewriter is a low-speed paper tape reader and punch. Such a device provides two forms of input (keyboard and paper tape) and two forms of output (printed form and paper tape).

The *line printer,* which is the most important hard-copy output device to be used with computers, prints a line at a time at a very fast rate. This device, shown in Figure 8–7, is used to produce reports, summaries, and

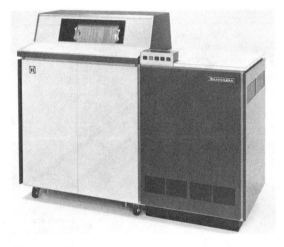

(Courtesy of Burroughs Corporation)

Figure 8–7 A line printer.

similar output on continuous paper forms. The paper may be blank, lined, or printed in any form.

There are two major categories of printing techniques. In *impact printing,* a type carrier contacts an inked ribbon and paper. In *electrostatic printing* or *nonimpact printing,* light-sensitive paper is exposed to a character image to form the printed character. Nonimpact printing is usually faster than impact printing because of simpler mechanical construction, but impact printing is the more common method.

There are six main types of impact printing devices: chain printers, incremental-bar printers, print-wheel printers, drum printers, comb printers, and wire matrix printers.

The *chain printer* consists of a rotating chain containing a series of type slugs (Figure 8–8). Hammers are activated behind the paper, forcing it against the ribbon and the rotating chain to form the printed character. The chain consists of five sections containing 48 different characters.

The *incremental bar printer* consists of a series of type bars, positioned side by side, with one type bar for each print position across the line. To print, a magnet releases a spring-loaded hammer at the proper time so that the positioned character is pressed against the ribbon and paper (Figure 8–9). This type of printing mechanism is rather slow and today it is used almost exclusively with accounting machines.

The *print-wheel printer* is similar to the incremental bar printer, except that the type bars of the bar printer have been put in a circle in the wheel printer. Most printers of this type include 120 print wheels. Each

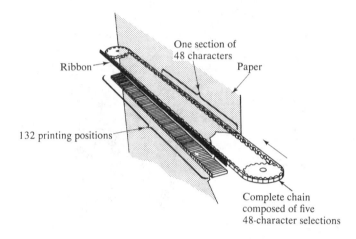

(Courtesy of IBM Corporation)

Figure 8–8   Print chain.

wheel has 48 characters of type, including numbers, letters, and special characters (Figure 8–10). At the time of printing, all 120 print wheels are correctly positioned to represent the information to be printed on one line. Printing of all 120 positions occurs simultaneously.

The *drum printer* uses a solid cylindrical drum, around which characters are embossed. The drum rotates at a constant speed. All characters of the same type, As, Bs, Cs, etc., are printed at one time by hammers

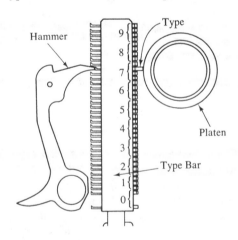

(Courtesy of IBM Corporation)

Figure 8–9   Incremental bar printer mechanism.

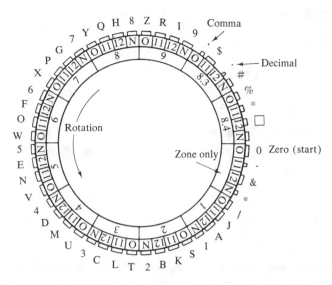

(Courtesy of IBM Corporation)

Figure   A print-wheel.
8–10

behind the paper striking the paper against the drum. One complete revolution of the drum is required to print each line (Figure 8–11).

The *comb printer* consists of a complete set of characters mounted on a horizontal bar placed in front of the paper form. Sliding from left to right, the bar passes in front of the paper, hammers striking the desired characters onto the form. After the bar has traveled the width of the paper form, it returns to its original or "home" position to print the next line.

In the *wire matrix printer*, each character is printed as a series of dots formed by the ends of small wires arranged in a 5 × 7 rectangular

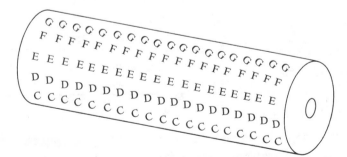

Figure   A print drum.
8–11

matrix (Figure 8–12). When a character is decoded, the appropriate wires are extended and pressed against an inked ribbon. A variety of different characters can be printed by this method.

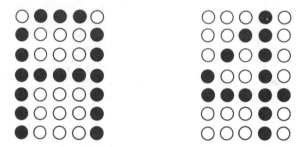

**Figure
8–12**   A wire matrix printer dot pattern for the letter A and digit 4.

The *electrostatic printing* method is much faster than the line-at-a-time impact printing; however, the major disadvantages are that special paper is required and only one printed copy at a time can be produced. Printing speeds of 2 000–5 000 lines per minute are common with electrostatic printing devices. The printing speed is limited only by the speed at which paper can be moved. Characters are printed by first placing spots of electricity (in the form of characters) on a special coated paper and then passing the paper through a powdered ink bath. The powdered ink clings to the paper wherever there is an electric spot. The ink is then permanently melted onto the paper by a heating process.

Review Questions

9. Name several types of printers.
10. Why is printing the most practical form of computer output?
11. What is meant by impact printing? by electrostatic printing?
12. Briefly describe the operation of the chain printer; of the drum printer.

Magnetic Ink Character Readers

The magnetic ink character reader is a special-purpose input device that was designed as an aid to the automation of the banking industry. This device can read card and paper documents inscribed with a special magnetic ink character type font. The printed check is the most common form of document that uses these printed characters.

The device, shown in Figure 8–13, is called a *reader-sorter*. It transmits information printed in MICR (Magnetic Ink Character Recognition) type font to the computer's memory. In addition, the reader-sorter can do a variety of sorting jobs. It can sort intermixed documents of various

(Courtesy of National Cash Register Company)

Figure   Magnetic ink character reader-sorter.
8–13

lengths, widths, and thicknesses. It can sort checks to any one of its pockets.

☐ Optical Mark and Mark Sense Readers

Optical mark and mark sensing is performed by detecting the presence or absence of pencil marks in specified positions on a form. Many areas of data collection are simplified by using preprinted forms that require only that the user fill in appropriate boxes with pencil marks. Such forms are commonly used for collecting inventory information, taking school attendance, conducting a census, recording a public opinion poll, or taking a test. Forms of this type may be read by *optical mark* and *mark sense readers*.

The mark detection system of an optical mark reader generally consists of a light source, mirrors, and light-sensitive photocells. A mark is detected when a drop occurs in the amount of light arriving at the photocells after being reflected by the document being scanned. In contrast, the mark detection system of a mark sense reader generally consists of sets of three brushes each of which make contact with marks. A voltage is applied to the outer two brushes of the sets and a mark is detected when a current passes through the graphite mark to the center brush. Documents that are to be read by an optical mark reader can be marked with standard lead pencils. Documents read by mark sense readers must be marked with special pencils containing soft and highly conductive leads. An optical mark reader is shown in Figure 8–14.

(Courtesy of IBM Corporation)

Figure   Optical mark page reader.
8–14

☐ Optical Character Readers

Another character-reading device that can be used as input to computers is the *optical character reader* (Figure 8–15). This device reads upper-case letters, numbers, and special characters that are printed on paper documents. Documents to be read are placed in a hopper, and then transported in the reader past an optical scanning position where a

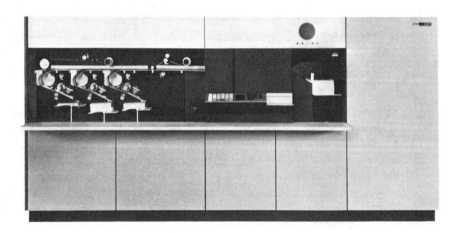

(Courtesy of IBM Corporation)

Figure   Optical character reader.
8–15

powerful light and lens enable the machine to distinguish the letters, numbers, and special characters as patterns of light. These light patterns are converted into electrical pulses for use by the computer.

There are four general types of optical character readers: (1) page readers, which read 215.9 x 279.4 mm (8½ x 11 inch) documents; (2) document readers, which read a line or two from small documents about 101.6 x 203.2 mm (4 x 8 inches) or 50.8 x 101.6 mm (2 x 4 inches); (3) reader/punches, which read data printed on a card and punch the data into the same card; and (4) journal tape readers, which read printed cash register or adding machine listing tapes.

Page readers tend to be large, expensive, multifont machines because of the flexibility required to scan the loose formats of varying pages. Document readers, journal tape readers, and reader/punches are somewhat smaller and cheaper because of a simpler transport mechanism and the smaller scanning areas required for their types of input. In the last section, we discussed the optical mark reader. Some optical character readers have the ability to read both alphabetic characters and marks.

Optical character readers are widely used by utility companies, oil companies, department stores, mail order houses, and credit card companies. The use of these readers simplifies the computer input process.

☐ Digital Plotters

Automatic plotting devices are used with computers to produce pictorial or graphic representations of information. The *digital plotter* is a device which can draw under control of the computer. Typical applications might be the drawing of graphs, weather maps, land contour maps, PERT charts, subdivision maps, computerized art, or highway maps.

The two most common forms of plotters are drum and flatbed types. The pen of a drum plotter is driven in one axis while the paper moves positively or negatively in the other axis. The flatbed plotter moves the pen in both the X and Y axes and the table is usually fixed. The computer provides pen movement and functional commands to the plotter in digital form, and these commands are then converted into pen motions. Figure 8–16 shows an IBM 1130 computer system that includes a digital plotter. Figure 8–17 illustrates this same plotter drawing a picture. The movement of the pen is under the control of the computer.

☐ Review Questions

13. What is magnetic ink character recognition?
14. How are MICR reader-sorters used in banks to process information?
15. What is the primary difference between an optical mark reader and a mark sense reader?

(Courtesy of TRW Equipment)

**Figure
8–16**   An IBM 1130 computer system that includes a card reader and digital plotter.

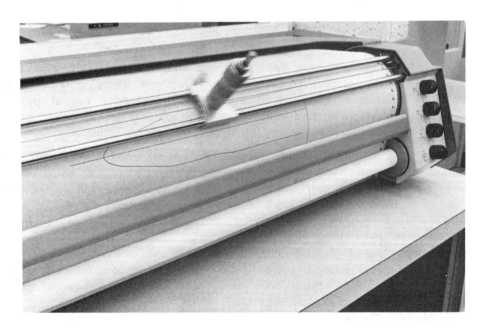

(Courtesy of TRW Equipment)

**Figure
8–17**   A picture being drawn by a digital plotter. The plotter pen moves as specified by the computer.

16. Name several uses for an optical character reader.

17. What is the difference between optical mark reading and optical character reading?

18. What is a digital plotter?

19. What output device was used to produce the picture shown in Figure 8-18?

(Courtesy of Houston Instruments)

Figure 8-18   World War I Flying Ace.

☐ Visual Display Units

One of the more popular input-output devices is the Cathode Ray Tube (CRT) display unit. This device, which resembles a television display, is used to enter data into the computer as well as to display output information. Associated with many CRT displays is a *keyboard* (Figure 8-19) or a keyboard and *light pen* (Figure 8-20).

A *light pen* is a photosensitive device which detects the presence of light on the display screen. When pointed at the screen, it will detect light and inform the computer. It can be used either to point at information which already appears on the screen or to designate a location at which information is to appear; or it could be used to enter information directly. A keyboard allows the user to compose messages or make inquiries in much the same manner as a typewriter.

(Courtesy of IBM Corporation)

Figure 8–19   Cathode ray tube display with keyboard.

Cathode ray tubes are used in airline reservation systems, management information systems, business systems, information retrieval systems, simulation systems, military defense systems, design automation systems, and computer-assisted instruction (CAI) systems. Much work with CRT

(Courtesy of IBM Corporation)

Figure 8–20   Cathode ray tube display system with keyboard and light pen.

displays and CAI systems has been done at universities, schools, and research organizations in recent years.

☐ Voice I-O

Voice recognition devices are available that will accept a very limited vocabulary of voice input. These devices convert audio signals to digital impulses for use by the computer.

Voice output is currently being used more than voice input. Audio response devices have been used successfully in banking, utilities, communications, and manufacturing. Voice output can be used by banks to give information on accounts, by brokerage firms to quote stock prices, by telephone utility companies to give changes in telephone numbers, and so on.

The Audio Response Unit shown in Figure 8–21 provides recorded voice responses to inquiries made from telephone-type terminals. This unit is attached to the computer, which, in turn, connects the computer to the telephone network. The audio response is composed from a vocabulary pre-recorded in a human voice on a magnetic drum within the unit. An

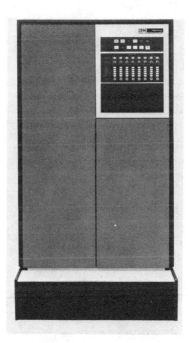

(Courtesy of IBM Corporation)

Figure Audio response unit.
8–21

inquiry consists of a series of digits from a terminal. The unit inputs these digits to the computer, which processes the inquiry and sends the response message back to the Audio Response Unit. The message, consisting of a series of addresses, selects the appropriate words from the vocabulary on the magnetic drum, and transmits the vocal reply back to the inquirer.

Although verbal input devices and audio response units are rather limited today, it is expected that great improvements will be made with verbal I-O equipment in the near future.

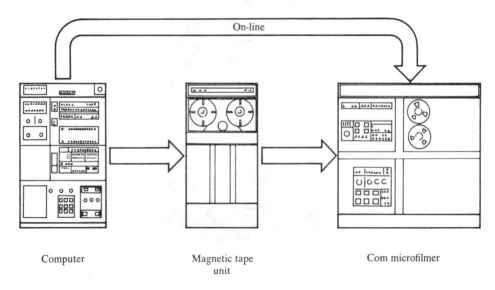

Computer	Magnetic tape unit	Com microfilmer

Figure 8–22   Schematic drawing of COM operation.

☐ Computer Output Microfilm

With the increasing calculating speeds of computers, a growing problem is how to obtain output from the computer. Printers have become faster, but are slow in comparison with the speeds at which computers may generate output.

Computer Output Microfilm (COM) has recently come of age. COM does not solve all problems associated with computer output, but it provides an additional option that system designers may consider. Figure 8–22 shows how the COM microfilmer interfaces with a computer.

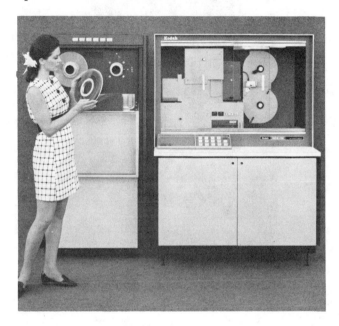

(Courtesy of Eastman Kodak Company)

Figure 8–23   The KOM-90 microfilmer converts computer output magnetic tapes to 16 mm microfilm. Data recording is accomplished at a rate up to 90 000 characters per second.

Instead of printing pages on the printer, the computer generates an output magnetic tape. This magnetic tape is used as input to a COM unit. (An example of a COM unit is Kodak's KOM-90 shown in Figure 8–23). The COM unit reads data from the magnetic tape, displays it on the face of a cathode-ray tube,* and photographs it onto 16 mm roll

---

* Most COM manufacturers employ a CRT to expose the film; however, some manufacturers have implemented other ways. One company uses a laser beam to write data on the film.

microfilm (see Figure 8–24). Data recording is accomplished at a rate up to 120 000 characters per second or 26 000 lines per minute—approximately equal to 300 printout pages per minute.

(Courtesy of Eastman Kodak Company)

Figure 8–24   This 4-ounce magazine of Kodak microfilm contains as much information as a computer output printer could produce on a 2 000-page report.

As shown in Figure 8–22, the COM Microfilmer can be directly connected to the computer (on-line), thus eliminating the necessity of recording the data on magnetic tape.

An alternative to the reel of microfilm is *microfiche,* a 10.16 x 15.24 cm (4 x 6 inch) strip of microfilm that contains 208 or more full pages of information (see Figure 8–25). You can make a simple mental comparison of a single, thin microfiche with a stack of hard copy printouts. Microfiche films are simple to file and quick to retrieve. When placed in a microfiche viewer, the single page needed is shown in full size on the screen for easy reading; and, if desired, a full-size photocopy of the single page may be printed out in seconds. Typical output speeds of computer-stored data to microfiche is one microfiche per minute, or approximately 12 000 pages per hour.

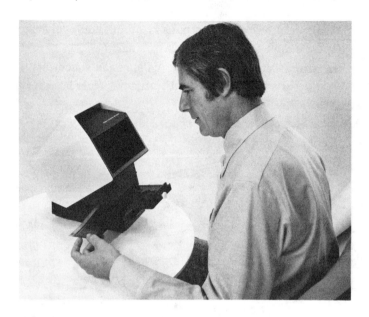

(Courtesy of Eastman Kodak Company)

Figure 8–25 A microfiche is a 10.16 by 15.24 cm (4 x 6 inches) sheet of microfilm that contains over 200 full pages of information. Shown here is a microfiche being placed in a microfiche reader.

Aperture cards (see Figure 3–10) are widely used for storing microfilm images of documents, including engineering drawings and specifications. When punched cards are used, they may be punched with pertinent information and sorted or processed by machine. Aperture cards are inserted into a reader for viewing. If the reader is equipped with a printer, a paper copy of the image can be made in seconds.

The uses for computer output microfilm are probably limitless. Microfilm reduces a high volume of documentary data to manageable proportions and frees the user from time-consuming searches and the computer from high-volume printing tasks.

Some fundamental applications of COM are the following:

- Business-oriented listings with a low or high frequency of reference, but with an infrequent need for updating.
- Computer-generated data bases, such as catalogs, indexes, directories, bibliographies, abstracts, and financial data.
- Libraries
- Engineering drawings, including plots, graphs, maps, charts, circuit designs, etc.

- Management information reports requiring both alphameric and graphic output for proper display of data.
- Insurance—examples are agents' commission statements, agents' digest system, positions' records, vendors' records, etc.
- Animated movies
- Educational and training films for industry, hospitals, businesses, government, and schools.

You know the old saying garbage in, garbage out.

☐ Intelligent Terminals

The term *intelligent terminal* designates a terminal in which a number of computer processing characteristics are physically built into, or attached to, the terminal unit. This enables the terminal to perform some functions normally handled by the computer, thus relieving the load on the computer system or data transmission lines. Specifically, the intelligent terminal detects and corrects certain operator errors, relieves the computer of some routine tasks, speeds up processing, and makes information available more easily and more quickly.

Intelligent terminals are usually cathode ray tube (CRT) units equipped with a keyboard, such as the Teletype Model 40 terminal shown in Figure 8–26. Units like this one are designed to operate as remote communication devices in connection with a computer system. They may be connected (interfaced) with a number of other input-output devices, such as card readers, printers, and cassette recorders. The intelligent terminal, coupled with other I-O devices, greatly increases a computer's capability.

An important function of the intelligent terminal is to capture and enter raw source data at the remote location of its origin, such as a sales office, branch office, or mobile office. Since the terminal can be programmed for specific applications, this assures that entries are made in the proper

(Courtesy of Teletype Corporation)

**Figure
8–26**   An intelligent terminal, which gives an operator control to review, send,
receive, print, and edit data for specific needs.

places in fill-in blanks. Operators always know exactly what is being
entered and where entries are to be made through visual verification
with the CRT display. Each entry is checked as it is made, and the
operator can make corrections before committing data to the computer
by simply rekeying the data.

Many of the intelligent terminals use *microcomputers* to control various
functions. These microcomputers can be programmed to perform many
unique and special functions that may be required for a special
application.

☐ Point-of-Sale (POS) Terminals

Computer users are starting to realize the potential advantages of capturing data at the source. Some of the benefits of a good data collection
system are: reduction of clerical costs; increased accuracy of information because of the elimination of the manual handling and transcribing

of data; more effective cost control; and sounder operating decisions by management, because they are getting timely management information, not history.

Useful data must have at least two characteristics; it must be accurate, and it must be timely. Neither of these characteristics can be overlooked. The person who is capturing the data should do the fewest number possible of the simplest things possible.

Characteristics of *point-of-sale* systems are: the input device should be installed as close as possible to the point where the data are generated; the device should be easy to operate by the person at that location who is familiar with the characteristics of these data and with the important effect of errors in the data; pre-coded information should be used when possible; a method of visual verification and correction is desirable.

(Courtesy of IBM Corporation)

Figure 8–27　Point-of-sale terminals are being used in many department stores to expand and speed sales floor service to customers. In a typical sale, for example, a salesperson merely passes a hand-held wand over the thin magnetic strip on a price tag, without removing it from the merchandise. The terminal then can read, record, and print information describing the item, display the price on a lighted panel, compute the amount due including applicable taxes, calculate change to be returned, and print a cash receipt.

Some cash registers have, for a number of years, been equipped with a paper tape punching mechanism to record the facts of each sale when these facts are entered on the machine's keyboard. For example, the sales clerk enters the amount of sale, tax, and other charges and credits if any. The clerk may also enter the stock number and unit quantity of merchandise sold as well as any other data desired. While this is being done, the machine punches a paper tape with the amount and identification of each item. At the end of the day or period, the punched tape is removed from the cash register and placed in a device that records the data from punched paper tape to magnetic tape to feed the day's sales to the computer, which updates the accounts receivable, cash on hand, and stock records, and produces sales-analysis reports for the store management.

This semiautomatic method of capturing data is certainly better than complete manual systems; however, there is still much room for improvement. Today, several companies are producing systems that eliminate the manual keying of data (an excellent place for errors to creep into a point-of-sale system).

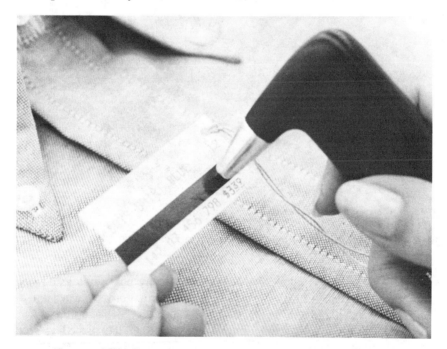

(Courtesy of IBM Corporation)

Figure 8–28 The hand-held wand of a point-of-sale terminal enables a salesperson to give improved customer service by electronic reading of magnetically encoded sales data directly from price tags. The device also helps a store ensure that accurate, comprehensive sales data are captured at the point of sale.

The IBM Point-of-Sale Terminal (see Figure 8–27) serves as both a cash register and a terminal and is linked with other terminals to a centrally located computer. The salesperson's job is automated through the use of a hand-held wand (see Figure 8–28) that senses information previously recorded on a thin magnetic strip on the price tag. The cash register terminal has a keyboard so that sales data not recorded on the magnetic strip can be entered.

Price tags are prepared by a ticket encoder and printer (see Figure 8–29) in two lines of information on a 6.35 mm wide magnetic strip running the length of the tag.

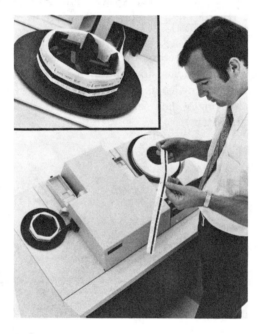

(Courtesy of IBM Corporation)

Figure 8–29   A sales tag encoder and printer produces price tags for merchandise.

When a sale is made, the salesperson merely passes the wand over the magnetic strip on the price tag. The information is printed on a cash sale or charge slip as well as on a journal log. The terminal, which is certainly an intelligent terminal (discussed in the preceding section), computes the amount due, including taxes, and calculates the amount of change to be returned.

With the terminal linked directly with the customer files in the store's computer center, the salesperson's entry immediately gets a return signal (on the control panel of the terminal) if a customer's credit card is out of date or invalid for some other reason.

(Courtesy of NCR Corporation)

Figure 8–30   A point-of-sale terminal that contains built-in computer logic to accept, record, and transmit sales data.

Another point-of-sale terminal (see Figure 8–30) manufactured by NCR Corporation also uses a tag reader to scan and read imprinted data at the point of sale. This intelligent terminal has built-in computer logic to accept, record, and transmit sales data.

Today, computerized supermarkets throughout the country are becoming rather common. The key to these checkout systems is an optical scanning device (see Figure 8–31) which "reads" an identification code placed on each item of merchandise and transmits this information to the store's computer. The computer uses this information to create a perpetual inventory control system.

The code used to identify products is the Universal Product Code, a 10-digit numbering system for identifying items sold by grocery stores (see Figure 8–32). The first five digits in the code identify the manufacturer; the second five digits identify that manufacturer's product. This 10-digit code is expressed in a symbol as a series of vertical bars that can be understood by computer equipment. This symbol will be printed on most of the 10 000 items sold in a typical supermarket. Upon receiving the code, the computer would immediately match it with product information, such as price. It would then relay this data to a cash register where it would be visually displayed to both the customer

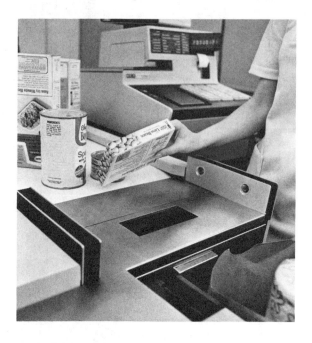

(Courtesy of NCR Corporation)

**Figure
8–31**   Computerized checkout systems speed grocery shopping and selling. As grocery items pass over the reading slot, the optical scanning mechanism reads the Universal Product Code data from a symbol affixed to the bottom of each product. This code is then transmitted to a computer. The computer then looks up the product code, matches the code with the latest price for that product, computes taxes, and sends this information to the cash register terminal. The cash register then visually displays the product name and price and prints a customer receipt.

and the checker. Simultaneously, this price would be printed on the customer's receipt along with the product name.

Placing the price in the store's computer memory eliminates the tedious job of price-marking items and also eliminates checkout errors that occur because of illegible price marks and ring-up mistakes. The store manager can also use the system to check the inventory of any product, to determine sales up to the moment at any checkstand or in any department, to know total sales, and to change prices of products.

We briefly discussed two areas (retail stores and supermarkets) where point-of-sale terminals are used. The capturing of data at its source is commonly referred to as *source data automation*. No additional steps are needed to transcribe the data to computerized form. Point-of-sale terminals, magnetic-ink character-reading devices (such as those used by banks), optical character-reading devices (such as those used by

Figure 8–32 A key feature of a computerized supermarket system is a high-speed optical scanner that reads the grocery industry's Universal Product Code (UPC) symbol. The symbol—the series of vertical black bars and numbers shown here—is printed on supermarket products. After an item has been pulled across the scanner's window, the information is sent to the computer.

utility companies) and other recognition devices, offer the possibility of preparing data only once, at the original source, and sending this data directly to the computer. There are many application areas that could be drastically improved by using source data automation systems.

The securities industry is typical of areas where source data automation can be of benefit. At least 40 000 terminals of various types are linked to computers for the purpose of transacting securities business. However, the real problem in the securities industry is that most of its transactions are still on manual or, at best, semi-automated systems. The two causes of operational problems are paper and segmentation. The paper certificate is the basic tool for recording and transferring ownership. Segmentation of the industry has caused the development of

That's right—I did rob a supermarket. How did you know?

many self-contained processes. Even where automation has been applied, it is not uncommon to end the process with a printout, hand carry the printout to the next segment in the process, and then keypunch the data all over again. What is needed are a device and a method that will allow the data to be captured once and then carried throughout the automated system.

☐ Data Communication Equipment

Data communications involves the transmission of information from one point to another. A system for data communications consists of some type of *terminal* that is used to generate and receive electronic signals transmitted over communication lines. In addition, a *data set* is often required. This device converts digital signals for transmission over communication lines. Information to be transmitted is first converted by the terminal into an intermediate form acceptable to a data set. The data set converts the signals to a form which can be transmitted over a common communications line (see Figure 8–33). At the other end of the communications line is another data set and another terminal to perform the conversions in reverse order.

A wide range of data transmission facilities are available to carry data from one point to another. Companies such as American Telephone and Telegraph and Western Union offer teletype lines, telephone lines, and high-speed telephone channels (facilities that carry many telephone calls simultaneously).

A variety of devices are currently available for use as terminals in a data communication system: a punched card reader, a teletypewriter, a

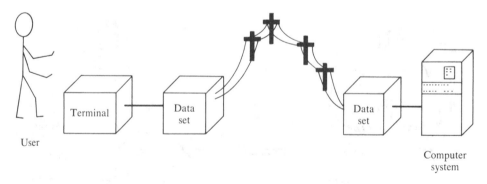

Figure 8–33   Data transmission between a user and a computer.

push-button telephone, a card-dialing telephone, graphic display devices, data collection equipment, a digital plotter, a paper tape reader, and others. Shown in Figure 8–34 is a UNIVAC DCT-2000 Data Communications Terminal. This device is a combination card punch, line printer, card reader, and operator's console which can send and receive information via telephone lines at speeds of 300 characters per second.

(Courtesy of Sperry Rand Corporation's Univac Division)

Figure 8–34 Data communications terminal that combines the functions of a card reader, line printer, card punch, and operator's console. It can send and receive information over common telephone lines at speeds of 300 characters per second.

▢ Data Synchronizers (Buffers)

Most input and output devices operate at slower speeds than the computer. Rather than slow down processing within the computer, *data synchronizers* are used to act as *buffers* between the I-O units and the computer. On input, the data is read into the buffer at the rate of an input unit. When all of the data is in the buffer, they are transferred to the computer at a faster rate. Similarly, on output, a buffer is used for the reverse operation between the computer and an output device (Figure 8–35).

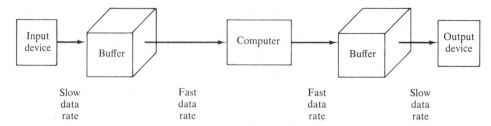

| Slow data rate | Fast data rate | Fast data rate | Slow data rate |

Figure 8–35   Schematic of buffering data between the computer and I-0 devices.

Data synchronizers are usually special-purpose devices with their own control and storage units. By using these devices, the I-O capacity of the computer is greatly increased.

"Well, don't just stand there, think of something!"

☐ Review Questions

20. Describe how a CRT display device could be used in a banking application; in an airline reservation system; in designing an automobile.
21. Name several applications where voice input-output could be used.
22. What is COM?
23. Briefly explain how a COM microfilmer is used.
24. What is a microfiche?
25. What is an aperture card? Give an example.
26. List six applications where COM equipment might be used.
27. What is an intelligent terminal?
28. Explain how and where intelligent terminals are used.
29. What is a point-of-sale terminal?
30. List several areas where point-of-sale terminals might be useful.
31. Explain how the Universal Product Code is used.

32. What is source data automation?
33. Briefly explain how data could be sent from a terminal located in New York City to a computer system located in Houston, Texas.
34. What is a data synchronizer? How is it used to dial in data communications between a computer and input-output devices?
35. Consider the devices described in this chapter. Name at least three in each of the following groups:
    (a) devices used only for input
    (b) devices used only for output
    (c) devices used for both input and output.

☐ Summary

Input and output devices are the means by which the computer communicates with the outside world: input units transfer data to the computer, while output units receive data from the computer.

When input or output units are controlled by the computer, they are considered to be *on-line*. When they are operating independently of the computer, they are *off-line*.

The input devices discussed in this chapter include the card reader, paper tape reader, typewriter, MICR reader, optical mark reader, mark sense reader, optical character reader, voice recognition device, data communication units, point-of-sale terminals, and intelligent terminals.

The output devices covered in this chapter include the card punch, paper tape punch, typewriter, line printer, digital plotter, CRT display, audio response unit, computer output microfilm (COM), data communication equipment, point-of-sale terminals, and intelligent terminals.

Key Terms

peripheral unit	optical mark reader
on-line	optical character reader
off-line	digital plotter
card reader	cathode ray tube (CRT) display
card punch	light pen
paper tape reader	audio response unit
paper tape punch	computer output microfilm (COM)
typewriter	data communications
line printer	terminal
impact printing	data set
electrostatic printing	data synchronizers
MICR reader	buffer
point-of-sale terminal	microfiche
source data automation	intelligent terminal

9

Computer Storage

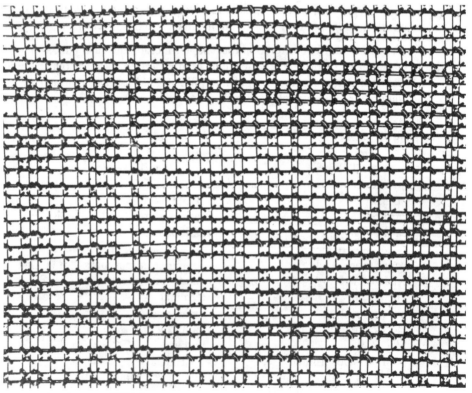

(Courtesy of IBM Corporation)

In the early nineteenth century, Charles Babbage conceived the Analytical Engine, the forerunner of the modern digital computer. Babbage's Engine contained all the functional parts of a computer, including storage. The Analytical Engine contained a *store* which, by mechanical means, was intended to hold numbers and the results of computations. All computers that followed the Analytical Engine have also used some form of storage to hold instructions, data, and intermediate calculations. Computer storage, sometimes called *memory,* is actually an electronic file where instructions and data are placed until needed. When data comes into a computer through an input unit, it is first placed in storage and remains there until it is called for by the control unit of the computer.

☐ Classification of Storage

Computer storage is divided into two classes: internal storage and auxiliary storage. *Internal storage** is an integral part of the Central Processing Unit and is directly accessible to it. *Auxiliary storage*** is used to supplement the capacity of internal storage and is of two types: sequential and direct access. *Sequential access,* such as that used with magnetic tape, involves examining sequentially all recorded data. This form of storage necessitates tape searching by starting at the beginning of the tape and continuing to search through all records until the desired information area is found. In contrast, *direct access**** devices provide immediate access to individual records and do not require reading from the beginning of a file to find a particular record.

Two terms used in the above paragraph demand further definition. A *record* refers to a group of logically related *items* read as a single unit into internal storage or written from storage in the same manner. The term *file* refers to a group of logically related records. For example, the name of an employee might be one *item.* All data about the employee (age, sex, marital status, work experience, number of children, etc.)

---

* Also called *primary storage* and *main storage.*
** Also called *secondary storage.*
*** Also called *random access.*

might be contained in one *record*. The data for all employees in a company might be contained on a *file*.

Sequential access storage is *nonaddressable;* that is, an operator cannot directly refer to the contents of a particular storage location. Direct access storage is *addressable*: a given item can be selected from anywhere in storage by simply specifying the address where it is located.

The *capacity* of a storage device is expressed as the number of words, bytes, characters, or bits it can store at one time. The cost of storage is directly determined by the capacity of the device and its type.

The time the computer takes to locate and transfer information to or from storage is called *access time*. Access to some storage units is so rapid it is measured in nanoseconds (billionths of a second).

The most widely used form of internal storage is *magnetic core,* although *thin film* and *integrated circuits* are being used on some of the recent machines. Auxiliary storage devices (Figure 9–1) include magnetic tapes,

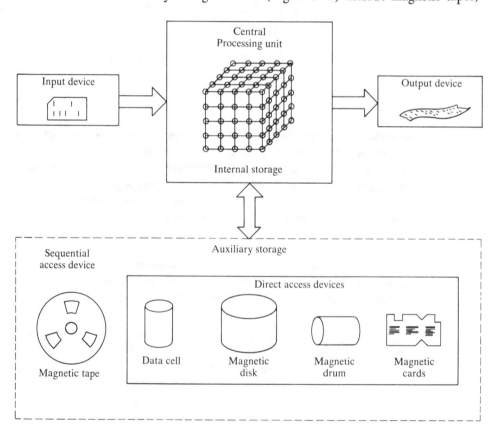

Figure 9–1   Auxiliary storage devices used to supplement the internal storage of a computer.

magnetic disks, magnetic drums, magnetic cards, and data cells. Magnetic tape is the only sequential storage device discussed in this book; all the other auxiliary storage devices are of the direct access type. These various forms of storage will be discussed in the remainder of this chapter.

Review Questions

1. What is the difference between internal storage and auxiliary storage?
2. What is meant by "access time"?
3. What is the most common type of internal storage used in modern digital computers?
4. Name three kinds of information normally contained in internal storage.
5. Describe the difference between the sequential and direct access methods of storage.
6. Define the following terms and give an example of data storage using these three terms.
   (a) record
   (b) file
   (c) item
7. What is the difference between addressable and nonaddressable storage?
8. What is meant by the "capacity" of a storage device?
9. Name three auxiliary storage devices of the direct access type.

Magnetic Core

A *magnetic core* is a tiny doughnut-shaped ring of ferromagnetic material with a hole diameter that may be less than .03 mm (.01 inch). Each core is about the size of the head of a pin. Figure 9–2 shows cores compared in size to grains of salt and a paper clip. Other than its compact size, low power consumption, and low heat dissipation, the magnetic core has another important characteristic. It can be magnetized at incredible speeds—billionths of a second—and will retain this magnetism indefinitely unless a deliberate change is made.

The cores are made by pressing a mixture of ferric oxide powder and other materials into the proper shape and baking the molded forms in an oven.

The cores are then placed on wire, like beads on a string. Passing electric current through the wires in one of two directions magnetizes the wires. The direction of the current determines the polarity or magnetic state of the core. Magnetism in one direction represents a *one,* while magnetism in the opposite direction represents a *zero* (Figure 9–3). For machine purposes, this is the basis of the binary system of storing information.

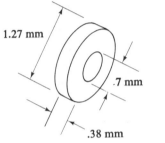

1.27 mm

.7 mm

.38 mm

Magnetic cores

Grains
of salt

(Courtesy of IBM Corporation)

Figure   The geometry and size of a magnetic core.
9–2

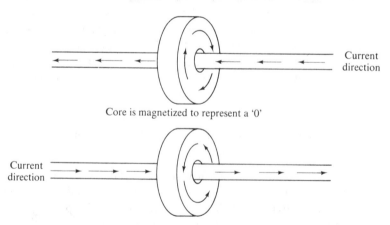

Current
direction

Core is magnetized to represent a '0'

Current
direction

Core is magnetized to represent a '1'

Figure   Polarity of magnetic cores.
9–3

Magnetic cores are strung together in planes, which are designed so that
only one core in each plane can be magnetized or sensed at any one time.
This core selection process is accomplished by running two wires through
each core at right angles to each other (Figure 9–4). When half the cur-

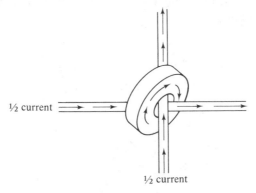

½ current

½ current

**Figure
9–4**   Process of selecting a core.

rent needed to magnetize a core is sent through each wire, only one core
at the intersection of the wires is magnetized. Other cores located on
the same wires are not affected. Using this principle, many cores can be
strung on a plane, yet any single core can be accessed without affecting
any other. A plane of magnetic cores is shown in Figure 9–5. This plane
contains 1 024 magnetic cores, arranged in a 32 × 32 array.

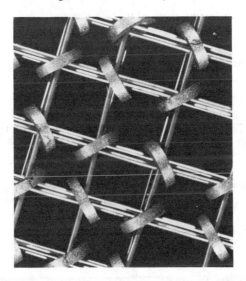

(Courtesy of IBM Corporation)

**Figure
9–5**   Plane of magnetic cores.

The storage unit of a computer consists of several planes, each containing several hundred cores. These planes are stacked on top of one another as shown in Figure 9–6. Each vertical column of cores is assigned an address where one piece of information can be stored. When the computer reads the contents of this address, it will read each of the cores in this column.

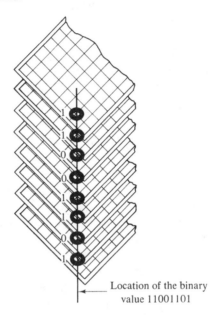

Location of the binary
value 11001101

Figure 9–6   Information as represented in core storage.

The number of planes used in a computer storage unit varies with the cost and size of the computer. A memory plane can hold only one bit at each location. To store a *byte* (8 bits) in one location, the computer needs 8 memory planes. To store a 16-bit *word,* it needs 16 memory planes. To store a 32-bit *word,* it needs 32 memory planes. Each bit of the word is stored on a different memory plane. When the computer writes or reads a word, all the bits in the word are selected simultaneously.

Magnetic core provides a *nonvolatile* storage for computers; that is, it retains its binary state when all power is removed from the equipment.

☐ Thin Film

Thin film storage, which utilizes concepts similar to those magnetic core storage is based on, has been used as internal storage for some recent computers. It is, however, more compact, more expensive, and faster in access time than is magnetic core storage.

One form of thin film memory consists of a series of metallic alloy dots, a few millionths of an inch thick, deposited on a glass, ceramic, or plastic plate. The metallic dots are connected by very fine wires and perform in the same manner as magnetic cores. Like magnetic cores, these dots can be magnetized in either of two stable preferred directions. Several thousand dots may be deposited on a one-inch square plane.

Because the thin films consist of so many small spots, the arrangement of circuits to perform reading and writing operations is difficult. A common method is to etch copper wires onto an insulating material. Then, by closely positioning these circuits, the spots can be magnetized and their direction of magnetization sensed.

Another form of thin-film utilizes short-rod memory elements. This type of memory is used in machines manufactured by the National Cash Register Company. The rods are made by depositing a thin metallic film and then a protective coating on a thin copper wire. This process yields a plated wire .15 mm in diameter, which is then cut into 2.79 mm lengths to form the rods. Each rod in a memory is individually addressable and can hold one byte of information (eight bits plus a parity bit, used for checking purposes). The basic memory plane is formed by inserting the rods into coils wound on a plastic frame. Then the entire plane is sealed between two sheets of plastic. Automated processes are used to plate the wire, cut the rods, wind the coils, insert the rods into the coils, and seal the planes. The result is a high-performance, low-cost memory.

Review Questions

10. Describe a magnetic core. How can it be used to store information?
11. What characteristics of magnetic cores make them especially suitable for use as internal storage components?
12. What is a memory plane?
13. What is meant by "nonvolatile storage"?
14. Thin film is used for what purpose?

Magnetic Tape

As described in chapter seven, magnetic tape is one of the more popular media for representing information. It is used not only as a fast way of getting information into and out of the computer, but also as auxiliary storage.

A tape unit reads from and writes on tape (Figure 9–7). Before the tape unit can perform read or write operations, it must be prepared for operation. This preparation involves loading two reels on the tape unit and threading the tape through the tape transport mechanism. Figure 9–8 shows an operator loading a magnetic tape reel on a tape unit.

(Courtesy of Texas Instruments Incorporated)

**Figure
9–7**   Magnetic tape units.

(Courtesy of Sperry Rand Corporation's Univac Division)

**Figure
9–8**   Operator loading a reel of magnetic tape on a tape unit.

During tape read or write operations, the tape moves from one reel across a read-write head to the other reel. Two types of read-write heads are used (Figure 9–9). Figure 9–9a shows a one-gap read-write head where reading and writing take place at the same gap. In the two-gap head (Figure 9–9b), tape being written passes over the write head to have data recorded and over the read head to be read.

Writing on tape is *destructive;* that is, as new information is written, old information is destroyed. Reading is *nondestructive;* the same information can be read again and again. Information is written on tape by magnetizing areas in parallel tracks along the length of the tape. There are both seven-track and nine-track tapes. In the tape unit, there is one read-write coil in the head for each recording track, where electrical current flowing through the coils magnetizes the iron oxide coating of the moving tape and erases previously written information. The execution of a "program write" command results in one or more records of data being written. A 15.24 mm *interrecord gap* (IRG) is left after each "write" has been completed (Figure 9–10). The gap serves to separate one record

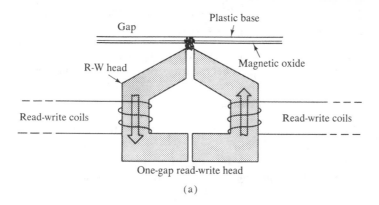

One-gap read-write head

(a)

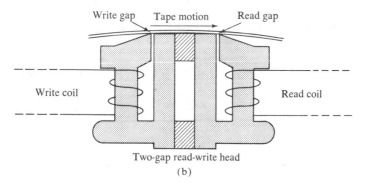

Two-gap read-write head

(b)

Figure 9–9   Read-write head unit of a magnetic tape unit.

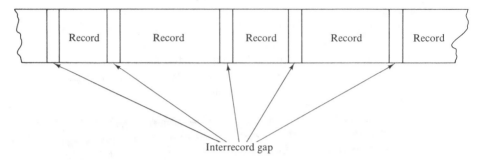

| Record | Record | Record | Record | Record |

Interrecord gap

Figure 9–10   Interrecord gaps and records on magnetic tape.

from another and allows distance for both stopping the tape after an operation and accelerating the tape to the proper speed when starting a new operation.

File protection rings are often used with magnetic tape to prevent the accidental writing of information on a tape. This ring, which is made of plastic, fits into a circular groove on the tape reel (Figure 9–11). Writing is prohibited whenever the ring is absent.

Magnetic tapes must have blank spaces at each end to allow for threading on the tape unit. Reflector spots or markers on each end of the tape enable the tape unit to sense the beginning or end of the tape. These spots, which are invisible, define the usable portion of the tape.

Magnetic tape units read tapes at speeds up to 285.8 cm (112.5 inches) per second. Information can be recorded on a tape up to 1 600 characters per inch. This is referred to as the "tape density." Data recorded at 1 600 characters per inch and reading at 285.8 cm per second allows

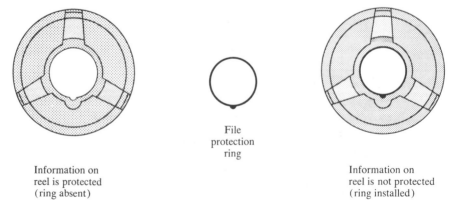

File
protection
ring

Information on
reel is protected
(ring absent)

Information on
reel is not protected
(ring installed)

Figure 9–11   Protection of information recorded on magnetic tape.

180 000 characters to be transmitted each second. This high-speed operation is the primary reason that magnetic tape is used as a primary input-output method for many medium and large computer systems.

Many businesses store all their information on magnetic tape, building up large *tape libraries* as shown in Figure 9–12. Data is often recorded

(Courtesy of **IBM** Corporation)

Figure A magnetic tape library.
9–12

on magnetic tape by using a *card-to-tape conversion* procedure or a *key-to-tape recorder*. In card-to-tape conversion, the source data are initially recorded on punched cards. Then, using the card reader, the computer, and a magnetic tape unit, the data are recorded on magnetic tape (Figure 9–13). The key-to-tape recorder (Figure 9–14) is a device that

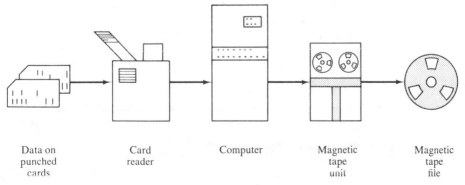

| Data on punched cards | Card reader | Computer | Magnetic tape unit | Magnetic tape file |

Figure Card-to-tape conversion procedure.
9–13

(Courtesy of National Cash Register Company)

Figure 9–14   Key-to-tape recorder.

can be used to record data directly onto magnetic tape just as a keypunch is used to record data on cards.

Also available are *hypertape* and *cassette/cartridge* tape units. *Hypertape* is a special type of magnetic tape with data recorded horizontally in ten parallel tracks on a tape that is 2.54 cm (1 inch) wide and 1 800 feet long. The tape density is either 1 511 or 3 022 eight-bit bytes per 2.54 cm (1 inch) and the tape speed is 285.8 cm (112.5 inches) per second. Its data transfer rate is up to 340 000 characters per second. Hypertape is enclosed in a special cartridge that contains both the feed and take-up reels (Figure 9–15). This cartridge protects the tape from dust and minimizes tape loading and unloading time.

In computer systems, there is often a requirement for large quantity storage of data that need be used only occasionally. In large systems, this requirement is often met by using a magnetic tape unit. Minicomputer systems often have these same requirements, although usually on a lesser scale. The magnetic tape units available for large systems, although a possible solution, are not often employed because their cost is generally higher than that of a minicomputer. Recently, several container-loaded magnetic tape units, designed as low-cost storage devices for minicomputers, have been made available.

A *cassette/cartridge* unit is a digital tape recorder which operates with tape (usually 3.175 or 6.350 mm (⅛ or ¼ inch) wide) that has been previously loaded in some form of container. The container is usually open at one end to permit insertion of magnetic heads and the drive mechanism. The remainder is completely enclosed. The containers come in two forms: *cassette,* which is a tape container in which two reels are mounted; and *cartridge,* which is a container in which the tape is stored

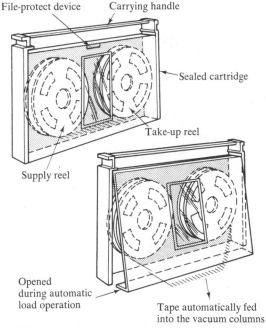

File-protect device   Carrying handle

Sealed cartridge

Take-up reel

Supply reel

Opened
during automatic
load operation
                        Tape automatically fed
                        into the vacuum columns

(Courtesy of IBM Corporation)

Figure   Hypertape cartridge.
9–15

in the form of an endless loop. Cassette/cartridge units are basically simple, modest-performance devices. They are relatively easy to operate and their cost is fairly low. Hence, these devices provide a low-cost solution to the problem of large capacity storage for small digital computer systems.

☐ Review Questions

15. List several advantages for using magnetic tape as a storage medium.
16. Briefly describe how information is read and written onto magnetic tape.
17. What is meant by "packing density"?
18. Discuss density and tape speeds with regard to transfer rate.
19. What is meant by "reading is nondestructive"?
20. What is an interrecord gap?
21. What are file protection rings used for?
22. What device can be used to directly record data on magnetic tape?

☐ Magnetic Drum

A *magnetic drum* is a metal cylinder coated with magnetically sensitive material on its outer surface. The drum rotates at a constant speed. The drum surface is divided into several *tracks or channels* (Figure 9–16).

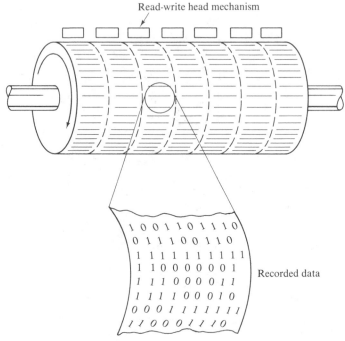

Figure 9–16   Schematic of a magnetic drum.

Each track has an associated read-write head mechanism that is used to read and write data on the drum surface. A read-write head is suspended a very slight distance from the drum surface, as shown in Figure 9–17. Whenever new data are recorded, the old data are automatically erased.

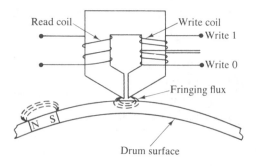

(Courtesy of IBM Corporation)

Figure 9–17   Read-write head recording on a magnetic drum surface.

As the drum rotates, reading and writing occurs when the specified area of the track (on some drums, a track is subdivided into several *sectors*) passes under the read-write mechanism for that track. Writing results in magnetized spots on the drum surface. Reading involves only sensing the magnetized areas. A magnetic drum is shown in Figure 9–18.

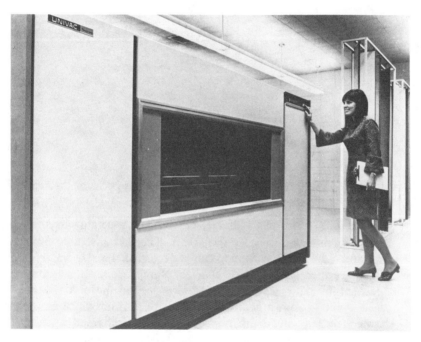

(Courtesy of Sperry Rand Corporation's Univac Division)

Figure   Magnetic drum.
9–18

☐ Magnetic Disk

Magnetic disks are rapidly becoming the most used type of auxiliary storage. The physical characteristics of all *magnetic disks* are similar. Each one is a thin metal disk coated on both sides with magnetic recording material (Figure 9–19). Disks are mounted on a vertical shaft and are slightly separated from each other to provide space for the movement of read-write assemblies. The shaft revolves, spinning the disks. Data are stored as magnetized spots in concentric *tracks* on each *surface* of the disk. Disk units have several hundred tracks on each surface for storing data. The tracks are made accessible for reading and writing by positioning the read-write heads between the spinning disks. The read-write head mechanism is hydraulically driven to move all heads simultaneously to any track position. After horizontal movement is completed to a specified

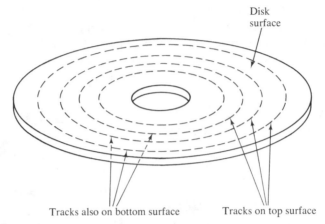

Figure   Schematic of a magnetic disk.
9–19

track, the read-write heads can be directed to perform the reading and writing on the track.

Figure 9–20 illustrates a disk assembly. This assembly is composed of six disks mounted on a vertical shaft. The disk assembly provides ten surfaces on which information can be recorded. The top and bottom surfaces are used as protective plates and are not used for recording purposes. Information is read from or written on the disks by read-write heads mounted on a comb-like access mechanism which has ten read-write heads mounted on five access arms. Each read-write head can either read or write information on the corresponding upper or lower disk surface. The entire access mechanism moves horizontally so that information on all tracks can be either read or written.

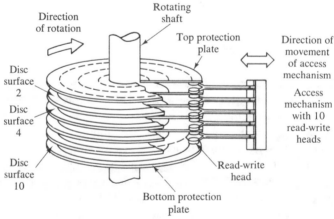

Figure   Schematic of a magnetic disk assembly of six disks.
9–20

Figure 9–21 shows a disk assembly of six disks in operation. The read-write heads are shown being relocated to a new track while the disks are revolving.

A magnetic disk assembly can have several disks. A disk unit with 25 disks can have a storage capacity of over 100 million characters of information. This information can be transmitted to and from a computer at rates of over 150,000 characters per second.

The magnetic disk data surface can be used repetitively. Each time new information is stored on a track, the old information is erased as the new is recorded. The recorded data may be read as often as desired; data remain recorded in the tracks of a disk until they can be written over.

The simplified disk assembly shown in Figure 9–20 illustrates the read-write head mechanism moving in a horizontal direction. In this manner, the disk mechanism is able to position itself at any specified track. The time required to locate a specific track is called the disk *access time*. This time is related to the lateral distance that the read-write head mechanism moves. In addition to access time, there is another timing factor associated with disk read-write operations. The *rotational delay time* is the time required for the disk to attain the desired position at the selected read-write head. The maximum revolution time for a disk is the time required for one full revolution. The average rotational delay time is one-half the disk revolution rate. For example, if the disk revolves at 2,400 revolutions per minute (a typical speed) then the average rotational delay time would be slightly over 11 milliseconds.

(Courtesy of IBM Corporation)

Figure 9–21   Read-write head assembly being relocated to a new track position as the disks revolve.

(Courtesy of IBM Corp.)

Figure   IBM 3340 disk storage.
9–22

Some disk units have removable and replaceable disk packs (Figure 9–22). These disk units are used as input-output units as well as storage devices. The disk pack is popular because it allows a user to move the data stored in one disk unit conveniently to another place so that they can

(Courtesy of Sperry Rand Corporation's Univac Division)

Figure   Ease with which a disk pack can be replaced on a disk unit.
9–23

be processed on various computer systems. Replacement of one disk pack by another takes less than one minute. Figure 9–23 illustrates the ease with which a disk pack goes on the disk unit.

The removable disk pack unit usually does not provide as much direct storage capacity as the larger disk units made up of many permanently located disks; however, the unit is much cheaper and provides an unlimited storage capacity simply by replacing one disk pack with a new one containing different information.

There is one other type of disk unit. This unit, called a *fixed head disk,* has a stationary read-write head for each track. These head-per-track devices are much faster than other disk units, since there are no moving parts—only the rotational delay time. In fact, access times of the fixed head disks are similar to magnetic drums. Fixed-head disk units are, however, more expensive than other type of disks.

A new type of disk, recently introduced, has proved to be a strong competitor with the previously mentioned disk units. These disks, called *floppy disks,* are flexible, made of oxide-coated mylar, and stored in paper or plastic envelopes. The entire envelope is inserted in the disk unit, effectively protecting the contents of the disk surfaces. The disk surfaces are rotated inside the protective covering. The disk head contacts the track positions through a slot in the covering.

(Courtesy of Digital Equipment Corporation)

Figure 9–24   A high school student inserting a diskette into a floppy disk unit.

The student in Figure 9–24 is placing a floppy disk (or diskette) into the disk unit. Disk units such as these are relatively inexpensive, and the disks themselves are cheap. It is estimated that eventually a diskette will cost around 50 cents. Because of their low cost and high speed, the floppy disk units are finding wide use, especially in minicomputer system applications.

☐ Review Questions

23. Describe magnetic drum storage.
24. Briefly describe the different types of magnetic disk units.
25. Which type of disk unit is commonly used as an input-output unit as well as an auxiliary storage device?
26. Describe a disk pack.
27. What is disk access time? rotational delay time?
28. How many read-write heads would be on a 200-track fixed-head disk?
29. What is a floppy disk unit?

☐ Magnetic Cards

Magnetic cards provide storage and direct access to data in a manner quite different mechanically from magnetic drums or disks. Cards are assembled in removable and replacable cartridges of several hundred cards per cartridge. The cards are made of the same plastic material as magnetic tape (although considerably thicker) and are coated with the same kind of magnetic oxide material on one side. Data is recorded in or read from magnetized spots on the card as the card moves past a read-write head. Any card may be selected from and returned to the cartridge under computer control. The cards are removed from their cartridge whenever data is to be recorded or retrieved. This is done automatically by the unit whenever the computer calls for a particular card.

The most popular magnetic card unit is CRAM (Card Random Access Memory). This unit uses a card measuring 8.87 cm by 35.56 cm (3.5 by 14 inches (Figure 9–25) and a cartridge which holds 384 cards. When the computer calls for a particular card, that card drops out of the chamber and wraps around a rotating drum, where it is held by air suction (Figure 9–26). The card is now like a magnetic drum, but an unusual drum in which the recording occupies only about two-thirds of the circumference. One-third of each drum-revolution is thus free for updating the information just read, so that it is ready for re-recording

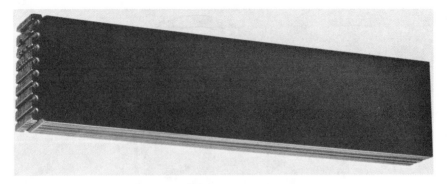

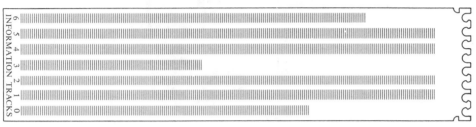

(Courtesy of National Cash Register Company)

Figure   Magnetic cards used in the CRAM unit.
9–25

during the next revolution. Consequently, the minimum processing (updating) time imposed by CRAM is one-third of a revolution, rather than the full revolution required by other rotating file devices. When the program has finished with a card, the card is returned via the top of the mechanism to the chamber, where it then occupies the outer right-hand position in the deck.

While the card is on the drum, data may be written or read in any one of seven information tracks during one revolution. No switching time is involved in changing from one track to another on successive revolutions, since the CRAM is provided with individual read-write heads for each track. While information is being recorded by the write head, the read head is performing a simultaneous validity check on the recorded information.

The CRAM unit, shown in Figure 9–27, can store over 125 million characters of information. The unit has access to any card from a cartridge in approximately one-eighth of a second.

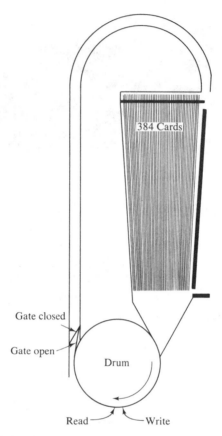

384 Cards

Gate closed

Gate open

Drum

Read — — Write

(Courtesy of National Cash Register Company)

Figure Schematic of a cartridge containing 384 magnetic cards.
9–26

☐ Data-Cell Drive

The *data cell drive* (Figure 9–28) is a device similar to the magnetic
card unit. It uses a magnetic strip, three times as thick as magnetic tape,
about 6.35 cm wide and 33.02 cm long (2.5 by 13 inches). Each strip
contains 100 tracks and can store 2 000 bytes (8-bits) per track. The
strips have a magnetic coating on one side. Ten strips are placed in a
subcell. The data cell drive contains ten removable data cells, each
containing twenty subcells (Figure 9–29). Thus, a complete drive
contains 2 000 strips.

When a particular location is required either for reading or writing, the
cells are rotated until the subcell containing the strip to be processed is
under a drum that is fixed in position above the array of cells. As the
drum continues rotating, the strip is taken from the subcell and wrapped

(Courtesy of National Cash Register Company)

Figure 9–27 CRAM (Card Random Access Memory) unit.

(Courtesy of IBM Corporation)

Figure 9–28 Data Cell Drive.

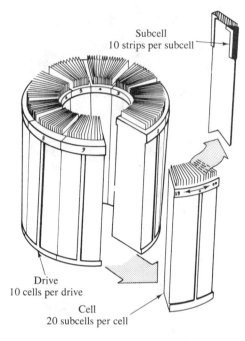

Subcell
10 strips per subcell

Drive
10 cells per drive

Cell
20 subcells per cell

(Courtesy of IBM Corporation)

Figure   Strip selection in the Data Cell Drive.
9–29

around a drum where reading or writing can occur. The strip remains attached to the rotating drum until another strip is selected. The strip is restored by reversing the direction of rotation of the drum. The strip drops back into its subcell position between the separated adjacent strips.

The access time of the data cell drive is more than the associated times of disks or drums. This is primarily because so much mechanical movement is required to gain access to a specific location. Nevertheless, this device can contain approximately 400 million bytes of information that are accessible to the computer at any one time. Thus, it offers an excellent way of storing large amounts of information at a relatively low cost.

☐ Magnetic Bubble Memory

The magnetic bubble memory is a technique now being developed by Bell Telephone Laboratories and other firms. This technique utilizes magnetic "bubbles" that move. The bubbles are locally-magnetized areas that can move about in thin plates of orthoferrite, a magnetic material. It is possible to control the reading in and out of this "bubble" within the plate and, as a result, a very high-capacity memory can be built.

Laser-Holographic Storage

As computers continue to grow in size and complexity, storage will have to be increased significantly at no sacrifice in speed. This means the information will have to be packed much more densely in whatever storage device is used. Holography is a technique that can further the development of large storage devices. With recent advances in holography and laser beam technology, computer developers are studying optical memories whose ultimate storage capacity may well be in excess of 100 million bits of data, and whose random access time may be as short as one microsecond. Holograms make use of a high-energy laser beam to store or display three-dimensional images. The image produced by a hologram can easily be read by a photodetector, and information can be stored redundantly.

A holographic memory is made on a special recording medium somewhat simular to conventional photographic film. The recording process starts with the construction of a data mask that represents the contents of a page. Each mask is basically an array of pinholes, blocked where zeros are to be recorded and transparent where ones are needed. Each data mask is recorded holographically, one at a time, on the recording medium. Information is retrieved from the memory by projecting the data recorded on the hologram onto a light-sensitive detector. The detector converts the optical information into electronic signals that the computer can process.

Several experimental laser-holographic memory systems have been developed. IBM has developed a system that stores more than 100 million bits of information on a nine square inch holographic plate. A system, developed by a Japanese firm, is capable of accomodating a telephone directory of 3 800 pages on 16 pieces of film, each measuring five square inches. It has a capacity much greater than present storage units, and is considerably faster than conventional magnetic tapes or disks in information read-out. Another system has been developed that can record over 70 866 bits of information onto a single cm of eight millimeter photographic film at a rate of over 10 million bits per second. Laser storage devices are still considered to be in the early experimental stages and will probably not become economically feasible in the near future.

Semiconductor Memories

A *semiconductor memory* (also called *integrated circuit memory*) uses silicon chips with interconnecting on-off switches (called flip-flops). The direction of the electric current passing through each cell determines whether the position of the switch is on or off; that is, whether the bit is 1 or 0. Each silicon chip is about 0.32 cm^2 (one-eighth of an inch square).

Semiconductor memories provide increased storage capacity and low access time. It is also possible to design logic into these memories.

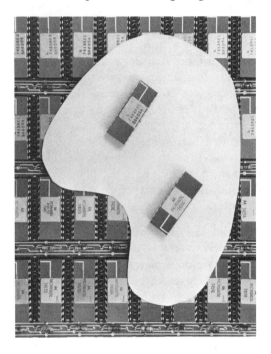

(Courtesy of Cincinnati Milacron)

Figure 9–30   Blowup of a metal oxide semiconductor memory board.

There are two types of chips—bipolar and metal oxide semiconductor (MOS) chips (see Figure 9–30). A single MOS chip contains 1 024 bits. A bipolar chip holds fewer bits but offers faster speeds than the MOS chip. The MOS chips are less expensive to produce.

Semiconductor memories can be found in many large computers such as the IBM System/370* as well as in small computers like the IBM System/32, NCR Century 151, and Univac 90/60. Semiconductor mem-

* The IBM System/370 Model 145 was the first major computer system to incorporate an all-integrated circuit memory.

ories are used as the internal memory in almost all minicomputers. We can expect to see wider use of this type of memory in future systems of all sizes. These memories are both faster and more compact than core memory.

Virtual Memory

System designers and programmers have typically had to be concerned with internal memory capacity to make sure that they could fit their computer programs and working data into the available space. If the programs were too large for memory, the programmer would segment the program, putting the first part in internal storage and the other segments in auxiliary or secondary storage. When the first section was complete, the second section would be brought into internal storage (overlaid in the same memory area that contained the first section). The use of overlays can be limited to smaller sections, so that a main segment is kept intact and smaller portions are overlaid.

The concept of *virtual memory* is to have the hardware and software *automatically* segment the program and to move segments into storage when needed. The auxiliary storage, usually disk units, is, in effect, utilized as an "extension" of the computer's internal memory. Virtual memory is the memory space defined by a range of addresses specified by the programmer and different from the addresses utilized by the memory system. A device is required for translating the addresses used by the program into the correct memory location addresses. The size of virtual memory is consequently limited only by the addressing capability of the computer and not by the number of locations in its internal memory. With virtual memory, the programmer has the illusion that the memory of the computer is larger than it really is.

The basic element of a virtual memory is a program segment or *page*— a fixed-size unit of storage, usually 2 048 or 4 096 bytes. The pages of memory are swapped back and forth in such a way that the internal memory (real memory) of the computer is expanded to many times its actual capacity. The process of swapping programs or data back and forth is referred to as *page-in,* since the page goes from disk to internal memory, and *page-out* as a page leaves the internal memory and is stored on the disk unit.

The difficult part of any memory organization is keeping track of what part of the program is in internal storage and what part is stored on the disk. A technique called *dynamic memory allocation* is used in the management of memory resources. This technique divides a selected area of internal memory into pages. Any available page may be assigned for different purposes, depending on the requirements of the moment. A control routine keeps account of which pages are free so that the available memory space can be immediately assigned as needed. This is accomplished by a technique wherein available pages are linked together in the form of a chain. When a memory page becomes available, it is appropriately added to the chain. The control routine shuffles programs or data from auxiliary storage into available memory pages as required.

An IBM virtual memory system has a special hardware device, called a *Dynamic Address Translation (DAT) device,* which is used to control the memory allocation assignments. Other computer manufacturers use software techniques (part of the Operating System) to control dynamic memory allocation assignments.

Virtual memory allows a programmer to write a program as if internal memory were limitless. With virtual memory, the computer takes care of the difficulty of scheduling the swapping of data and programs.

Sure, it's depressing. This thing has a memory of 16 trillion bytes, and I can't recall what I had for breakfast.

☐ Review Questions

30. Briefly explain the operation of a magnetic card unit.
31. Explain why the access time of a Data-Cell Drive is longer than the access time of a magnetic drum.
32. Identify an application where a magnetic card unit or Data-Cell Drive could be used.
33. What are some of the advantages of direct access storage devices as compared to a magnetic tape unit?
34. What is a semiconductor memory?
35. Why are many of the newer computer systems using semiconductor memory as the computers' internal memory?
36. Why does the virtual memory concept permit the user to run larger programs than could be run without virtual memory?
37. What is a "page"?
38. What is meant by "page-in"? "Page-out"?
39. What is dynamic memory allocation?

☐ Summary

Computer storage is actually an electronic file where instructions and data are placed until needed. *Internal storage* is an integral part of the Central Processing Unit and is directly accessible to it. This storage holds programs and data currently being manipulated. *Auxiliary storage* is used to supplement the capacity of the internal storage. Programs or data stored in auxiliary storage cannot be used by the computer until they are brought into the computer's internal storage.

Magnetic core storage is the most widely used method for internally storing data in a computer. Other popular methods use thin-film techniques and integrated circuit memory.

Auxiliary storage devices covered in this chapter include magnetic tape units (such methods using hypertape, cartridges or cassettes), magnetic disk units, magnetic drums, magnetic card units, and data-cell drives.

Computer memories of the future may very well include thin film memories, semiconductor memories, laser-hologram memories, and magnetic bubble memories.

Key Terms

memory	hypertape
internal storage	tape cassette
auxiliary storage	tape cartridge
sequential access	magnetic drum
direct access	track
record	channel
file	sector
capacity	magnetic disk
access time	disk surface
magnetic core	rotational delay time
thin film	fixed head disk
memory plane	disk pack
nonvolatile	magnetic card
magnetic tape	data cell drive
destructive	magnetic bubble memory
nondestructive	laser-holographic storage
interrecord gap	microcircuit
file protection ring	Large Scale Integrated (LSI) circuit
semiconductor memory	virtual memory
dynamic memory allocation	page
	page-in
	page-out

10

Representative Computer Systems

In this chapter, computer systems are classified into the following major types:

(1) large scale systems
(2) medium scale systems
(3) small scale systems
(4) minicomputer systems
(5) business minicomputer systems
(6) microcomputers

These groupings are neither clearly defined nor sharply divided and are more or less relative to one another. Instead, purchase price of the various computer systems was the determining factor in classification of the six types. A large scale system leases for over $100 000 per month, while a small scale system can be leased for as little as $1 000 per month. Minicomputer systems are generally not leased; however, their purchase price is usually quite low, often less than $10 000. A microcomputer is priced around $1 000.

The following abbreviations will be used in describing these systems.

bps — bytes per second
cpm — cards per minute
cps — characters per second
lpm — lines per minute

□ Large Scale Computer Systems

Representative of computer systems in the large scale class are the IBM System 370, Models 155, 158, 165, 168, and 195; IBM System 360, Models 65, 67, 75, 85, and 195; Control Data 6800 and 7600; Burroughs B7500 and B6700; Honeywell 6080, 6070, and 6060; Univac 1108 and 1110; and the Illiac IV. These systems are valued at several million dollars and usually lease for several hundred thousand dollars per month. Discussed in this chapter are the System/360 Model 195 and the UNIVAC 1110.

Know anybody who'd like to buy a new minicomputer?

IBM System/360 Model 195

The IBM System/360 (Figure 10–1) is the largest and broadest line of computer equipment ever introduced, and is, by far, the most widely used equipment in the world. As such, it has become the universal standard of comparison, and many of its characteristics and facilities have become virtual industry standards. System/360 now consists of 12 different central processors, more than 50 peripheral devices, and a uniquely broad array of supporting software. The smallest member of the System/360

(Courtesy of IBM Corporation)

Figure
10–1   Control panel of the IBM System/360 Model 195—one of the largest computers ever manufactured.

family of computers is the Model 20, discussed later in this chapter. The largest member of the family is the Model 195. Ranging between these two computers are Models 22, 25, 30, 40, 44, 50, 65, 67, 75, and 85.

The System/360 Model 195 is the largest "super-computer" from IBM. It is program-compatible with the smaller general-purpose models. It has a 54 nanosecond memory cycle time and uses extensive overlapping of operations to provide extremely fast processing. Floating-point arithmetic operations can be performed at nanosecond speeds—e.g., a floating point addition takes only 108 nanoseconds.

The circuitry used in the Model 195 is called Monolithic Systems Technology (MST) and it packs approximately 20 866 circuit components into one cm^2.

A wide selection of peripherals (input-output devices) are available for use with the Model 195, as well as an extensive software facility. Several different operating systems are available and users can do their programming in PL/I, COBOL, BASIC, APL, FORTRAN, or RPG, as well as in assembly language.

Monthly rentals for Model 195 systems will range from about $165 000 to $300 000. Purchases prices will range from about $7 to 12 million.

The Model 195 is designed to help solve the most complex commercial and scientific problems from nationwide airline reservations handling to global weather forecasting. It is so fast that it can process an instruction in just 54 billionths of a second. In that time, light—traveling at 344 991 km (186 281 miles) a second—can move only 16.15 m (53 feet). The Model 195 is capable of processing as many as 15 different problems simultaneously. Many programmers, users, and computer personnel (Figure 10–2) are required to feed and use the data processed by such a powerful computer system.

UNIVAC 1110

The Univac 1110 is the largest member of the Univac 1100 family of computers. The first member of this family was the 1107. More recent members of the family include the UNIVAC 1106 and 1108 systems.

The 1110 system (Figure 10–3) is designed to perform in a broad range of scientific, business, commercial, and real-time applications. The system retains virtually all of the processing facilities, peripheral equipment, and software of the UNIVAC 1108 system, while providing greatly increased processing power.

The internal storage of the 1110 is plated-wire memory (a type of memory to be described in detail later in the chapter). The nondestructive readout capability of the plated-wire memory yields a cycle time of 320 nanoseconds per word for reading and 520 nanoseconds for writing. A second level of storage for the 1110 that can be addressed directly

(Courtesy of McDonnell Automation Company)

Figure 10–2   The IBM System/360 Model 195 is designed to help solve the most complex commercial and scientific problems. It is so fast that it can process an instruction in just 54 billionths of a second. In that time, light—traveling at 344,991 km a second—can move only 16.15 m. Shown here are a programmer and computer operator looking at data produced by this powerful computer.

is provided by conventional magnetic core storage in a choice of 750 nanosecond or 1.5 microsecond cycle times. A maximum of 1 048 000 words of storage can be used.

UNIVAC 1110 systems can include a wide variety of peripheral devices, including several mass storage devices with storage up to 114 million characters of data. Software support for the 1110 includes an operating system and programming language translators for COBOL, FORTRAN, Conversational FORTRAN, APL, BASIC, ALGOL, JOVIAL, and assembly languages.

System rentals for the UNIVAC 1110 begin at approximately $60 000 per month and extend upward to over $150 000.

☐ Medium Scale Computer Systems

The medium scale computer system provides considerable computing power for most business applications. The monthly rental price of this

(Courtesy of Sperry Rand Corporation's Univac Division)

Figure 10–3 The Univac 1110, largest member of the Univac 1100 family of computers.

class system is usually several thousand dollars. There are many computer systems that fall into this class. A few systems are: Burroughs B4700 and B3500; Control Data 3500; Digital Equipment DEC System-10 family; Honeywell 2200, 6050, 6040, and 6030; IBM System/370, Models 135 and 145; IBM System/360, Models 40 and 50; NCR Century 200 and 300 and Univac 9700 and 9400. Briefly discussed in this chapter are the IBM System/370 Model 145, NCR Century 200, and Univac 9400.

IBM System/370 Model 145

The System/370 (Figure 10–4) is the successor to the System/360 as IBM's current line of medium-to-large scale computer systems. It now consists of seven basic central processor models designed to handle a broad range of business and scientific applications. The processors can be supported by more than 40 peripheral devices and a broad array of software facilities. Shown in Figure 10–5 is the computer console.

The System/370 Model 145 is truly an advanced computer. In addition to being the first commercial computer from a major manufacturer to use an all integrated circuit internal memory, Model 145 extended the concept of microprogrammed control to a new high degree of flexibility.

The Model 145 uses *virtual storage,* which is a storage allocation scheme in which the addresses used by a program to identify information are distinguished from the addresses used by the storage system to identify

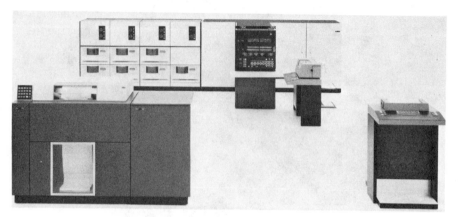

(Courtesy of IBM Corporation)

**Figure
10–4**   IBM System/370 Model 145.

physical storage location; all program-generated (virtual) addresses are automatically translated to the corresponding physical storage (real) addresses.

As implemented in the System/370, virtual storage permits programmers and operators to work with their computer as if it had up to 16 million bytes of internal storage—even though the real internal storage capacity may be only a small fraction of that size. The secret, of course, is that only those portions of a program that are actually required at any given

(Courtesy of IBM Corporation)

**Figure
10–5**   This console is part of the IBM System/370 computer system shown in Figure 10–4.

time need to be present in internal storage. The rest of each program is kept on a disk file, ready to be loaded into internal storage when needed.

Model 145 is designed to serve current users of the System/360 Models 30 and 40 as a machine to upgrade their systems effectively. It offers internal processing speeds three to five times as fast as the Model 40 and 5 to 11 times as fast as the Model 30, plus internal storage capacities of up to 524 288 bytes—twice the maximum capacity of the Model 40 and eight times that of the Model 30.

Monthly rentals for typical Model 145 configurations range from about $14 700 to $45 000, with purchase prices ranging from about $690 000 to $2 150 000.

System/370 computers can utilize most of the approximately 50 System/360 peripheral devices. In addition to the wide array of System/360 peripheral equipment, IBM has developed a number of mass storage and input-output units primarily for use with the System/370. Examples are a high performance disk storage facility, an economical disk storage facility, a 2 000 lpm printer, a low-priced magnetic tape system, a 96-column card reader-punch, an optical mark reader, and other card handling units.

Users of the virtual-storage Model 145 can choose from as many as seven operating systems and several programming languages, including COBOL, RPG, FORTRAN, PL/I, APL, and assembly language. Most application programs written for the System/360 system can run on a System/370 with little or no modification and, in most cases, without recompilation.

NCR Century 200

The basic Century 200 system (Figure 10–6) includes 32 768 bytes of rod memory, an I-O writer, a dual drive disk unit, a 1 500 lpm line printer, and either a 300 cpm card reader or a 1 000 cps paper tape reader. This system rents for about $4 000 a month and sells for just under $200 000.

Two unique features of the Century 200 are the requirement that every system contain at least one dual disk unit and the use of thin film rod storage rather than the traditional magnetic core storage. The rods are made by depositing a thin metallic film covered by a protective coating on five-mil copper wire. This process yields a plated wire 0.15 mm in diameter, which is then cut into lengths to form the rods. The basic memory plane is formed by inserting the rods into solenoid coils wound on a plastic frame. The entire plane is then sealed between two sheets of plastic.

The Century 200 dual drive disk unit is the key device in the system. Each disk unit has two vertical spindles, and each spindle drives a re-

(Courtesy of Sperry Rand Corporation's Univac Division)

Figure 10–6   A Century 200 computer system. A dual disk unit is located in front, a printer at the rear left.

movable disk pack that provides on-line storage for 4 194 304 bytes of information. A magnetic card storage system can also be added to a Century 200 to provide additional auxiliary storage. This unit, called CRAM (Card Random Access Memory), has a storage capacity of 124.4 million bytes per single changeable cartridge.

The Century 200 has 39 instructions available for performing addition, subtraction, code translation, editing, bit and character testing, and scanning. Optional instructions for floating point and fixed point arithmetic are available.

NCR offers a fairly broad range of input devices for use with the Century 200, including the following: a 300 cpm photoelectric card reader, a card read/punch which can read at 750 cpm and punch at 240 cpm, 1 000 and 1 500 cps, photoelectric paper tape readers, a 200 cps paper tape punch, several line printers with printing speeds ranging from 300 lpm to 1 500 lpm, several magnetic tape units, two MICR sorter/readers with rated speeds of 600 and 1 200 documents per minute, and an optical journal reader, along with several data communication devices.

Software for the Century 200 includes a disk operating system, an assembler, COBOL and FORTRAN compilers, utility routines, sort routines, and application packages to perform the following functions: general payroll, hospital payroll, in-patient accounting, general reporting, order billing, utility billing, budgetary accounting, general accounts receivable, retail accounts receivable, general accounts payable, retail accounts payable, commercial bank central information file system, life insurance management, and production scheduling.

UNIVAC 9400

The UNIVAC 9400 computer (Figure 10–7) is best suited for business data processing and its instruction set of 70 instructions has clearly been chosen to maximize its performance in typical commercial applications. The general design of the 9400 computer is comparable to that of the IBM System/360 system. The 9400 uses a plated-wire memory rather than the traditional magnetic core memory, and monolithic integrated circuitry. The computer uses 32 general-purpose registers and has strong communications capabilities. Monthly rentals range from about $6 000 for a four-tape system to $20 000 for a combined disk/tape system.

Plated-wire internal storage for the 9400 (available in capacities of 24 576, 32 768, 49 152, 65 536, 98 304, and 131 072 bytes) has a cycle time of 600 nanoseconds per access. It is a magnetic storage device of the thin film type.

The 9400 disk system consists of a disk controller and from one to eight removable disk units. Each disk pack of six disks can contain 7.25 million bytes of data, yielding a maximum on-line capacity of 58 million bytes.

(Courtesy of Sperry Rand Corporation's Univac Division)

Figure 10–7   UNIVAC 9400 computer system.

The UNIVAC 9400 input-output devices include a 600 cpm card reader, a 250 cpm card punch, 900 and 1 100 lpm line printers, three magnetic tape subsystems, a paper tape system, a disk storage system, three data communication subsystems, and on-line Univac 1004, 9200, or 9300 computers. The 9400 is also capable of accommodating remote terminal devices such as the Uniscope 300 and the DCT 2000. The control console for the 9400 is shown in Figure 10–8.

(Courtesy of Sperry Rand Corporation's Univac Division)

Figure   Control console for the Univac 9400 computer.
10–8

Software for the UNIVAC 9400 includes tape and disk operating systems, an assembler, a FORTRAN compiler, a COBOL compiler, RPG, service and utility programs, a sort/merge program, a system library service, and a linkage editor.

☐ Small Scale Computer Systems

Physically, today's typical small scale computer system is made up of a processor with an internal main storage unit for data and programs, a keyboard device for data entry, a printer to record the results produced, and a magnetic disk unit for secondary (i.e., low-cost and relatively large-capacity) data storage. These four elements constitute the *input* (keyboard data entry), the *logic* (processor), the *memory* (main storage and disk), and the *output* (printer), which are the classic elements of every computer system.

Substitutions can be made for the input device (e.g., a CRT display unit with keyboard or a punched card reader instead of a typewriter) and for the output device (e.g., a card punch instead of the printer). Many systems lack the disk storage unit, while others add magnetic tape units for secondary storage and/or high-speed data input and output.

These low-cost business data processing systems have various names, such as electronic accounting machines, office computers, electronic billing computers, and magnetic record computers. To simplify matters, we will use the generic term *small scale computer system* throughout this book.

As for operating characteristics, the internal speed of the processor and the transfer rate of its main storage unit typically permit computational speeds in the range of thousands of calculations per second. The rated speeds of the associated input devices will usually range from about 10 to 200 characters per second, while the rated output speeds will typically range from about 10 to 500 characters per second. (By contrast, the average speed of even a first-rate typist will seldom approach 10 characters per second.)

In price and performance, the small scale computer systems span a wide range that fills the gap between conventional accounting machines at one extreme and medium scale computer systems at the other. Though the current small computer systems differ widely in their architecture, data formats, peripheral equipment, and software, they are generally characterized by purchase prices in the $30 000 to $100 000 range and by a storage orientation, in both their equipment and software, toward conventional business data processing applications. Monthly leasing charges on small scale systems vary between $500 and $5 000.

There is general agreement throughout the business world today that the time of the small business computer has arrived. Compact, low-cost business data processing systems will be nearly as common and indispensable in most offices as typewriters and telephones are. The ever-increasing costs and complexities of doing business are forcing small businessmen to find new ways to cut their labor costs and gain tighter control over their operations. A wisely chosen small computer can help immeasurably in both these critical areas.

A small business computer can calculate and print a company's payroll checks, customer invoices, and inventory status. It can print directories or sales forecasts. It can keep track of stock on hand, stock on order, and supplies to be ordered. It can help to administer hospitals, hotels and motels, wholesale operations, retail establishments, meat packing houses, etc. In short, it can perform virtually any information-handling or record-keeping operation that most businesses do now, plus many desirable operations that cannot economically be performed by manual methods.

Leading suppliers of small scale computer systems include Burroughs Corporation, IBM, NCR Corporation, Univac, and Nixdorf. Several smaller companies, including Basic/Four, Datapoint, Quantel Corporation, Ultimac Systems, and numerous others, offer small business systems based on minicomputers (see the section on Business Minicomputer Systems) with comparatively powerful internal processing capabilities.

Small scale systems include Burroughs L Series, Burroughs TC Series, IBM System 3, IBM System 32, IBM System/360 Model 20, IBM 1130, NCR 399, NCR Century 50 and 100, Nixdorf 800 Series, Univac 9200 and 9300, and Wang 2200B. Described in this chapter are the IBM System 3, IBM System 32, IBM System/360 Model 20, IBM 1130, Nixdorf 800 820/840, NCR Century 8200, and NCR Century 100.

IBM System/360 Model 20

The Model 20 is the smallest member of the IBM System/360 computer line (Figure 10–9). It is a card-oriented system designed primarily to serve as a first step upward from unit record machines. A Model 20 system that includes a Multi-Function Card Machine and a printer can be rented for around $1,300 per month, though monthly rentals for most Model 20 systems will range from about $1,500 to $4,000.

(Courtesy of IBM Corporation)

Figure 10–9   IBM System/360 Model 20.

The Model 20 uses the same basic instruction and data formats as the larger System/360 models. The instruction repertoire is a compatible subject of the full System/360 repertoire, except that the I-O instructions and some control instructions are unique to the Model 20. Because of these unique instructions, programs written for a Model 20 system cannot be directly executed on a larger System/360 model.

A Model 20 can contain from 4 096 to 32 768 bytes of core storage. The core cycle time is 3.6 microseconds. The computer includes eight 16-bit general registers that can be used as accumulators or as index registers.

A control panel, built into the top of the Model 20 central processing unit cabinet, provides the switches, keys, and lights required for manual control of the system. An optional printer-keyboard is available which provides keyboard input and typewriter facilities.

A System/360 Model 20 system can include up to three punched card I-O units, one line printer, one magnetic character reader, one printer-keyboard, one magnetic tape controller with up to six tape units, and four removable disk units.

The Multi-Function Card Machine is a unique punched card I-O unit developed especially for the Model 20. Equipped with two 2 200-card input hoppers, a reading station, a punching station, and five 1 300-card radial stackers, the unit combines many of the facilities of a card reader, card punch, collator, interpreter, and card document printer in a single unit under stored program control.

The removable Model 20 disk unit provides 5.4 million bytes of storage with 75 millisecond average positioning time. The unit has a rotational delay of 12.5 milliseconds, and a data transfer rate of 156 000 bytes per second.

Software systems are available for card, tape, and disk-oriented systems. The card-oriented software requires a Model 20 with 4 096 bytes of core memory, punched card I-O equipment, and a printer. The tape-oriented software requires an internal core storage of 8 192 bytes, four magnetic tape units, card I-O equipment, and a printer. The minimum disk-oriented equipment requirements include a CPU with 12 288 bytes of core storage, one disk unit, card I-O equipment, and a printer. Software components include an assembler, a Report Program Generator (RPG), an input-output control system (IOCS), utility routines, and a Sort/Merge program (for use with tape and disk-oriented systems). IBM emphasizes the use of RPG as the primary programming system. The Model 20 RPG is a generalized program designed to generate coding to perform most of the routine business data processing functions. Most programs written in the Model 20 RPG language can be generated and run on the larger System/360 computers, provided that an equivalent configuration of I-O equipment is available. IBM has also developed several program packages that perform the following functions: hospital billing, telephone revenue accounting, bill-of-material processing, and wholesale inventory management.

IBM System 3

With more than 30 000 installations at the end of 1975, the System/3 family ranks as one of the most successful computer systems in history.

The System/3, shown in Figure 10–10, is a low-priced IBM computer system that employs the 96-column punched card that was described in Chapter 3 and is shown in Figure 10–11. Hardware rental prices for System/3 begin at less than $1 000 a month.

(Courtesy of IBM Corporation)

Figure 10–10   IBM System/3 Model 8 installation.

There are five versions of the System/3. The System/3 Model 6, introduced in 1970, is a keyboard-oriented system designed to appeal to current users of accounting machines or time-sharing terminals. The System/3 Model 8, announced in 1974, is a batch processing system without punched card functions. The System/3 Model 10, the original member of the System/3 family, was announced in 1969. It offers file-oriented data processing, in contrast to the transaction-oriented data processing orientation of the System/3 Model 6. Moreover, the Model 10 provides substantially higher throughput rates in most applications and a greater choice of peripheral devices. The System/3 Model 12, announced in mid-1975, is essentially an improved MOSFET (Metal Oxide Semiconductor Field Effect Transistor) memory version of the older Model 10. The Model 12 features disk-file-oriented data processing, with magnetic tape and punched card I/O available. The System/3 Model 15 incorporates a multiprogramming capability and has an internal memory (MOSFET) of up to 262 144 bytes and a disk storage of up to 164 million bytes. The Model 15 represents, in most respects, a bigger, better, and more costly System/3 Model 10.

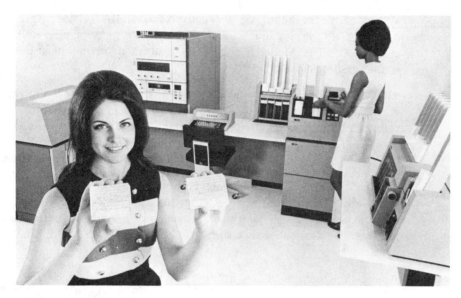

(Courtesy of IBM Corporation)

Figure 10–11 Card reading equipment for the IBM System/3 computer system reads the small 96-column card. Shown here is an operator placing cards in the reader.

The System/3 has been kept fresh during its life span through the introduction of semiconductor memory, larger memory capacities, and larger and faster disk units. Although the orientation of the System/3 family now is principally toward batch processing, the capability to interface multiple local CRT terminals and printers is available on the Model 8, 12, and 15. On the Model 8 and 12, up to 12 devices can be attached; the Model 15 feature expands the capacity to 30 devices.

The System/3 central processing unit is byte oriented and uses Monolithic Systems Technology as its basis. It has a microminiature circuit which allows up to five circuits in a module and switching speeds of 8 to 12 nanoseconds. The internal speed of the System/3 is high, with a cycle time of 1.52 microseconds. It can perform an addition in 24.4 microseconds.

The System/3 Model 6 can be used in two radically different ways. As "the office computer," the Model 6 is a low-cost, stored-program computer, using disk drives for on-line file storage and featuring an Operator Keyboard Console for both data entry and system control. Ledger card processing is also an option. All programming of standard business applications is to be normally done in the RPG II language. As "the problem solver," the System/3 Model 6 is a fast arithmetic processor designed to permit engineers, scientists, and other technicians to use the system at the keyboard via the conversational BASIC language. An optional CRT display unit is offered for quick display of the results of calculations. The Model 6 also offers features to permit its use as a simple desk calculator.

The Model 6 offers full operator control of the system via the Operator Keyboard Console. Input data is directly entered at the keyboard, with printing taking place on conventional (nonmagnetic) ledger cards. This equipment is designed to seem familiar and comfortable to most small businessmen, as is the design approach used in setting up the applications.

The basic System/3 Model 6 configuration consists of a processing unit (with 8K, 12K, or 16K bytes of core storage), an Operator Keyboard Console, an 85-cps serial printer (available in unique bidirectional-printing models), and a disk storage subsystem of 2.45 to 9.83 million bytes.

Applications such as billing, inventory control, accounts receivable, and sales analysis are the "bread and butter" uses of the Model 6 in the RPG II-based, business-oriented environment. Under BASIC, the typical application areas are engineering/scientific, financial (such as bond analysis, lease analysis, and rate of return calculations), and general business (sales forecasting, cash flow analysis, overhead distribution, etc.).

The System/3 Model 10 computer is compact and well designed. The basic system, consisting of processing unit, printer, and Multi-Function Card Unit (MFCU), requires only 150 square feet of floor space. The MFCU, like the Multi-Function Card Machine used in the System/360 Model 20, can perform the functions of card reading, punching, collating, and interpreting. Consolidation of all these functions into a single compact unit leads to reduced equipment costs and card-handling time.

IBM software support for the System/3 Model 10, while far from sophisticated, is well tailored to complement the system's modest hardware capabilities. A set of System Control Programs, designed to handle basic operating and data management functions, is supplied to Model 10 users at no extra charge. The System Control Programs for disk-oriented systems include a supervisor and scheduler that perform the functions of a simple operating system. All other System/3 software is separately priced.

IBM is encouraging most System/3 users to do their application programming in the RPG II language. RPG II is available for both card and disk systems. The language is an extended version of System/360 RPG that is capable of handling most business programming requirements quite effectively. ANSI COBOL and FORTRAN compilers are also available for the System/3 Model 10. Thus, System/3 Model 10 users can elect to write their programs in any of three languages—RPG II, COBOL, or FORTRAN.

The basic System/3 Model 12 (see Figure 10–12) system consists of a 32 768 byte processing unit, an IBM 3340 Direct Access Storage Facility (see Figure 10–13), a printer, and either a MFCU or a card read-punch. The performance of the basic system can be enhanced through the addition on other peripherals, including magnetic tape units, magnetic character readers, optical mark readers, and several terminal devices.

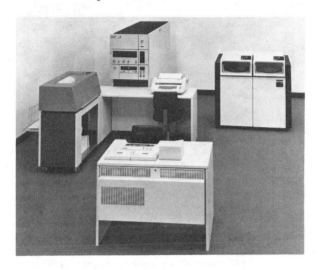

(Courtesy of IBM Corporation)

Figure 10–12   Overall view of a System/3 Model 12 installation.

The System/3 Model 15 (see Figure 10–14) uses a CRT operator console and can support the 80-column Multi-Function Card Machine and 80-column card reader. Thus, the Model 15 offers Model 10 users a natural growth path with minimum effort.

IBM System/32

The IBM System/32 is a low-cost, easy-to-operate, desk-sized computer (see Figure 10–15). Developed for first-time computer users in small businesses, the System/32 comes equipped with preprogrammed Industry Application Packages designed to eliminate the need for an in-house programming staff. The System/32 can be rented for less than $1 000 per month. IBM defines the typical System/32 prospect as a business with sales in the range of from $1 million to $10 million and up to 250 employees.

IBM expects the System/32 to be the biggest-selling computer system ever announced.

(Courtesy of IBM Corporation)

Figure   IBM 3340 Direct Access Storage Facility.
10–13

The System/32 is the easiest to operate, smallest, and lowest-priced general business computer ever announced by IBM. It achieves its small size through the use of state-of-the-art components and its ease of use through IBM-supplied software packages that are delivered already compiled and debugged.

(Courtesy of IBM Corporation)

Figure   The System/3 Model 15 computer system.
10–14

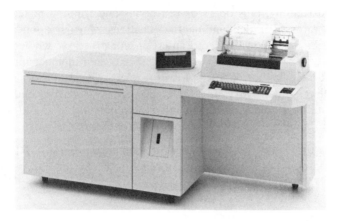

(Courtesy of IBM Corporation)

Figure 10–15 The IBM System/32 consists of a central processing unit, memory disk storage capacity, a diskette data read/write facility, an operator console with visual display, keyboard, and print capability—all in a single desk-sized unit.

The System/32 can be programmed to perform either interactive or batch processing, using data entered either through the on-line operator keyboard or via diskettes prepared off-line. Optional communications capabilities also allow it to operate as a remote terminal or as a satellite system within a communications network including larger IBM computers.

The System/32 is packaged as a compact, desk-sized configuration that includes all the components of the system—the central processing unit, memory, keyboard, CRT display, printer, disk storage unit, and diskette drive. It requires no special flooring, air conditioning, or power supplies. Since the computer can be located in an office and is no longer sheltered in a computer room environment, security from unauthorized access is provided by an optional keylock for turning on the system.

Ten models of the System/32 are available; they are distinguished by their various printing capabilities and disk storage capacities. The basic System/32 consists of a central processing unit with 16 384 bytes of metal oxide semiconductor (MOS) internal memory, 5 million bytes of nonremovable disk storage, a printer, keyboard console, CRT display screen, and single diskette I/O drive. Internal memory for all central processor models can be increased to a maximum of 32 768 bytes, in 8 192 byte increments.

The System/32 is designed to be operated by office clerical personnel with a minimum of training and will not require the services of a programming staff. To make that possible, IBM is supplying software packages that contain all the coding necessary to get a user installation up and running, plus operator run books and training materials to aid the operator in understanding the functions of each application package. Packages are available for users in construction, wholesale paper and office products, wholesale food, hospitals, and membership organizations and associations. These software packages include programs to perform billing, order entry, invoicing, accounts receivable, and payroll, plus additional functions such as inventory control, job costing, and membership mailing lists, that are unique to each industry area.

For those users who wish to write their own programs, RPG II, the only programming language announced for the System/32, is available.

This above all, my son: stock up on spare parts for your System/32.

The equipment rental prices for a basic configuration range from less than $800 to $1 085 per month. The System/32 promises to be a strong contender in the race to woo small businesses into the fold of computer-based data processing.

Figure 10–16 shows the System/32 being used in a small food-distributing business. The system is used for billing, inventory control, accounts receivable, and sales analysis.

To use the system, the operator turns the machine on and presses a program load key. The programs may be either in the machine or on a diskette. If the operator plans to do a company's accounts receivable, for example, the system is instructed, in simple understandable terms through its typewriter keyboard, to "load" the receivables program.

The system, in turn, notifies the operator through a message on its visual display screen that it is ready or that additional instructions are required (see Figure 10–16a). The operator then types another command to

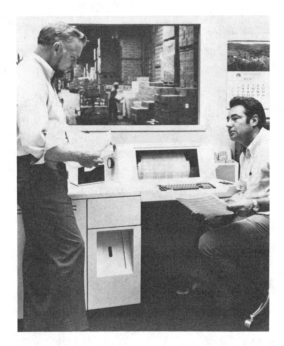

(Courtesy of IBM Corporation)

Figure   An IBM System/32 computer system may be used by a small food-
10–16   distributor to provide support in managing areas, such as billing, inven-
             tory control, accounts receivable, and sales analysis.

indicate the exact information wanted, such as delinquent accounts. In this manner, the operator is guided step-by-step through the task being performed.

The system contains a broad range of application capabilities. Post-billing, for example, includes a credit check, according to the limits set by the merchant or the credit manager. It handles either quantity break markups or discounts and can produce invoices with tear-strips costed for each item.

The system also handles contract or negotiated prices and automatically updates all records affected during billing. A range of information is captured for later use.

Daily reports include a standard invoice register and sales recap by salesperson, showing the orders shipped for each salesperson, commissionable orders, total sales for the day, and profitability on each invoice.

IBM 1130

The IBM 1130 is a desk-size, 16-bit word-oriented computer intended primarily for small-scale scientific applications. It can also serve as a low-cost processor for certain business applications that do not require

(Courtesy of IBM Corporation)

Figure 10–16a To operate the System/32, the user turns the machine on and pushes a program load key. The operator then types in a word or term, indicating the task to be performed by the computer. The visual display screen shown here, upper left, provides the operator step-by-step instructions, simplifying the job of operating the system.

high input-output speeds. System rentals vary from about $700 per month, with minimum storage and input-output equipment, to about $2 000, with disk storage and a full complement of input-output equipment.

The IBM 1130 system offers a choice of models with 16 384 or 32 768 words of core storage with a 3.6 microsecond cycle time and 8 192, 16 384, and 32 768 words of core storage with a 2.2 microsecond cycle time. Each of the models includes a disk unit that can store 512 000 words. Core storage and the disk unit are housed in the desk console which is an integral part of the IBM 1130 Central Processing Unit. Figure 10–17 shows a user placing a disk cartridge in the disk unit. The removable disk cartridge stores up to 512 000 words on a single disk. The average access time to randomly placed data is 790 milliseconds.

Input-output devices for the IBM 1130 include a 60 cps paper tape reader; a 14.5 cps paper tape punch; 300 and 400-card read punches; 600 and 1 000 cpm card readers; 91 cpm card punch; 110, 340, and 600 lpm line printers; a digital plotter; an optical mark reader; and a communications adapter. One interesting use of an IBM 1130 is as a remote terminal connected by a communications link to a larger central computer facility.

The keyboard and printer of the IBM 1130 (Figure 10–18) provide for input of data into the computer and printed output from the computer. The console printer provides output at a maximum rate of 15.5 characters per second.

Punched card, paper tape, and disk-oriented software systems are available. A Monitor System is available for the disk-oriented system which reduces the need for operator intervention by providing automatic handling of run-to-run supervision. The available software includes an assembler, a FORTRAN compiler, utility routines, several application packages to aid in solving petroleum exploration and engineering problems, a package for civil engineering problems, as well as programs for

(Courtesy of IBM Corporation)

Figure 10–17 An IBM 1130 computer system. Paper tape units and a digital plotter are shown on the far left, with a card read punch in the center and line printer in the left rear.

type composition, statistical and numerical routines, and a business application package.

(Courtesy of TRW Equipment)

Figure Keyboard and printer of the IBM 1130. These devices provide for
10–18 limited data input and output.

NCR Century 8200

The Century 8200 (see Figure 10–19) is a business computer system designed primarily for small- to medium-sized firms that wish to have their data processing fully automated.

The initial models of the Century 8200 are intended for four segments of the business community: manufacturing, wholesale/distribution, construction and contracting, and transportation.

Operation of the Century 8200 is simple and straightforward. Conversation between the operator and the system is established by a program, which displays a list of all possible operations, in menu fashion, on the console terminal screen. The operator selects the desired operation by entering the number associated with each task via the keyboard. If there are other decisions to make, similar lists appear; and options are selected in the same manner until the system is prepared to receive input data. Changes in operation are effected by returning to the display control function and selecting another task.

(Courtesy of NCR Corporation)

Figure
10–19
NCR Century 8200 computer system provides on-line order entry, inventory control, and accounts receivable applications. System above has (left to right) two disk units, CRT terminal through which on-line entries and inquiries are made, central processing unit, card reader, and printer.

NCR offers two models of the Century 8200 system, which differ only in the number of video terminals each supports. Purchase price for a minimum system with one terminal is around $40 000, while the multi-terminal system starts at around $43 000. Respective monthly rentals begin at $1 285 and $1 385 per month. The prices of additional video (CRT) terminals ($2 000 purchase or $80 per month each) must be added to the multiterminal system.

One large NCR Century 8200 system is used by the Sumitomo Bank in Toyko, one of the world's largest banks. This system controls over 3400 on-line teller terminals plus more than 600 automated teller terminals located throughout Japan.

NCR Century 100

The NCR Century 100 (Figure 10–20) is a small scale disk-oriented system that includes 16 384 bytes of magnetic core storage, a line printer, a dual removable disk unit, and either a card reader or a paper tape reader. This system leases for about $2 000 per month or sells for slightly over $100 000.

The Century 100 uses the byte to store data. Bytes can be addressed and manipulated individually, or consecutive memory locations can be grouped to form decimal or binary fields up to 256 bytes in length. The storage for the Century 100 is thin film rods. Each rod is individually addressible and can hold one byte.

(Courtesy of National Cash Register Company)

Figure 10–20   The basic NCR Century 100 system, with 450 lpm printer at left, 300 cpm card reader and control console at center, and a dual removable disk unit at right.

All software for the Century 100 is disk-oriented. Principal software components are a basic operating system and compilers for COBOL, FORTRAN, and NEAT/3 (NCR's own language) programming languages. The Century 100 has a repertoire of 19 instructions: decimal add and substract, binary add and subtract, move, compare, pack, unpack, repeat, wait, input-output, and branch.

The most distinctive characteristic of the Century 100 is the requirement that every system shall include at least one dual removable disk unit. Figure 10–21 illustrates a user placing a disk pack on one of the disk units. The disk units have a revolution time of 41.6 milliseconds and can transfer information to and from the computer at a rate of 108 000 bytes per second. Each disk pack is approximately 35.5 cm (14 inches) in diameter and 12.7 cm (5 inches) deep, weighs less than 10 pounds, and has 12 disk surfaces each containing 192 tracks. Each disk pack provides storage for 4 194 304 bytes of information. If only BCD numerical data is being stored, the pack will hold 8 388 608 digits.

Input-output devices for the Century 100 include a 300 cpm photo-electric card reader, a 1 000 cps photoelectric paper tape reader, and a 450 lpm line printer. The card reader reads standard 80-column cards.

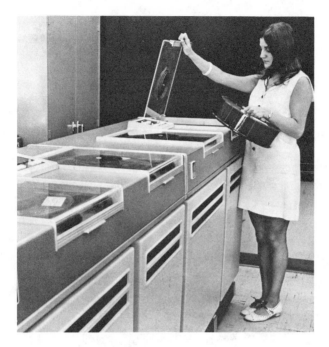

(Courtesy of National Cash Register Company)

Figure   Disk pack being placed on a Century 100 disk unit.
10–21

Both the feed hopper and output stacker have a capacity of 1 000 cards each. The paper tape reader can read five, seven, or eight channel paper or Mylar tape in strips or rolls up to 106.7 m (350 feet) in length. The printer uses a 64-character set and can print up to 132 positions on a single line.

A console control panel (Figure 10–22) is an integral part of the Century 100. Panel switches are used to select registers and functions and to enter data into the computer. Pushbuttons and toggle switches control a variety of system functions. Lights provide binary display of the contents of memory locations and registers.

An Input-Output Writer (Figure 10–23) which is basically a character-at-a-time teletype printer and keyboard is an optional feature for the system. When used, the I-O writer is integrated into the console.

☐ Minicomputer Systems

During the past decade, minicomputers have received more attention than any other single subject in the fast-moving world of electronic data processing. Today, these compact yet surprisingly powerful computers

(Courtesy of National Cash Register Company)

**Figure
10–22**   Operator adjusting a dial on the control panel of the Century 100.

are being delivered at an ever-increasing rate for use in a steadily broadening spectrum of applications. Here are just a few reasons:

- Innovations in technology and manufacturing are resulting in the availability of minicomputers with steadily lower price tags and/or increased capabilities.
- Economic pressures are forcing computer users to strive to achieve maximum performance at minimum cost.
- Increasing software consciousness on the part of both minicomputer makers and users is spurring software development along avenues undreamed of only a few years ago.
- Increasing emphasis upon distributed processing, in which large, centralized computers are augmented or replaced by multiple smaller computers located wherever there is data to be processed, is causing even the largest computer users to take a hard new look at the minicomputers.

The low prices and impressive capabilities of the current minicomputers are naturally attracting the attention of the businessmen, scientists, educators, and government officials who are responsible for deciding what types of information processing equipment to use in their operations.

But what, exactly, is a minicomputer? Well, there is some disagreement within the industry itself as to just what constitutes a minicomputer. In this book, we will simplify the picture by classifying minicomputers as digital computers which are suitable for general purpose applications and are priced below $15 000 in their minimum configurations. The primary emphasis in this section is on the "classical" or scientifically oriented minicomputers; the numerous minicomputer systems designed specifically for business data processing are discussed in the next section.

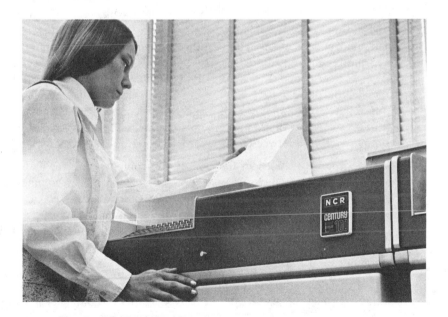

(Courtesy of National Cash Register Company)

Figure 10–23 The input-output writer enables the operator to enter instructions and data into the Century 100 and receive printed output.

Although the currently available minicomputers exhibit a wide variety of characteristics and capabilities, there are enough similarities and common traits to make it possible to define a *typical minicomputer* whose characteristics are reasonably representative of most of the machines on the market today.

(Curtesy of Interdata)

Figure 10–24   The typical minicomputer has a word length of 16-bits, weighs less than 50 pounds, and can be set on top of a table or desk.

The *typical minicomputer* is a parallel, binary processor with a 16-bit word length (though 8-bit, 12-bit, 18-bit, 24-bit, and 32-bit word lengths are also fairly common). It uses integrated circuits and is housed in a compact cabinet suitable for either tabletop use (see Figure 10–25) or mounting in a standard rack (see Figure 10–26). It weighs less than 22.68 kg (50 pounds), consumes less than 500 watts of standard 115-volt electric power, and requires no special air conditioning. It offers from 4 096 to 32 768 words of magnetic core or semiconductor storage with a cycle time of 0.8 to 1.5 microseconds. Today's typical minicomputer can add two 16-bit operands in 1 to 3 microseconds.

Input/output operations in the typical minicomputer are facilitated by an optional direct memory access (DMA) channel, which accommodates I/O data rates of up to about 1 000 000 words per second. The typical complement of standard peripheral equipment consists of a teletypewriter, disk unit, magnetic tape drive, card reader, paper tape reader and punch, line printer, and an assortment of interface for communication and control applications.

Software support for today's typical minicomputer is limited to a symbolic assembler; a BASIC, FORTRAN, or RPG compiler, a simple batch-mode operating system or real-time monitor; and a modest assortment of utility routines. The list purchase price of the basic system, including 4 096 words of internal storage but no input/output

(Courtesy of Digital Equipment Corp.)

Figure 10–25 Minicomputer and high-speed paper tape reader mounted in a standard 19″ rack.

devices, is likely to be well under $5 000. By all previous standards of value in the computer field, it is a truly impressive little package of computing power for the price.

A variety of input-output devices than can be connected to a minicomputer is as numerous as the variety that can be connected to a large computer. Teletypewriters are perhaps the most useful and the most frequently used input-output device for minicomputers, both from a functional and cost standpoint. Most minicomputer manufacturers offer a wide variety of miniperipheral (input-output devices for minicomputers) devices which may be included in minicomputer systems: card reader (see Figure 10–26), magnetic tape cassette units (see Figure 10–27), magnetic tape cartridge units, minitape units, removable disk pack units (see Figure 10–28), floppy disk units, printers (see Figure 10–29), digital plotters, CRT display devices (see Figure 10–30), punch card units, and optical card readers (see Figure 10–31).

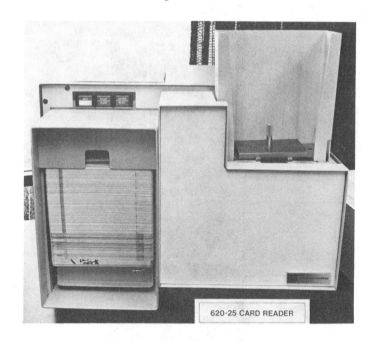

(Courtesy of Varian Data Machines)

**Figure
10–26**   Card reader.

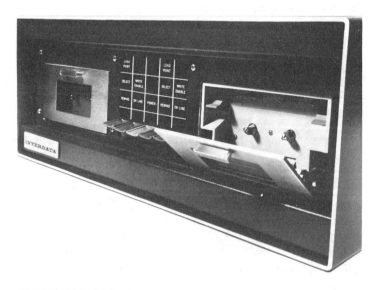

(Courtesy of Interdata)

**Figure
10–27**   Magnetic tape cassette system.

(Courtesy of Hewlett-Packard)

Figure   Direct-access moving-head disk unit with single removable cartridge.
10–28

(Courtesy of Digital Equipment Corp.)

Figure   Printer.
10–29

(Courtesy of Digital Equipment Corp.)

Figure 10–30   CRT display device.

(Courtesy of Hewlett-Packard)

Figure 10–31   Optical Mark Reader.

Miniperipherals are characteristically relatively small and can be placed on a tabletop or be rack mounted. The only exceptions are medium-speed line printers moveable head disk units, and magnetic tape cartridge devices which usually are freestanding units.

Many minicomputer systems consist of a minicomputer and one or two miniperipheral devices. Minicomputer systems, however, can be configured using a large number of input-output units. The minicomputer system shown in Figure 10–32 is composed of a minicomputer, two disk units, two CRT displays, and a magnetic tape unit. Figure 10–33 shows a system consisting of a printer, CRT display, two disk units, and a minicomputer.

(Courtesy of Microdata Corp.)

Figure 10–32   Minicomputer system consisting of a minicomputer, two desk units, two CRT displays, and a magnetic tape unit.

Most of the currently installed minicomputers are being used in industrial control and laboratory instrumentation. These areas are where it all began. The minicomputer boom started when it became apparent that the impressive recent advances in semiconductor and magnetic technologies had made it possible to construct general-purpose computers at a lower cost than the single-purpose, hardwired controllers which were formerly used in these specialized applications. The added flexibility of stored-program computer control was a welcome bonus that helped to ensure the rapid acceptance of the minicomputers.

During the past decade, the capabilities of the minicomputers have been steadily increasing while their costs have been steadily decreasing. The proliferation of these small, economical, and surprisingly fast computers has led to an ever-widening range of applications for them.

(Courtesy of Digital Computer Corp.)

Figure Minicomputer system consisting of a printer, CRT display, two desk
10–33 units, and a minicomputer.

Among the largest current markets for minicomputers are industrial control, research, engineering and scientific computation, data communications, and education. Specific applications in which minicomputers are already being widely and successfully used include:

- Traffic control
- Shipboard navigation control
- Message switching
- Communications controllers for larger computers
- Communications line concentrators
- Programmable communications terminals
- Peripheral controllers for larger computers
- Control of multistation key-to-tape/disk systems
- Display control
- Computer-aided design
- Typesetting and photocomposition
- Computer-assisted instruction
- Engineering and scientific computations
- Time-sharing computational services
- Business data processing
- Process control
- Numerical control of machine tools

- Direct control of machines and production lines
- Automated testing and inspection
- Telemetry
- Data acquisition and logging
- Control and analysis of laboratory experiments
- Analysis and interpretation of medical tests

The major manufacturers of minicomputers are Digital Equipment Corp., IBM Corp., Data General Corp., Interdata, General Automation, Varian, Hewlett-Packard Co., and Computer Automation. Popular models include the IBM 5100, PDP-8 series, PDP-11 series, NOVA series, Varian 73/74, and INTERDATA 7/32. Briefly described in this section are the IBM 5100, the Digital Equipment Corporation's PDP-11 series minicomputers, and the Varian 73.

IBM 5100 Portable Computer

If you are presently using data tables to look up values of elliplic integrals of the second kind, hyperbolic functions, or chi-square values, be sure to hang onto the books they come in. In a few years, they may have some value as rare curiosities. The IBM 5100 Portable Computer, announced in 1975 (see Figure 10–34), eliminates the necessity for having books of tables by placing a computer on your desk. However, you can buy a lot of books of tables for the 5100's beginning price of just under $9 000. To pay for itself and make it worthwhile to acquire, the 5100 must save you time, allow you to do calculations you could not do manually, and/or replace a more expensive method.

(Courtesy of IBM Corporation)

Figure 10–34   IBM 5100 Portable computer consists of a combination typewriter-like electronic keyboard and a 10-key calculator pad for data entry, a 1024 character display, a processing unit, and a magnetic-tape cartridge capability for storing programs and data. The 5100 weighs about 50 pounds.

The 5100, which is built around a microprocessor*, provides up to 65 536 bytes of 530-nanosecond MOSFET internal memory, a CRT display, and an integral magnetic-tape cartridge drive capable of accessing up to 204 800 bytes of data. The programming facility is provided by a BASIC or APL interpreter, or both, stored in read-only memory.

A printer and a second magnetic tape cartridge drive can be added to the 5100.

Supporting the system are three application libraries: one for business functions, one for scientific/engineering computations, and one for statistical functions. These capabilities are supplemented by the mathematical functions built into the BASIC and APL programming languages. Thus, the basic tools for numerical computation are provided. But any procedures peculiar to specific disciplines will have to be programmed by the user through the facilities of BASIC or APL.

The IBM 5100 is not intended to support conventional business data processing. The absence of a direct-access device and the slow speed

---

* Microprocessors are discussed in a later section.

of its peripheral devices prevent the 5100 from being used effectively to maintain a file of records, as would be required to process a payroll, for example. It could, however, be used to compute and print business documents, such as invoices, paychecks, and sales analysis reports, one at a time with manual entry of information; but the inability to effectively maintain a file of records eliminates most of the advantages gained through the use of a computer.

Memory sizes of the 5100 range from 16 384 bytes to 65 536 bytes in 16 384 byte increments. For each memory size, there is a corresponding 5100 model for the BASIC language, for the APL language, and for a combination of BASIC and APL. Switching between the languages in the combined models is accomplished through a front panel switch.

The BASIC language is widely known and used. Its English-like statement keyword structure makes it an easy language to learn and a logical choice for first-time users. BASIC also provides convenient facilities to handle alphanumeric strings for annotating tables. The APL language is more suited to expressing complex mathematical relationships.

The 5100 is also novel in the way IBM is supporting it. The support is similar to that provided for the company's typewriters. No customer engineer shows up when you install the 5100. You read the instruction book that comes with it and set it up yourself. Lease plans are not available for this unit; it is offered on a purchase-only basis. Maintenance agreements are available, naturally, just as with typewriters.

IBM's entry into the field of personal or desk-top computers, timed as it is at the beginning of the whole availability of microprocessors, may herald the start of a highly competitive market segment. If that is the case, you can expect to see many specialized models announced by many vendors, each tailored to a specific type of computational problem.

The IBM 5100 Portable Computer was designed to put the power of a programmable computer at the fingertips of financial analysts, planners, statisticians, and other problem-solvers concerned with profits, schedules and productivity (see Figure 10–35).

Combining stand-alone computing facilities with desk-top compactness, the IBM 5100 can be used in many business environments. Problem-solvers using the 5100 can handle high-priority problems, resolve financial data, and explore more options for critical business solutions— all aimed at improving the bottom line of the business.

Professionals, whose work involves analyses of complex data, can be productive quickly with the Portable Computer. With its interactive

(Courtesy of IBM Corporation)

Figure 10–35   The IBM 5100 Portable Computer being used by business planners to help them solve problems with the company's profits, schedules, and productivity.

BASIC and/or APL programming languages, the user does not have to become a computer specialist to use it.

Posing on top of sugar crystals in a teaspoon (see Figure 10–36) are five tiny IBM computer circuitry chips. Each chip is approximately 5.84 mm (0.23 inch) square. These small Metal Oxide Semiconductor Field Effect Transistor (MOSFET) circuitry chips are one of the reasons that so much power can be packaged into a small 50-pound unit.

PDP-11 Family

The Digital Equipment Corporation's PDP-11 family of minicomputers has evolved into the industry's broadest series of processors, supported by a family of common peripherals, operating systems, and application software. The central processors are ordered in incremental steps of speed and size, so that users can match their needs with the required levels of processor power.

(Courtesy of IBM Corporation)

Figure 10-36 The IBM 5100 Portable Computer uses MOSFET circuitry. The circuit density achieved on each chip—as shown here with sugar crystals in a teaspoon—is 49 152 bits. Each chip is approximately 5.84 mm (0.23 inch) square.

There are currently nine different models in the PDP-11 computer family*. The LSI-11 is a board-level microcomputer product specifically designed for sophisticated users who can incorporate the LSI-11 into a product. The PDP-11/04, 11/05, and 11/10 minicomputers provide solutions to dedicated applications in which the computer is used to solve one or two problems and run one or two programs. They are used, for example, in data acquisition, to convert analog signals to digital signals, to analyze pulse heights, and to sort data on magnetic tape. As little as 4 096 words of memory can suffice in straightforward applications, but the system can be expanded to up to 28 672 words in order to handle more complex applications, perhaps coded in BASIC or FORTRAN language.

---

* The original models in the PDP-11 family, Models 11/15 and 11/20, are no longer actively marketed by Digital Equipment Corporation.

William! Where do you want the minicomputer?

The PDP-11/35, 11/40, 11/45, and 11/50 minicomputers are used in multiple-task applications, where the computer must solve many problems or run multiple programs. They are being used to automate entire industrial processes, for example, monitoring and controlling multiple operations in real-time while preparing and printing production reports for management. Memory sizes can range from 8 192 to 126 976 words to accommodate several programs in memory simultaneously.

The multifunction PDP-11/70 can handle simultaneous batch, real-time, and time-sharing applications in its larger configurations, or pairs of these in smaller configurations.

Hallmarks of the PDP-11 family are its common physical architecture and software compatibility. All PDP-11 processors use the same basic instruction set.

From an applications point of view, practically no area of business or industry has been neglected for automation by some member of the PDP-11 family: commercial, batch processing and multiprogramming, commercial, scientific, and educational time-sharing networks; communications front-end processing, intelligent terminals, process controllers; laboratory instrumentation; etc. In these varied applications environments, Digital Equipment Corporation offers a multitude of application-oriented packaged systems for all models. They include packages for typesetting, communications, industrial controllers, laboratory monitoring, educational time-sharing, and others.

Varian 73

The Varian 73 minicomputer is a machine designed for solving a wide range of applications. It is available with either semiconductor or magnetic core memories, or any combination of the two. Up to 262 000 words of memory can be included in a Varian 73 system. Instructions can be executed in either 330 or 660 nanoseconds, depending upon the type of memory used.

Varian 73 software includes several operating systems, compilers for RPG, BASIC and FORTRAN, assembler, diagnostic programs, and several utility and service routines

Peripheral devices for the Varian 73 include fixed head disks, moving head disks, drum storage units, magnetic tape units, teletypewriters, paper tape readers and punches, a card reader and punch, line printers, CRT displays, a digital plotter, and data communication equipment. A Varian 73 processor is shown in Figure 10–37.

(Courtesy of Varian Data Systems)

Figure   Varian 73 minicomputer.
10–37

☐ Business Minicomputer Systems

Theoretically, the minicomputer's capabilities and economy should make it an ideal solution to the information processing needs of nearly every small business. In retail stores of all kinds, a minicomputer could handle the bookkeeping, inventory control, labeling, billing, payroll, and a variety of other useful functions. And it could do all this at roughly the cost of a single clerk! Yet, minicomputers are just beginning to be used in conventional business data processing applications. This user area is certainly the largest potential market for minicomputers.

The reason, of course, is software. Programming minicomputers, with with their short word lengths, limited storage capacities, and lack of sophisticated software aids, is more difficult than producing software for larger machines. As a result, it is common in minicomputer applications for programming costs to far exceed the cost of the hardware itself.

But help for the businessman is definitely on the way. A few manufacturers have introduced minicomputer-based systems designed primarily for business data processing applications. Several small system companies have designed hardware/software systems to handle specific business applications. These companies offer package systems to handle a wide range of applications, such as general accounting, billing, order processing, inventory control, payroll, text editing, hospital data processing, credit authorization, stock brokerage accounting, and many more. The system houses are accelerating the use of minicomputers by penetrating new markets and making it easier for unsophisticated users to get started in Electronic Data Processing. These trends, together with the increasing emphasis on distributed processing and the steadily decreasing price tags of the minicomputers themselves, make it clear that minicomputers will have an ever-increasing impact in the business data processing world. At the same time, enough problems remain to be solved to make it safe to predict that the widely discussed day when there will be a computer in every business is still quite a few years away.

As discussed previously, large computer manufacturers such as IBM offer small scale data processing systems, such as the System/32 and System/3, which are designed as low-cost business systems. Minicomputer manufacturers such as Digital Equipment Corporation offer business computer systems that incorporate their PDP-8 and PDP-11 minicomputers. About a dozen smaller companies, including Qantel, Basic Four, Datapoint, Basic Timesharing, Mini-Computer Systems, Custom Computer, and Ultiman, offer small business data processing systems based upon minicomputers with comparatively powerful internal processing capabilities.

The Digital Equipment Corporation DATASYSTEM and the Qantel Business Systems are briefly discussed in the following sections.

DEC Datasystem Family

The DEC Datasystem 300 family of packaged systems is based on PDP-8 and PDP-11 minicomputers. The Datasystem 310 is based on the PDP-8/A microcomputer. The Datasystem 340 uses a PDP-8 minicomputer. The newer Datasystem 350 is a disk-based system that uses the PDP-11 minicomputer.

The DEC Datasystem 500 family of business computer systems offers compatible growth through five models based on three PDP-11 minicomputers. Capabilities range from small single-user systems to multi-terminal, time-shared, interactive systems that can be connected into distributed processing networks. The Datasystem lineup includes the

Model 530 system for small scale users; the 540, 550, and 560 systems that can be used for heftier batch operations, for time-sharing with as many as 32 users, and for data base processing of data bases up to 704 million bytes; and the 570 system for up to 63 time-shared users and connection into a distributed processing network.

FORTRAN, BASIC, RPG II, and COBOL (subset of ANSI COBOL-74) programming languages are available on the Datasystem 500's. Another available language, called MUMPS-II, is a highly specialized language for on-line interactive systems with large data bases. It has data base management characteristics rather than file management characteristics. With this structure, records can be accessed by multiple users for continuous updating, examination, etc.

Qantel Business Computer Systems

The Qantel Corporation offers four upward-compatible business computers designed with the first-time user in mind. Prices start at less than $20 000 for the minimum packaged system.

The bottom model of the line is the System 800, which leases for about $600 per month including maintenance. The system includes an 8 192 byte user memory, a 16 384 byte reserved area for an operating system, a 6-megabyte disc file, and a combination printer/input keyboard.

Similar in configuration to the System 800, the System 900 includes a standard video terminal and has a price tag of about $25 000, while leasing with maintenance costs of less than $800 per month.

The System 950 is the next model up the scale and the first to allow for user memory expansion from the supplied 8 192 bytes: one 8 192 byte segment can be added to the basic memory. The 950 sells for less than $30 000.

At the top of the Qantel line is the System 1200. It has a user memory of 8 192 bytes (expendable in 8 192 byte segments to 32 768 bytes), a printer, a disk drive, the capability to accommodate up to eight video or video inquiry terminals and several peripherals, and the ability to run up to four jobs simultaneously. The 1200 is priced at about $35 000 for a basic configuration, with a monthly lease and maintenance charge of about $1 000.

☐ Microcomputers

A *microcomputer* consists of a central processing unit with about 1 024 words of memory (usually 8, 12, or 16 bits) and costs about $1 000 or less. A microcomputer contains at least one *microprocessor*.

He might look like a singer to you, but he looks like a programmer to me.

A *microprocessor* is usually an LSI (large scale integration) chip, or MSI (medium scale integration), or SSI (small scale integration) transistor logic circuits on boards. A very popular microprocessor is the 8080, manufactured by Intel.

Microcomputers come in varying shapes and sizes. Digital Equipment Corporation offers the LSI-11 and the PDP-8/A microcomputers. Fabri-Tek, and Intersil, Inc. both offer PDP-8 compatible microcomputers. Computer Automation, Inc. offers the "Naked Milli", and Microdata Corporation manufactures the Micro One, shown in Figure 10–38.

Microcomputers are developing along much the same path taken by minicomputers and, earlier, by general purpose computers. That is, the same type of operating software, development software, and application software are being created; peripherals of the proper scale are being introduced, common interfaces types are being used; and certain architectures are becoming quasi-standards.

It is now possible to obtain directly from the manufacturer a fairly complete operating system for a microcomputer. National Semiconductor has a disk operating system, and Fabri-Tek has a real-time operating system.

Standard interfaces will come to mean that users will be able to choose their own peripherals. This factor, whether the peripherals are manufactured by the microcomputer manufacturer or not, may someday be the only real distinction between minicomputer and microcomputer manufacturers. The former will tend to be in firm control of their peripheral designs and costs and will increasingly tend to supply complete system configurations. Microcomputer manufacturers, meanwhile, will allow users to purchase peripherals from any vendor.

(Courtesy of Microdata Corp.)

Figure 10–38 Microdata's Micro One microcomputer. It contains a bipolar central processing unit and 120 chips on the board.

☐ Review Questions

1. List the classifications of computer systems.

2. Briefly explain the difference between a large scale computer system and a small scale system.

3. The IBM System/360 Model 195 computer can perform an operation in _____ nanoseconds.

4. What is virtual storage?

5. What is a minicomputer?

6. What was the first computer system to use integrated cricuits as an integral memory?

7. Compare the minicomputer with a medium scale computer system.

8. Briefly explain how a small scale computer system might be used in some business application.

9. What is a microcomputer?

10. In what way does a microcomputer differ from a minicomputer?

11. What is a microprocessor?

12. Do you feel that someday microcomputers or minicomputers will be used in small businesses? In the home? In schools?

☐ Summary

Computer systems can be classified into six categories: large scale, medium scale, small scale, minicomputers, minicomputer business systems, and microcomputers.

Large scale computer systems are valued at several million dollars and often lease for several hundred thousand dollars per month. These computer systems often consist of a large scale computer with many input-output devices. Described in this chapter are two large scale systems: the IBM System/360 Model 195 and the UNIVAC 1110.

The IBM System/370 Model 145 is a representative medium scale system. This system, along with the NCR Century 200 and UNIVAC 9400, are briefly described in this chapter. Medium scale computer systems provide considerable computing power for most business applications. The monthly rental price for systems in this class is usually several thousand dollars.

Small scale computer systems are often card-oriented. The IBM System/3 uses the small 96-column card. Other small-scale systems use the standard 80-column card. Small scale systems rent for as little as $1 000 per month. Described in this chapter are the IBM System/360 Model 20, IBM System/3, IBM System/32, IBM 1130, NCR Century 8200, and the NCR Century 100.

Minicomputers are general-purpose digital computers that cost less than $15 000. A typical minicomputer uses a 16-bit word, is built from integrated circuitry, weighs less than 50 pounds, usually has between 4 096 and 16 384 words of storage, and has a storage cycle time of about 900 nanoseconds. Described in this chapter are the IBM 5100 Portable Computer, the PDP-11 family, and the Varian 73.

Several minicomputer systems have been configured as business systems. Discussed in this chapter are Digital Equipment Corporation's Datasystem and the Qantel Business Systems.

A *microcomputer* consists of a CPU with about 1 024 words of memory and costs about $1 000. It contains at least one microprocessor, usually an LSI chip or MSI/SSI transistor logic circuit boards. Microcomputers are finding expanding uses in all phases of business.

I now pronounce you husband and wife.

Key Terms

bps	minicomputer
cpm	large scale computer-system
cps	medium scale computer system
lpm	small scale computer system
virtual storage	minicomputer business system
LSI	microcomputer
MSI	microprocessor
SSI	

five

Computer Programming Fundamentals

11

The Program
Development Cycle

Courtesy of Honeywell, Inc.

Programming is the process by which a set of *instructions* is produced for a computer to make it perform some specified activity. The activity can be anything from the production of a company payroll to the solution of a complex mathematical problem. The set of instructions that control the computer is called a *program*.

Preparing a computer program and checking it out are both time-consuming and important operations. Since the computer does not do any thinking and cannot make unplanned decisions, every step of the problem has to be accounted for by the program. A problem which can be solved by a computer need not be described by an exact mathematical equation, but it does need a certain set of rules that the computer can follow. If a problem needs intuition or guessing, or is so badly defined that it is hard to put into words, the computer cannot solve it. A great deal of thought must be put into defining the problem and setting it up for the computer in such a way that every possible alternative is taken care of. A computer cannot be expected to perform any task adequately unless the problem it is required to solve has been specified correctly in every detail, and the instructions it is asked to obey define in complete detail each step of the solution.

It should always be remembered that computers are used to implement the solutions to problems. Computers do not solve problems—*people* solve problems. The computer carries out the solution as specified by people.

The main steps (Figure 11–1) which have to be covered before a program is completed are:

Understand the problem, and plan the solution

Prepare a flowchart of the problem

Prepare the computer instructions in coded form

Test the program until it is working properly

Prepare detailed documentation of the program and instructions on its operation.

The amount of time spent on each of the previous steps will largely depend on the type and complexity of the problem being programmed;

279

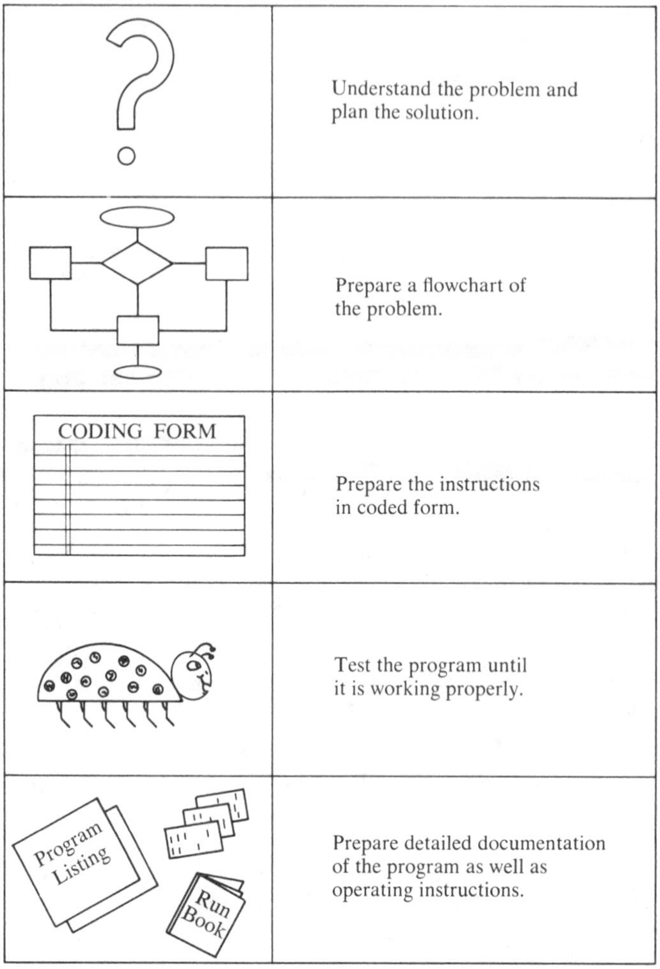
Understand the problem and plan the solution.
Prepare a flowchart of the problem.
CODING FORM
Prepare the instructions in coded form.
Test the program until it is working properly.
Program Listing
Run Book
Prepare detailed documentation of the program as well as operating instructions.

Figure 11–1 The Program Development Cycle.

however, some attempt to implement each of these steps is required for practically every program. Even though the steps are indicated as isolated and distinct steps, they are not this clearly defined. Actually, the steps interact, intertwine, and recycle.

☐ Understanding The Problem

Understanding the problem to be solved by a computer is of fundamental importance. Often one must ask himself questions of the following type.

Is the problem worth doing?

Can the problem be solved with a computer?

Do we know how to solve the problem on a computer?

Can the computer in question solve the problem?

What are the inputs and outputs?

What programming language will be used?

Have parts of the problem already been programmed?

After questions of this type are answered one can better determine if a problem should be solved by a computer.

In many cases, the programmer will work from a detailed program specification prepared by someone else. This specification includes all of the input to be processed by the program, the processing required, and details of all output from the program. The programmer must satisfy himself that all possible conditions have been covered, or that any conditions not specified can be adequately handled. Having agreed to the specification of the problem, the programmer must then develop a "strategy" to be used in writing the program. The strategy will greatly depend on the programmer's experience, the capacity of the computer, the type of programming language to be used, and the complexity of the problem.

The process of understanding the problem is called *problem analysis.* The goal of this process is the formal and logical presentation of the problem for computer solution.

Flowcharting

After it has been determined exactly what the problem is and just how to solve it, a *flowchart* is made of the logic of the solution. A flowchart is basically a pictorial view of how the computer will solve a problem. It is composed of simple descriptions contained in special symbols, all connected by straight lines. Figure 11–2 shows a flowchart to read three numbers from a card, determine the largest of the three, and print it.

The flowchart is used as a guideline for coding the program. The process of flowcharting is discussed in chapter 12.

Review Questions

1. Briefly define the following terms:
   (a) programming
   (b) program
   (c) flowchart

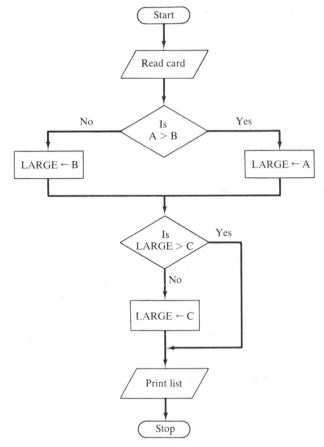

Figure 11–2   A flowchart to read three numbers from a card, determine the largest of the three, and print it.

2. What are the main steps that are used in the preparation of a computer program?
3. What is meant by "problem analysis"?
4. List two or three applications in which a computer cannot be used to solve problems.
5. What is the purpose of preparing a flowchart?
6. What must a programmer do before writing computer instructions?

☐ Coding

Coding is the writing of instructions in a language or code which the computer can accept. Normally, one codes from flowcharts. There is not a one flowchart symbol to one program step correspondence, however. One flowchart symbol may become several computer instructions or statements in a coded program.

The program will be coded in either an *assembler language* (see Figure 11-3), or in a *compiler language* (see Figure 11-4). The choice of language will depend on the complexity of the problem, the capacity and resources of the computer to be used, and the programmer's familiarity with specific programming languages.

Line 3 5 6	Label	Operation 15 16 20 21 25 30 35 40	OPERAND 45
0 1		MCW	@TOTAL@,245
0 2		MLCWA	EDIT1,281
0 3		MCE	ACTTOT,281
0 4		W	
0 5		CS	
0 6		CS	
0 7		B	WRTHDR
0 8		MCW	@FINAL TOTAL DEBITS@,258
0 9		MLCWA	EDIT1,281
1 0		MCE	DRTOT,281
1 1		MCW	@**@,283
1 2		W	
1 3		CS	
1 4		CS	
1 5		CC	J
1 6		MCW	@FINAL TOTAL CREDITS@,259
1 7		MLCWA	EDIT1,281
1 8		MCE	CRTOT,281
1 9		MCW	@**@,283
2 0		W	
2 1		CS	
2 2		CS	
2 3		CC	J
2 4		A	CRTOT,DRTOT
2 5		MCW	@FINAL TOTAL NET@,255

Figure 11-3 Program written in assembler language.

The more sophisticated and easier to use a language is, the less control a programmer will have over the final form of the program that is actually executed by the computer. Thus, some loss of efficiency in running time or an increase in the size of the program may occur. These penalties are counterbalanced by the speed of writing a program in an easy-to-use compiler language and the likelihood of fewer mistakes.

Whatever programming language is used to write a program, the programmer's goal is to reproduce the logic of the program as described in a flowchart as simply, economically, and efficiently as possible.

```
    BIG: PROCEDURE OPTIONS (MAIN);
    DECLARE (A, B, C, LARGE) FLOAT;
    GET LIST (A, B, C);
    IF A>B THEN DO;
    LARGE=A;
    GO TO CHECK;
    END;
    LARGE=B;
    CHECK: IF LARGE>C THEN GO TO OUTPUT;
    LARGE=C;
    OUTPUT: PUT SKIP LIST (LARGE);
    STOP;
    END BIG;


    1,3,-2
```

Figure 11–4   Program written in PL/I compiler language. The flowchart used to code this program is shown in Figure 11–2.

The flowchart shown in Figure 11–2 was used to code the program shown in Figure 11–4. The programming language used in this program is called PL/I. There are several other languages that are used to develop business programs. COBOL, FORTRAN, and BASIC are the names of only a few of them. Programming languages are discussed in chapter 13.

After a program is coded, it is usually keypunched onto cards in exactly the same way it is written on the coding form. If the coded program con-

"And now I want you to meet our computer science teacher."

tains 15 instructions (15 lines of coding), then 15 cards will be keypunched (see Figure 11–5). In keypuncning, the operator punches information into the card in specific locations, just as they appear on the coding sheet.

After the program has been keypunched on cards, it is often a good idea to obtain a *listing* (Figure 11–5). This is a printed copy that shows what has been punched into the cards and other related information, such as the number of cards in the card deck. The programmer uses the listing to make sure there were no keypunching errors in the program. Listings are usually prepared on unit record machines or off-line computer systems.

```
BIG: PROCEDURE OPTIONS (MAIN);
DECLARE (A,B,C,LARGE) FLOAT;
GET LIST (A,B,C);
IF A>B THEN DO;
LARGE=A;
GO TO CHECK;
END;
LARGE=B;
CHECK: IF LARGE>C THEN GO TO OUTPUT;
LARGE=C;
OUTPUT: PUT SKIP LIST (LARGE);
STOP;
END BIG;
```

**Figure
11–5**   Printed listing of a program.

Before a program can be executed on a computer it must be *translated* into a language that the computer understands. The computer does not directly understand programs written in *symbolic programming languages,* such as assembly languages or compiler languages (COBOL, PL/I, etc.). Programs written in these languages, called *source programs,* must be *assembled* or *compiled* into *object programs.* These object programs can then be executed on the computer. The program translation process is discussed in chapter 13.

☐ Testing

Mistakes in computer programs are common. The process of finding and removing mistakes from a computer program is called *debugging* (Figure 11–6). It is during the testing or debugging process that one determines whether a program is working properly and, if it is not, makes the necessary program changes to make it work properly.

(Courtesy of IBM Corporation)

Figure 11–6   Detecting mistakes in a program is a time-consuming and necessary task. Shown here is a programmer comparing punched card statements with flow chart logic in an effort to locate a program *bug*.

Mistakes or errors in a program are known as *bugs* and are of two main types: mistakes due to the incorrect use of the programming language and mistakes due to incorrect logic in the solution of the problem. Programming is an exercise in logical thinking. There is no place for loose ends or fuzzy thinking. Nevertheless, program mistakes are bound to occur and will show up during the testing process.

Programs are often tested with samples of the data normally expected to be input to the program and the results obtained compared with calculated results obtained manually from this test data. When the results obtained by the program agree with the expected results, and when the program operates as specified, the program may be said to be working properly.

Many program mistakes are detected during the program translation process. Assemblers and compilers detect and indicate to the user mistakes in source programs. These program translators provide the programmer with a listing of the program accompanied by *error messages*—

*"Before you say anything, Daddy, I think you should know he's
making $50,000 a year with his own minicomputer
software company."*

called *diagnostics*—and references to potential sources of error in the
program. The programmer examines the printout and takes appropriate
action to eliminate the mistake. For example, a program correction usually involves making changes in the coding form, repunching the cor-
rected statements in new cards, and inserting them in the program card
deck. After corrections are made, the revised card deck is again translated into an object program and the process is repeated until the listing
indicates that the program is free from obvious mistakes. The process of
making changes to a computer program is called *patching* or *program
updating.*

Computer manufacturers often offer software to help test programs.
Programs such as trace routines, memory dump routines, and register
dump routines are often helpful in testing programs. Debugging systems
are available on many computers. Such a system provides the user with a
program designed specifically to help him detect program errors. This
system allows the programmer to specify breakpoints, where the computer will stop, and then allows him to use the typewriter to enter data
into the computer and to receive printouts. These debugging aids help
in obtaining clues to the problem.

Before coding a program, it helps to remember some of the so-called
axioms of programming:

> Every computer program contains at least one bug.
>
> If there is a bug, the computer will find it.
>
> If anything can go wrong, it will.

With these axioms in mind, happy debugging!

☐ Documentation

A tested computer program is often stored as a pattern of magnetic bits on a tape or disk, or as holes punched in cards or tape. This program is capable of being placed in the computer and obeyed. The program may be capable of successfully fulfilling the task it has been designed for, but it will be impossible to use it unless one knows the *input* necessary for the program, the *output* it produces, and the way the computer must be operated. Some form of *documentation* must accompany a program; otherwise, it is useless.

Documentation of programs contributes to their useful value. Well-documented programs are extremely valuable whenever the program is to be rewritten for another computer or whenever someone other than the originator is to modify the program. There is no excuse for poorly documented programs.

Program documentation often includes:

An English-language description of the problem
A flowchart
A symbolic listing of the program
A list of instructions needed to operate the program, including computer console switch settings
Description of files and record layouts
Test cases and sample results
A list of error conditions
A deck of punched cards, a roll of punched paper tape, or magnetic recording on either a tape or disk.

☐ Review Questions

7. Explain coding.
8. What is meant by "program translation"? Give an example.
9. What is the difference between a source program and an object program?
10. What is a listing? In what way is it used?
11. Why is it necessary to test or debug a program?
12. What are diagnostics? How are they used in the testing process?
13. What is meant by "patching" a program?
14. Why is it necessary to document a program?

☐ Summary

Programming is the process by which a set of instructions is produced for a computer to make it perform some specified task. The set of instructions produced is called a *program*. This chapter describes the five steps required in the development of a program. These steps are:

1. Understand the problem.
2. Represent the problem solution in flowchart form.
3. Use the flowchart to write a program.
4. Test the program to insure that it is working properly.
5. Document how the program is to be used.

Flowcharting is covered in detail in the next chapter.

Key Terms

programming
program
problem analysis
flowchart
coding
listing

translated
debugging
bugs
diagnostics
patching
documentation

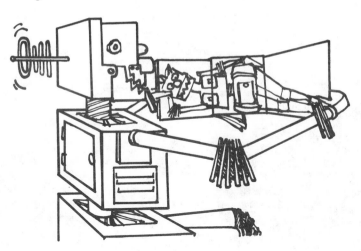

Cartoon from "Computer Science Mathematics"

12

Flowcharting

Courtesy of IBM Corporation

⬜ The Program Flowchart

A *program flowchart** is a drawing showing the steps required in the solution of a problem. It is perhaps the best method available for expressing what computers can do—or what you want them to do. Flowcharts are easy to prepare, easy to use, and free of ambiguities. There are many reasons why flowcharts are used, especially when a problem is complex and involves the work of more than one programmer. Some of the uses of the flowchart in computer applications are:

1. To present the logic used in solving a problem in pictorial form. It breaks the problem down into logical elements and subdivisions.
2. To provide a way of communicating the program logic to other people.
3. To aid in coordinating the efforts of two or more programmers working on the same application.
4. To provide a means of refreshing the programmer's concept of a program when he returns to a program which has remained static for some time.
5. To provide a common language between programmers not necessarily using the same computing equipment.
6. To provide a visual description of the data process, which allows better control over computer operations.
7. To provide a detailed blueprint to be used in writing a computer program.
8. To point out areas of the problem which need further clarification, analysis, and definition.
9. To divide a large problem into several smaller manageable segments.

A flowchart is basically a diagram composed of symbols, directional lines, and information about how the computer will be used to solve a problem. It shows *what* is to be accomplished, rather than *how* it is ac-

---

* Sometimes called a *flow diagram, block diagram,* or simply *flowchart*. Throughout this book, the term *flowchart* will be assumed to mean *program flowchart*. Another type of flowchart, called the *system flowchart,* is discussed in chapter 21.

complished. Figure 12–1 illustrates a humorous flowchart* which shows some of the symbols used and the step-by-step manner in which even a simple procedure, like calling someone on a telephone, can be analyzed.

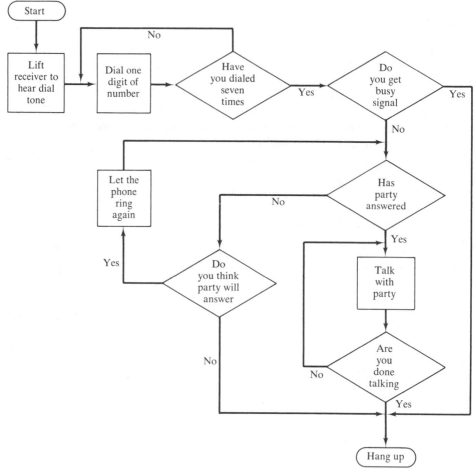

Figure 12–1   Flowchart of a person calling a party on a telephone.

▢ Flowcharting Symbols

Shown in Figure 12–2 are the symbols most commonly used in flowcharts. Different symbols mean different operations. The use of symbols with different shapes helps the programmer to organize the flowchart and makes the resulting diagram easier to read.

---

* Adapted from *Computer Oriented Mathematics,* National Council of Teachers of Mathematics, Washington, D.C., 1963, p. 7.

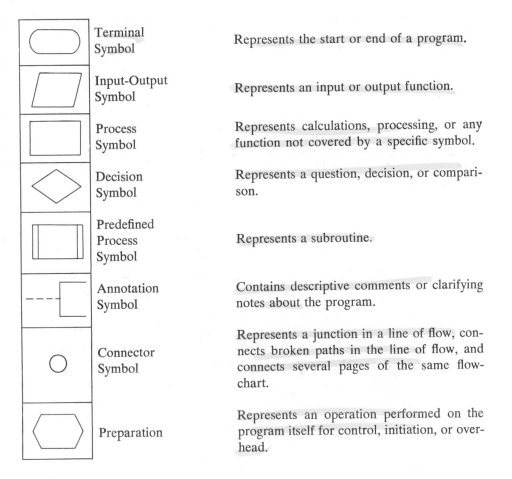

Terminal Symbol	Represents the start or end of a program.
Input-Output Symbol	Represents an input or output function.
Process Symbol	Represents calculations, processing, or any function not covered by a specific symbol.
Decision Symbol	Represents a question, decision, or comparison.
Predefined Process Symbol	Represents a subroutine.
Annotation Symbol	Contains descriptive comments or clarifying notes about the program.
Connector Symbol	Represents a junction in a line of flow, connects broken paths in the line of flow, and connects several pages of the same flowchart.
Preparation	Represents an operation performed on the program itself for control, initiation, or overhead.

Figure 12–2   Flowcharting Symbols.

The beginning or end of a program is indicated by the terminal symbol. Thus,

is to be used at the beginning of a program and

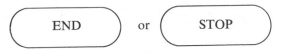

is to be used at the termination of a program.

A parallelogram is used to represent any input or output function. The symbol

could be used whenever information on a punched card is to be input to the program. The symbol

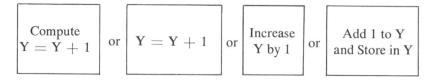

could be used to indicate the writing or printing of data from computer storage.

A rectangle is used to indicate computer processing, such as computations or movement of data within computer storage. "Add X + Y," "Move A to B," and "Compute Y = Y + 1," are examples of processing and would be represented in flowchart notation as follows:

Add X + Y	Move A to B	Compute $Y \leftarrow Y + 1$

The last example uses the symbol ← which is often used when making variable assignments. Other ways of representing this same computation follow.

Compute $Y = Y + 1$	or	$Y = Y + 1$	or	Increase Y by 1	or	Add 1 to Y and Store in Y

An open-ended rectangle symbol is used to provide descriptive comments or explanatory notes for clarification. For example, the following symbol

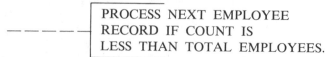

could be used to add a clarifying comment to a flowchart. Note that it is connected to the program flow by a dashed line.

Mathematical symbols are also used in flowcharts. Some of the more common ones are:

$:$ Compare $(X : Y)$

$=$ Equal to $(X = Y)$

$\neq$ Not equal to $(X \neq Y)$

$>$ Greater than $(X > Y)$

$<$ Less than $(X < Y)$

$\geq$ Greater than or equal to $(X \geq Y)$

$\leq$ Less than or equal to $(X \leq Y)$

Y   Yes

N   No

The *connector* and *predefined process symbols* will be discussed in examples later in the chapter, and the remainder of the chapter will deal with using flowcharting symbols in the construction of flowcharts.

Flow Direction

All the flowchart symbols discussed in the previous section are connected together by directional flow lines—i.e., straight lines with arrows. The normal direction of flow is from left to right and from top to bottom. In certain cases, however, it is not possible to conform to the normal flow direction. Arrowheads are then included on the flow lines to indicate direction.

Figure 12–3 shows a flowchart of a procedure for crossing the street at a traffic intersection. This example illustrates the use of three different flowchart symbols and the placing of directional lines to indicate the program flow.

Flowcharting Guidelines

Although there are many different levels of flowcharts, five general rules should be followed in the preparation of all flowcharts, regardless of the complexity of the problem.

1. Use standard symbols.

2. Develop the flowchart so that it reads from top to bottom and left to right whenever possible. Do not cross flowlines. Use arrowheads to indicate direction.

3. Keep the flowchart clear, readable, and simple. Leave plenty of room between the symbols. If a problem solution is large or complex, break it down into several flowcharts.

4. Write simple, descriptive, to-the-point messages in the flowchart symbols.

5. Be legible—print clearly and use a programming template to draw the symbols.

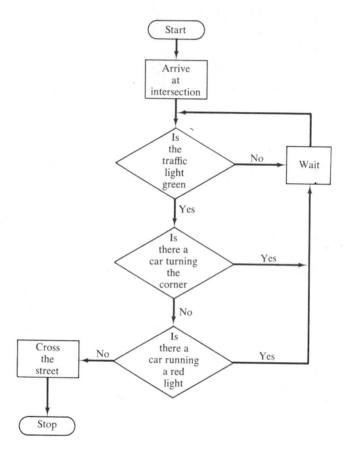

Figure 12–3   Procedure for crossing the street at a traffic intersection.

☐ Flowcharting Template

A flowcharting *template* (Figure 12–4) is a simple means of drawing the various symbols needed for a flowchart. This template, usually made of plastic, contains cutouts for each of the flowcharting symbols. Templates are available in most college bookstores and office supply stores and are often obtainable from computer manufacturers.

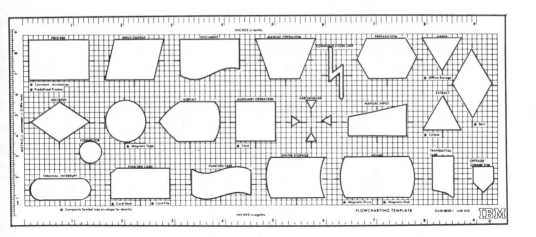

**Figure
12–4**   Flowcharting Template.

Figure 12–5 shows a programmer using a template to draw a flowchart. By using a template, anyone—regardless of his drawing ability—can prepare legible, clear, understandable flowcharts.

**Figure
12–5**   Programmer using a template to draw a flowchart.

☐ Review Questions

1. What is a program flowchart? Give an example.
2. List several reasons for using flowcharts.
3. Identify the following symbols:

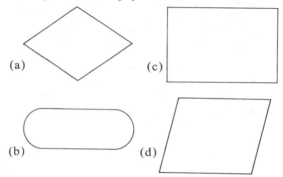

(a)

(c)

(b)

(d)

4. What is the meaning of the following symbols?
   (a) $<$ (c) $\neq$
   (b) $\geqq$ (d) :
5. What is the annotation symbol used for?
6. What is the proper direction of flow?
7. What is a template?
8. When will the following program terminate?
   (a) at symbol F   (c) never
   (b) at symbol B   (d) at symbol A

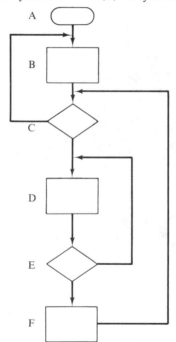

☐ Construction of the Flowchart

Flowcharts can be prepared showing any degree of detail. It is common to begin with very simple diagrams—often just a sketch on paper showing the gross logical structure—and then to amplify gradually each of the boxes in successive redrawings of the same flowchart until the required amount of detail is obtained.

Since much of the detailed computer program is devoted to *housekeeping functions,** it is generally reasonable to assume that the first flowchart will omit these functions. Thus, the first flowchart would most likely consist of the basic series of logical operations necessary to perform the solution to the problem. A rough sketch of a procedure is shown in Figure 12–6. This flowchart was drawn without a template. A final com-

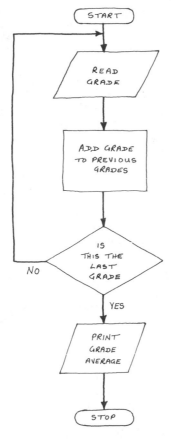

Figure 12–6   Rough sketch of the "Compute an Average" program.

* The part of a program that is devoted to set-up operations: clearing computer storage areas, initializing input-output devices, inserting constants, setting of entry conditions, etc.

plete flowchart, including housekeeping functions, is shown in Figure 12–7. The procedure shown in these flowcharts is rather simple and involves only the computation of an average (arithmetic mean) of the grades made on 25 test scores. A more complex procedure may possibly require the drawing of several intermediate flowcharts before the program logic is clearly defined.

The hierarchy of a flowchart tends to force the programmer to think in a logical manner, from a general solution of a problem to a detailed description of the program logic.

A *loop* is a series of operations which is performed repeatedly until some specified condition is satisfied; whereupon, a branch operation is obeyed

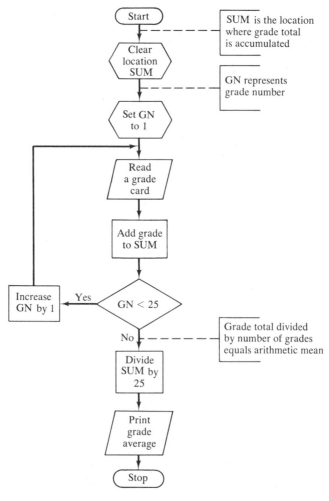

Figure 12–7   Final flowchart of the "Compute an Average" program.

to exit from the loop. Repeating a set of operations by returning to the beginning of a set of operations is called *looping*.

The flowchart in Figure 12–7 contains a program loop. This loop is repeated until 25 graded cards have been read.

Most programs contain one or more loops. Figure 12–8 illustrates the flowchart of a procedure that computes the final score for each of six students in an accounting course. Final grades for the course are based on five examination scores. This flowchart uses two loops.

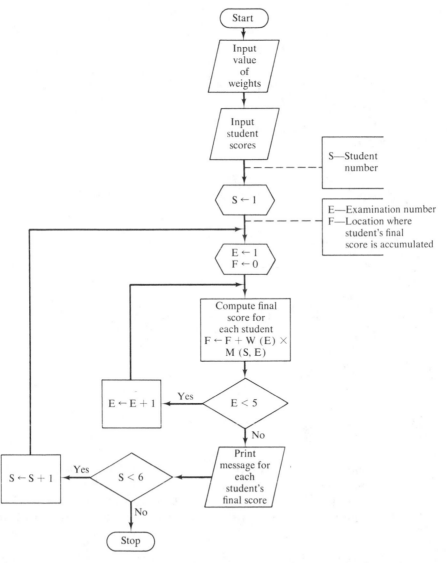

Figure 12–8   Flowchart with two loops.

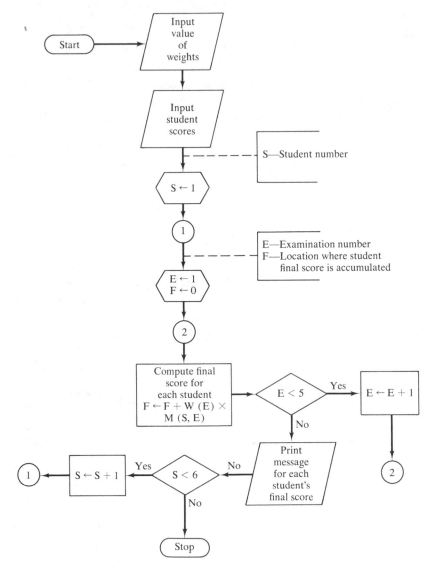

Figure   Flowchart using connector symbols.
12–9

A *connector symbol* may be used to eliminate long looping lines on a flowchart. For example, the flowchart shown in Figure 12–8 can be changed as indicated in Figure 12–9, using two connector symbols. Other uses of the connector symbol are illustrated in the examples at the end of this chapter.

When working with punched card records, the flowchart usually includes a test for the last card. This test may be placed at the beginning or at the

end of the flowchart, as shown in Figure 12–10. The last card usually
has some specific code which the program will test for. For example, the
last card in the card file shown in Figure 12–11 includes a negative
employee ID number. The program would simply test each card for a
−99 ID number. When this card is reached, the program knows it is
the last card in the file. Program counters can also be used if the number
of cards to be read is known. This is somewhat simpler and can easily be
implemented with a program loop. The number of loops will equal the
number of cards in the card file.

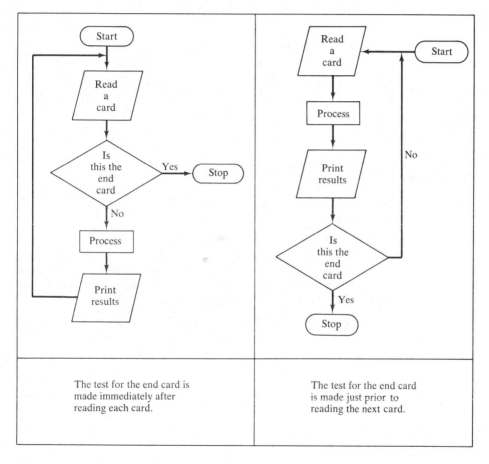

The test for the end card is
made immediately after
reading each card.

The test for the end card
is made just prior to
reading the next card.

Figure   Procedure for testing for the last card of a card file.
12–10

When working with magnetic tape files, the test is for end-of-file instead
of last card. Figure 12–12 illustrates this process.

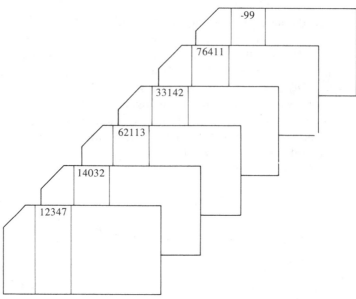

Figure Card file containing a stop or end card.
12–11

☐ Review Questions

9. What is meant by "housekeeping function"?

10. Define "looping" and give an example.

11. How is the connector symbol used? Give an example.

12. Draw a flowchart of a program that could be used to read the following card file. The program is to add 10 to the value punched onto each card and print the new total for each card. The end card has a −99 punched in the value field.

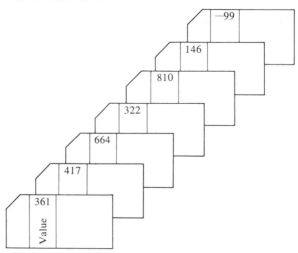

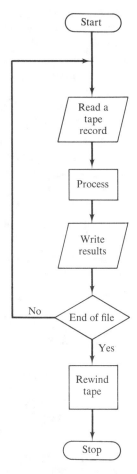

Figure   Procedure for testing for EOF (end of file).
12–12

☐ Subroutines

A *subroutine* is a set of instructions that directs the computer to perform some specific operation. It may be used over and over in the same program or in different programs. It is written separately from a program and is often kept in a *library* until it is needed, at which time it is integrated into a program for proper use.

A subroutine is entered by a branch or jump from a program and provision is made to return control to the program at the end of the operation.

Subroutines are used to avoid wasteful reprogramming. For example, assume that a programmer wanted to compute the square root of a number in his program. He could, of course, write the instructions needed to perform the computation. An easier method, however, would be to use a square root subroutine that is available for all programs. The program merely uses the subroutine by *calling* it by its predetermined name (say SQRT). After the subroutine calculates the square root, it returns program control back to the calling program. This calling process is illustrated in Figure 12–13. Instructions in the program are executed sequentially until the CALL SQRT instruction is reached. At this point, program control is transferred to the subroutine. The subroutine computes the square root and then returns control to the instruction following the CALL SQRT instruction. Instructions in the program are then again executed in sequential order.

Subroutines are indicated on flowcharts by using the *predefined process symbol*. For example, a flowchart reference to a square root subroutine might appear as that shown in Figure 12–14. The flowcharting symbol contains the name of the subroutine.

"And now, gentleman, if I may have your attention,
I'd like to go over this new subroutine with you . . ."

☐ Review Questions

13. What is a subroutine? Give your own example of how one could be used.

14. What flowchart symbol is used to represent a subroutine reference?

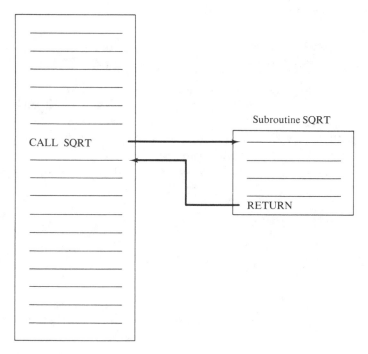

Figure   Subroutine reference.
12–13

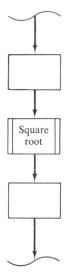

Figure   Predefined process symbol indicating a reference to a square root
12–14   subroutine.

☐ Computer-Drawn Flowcharts

Computers are widely used for making graphs, charting weather, and even drawing pictures of Snoopy. They can also draw *flowcharts*.

Several computer programs are available that accept a coded computer program (in a computer language such as FORTRAN or COBOL) as input and produce as output a printed (line printer) or drawn (digital plotter) flowchart of the program. The computer-drawn flowcharts are often not as legible and neat-looking as a hand-drawn flowchart; however they do provide a method of producing consistent flowcharts for program documentation and debugging purposes. Figure 12–15 shows a computer-drawn flowchart.

☐ Flowcharting Examples

Several sample flowcharts are presented here to illustrate the flowchart development process and the proper use of the flowcharting symbols.

Example 1

This example shows the method of computation for the weekly wage of an employee. The procedure computes the weekly wage and prints the computed value along with the employee's identification number. Input to the procedure is a data record containing the employee's ID number, hours worked, standard weekly pay rate, and overtime rate. After determining the number of hours that the employee worked, the procedure determines the wage using either the standard rate or the overtime rate. If the number of hours exceeds 40, then the procedure uses the overtime rate for all hours over 40 and the standard rate for the first 40 hours. If the number of hours was 40 or less, then the program multiplies the number of hours by the standard rate. A flowchart of this problem is shown in Figure 12–16.

Example 2

It is possible to perform the same computation described in Example 1 for 250 employees. The flowchart shown in Figure 12–17 illustrates how the Example 1 flowchart can be altered to effect this computation.

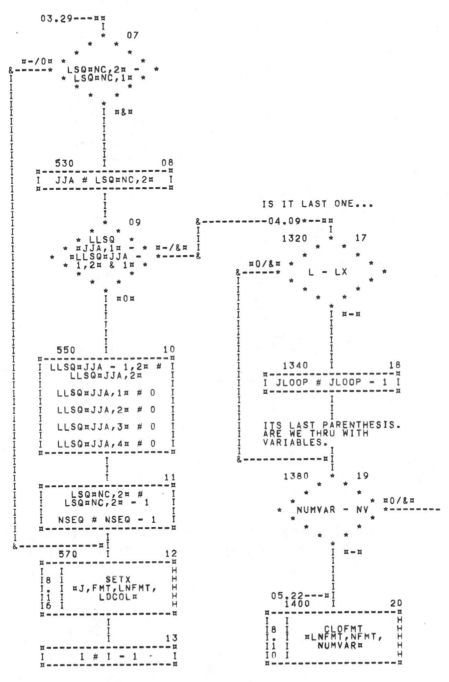

Figure Portion of a computer-drawn flowchart.
12–15

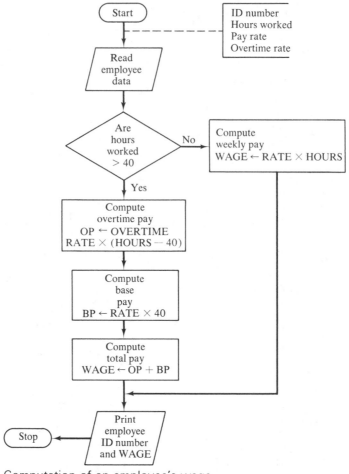

Figure 12–16   Computation of an employee's wage.

Example 3

A card file is prepared for all people living in Greenfelt, Kansas. Each card contains the person's age and income in the following format:

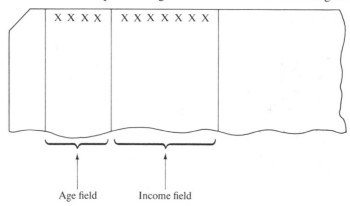

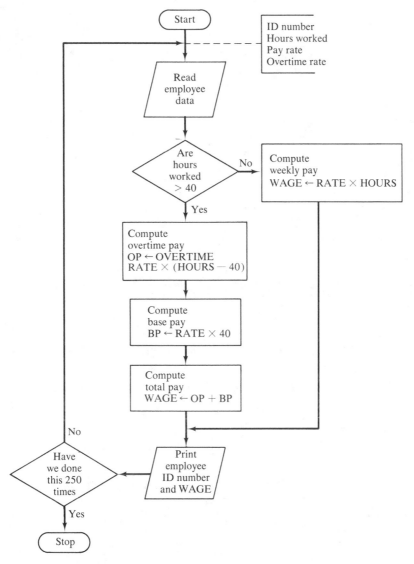

Figure   Wage computations for 250 employees.
12–17

The last card in the file is used as a *stop* card and contains 9999 in the age field. The flowchart, shown in Figure 12–18, describes a procedure that computes the average salary of the people in each five-year age group (0 to 4, 5 to 9, 10 to 14, . . . , 60 to 64) and prints out the following information.

Lower age limit for each group (0, 5, 10, . . . , 60)

Average annual salary for that group

Number of people in each group.

Example 4

The ABC Loan Company wishes to use a computer to solve a simple accounting problem. An automobile worth $9 000 is to be depreciated over eight years by the use of a double declining-balance depreciation.

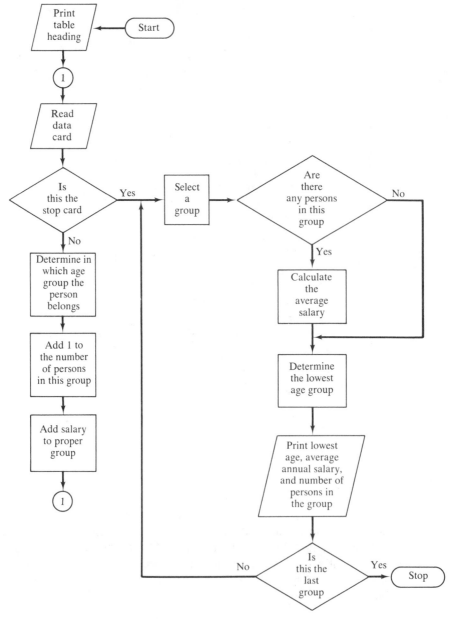

Figure 12–18   Average salary computation procedure.

Figure 12–19 shows a flowchart that describes this problem. This procedure would produce a table, such as the one that follows.

YEAR	DEPRECIATION	BOOK VALUE
1	900.00	8100.00
2	810.00	7290.00
3	729.00	6561.00
4	656.10	5904.90
5	590.49	5314.41
6	531.44	4782.97
7	478.30	4304.67
8	430.46	3874.20

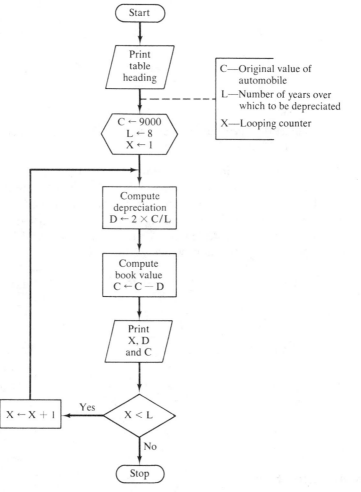

Figure 12–19   Accounting Problem.

Example 5

The following three lists are composed of all positive numbers, all negative numbers, and mixed positive and negative numbers, respectively.

List A	List B	List C
36	−4	−14
14	−11	3
4	−28	22
27	−17	−9
9	−6	6
18	−21	11
26	−36	−29
32	−14	32
41	−12	−8
7	−9	38
11	−43	24
16	−19	42
29	−24	−13
18	−2	18

A flowchart of a procedure to arrange the three lists in ascending order is shown in Figure 12–20.

The technique used in this procedure first compares A_J (first number in List A) to A_{J+1} (next number in List A). If A_{J+1} is smaller than A_J, then A_J and A_{J+1} are interchanged, and the comparison is similarly repeated for all remaining numbers in the list. After list A is processed, the same comparison technique is used on numbers in Lists B and C. Output from this procedure would be three sorted lists.

List A	List B	List C
4	−43	−29
7	−36	−14
9	−28	−13
11	−24	−9
14	−21	−8
16	−19	3
18	−17	6
.	.	.
.	.	.
.	.	.

☐ **Review Questions**

15. Draw a flowchart of a procedure to read the cards in Review Question 12, but omit the end card.

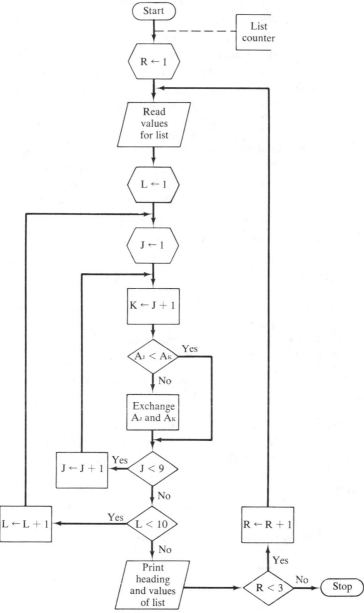

Figure 12–20 Sorting Problem.

16. Draw a flowchart for a process that you go through everyday, such as

driving a car through an intersection,
getting to class,
adding numbers,

going to the supermarket,
taking a test,
making coffee,
solving a business problem.

17. You are given eight coins, numbered 1 through 8, seven of which weigh the same. The eighth is heavier. Draw a flowchart that will detect the heavy coin with only two uses of a balance scale.

18. You are a clerk in a store and a woman hands you a $10 bill to pay for a purchase of x dollars. Draw a flowchart of a procedure that will determine what bills and coins she should receive in change.

19. A stack of 40 punched cards contains the final exam grades for a class of 40 biology students. Draw a flowchart of a procedure that will count how many grades below 70 there are and print this number.

☐ Summary

There are two basic types of flowcharts: *program flowchart* and *system flowchart*. A program flowchart is a drawing showing the steps required in the solution of a problem. The program flowchart is covered in this chapter. The system flowchart is covered in chapter 21.

The program flowchart is basically a diagram composed of symbols, directional lines, and information about how the computer will be used to solve a problem. A program flowchart shows what is to be accomplished. The flowcharting symbols and procedures used in this book conform to the flowcharting standards established by the American National Standards Institute.

Key Terms

program flowchart   loop
flowcharting symbol   looping
template   subroutine
housekeeping function   library

13

Introduction to Computer Programming

Courtesy of Sperry Rand Corporation's Univac Division

People use language to communicate with one another. In the same way, languages of one sort or another are used to communicate instructions and commands to a computer.* The unique feature which distinguishes a computer from other manufactured tools and devices is its versatility in dealing with different problems. A variety of programming languages** have been developed to provide a range of methods for communicating these problems to the computer.

The different types of programming languages are discussed in this chapter. Also included is a brief presentation of the six most popular programming languages: BASIC, FORTRAN, COBOL, PL/I, RPG, and APL.

The Three Levels of Language

The key to the successful use of a computer is *programming*. The computer cannot add two numbers unless it has been so directed. In fact, the simplest task can be a major problem for the computer if poorly programmed; paradoxically, however, the most complex problem can be a simple task when properly programmed.

Programming involves writing a set of instructions in a sequence that will produce a desired result when the sequence is executed on the computer. These instructions are stored in the internal memory of the computer. The data, or information upon which these operations are performed, is also stored in the internal memory of the computer.

As stated in Chapter 11, writing sequences of instruction is called *coding*. Coding can take place at various levels, ranging from machine language (basic language of the computer) to problem-oriented language (programming language in problem terminology). These different levels are:

---

* Languages devised for people-computer communications are called *artificial languages*.

** Also called *computer languages*.

- *Machine language*
- *Assembler language* (low-level language)
- *Higher-level language*

All coding levels except machine language are symbolic and must be translated into machine-language instructions. The computer operates at the level of machine coding; therefore, all other codes must eventually be translated into that form.

☐ Machine Language

Machine language is the common language of the particular computer; hence, this language does not require further modification before execution by the computer. After the proper definition of the problem, the computer user proceeds to code the operation, using codes that the computer can interpret.

Basic instructions to a computer consist of operations such as *add, subtract, multiply, divide, store, load, read, write,* and *shift.* A machine-language instruction consists of an *operation code* and one or more *operands.* Figure 13–1 illustrates a machine-language instruction with two operands.

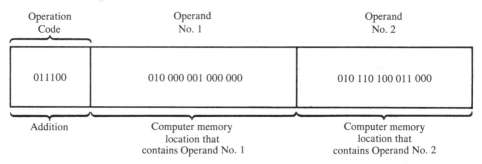

Figure 13–1   A machine language instruction.

The operation code refers to the part of the instruction that specifies the operation to be performed, such as add or read. The operands refer to the part of the instruction that references a location within the computer where the data to be processed is stored. In the example, the operation code (011100) indicates that the computer is to perform an addition operation. The operands (10000001000000 and 10110100011000) specify the computer memory locations of the data to be added.

A *program* is a meaningful sequence of instructions or statements, possessing an implicit or explicit order of execution. A program written in machine language is a sequence of binary numbers, such as that shown in Figure 13–2.

Machine language coding form			
Oper	OP 1	OP 2	Comments
100010	000 000 000 000 011	010 110 100 000 000	Load register with C
001100	000 000 000 000 011	011 010 000 000 000	Multiply by B
011100	000 000 000 000 011	010 101 011 000 000	Add A
010111	000 000 000 000 011	100 001 000 000 000	Store as D

**Figure
13–2**   Machine language program to compute $d = a + b \times c$.

Although machine languages provide for economy of construction, they are usually inconvenient for direct human use. Machine languages also require that the user have a thorough knowledge of the computer, its peculiarities, and its intricate details. It was inevitable that languages had to be developed that were easier to learn, easier to write, and easier to remember. It was also inevitable that numbers be replaced by symbols and words that the human user could better understand.

Now, all together—say *it's not the program's fault.*

☐ Symbolic Languages

Symbolic languages were developed to overcome the many inconveniences of machine languages. Symbolic coding involves programming a computer to recognize instructions in a language more easily understood by the user, and then translating these expressions into machine language. This concept has led to the development of a large number of different symbolic programming languages that are easy to use and understand.

Before looking at the various types of symbolic languages, let us define several terms. As stated earlier, a *program* is a meaningful sequence of *statements*. Statements, in turn, are strings of symbols from a given alphabet composed of letters, digits, and special characters. The form of each statement obeys a set of rules (*syntax*) and possesses an operational meaning (*semantics*). Collectively, the alphabet, syntax, and semantics are termed a *language*.

A *source program* is a computer program written in a symbolic language. The instructions or statements of a source program are processed in the computer to produce a program that can eventually be executed on the machine. This processing function is called *translating,* and the processor program is called a *translator*. Thus, the translator converts a program written in a symbolic source language into machine language. This machine-language program is called an *object program*. A translator, then, converts a source program into an object program. The object program is the program that is run on the computer to produce the desired results.

Symbolic languages are more suitable for human use than are machine languages. They are designed to facilitate computer programming, and they tend to be associated in some sense with the problems under consideration. One of the features that hastened the widespread acceptance of programming languages is that computer programs written in this more convenient form could be translated to machine language by another computer program running on the same or possibly a different computer. One of the significant aspects of the philosophy behind the use of symbolic languages and translator programs is that the same computer may process programs written in many different languages, provided that a translator program has been written for each language.

Assembly Language

An *assembly language* is a *low-level* symbolic language used for developing computer programs which must go through an *assembly* in order to be converted into a machine code required for operation on a computer. It is called a low-level language* because it closely resembles the machine code of a computer rather than the language of a problem.

---

* Assembly languages are also called *one-for-one languages* which indicates that there is a line of symbolic coding for each machine instruction in a program.

Programming in an assembly language offers a number of important advantages over programming in machine code. In assembly language, all operation codes of the computer are given mnemonic designations. For instance, the actual operation code for the instruction *add* may be 100110. In the assembly language, one need only write the mnemonic operation code ADD. Most programmers never learn the actual machine codes. All data and machine addresses in the commands are written using symbolic notation. The programmer is thereby relieved of potential problems in the effective allocation of computer storage. The use of symbolic addresses reduces the clerical aspect of programming and eliminates many programming mistakes. Because the symbols are chosen to be meaningful, the program is also much easier to read and understand than if it were written with numerical addresses.

As stated earlier, an assembly language program can not be directly executed by a computer. The mnemonic operation codes and symbolic addresses must be translated into a form the machine can use. This is the function of the *assembler*.

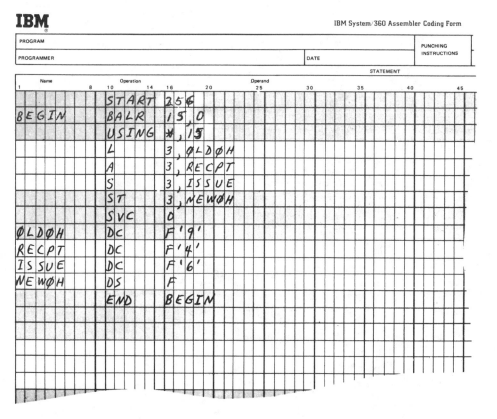

Figure 13–3 A program written in assembly language.

The assembly process begins with a source program written by the programmer. Ordinarily, a special coding form is used, such as that shown in Figure 13–3 (we shall examine this program later). Cards are punched from this form, making up the *source program deck*. This source program deck becomes the primary input to the assembly process, as shown in Figure 13–4. The assembly is done, in this case, by a computer under control of the assembler. The assembler, which is simply a pro-

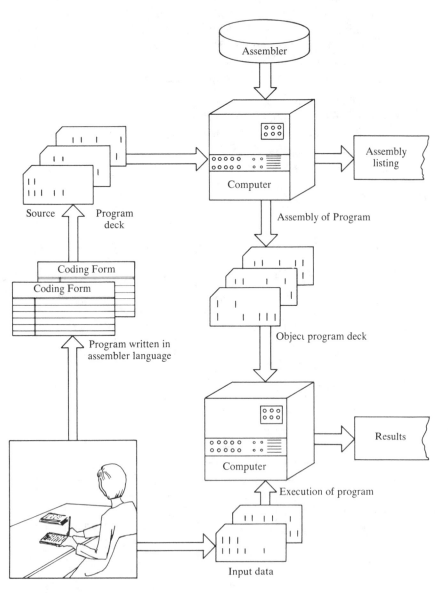

Figure 13–4   The assembly process—creating, assembling, and executing a program written in assembler language.

gram itself, converts each assembler language statement into a machine code. When all statements have been converted, an *assembly listing* and object program are produced. The object program consists of actual machine code corresponding to the assembler language statements written by the programmer. In many cases, the object program is punched into cards; in other cases, it is recorded on magnetic disks, magnetic tape, or punched paper tape. The *assembly listing* shows the original source program statements side by side with the object program instructions created from them. After an assembly listing is printed, most programmers refer to this listing rather than using their coding sheets again. An assembly listing of the program shown in Figure 13–3 is shown in Figure 13–5.

```
                                              START   256
000100   05 FO                        BEGIN    BALR    15,0
                            000102              USING   *,15
000102   58   30   F 012                        L       3,OLDOH
000106   5A   30   F 016                        A       3,RECPT
00010A   5B   30   F 01A                        S       3,ISSUE
00010E   50   30   F 01E                        ST      3,NEWOH
000112   0A 00                                  SVC     0
000114   00000009                      OLDOH    DC      F'9'
000118   00000004                      RECPT    DC      F'4'
00011C   00000006                      ISSUE    DC      F'6'
000120                                 NEWOH    DS      F
                                                END     BEGIN
```

Figure 13–5   Assembler listing for the program shown in Figure 13–3.

Consider an example of a simple inventory calculation. The programmer begins the calculations with an on-hand quantity, a receipt quantity, and an issue quantity. The new on-hand quantity can be computed using the following formula:

$$\text{NEW OH} = \text{OLD OH} + \text{RECPT} - \text{ISSUE}$$

The assembly language program to perform this computation is shown in Figure 13–3. The first three lines of coding are housekeeping instructions. The processing instructions start with the mnemonic operation code for *load*. This L is converted by the assembler into the actual machine code for Load, Hexadecimal 58 (binary 01011000). The 3 is the number of the computer register in which a word from storage is to be loaded. OLDOH is the symbolic address of the word in storage to be stored into computer register 3. The assembly listing for this program, shown in Figure 13–5, shows both the source language statement and the associated machine code. The translation of the other processing instructions—A for *add,* S for *subtract,* and ST for *store*—can be examined in Figure 13–5. The SVC instruction is used to inform the computer that there are no more computations in this program. The three DC instructions are used to establish numerical values for OLDOH, RECPT, and ISSUE. The DS instruction is used to identify NEWOH, where the computer result will be stored. The END instruction informs the assembler that the termination of the program has been reached.

The assembly language presented in the previous example was for use on the IBM System/370 computer. Assembly languages for other computers are different and therefore prevent a program written in the assembler language of one machine to be used on another machine.*

Some assembly languages include instructions which are equivalent to a specific set of one or more ordinary instructions in the same language. These instructions are called *macroinstructions,* or simply *macros;* and, when assembled, they are expanded into a predefined set of fundamental instructions. The assembler that processes macros is often called a *macro assembler* and the language that contains these macros is likewise called a *macro assembly language*.

An example of a macro would be a MOVE instruction. This instruction is assembled into two machine code instructions: MOVE A, B, would cause the macro assembler to generate *Load A* and *Store A at B* instructions.

☐ Review Questions

1. Name three levels of programming languages.
2. Briefly define the following terms:
   (a) coding
   (b) program
   (c) symbolic languages
   (d) machine language
   (e) source program
   (f) translator
   (g) object program
3. What is an assembly language?
4. Explain how an assembler is used.
5. What is a source program deck?
6. What is an assembly listing?
7. Explain how a program written in assembly language differs from a machine language program.
8. Discuss some characteristics of assembly language.
9. What is a macro assembler? A macroinstruction?

---

* Compatibility between assembler languages exists within a family of computers produced by one manufacturer.

☐ Higher-Level Languages

In contrast to assembly languages and machine languages, in which the source language is still highly dependent upon a particular hardware system, higher-level languages* relate to the procedures being coded and are thus relatively machine independent. Therefore, a program coded in a higher-level language can be executed on any computer system that has a translator available for that programming language.

Essentially, higher-level languages are completely general in application, although among the contemporary systems several are clearly better adapted to numeric-type problems and others are better adapted to nonnumeric-type applications. Three of the more popular numeric-type languages are FORTRAN, BASIC, and APL; while popular languages for nonnumeric-type applications are COBOL and RPG. A higher-level language designed for multipurpose use is PL/1.

Many higher-level programming languages have been introduced in recent years, primarily because this type of language simplifies the programming task. The use of a higher-level language reduces the requirement that the user have a detailed knowledge of digital computers. This, in turn, allows the user to concentrate more deeply on steps that are more closely related to the problem. Higher-level programming languages are widely accepted and used by people not having a strong background in computer programming.

A program can be written in a much shorter time when a higher-level language is used, primarily because the language includes a set of very powerful instructions. A higher-level language instruction may accomplish the same operation as several lower-level machine instructions. Both the coding and debugging tasks are simplified when one uses a higher-level language. Many of these languages are self-documenting; i.e., a listing of the program will suffice for documentation purposes. However, this usually applies only to very small computer programs.

A *compiler* is used to translate a program written in a higher-level language into the basic language of the computer.

As in the assembly process, the process of carrying out a particular computation consists of two stages. First, the source-language program is translated, or compiled, into the equivalent object program; second, the object program is executed. The two stages are kept separate. Compilation is completed before any actual computation begins, and, in fact, the entire object program is stored away before any part of it is executed.

At the completion of the compilation, one of two things may happen. The object program may be immediately executed, or it may be re-

---

* Also called *procedure-oriented languages, problem-oriented languages,* and *compiler languages.*

corded on some suitable medium, such as punched cards, punched paper tape, magnetic tape, or magnetic disk for use later (as shown in Figure 13–6). In the latter case, the object program must be read back into the main computer memory before the computer can execute the program. The two-stage process provides for the source-language program to be compiled on one computer and later executed on the same or a different computer. The compile-and-immediately-execute process is often called the *compile-and-go* process.

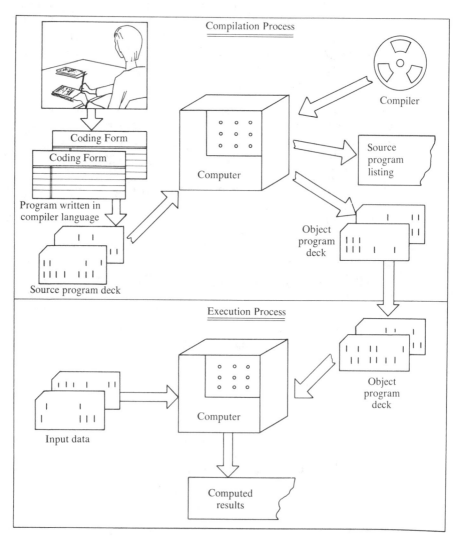

Figure 13–6   Creating, compiling, and executing a program written in a higher-level language.

Both assemblers and compilers provide auxiliary functions that assist the user in documenting and correcting the instructions written. These functions include program listings and error indications that are detected during the translating process. The errors detected by the assembler or compiler are called *diagnostics*. The process of correcting errors is commonly referred to as *program debugging*.

All I want you to tell me is which programming language to use.

☐ Interpretive Languages

Interpretive coding permits programming in a language that is easier to learn than machine language. Many of the earlier interpretive languages were similar to machine language; however, they provide a feature and operations that were not inherent in the computer used for executing the program. Interpretive systems are used primarily on computers that are too slow to permit efficient use of algorithmic languages, and on small computers (especially minicomputers and microcomputers) that have implemented higher-level programming systems such as BASIC or FORTRAN. They are also commonly used on small computers to provide a language that resembles machine language but is actually much easier to learn and use. A program written in such a language is ordinarily executed one statement at a time by a translator called an *interpreter*. The interpreter is a computer program that must be entered into the memory of the computer and remain there during the execution of a program written in interpretive language.

They are usually lengthy programs that can occupy several hundred or even several thousand locations of computer memory. Hence, an interpreter may occupy a major portion of the memory of a small computer.

☐ The Major Higher-Level Programming Languages

The major higher-level programming languages are BASIC, FORTRAN, COBOL, and to a lesser extent PL/1, RPG, and APL. These languages were developed by computer manufacturers and by committees consisting of representatives from manufacturers and users to make the computer available to the user directly without his or her having to work through an intermediary symbolic or machine language programmer. The ease of learning and the ease of coding make it possible for a computer user to learn programming in a short time. Through the use of a terminal or by coding the program on the proper coding form, the user can run the programs and produce the answer with little effort.

A brief description of these languages is contained in the following sections. A more complete description of each language is contained in Chapters 14 through 19.

☐ BASIC

BASIC, an acronym for Beginner's All-purpose Symbolic Instruction Code, was designed primarily for *conversational* (interactive) computing on a time-sharing computer system. The language was designed and developed at Dartmouth College for people who have had no experience with using computers or writing computer programs. Although all the higher-level languages are easy to learn and use, this is especially true of BASIC. Today, BASIC is available on all time-sharing computer systems, most minicomputers, many large and middle-scale machines, and some microcomputers.

A program written in BASIC is usually submitted directly to the computer from a terminal, usually a teletypewriter or a typewriter. In BASIC systems, compilation of statements occur as the user types them. To use a BASIC system, the user simply types his program (or enters it via paper tape) on the terminal and issues a command—such as RUN—to execute the program. Program answers are produced immediately. One can easily see that the interactive problem-solving capability available with BASIC can be extremely valuable to the user.

The BASIC language consists of about 20 statement types, such as GO TO, LET, FOR, PRINT, READ, and END. It is the easiest of all computer languages; it can be learned in a matter of hours and mastered in a matter of days. Each statement in a BASIC program has a line number which serves to identify the line and specifies the order in which the statements are executed by the computer.

Consider a program for computing the compound interest of an initial bank deposit of $2 000 invested at 5% interest for 5 to 20 years. The compound interest formula is

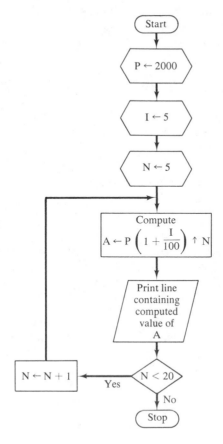

Figure 13–7   Compound interest problem.

$$a = p \left(1 \times \frac{i}{100} \right)^{n}$$

where p is the principal (the amount originally invested), i is the yearly rate of interest, n is the number of years, and a is the amount (principal + interest). A flowchart for performing the required calculations is shown in Figure 13–7, and a BASIC program and printed results are shown below.

```
100   REMARK COMPOUND INTEREST PROBLEM
200   LET P = 2000
300   LET I = 5
400   REMARK CALCULATE VALUES FOR 5–20 YEARS
500   FOR N = 5 TO 20
600     LET A = P * (1 + I / 100) ↑ N
700     PRINT "IN"; N; "YEARS, THE AMOUNT WILL BE"; A
800   NEXT N
900   END
```

This program illustrates a simple loop. The statements numbered 200, 300, and 900 are executed only once, whereas statements 500, 600, 700, and 800 are executed 16 times (for N = 5, 6, 7, 8, . . . , 20).
Output produced by this program is as follows:

```
IN  5 YEARS, THE AMOUNT WILL BE 2552.56
IN  6 YEARS, THE AMOUNT WILL BE 2680.19
IN  7 YEARS, THE AMOUNT WILL BE 2814.2
IN  8 YEARS, THE AMOUNT WILL BE 2954.91
IN  9 YEARS, THE AMOUNT WILL BE 3102.66
IN 10 YEARS, THE AMOUNT WILL BE 3257.79
IN 11 YEARS, THE AMOUNT WILL BE 3420.68
IN 12 YEARS, THE AMOUNT WILL BE 3591.71
IN 13 YEARS, THE AMOUNT WILL BE 3771.3
IN 14 YEARS, THE AMOUNT WILL BE 3959.86
IN 15 YEARS, THE AMOUNT WILL BE 4157.86
IN 16 YEARS, THE AMOUNT WILL BE 4365.75
IN 17 YEARS, THE AMOUNT WILL BE 4584.04
IN 18 YEARS, THE AMOUNT WILL BE 4813.24
IN 19 YEARS, THE AMOUNT WILL BE 5053.9
IN 20 YEARS, THE AMOUNT WILL BE 5306.6
```

Although far from being as powerful as FORTRAN or PL/I, BASIC is a language adequate for many scientific and business problems. BASIC is discussed further in Chapter 14.

Cartoon from "Computer Science Mathematics"

☐ COBOL

COBOL is an acronym for COmmon Business Oriented Language. It is an internationally accepted programming language developed for general commercial and business use. COBOL is a high-level compiler language in which the source program is written using statements in restricted English, but in readable form. A program coded in COBOL bears little resemblance to a computer's machine code. For example, in an accounting program, where new stock received is added to inventory, the COBOL statement might appear as ADD RECEIPTS TO STOCK ON HAND.

The COBOL compiler would examine each word of this statement separately. ADD becomes an operating instruction. RECEIPTS is a location where data are located. TO directs attention to what follows, STOCK ON HAND. STOCK ON HAND represents data stored somewhere in computer storage. After thus analyzing this statement, the COBOL compiler would generate several machine code instructions which could be used to carry out this specific calculation (Figure 13–8).

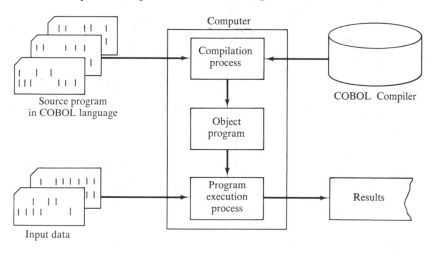

Figure 13–8 Compiling and executing (compile-and-go) a source program written in COBOL.

COBOL provides facilities for describing the program, specifying the computer it is to be run on, indicating the data formats and files it will use, and stating the operations to be performed on the data. Each COBOL program is broken down into four major divisions:

Identification Division—Used to identify the programmer's name, the name of program, the outputs of the compilation, along with the date, location, and security classification of compilation.

Environment Division—Used to identify the equipment needed for compiling the source program and for executing the object program.

Data Division—Used to describe the files and records that the object program is to manipulate or create.

Procedures Division—Used to tell the computer the steps to be performed using data described in the data division in order to solve the problem.

COBOL PROGRAM SHEET

Program Name: SORT
Programmer: D. D. SPENCER

Program No.:   Pay No.:   Charge No.:   Ext.:

Graphic: Punch:

Sheet 2 of 2   Date MAR 12

SEQUENCE (Page / Serial)	A (7–8)	B (12–)
1 0 0 0 2 6		DATA RECORD IS INPUT-RECORD
1 0 0 0 2 7		LABEL RECORDS ARE OMITTED
1 0 0 0 2 8		RECORDING MODE IS F.
1 0 0 0 2 9	01	INPUT-RECORD PICTURE X(80).
1 0 0 0 3 0	FD	OUTPUT-FILE
1 0 0 0 3 1		DATA RECORD IS OUTPUT-RECORD
1 0 0 0 3 2		LABEL RECORDS ARE OMITTED
1 0 0 0 3 3		RECORDING MODE IS F.
1 0 0 0 3 4	01	OUTPUT-RECORD PICTURE X(80).
1 0 0 0 3 5		PROCEDURE DIVISION.
1 0 0 0 3 6		DO-SORT.
1 0 0 0 3 7		SORT SORT-FILE ON ASCENDING KEY MAJOR-KEY,MINOR-KEY
1 0 0 0 3 8		USING INPUT-FILE GIVING OUTPUT-FILE.
1 0 0 0 3 9		STOP RUN

ID/UPDATE SEQ — Key (73) — Serial (80)

334

COBOL PROGRAM SHEET

Program Name SORT
Programmer D. D. SPENCER
Sheet 1 of 2
Date MAR 12

SEQUENCE (Page) (Serial)	B	
1.0.0.0.1	IDENTIFICATION DIVISION.	
1.0.0.0.2	PROGRAM-ID. 'SORT'.	
1.0.0.0.3	AUTHOR. D. D. SPENCER.	
1.0.0.0.4	REMARKS.	
1.0.0.0.5	BASIC SORT PROGRAM.	
1.0.0.0.6	ENVIRONMENT DIVISION.	
1.0.0.0.7	CONFIGURATION SECTION.	
1.0.0.0.8	SOURCE-COMPUTER. IBM-370.	
1.0.0.0.9	OBJECT-COMPUTER. IBM-370.	
1.0.0.1.0	INPUT-OUTPUT SECTION.	
1.0.0.1.1	FILE-CONTROL.	
1.0.0.1.2	SELECT INPUT-FILE ASSIGN TO 'SORTIN' UTILITY.	
1.0.0.1.3	SELECT OUTPUT-FILE ASSIGN TO 'SORTING UTILITY	
1.0.0.1.4	DATA DIVISION.	
1.0.0.1.5	FILE SECTION.	
1.0.0.1.6	SD SORT-FILE	
1.0.0.1.7	RECORDING MODE IS F	
1.0.0.1.8	DATA RECORD IS SORT-CARD.	
1.0.0.1.9	01 SORT-CARD.	
1.0.0.2.0	02 FILLER PICTURE X(35).	
1.0.0.2.1	02 MAJOR-KEY PICTURE X.	
1.0.0.2.2	02 FILLER PICTURE X(25).	
1.0.0.2.3	02 MINOR-KEY PICTURE 99.	
1.0.0.2.4	02 FILLER PICTURE X(17).	
1.0.0.2.5	FD INPUT-FILE	

Figure 13-9 COBOL Program.

COBOL uses a large number of reserved words that have special meanings. For example, reserved words such as MULTIPLY, EXAMINE, FLOAT, and ASSIGN have special meaning to the COBOL compiler and must be used according to COBOL language rules. These words, which number about 250, are an inherent part of the COBOL language and are not available for use as data or procedure names. In the statement

ADD OVERTIME TO NORMAL HOURS

the reserved words are ADD and TO which instruct the COBOL compiler to generate the machine code necessary to perform addition. OVERTIME and NORMAL-HOURS (defined in the Data Division) will be names or labels referring to units of data.

Figure 13–9 is a sample COBOL program. It is easily read—even by a non-programmer—because of its similarity to English. Since COBOL programs are relatively machine-independent, they can be compiled and run on a variety of different machines. Many users develop all their programs in this language, mainly to bridge the gap between the computer they are using today and computer systems that will eventually replace them. COBOL is discussed further in Chapter 16.

I guess it didn't like that COBOL program.

☐ PL/I

PL/I is a general-purpose or multi-purpose programming language which can be used for both commercial and scientific applications. PL/I aims at combining the problem-solving facility of scientific languages, such as FORTRAN, with the data-handling capabilities of commercial business languages—such as COBOL—in order to produce a language that may be used equally well in either application.

PL/I can be a very simple language to use; nevertheless, it can be employed to handle extremely complex computing problems. One of its most important characteristics is its modularity—that is, the presence of different subsets of the language for different applications at different levels of complexity. The language has a block structure which allows program segmentation into blocks of language statements or subroutines of a total program. PL/I is versatile enough to process a wide variety of data types, such as fixed and floating point numbers and character and bit strings. The language structure is *free form*. No special forms are needed for coding, since the significance of each statement depends upon its own format and not on its position within a fixed framework. Each PL/I statement terminates with a semicolon (;). Because the PL/I compiler recognizes the semicolon as a terminator, part of a statement or many statements can be written on one coding line.

PL/I has the best debugging capability of all existing programming language. A "default feature" by which every error or unspecified option is given a valid interpretation minimizes the effects of programming errors. For example, a PL/I compiler, when confronted with an unmatched left parenthesis, will automatically insert a right one in the proper place.

Figure 13–10 below shows a PL/I program that will read the maximum and minimum temperature for every day of the week, and calculate and print the average temperature for each day of the week.

PL/I is discussed further in Chapter 17.

```
WEATHER: PROCEDURE;
     DECLARE MAXDAY(7), MINDAY(7), AVERAGE(7);
     READ LIST ((MAXDAY(I), MINDAY(I)) I = 1 TO 7);
     AVERAGE = (MAXDAY + MINDAY) / 2;
     WRITE ((MAXDAY(I), MINDAY(I), AVERAGE(I))
     I = 1 TO 7) (2F(5), F(8, 1), SPACE);
END WEATHER;
```

Figure 13–10 A PL/I program to compute average temperature.

☐ FORTRAN

FORTRAN is an acronym for FORmula TRANslation. It is a high-level language for scientific and mathematical use, in which the source program is written using a combination of algebraic formulas and English statements of a standard but readable form.

As with COBOL and PL/I, the source program written in FORTRAN language defines the operation that the computer must perform. Operations and data are stated, although the arrangement may be in the form of an equation rather than a sentence. For example, the COBOL statement

MULTIPLY RATE TIMES HOURS TO GET GROSS PAY

may be expressed in FORTRAN as

GRPAY = RATE * HOURS

or may even be abbreviated to:

GP = RT * HRS

A FORTRAN program consists of executable statements, non-executable statements, and data items. Data items in FORTRAN are either variables (A, X, HOURS) or constants (26, 103.7, 63E2). The actual operations of the program are expressed by means of executable statements (such as X = X + 1, or DO 40 K = 1, 7).

The language of FORTRAN consists largely of mathematical notation. The formation of expressions in FORTRAN is quite similar to an expression in algebra. For example, the mathematical expression

$$y = 3x^3 - 4x^2 + 12x - 34$$

is represented in FORTRAN as

Y = 3 * X ** 3 − 4 * X ** 2 + 12 * X − 34

The symbol for multiplication is an asterisk (*); the symbol for exponentiation is a double asterisk (**). Other arithmetic operators in FORTRAN are addition (+), subtraction (−), and division (/).

Consider the following problem. An airplane flying at altitude A passes directly over a point P. If its speed is S, compute its distance from point P at times T = 1, 2, 3, . . . , 60 seconds after the pass. The reader may wish to refer to the following figure.

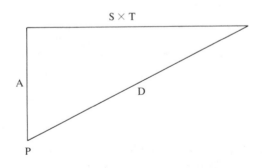

The distance travelled by the airplane after passing over point P is S × T, and the required distance is D. The formula

$$D = \sqrt{A^2 + (S \times T)^2}$$

can be used to compute the required distance.

A FORTRAN program to compute D is shown in Figure 13–11.

An examination of the program shown in Figure 13–11 more or less points out that the FORTRAN language may be more useful to mathematicians or engineers than it would to a programmer of business problems. This is certainly true, primarily because of its mathematical-like notation; however, FORTRAN is used by many business users to solve commercial problems.

FORTRAN is discussed further in Chapter 16.

Say something in FORTRAN.

☐ RPG

Report Program Generator (RPG) computer language provides a simple method for writing instructions for a computer to accomplish a variety of commercial data processing jobs. The purpose of a RPG is simply to generate a report program. This program in turn is used to write the desired report.

RPG is used extensively in small scale computer systems and is even finding acceptance in larger computer installations where there is a need for the production of business reports. There are two common versions of RPG: RPG-I is used with the IBM System/360, Univac 9000 series, IBM 1130, and IBM 1800. RPG-II is somewhat more flexible and used with IBM System/3, IBM System/32, and other computers. The lan-

FORTRAN CODING FORM

Program	AIRPLANE DISTANCE COMPUTATION		Punching Instructions								Page 1 of 1	
			Graphic						Card Form #	*	Identification	
Programmer	D. D. SPENCER	Date	Punch								73 80	

```
C       AIRPLANE DISTANCE COMPUTATION
        S = 1.0
        A = 3.0
        DO 10 I = 1,60
        T = I
        D = SQRT(A**2 + (S*T)**2)
10      WRITE(6,20) T,D
20      FORMAT(F5.0,F10.3)
        STOP
        END
```

ASD 656

Figure 13–11   A FORTRAN program to compute an airplane's distance from a given point.

guages are so similar that differences between them are of more academic than operational interest.

RPG is an easy language to learn and use. It is capable of handling several input files, selecting certain records from the files, performing limited mathematical computations, and producing the desired report from the records. During the process, it can also update records from the master file.

The use of RPG is restricted to situations where a simple report is desired from the computer rather than some complex processing or multiple output. It is a highly formalized language with very rigid specifications. Unlike other compiler languages where instructions are given, in RPG the programmer need only furnish data, specifying conditions and processing desired on special specification forms. Generally, four different types of specification sheets are used in writing RPG programs. They specify

(1) the form of input data,
(2) the input-output devices to be used in executing the program,

(3) the calculations that are required,

(4) the form of output data.

A program specified on these special forms is translated by RPG into machine code instructions.

RPG is discussed further in Chapter 18.

☐ **APL**

APL is a language for describing procedures in the processing of information. It can be used to describe mathematical procedures having nothing to do with computers, or to describe (to a human being) how a computer works. Most commonly, however, it is used for programming in the ordinary sense of directing computers how to process numeric or alphabetic data.

The language was invented by Dr. Kenneth E. Iverson and described in a book entitled *A Programming Language* (published by John Wiley & Sons in 1962).

APL is one of the most concise, consistent, and powerful programming languages ever devised. Operations on single items extend simply and naturally to arrays of any size and shape. Thus, for instance, a matrix addition that in other higher-level languages (such as BASIC or FORTRAN) might require two loops and a half-dozen statements, becomes simply $A + B$ in APL.

The language is very mathematically oriented. It is, however, finding widespread acceptance among a variety of users, many of them in business and education.

APL is discussed further in Chapter 19.

☐ **Comparing Programming Languages**

The successful application of computing equipment to a problem solution may be critically affected by the software skills of the programming staff. Return on the investment of computing equipment is partly a function of expressing instructions in a language powerful enough to obtain useful results at a reasonable cost. Thus, choosing a programming language has become a major task in many installations and among many communities of computer users. The choice of language can often have more effect on the success of a project than the choice of computer. Let us now look at some of the problems one faces when choosing a programming language.

Programming Languages Are Not Standard

It is difficult to compare any two languages adequately, since neither is defined precisely enough so that direct comparisons can be made.

Compilers Are Not Standard

There is usually more than one compiler for each language, which implies that more than one version of the language is actually implemented. This is more often true when the compilers are on two different compilers for the same language are for the same computer.

Users Are Not Standard

One must consider the language preferences of the different users. One group of users may prefer using a language that is disliked or ignored by another set of users. This preference is often due to different educational backgrounds, professional backgrounds, stubbornness, or company preference.

Operating Systems Are Not Standard

One must consider the operating system under which the processor and translated program operate. Many systems allow on-line use of languages, while other systems allow programs to run off-line.

Benchmarks

The following benchmarks must be considered when comparing programming languages:

1. Fast Object Code and Efficient Storage Utilization—Assembler-language coding (on any computer) written by an experienced programmer produces the "best" code. "Best" here implies faster operating time and less storage space. A good compiler cannot produce as good coding as a good machine-language programmer can; however, a good compiler can produce more efficient coding than an inexperienced programmer can. A rule-of-thumb estimate is that good assembler-language programs often run three or four times faster than compiler-produced codes and take about half as much storage.

   Most higher-level languages manipulate words (groups of bits) rather than single bits or characters, thus making a very poor memory-utilization comparison with assembler languages, where data is always packed in the minimum amount of storage.

2. Ease of Learning—Higher-level languages are generally best for most users. These languages are easier to learn than are assembler languages of the same complexity.

3. Self-Documenting—Documentation is a discipline in which all those who write programs must become adept, regardless of the programming language used. Higher-level programming languages can be written so that the programs are often self-documenting. To do this, however, the user must use comment statements describing operations, variables, and the functions of different program paths.

4. Ease of Coding and Understanding—It is easier to code programs in higher-level languages since the notation is considerably more problem-oriented. It is also much easier to understand the programs after they have been written.

5. Ease of Debugging—Freedom for the user is the salient feature of assembly languages. This means freedom to improve efficiency and sophistication and to make sophisticated errors. Higher-level languages provide safeguards that protect the user from his or her own failings.

   A problem written in a higher-level programming language is generally easier to debug than one written in an assembler language. One reason is that the notation is more natural, and more attention can be paid to the logic of the problem being solved, with less worry about the details of assembler coding. Another reason is that the source program will generally be shorter, thereby reducing the chance for additional errors.

6. Ease of Maintaining—Because of the notation, higher-level language programs are easier to modify. One of the great difficulties in modifying assembler-language programs is to make sure that a change in one instruction does not create major problems elsewhere in the program.

7. Ease of Conversion—The costs associated with converting a library of existing programs from one computer to another are very high. Higher-level programming languages are relatively machine independent, thereby relaxing the conversion task between different hardware systems.

8. Program Development Time—The use of higher-level programming languages will reduce the total amount of elapsed time from the inception of a problem to its solution. This is the greatest single overall advantage of higher-level languages. On large problems the elapsed time may be reduced from months to weeks, while on smaller problems the elapsed time may be reduced from days to hours.

9. Translating Time—The computer time required for translating source-language assembler programs is much less than that required to compile higher-level, source-language programs

into machine code. The compilation time varies with each processor; however, it is a significant factor that must be considered when developing programs with a higher-level programming language.

10. Inability of the Language to Express All Needed Operations—Some higher-level programming languages do not allow one to do all the operations that are required for the proper solution to a given problem. Many of the higher-level languages have weak or inadequate input/output facilities, no bit-handling capabilities, inabilities to manipulate characters of information, etc. This problem usually occurs when a user has chosen the language unwisely for a particular application.

11. Control Over Program and Data Location—Many small computers depend on the location of programs and data for efficiency in both execution time and memory utilization. Higher-level languages offer less flexibility than do assembler languages in specifying program layout and data storage.

Choosing a Programming Language

In the early days of electronic computing, there was no choice of programming languages. By choosing a computer, one automatically chose the assembler language and machine language that went with it. Today, however, a variety of programming languages are available for most of the existing computers. Following is a list of types of languages presently available:

- *Machine Language*—All computers can be programmed in the basic language of the computer.

- *Assembler Language*—All computer manufacturers offer a symbolic assembler language for each computer. Many computers have assembler languages of different levels.

- *Business-Oriented Language*—COBOL and RPG are not the only business-oriented programming languages; however, they are the best known and are definitely becoming more common.

- *Scientific-Oriented Language*—FORTRAN and BASIC are available on all large- and medium-scale machines, many small-scale machines, and several minicomputers. APL is available on the IBM System/360, System/370, IBM 5100, and several other machines.

- *General Languages*—PL/1 is commercially available on the IBM System/360 and System/370 as well as on several other machines.

- *Conversational Languages*—Several programming languages have been implemented as on-line conversational languages. BASIC, APL, and FORTRAN have been implemented on many machines.

The choice of language narrows somewhat when the user selects a specific computer. Some machines have two or more assembly languages. Some machines have more than one scientific-oriented language; e.g., FORTRAN, BASIC, and APL may be available. In short, the choice appears narrow, but the user does have a wide choice as to what type of language to use—assembler language or higher-level language, business-oriented language or scientific-oriented language, on-line conversational language or batch-processing language, or general programming language or COBOL/FORTRAN combination.

Some criteria that should be considered in the selection of a programming language follow.

Ease of Use

Languages such as BASIC, APL, FORTRAN, RPG, COBOL, and PL/1 are the easiest to use. Less convenient are the symbolic assembler languages, and one should never even consider using machine language. For convenience in learning, the higher-level languages are favored because the user need not have a detailed working knowledge of the computer.

Personnel Competence

The chosen language is often the language best known at a particular facility. If most of the employees of a business know COBOL, then it is a simple task to produce a working program. If the staff is more familiar with assembler language, FORTRAN, BASIC, or PL/1, then that language is the logical choice.

Language Suitability for Problem

The language chosen should contain all the elements needed to solve the particular class of problems for which it is being considered. For example, a language that provides good computational facilities (FORTRAN) may not provide the alphanumeric character-manipulating ability required for a specific inventory control problem. Conversely, a language that contains too many facilities is not desirable, since the user pays a heavy price for the facilities not needed for the specific problem.

Availability

Before the user selects a programming language, he or she should make sure that the language has been implemented on the machine configuration being considered. It is useless to select a language and then find out that the compiler will not run on a specific hardware system because it lacked a tape transport, card reader, disk file, etc.

Speed of Operation

Some high-level language compilers produce object programs that are as efficient as those obtained from an intermediate-level programmer using an assembler language.

Speed of Compilation and Programming

Compiling time is worth money, and this time varies between different languages and different implementations of the same language. Although generally slower in compilation speed than the assembler languages, the higher-level languages allow programming work to be done more rapidly than is possible with the assembler languages.

History of Previous Use

When a user has tentatively selected a language and has determined that a compiler is available for a specific hardware configuration, he or she should then investigate the history of use of this language. Were previous users satisfied with the language? How difficult is it to train people to use the language? What conversion problems will there be if this language choice is finalized?

Nature of the Job

Certain languages are better suited for certain specific applications. Business problems, which usually require a small amount of computation and a large amount of input/output data handling, can best be programmed in either PL/1, COBOL, RPG, or assembler language. In scientific programming, where the problem can conveniently be expressed in mathematical notation, languages such as FORTRAN, PL/1, BASIC, or APL are usually chosen.

▢ Review Exercises

10. What is a higher-level programming language?
11. List six higher-level languages.
12. What is the function of a compiler?
13. What kinds of applications are more suitable for COBOL? For FORTRAN? For PL/1?
14. Discuss the similarities and differences of assembly languages and higher-level languages.
15. What is the *compile-and-go* process?
16. What benefits would users realize if a common programming language were developed which could be used for all applications?

17. What is an interpreter?
18. Explain how an interpreter differs from a compiler.
19. Give the full name for each of the following acronyms:
    (a) COBOL
    (b) BASIC
    (c) FORTRAN
    (d) RPG
    (e) APL
20. Discuss some of the characteristics of the COBOL language.
21. Why is COBOL more appropriate for solving business problems than FORTRAN?
22. What is the name of a general-purpose programming language that can be used for solving many different types of problems?
23. What programming language is designed to work in an interactive environment?
24. List some of the problems one encounters when comparing programming languages.
25. List some factors that one may use in the selection of a programming language.

☐ Summary

For a computer to carry out a processing function, it must be provided with a set of instructions. These instructions (called a program) state precisely what must be done to accomplish the job.

Computer programs can be prepared using a variety of programming languages. The lowest form of language is called machine code. This language, which is the basic language of the computer, is difficult and inconvenient for direct human use and is never used in programming today's computers. The next level language is *assembly language*. In this language, each machine instruction is represented by a symbolic equivalent. A program written in symbolic assembly code is later translated into machine code by an *assembler*.

Higher-level programming languages are often called *compiler languages*. These languages are less machine-dependent than assembly languages. Higher-level languages are widely used by people who do not have a detailed knowledge of computers or assembly language programming. Programs written in these languages are translated into machine code by a *compiler*.

A brief overview of six popular programming languages has been presented in this chapter. The purpose has been to acquaint you with the general structure of each language and to introduce you to some of their characteristics. Each language has strengths and weaknesses. COBOL and RPG, for example, are better suited than FORTRAN or APL for data processing applications that involve the manipulation of large business files. FORTRAN or APL, on the other hand, are easier to learn than COBOL and RPG and are well suited to processing scientific data. PL/I combines features of both FORTRAN and COBOL and introduces additional features not found in either of those languages. BASIC is the easiest language of the six to learn and use.

Key Terms

machine code	interpreter
symbolic language	conversational computing
source program	interactive computing
object program	macroinstructions
assembler	macros
compiler	macro assembly language
assembly listing	COBOL
programming	RPG
coding	PL/I
higher-level language	FORTRAN
program	BASIC
syntax	APL
semantics	compile-and-go
translator	diagnostics
assembly language	program debugging
source program deck	

six

Programming Languages

14

BASIC

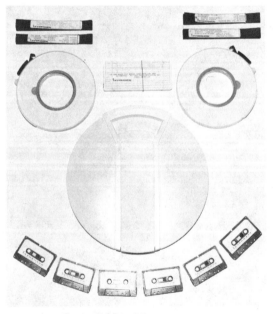

Courtesy of Interdata

BASIC is a language designed for solving mathematic and scientific problems: however, it can be used to solve problems in business and social sciences. Since BASIC has a relatively small set of instructions and few rules for correct coding, it is an easy language to learn and use.

The primary purpose of this chapter is to provide the reader with an elementary knowledge of BASIC so that he or she may write programs which will instruct the computer to solve simple problems in business, science, mathematics, or social sciences.

☐ Introduction

The BASIC language includes eleven built-in algebraic functions and eleven matrix functions that are easily available to the user. The algebraic functions include the computation of sine, cosine, exponent, square root, absolute value, natural logarithm, etc. The matrix functions (not included in this chapter) include add two matrices, print the entire matrix, multiply two matrices, invert a matrix, etc. Many computer users find these features of BASIC to be a great advantage and use them in solving many of the more complex algebraic problems found in their daily work.

The most common statements in BASIC are:

```
REM        IF THEN      END
LET        FØR          PRINT
READ       NEXT         GØ TØ
DATA       INPUT
```

These statements are used to form BASIC programs.

Consider the following problem. A sheet of paper is 0.5 mm thick. A stack of sheets of paper was started by laying down 2 sheets. The next addition to the stack was double the first, or 4 sheets. The third addition was double the second, or 8 sheets. If this process continued until 32 additions had been made, how high would the stack be? The program shown in Figure 14–1 computes this value and illustrates some of the more commonly used BASIC statements.

```
10   REM MØUNTAIN ØF PAPER
15   PRINT "NUMBER", "HEIGHT"
20   PRINT "ØF SHEETS", "IN MILLIMETERS"
25   PRINT
30   LET S=2
35   LET A=2
40   FØR D=1 TO 32
45   PRINT S, S*.5
50   LET A=2*A
55   LET S=S+A
60   NEXT D
65   END

RUN

NUMBER          HEIGHT
ØF SHEETS       IN MILLIMETERS

2               1
6               3
14              7
30              15
62              31
126             63
254             127
510             255
1022            511
2046            1023
```

4094	2047
8190	4095
16382	8191
32766	16383
65534.	32767
131070.	65535.
262142.	131071.
524286.	262143.
1.04857E+06	524287.
2.09715E+06	1.04857E+06
4.19430E+06	2.09715E+06
8.38861E+06	4.19430E+06
1.67772E+07	8.38861E+06
3.35544E+07	1.67772E+07
6.71089E+07	3.35544E+07
1.34218E+08	6.71089E+07
2.68435E+08	1.34218E+08
5.36871E+08	2.68435E+08
1.07374E+09	5.36871E+08
2.14748E+09	1.07374E+09
4.29497E+09	2.14748E+09
8.58993E+09	4.29497E+09

**Figure
14–1**   Mountain of paper program.

Although all BASIC program statements must have line numbers assigned by the program writer, *system commands* enable the user to communicate with the operating system of the computer. Thus, the command RUN at the bottom of the program in Figure 14–1 is a system command that instructs the computer to process the program. The printed answer following RUN is the computer's response to this command.

The program determines that the stack of paper is 4.29497E + 09, or 4 294 970 000 millimeters high. This converts to 4 294 970 meters, or about 4 294 kilometers, high. This stack of paper is 1 451 times as high as the Sears Tower, the tallest building in the world.

The first statement in the program is a REM (Remark) statement, which enables us to insert a program name or clarifying information into the program. The REM statement is not executed by the computer; it merely provides information to anyone reading the program. The general form of the REM statement is

line number   REM   *comment*

where *line number* is an integer between 1 and 9 999 and *comment* can be any arrangement of numbers or alphabetic characters.

Every statement in a BASIC program must have a line number. The computer will process the program in line number order—line number 10 first, line number 15 second, line number 20 next, and so on.

In BASIC, a *variable name* is either a single letter, such as A, B, C, . . . , Z, or a letter followed by a single digit, such as A0, A1, A2, . . . , B0, B1, B2, . . . , and so on. Symbols such as *, +, or • are not allowed in variable names.

Special symbols include those that have particular meaning in arithmetic operations and those used for punctuation.

Arithmetic Symbols

↑	Exponentiation (raising to a power)
*	Multiplication
/	Division
+	Addition
−	Subtraction

Punctuation Symbols

.	Period (or decimal point)
,	Comma
:	Colon
;	Semicolon
$	Dollar sign
"	Quotation marks
'	Apostrophe
(	Left parentheses
)	Right parentheses
&	Ampersand
?	Question mark
%	Percent sign
#	Number sign

BASIC is capable of handling decimal numbers up to six digits in length. These numbers may or may not be signed and may or may not contain a decimal point.

Examples

$$12 \quad -63 \quad 4.390 \quad -.007 \quad 634217$$

Numbers appearing this way in a program are called *constants,* as their meaning does not change. Numbers larger than six digits are represented in another way, by means of what is known as *E notation.* The letter E actually means "times 10 to the power of," and it is particularly valuable for representing very large or very small numbers.

Examples

16 500 000 is represented in E notation as 16.5E + 06
.000 012 7 is represented in E notation as 1.27E − 05

The computer normally performs its operations according to a hierarchy of operations. The system will search through an arithmetic formula from left to right and do specific operations according to the following pattern:

1. Exponentiation
2. Multiplication and division
3. Addition and subtraction

One can alter this order of operations by using parentheses in the formula. The parentheses have no effect on the formula itself other than to direct the order of operations. The computer will always find the innermost set of parentheses and evaluate the part of the formula it finds according to the hierarchy of operations.

Examples

$A + B * C \uparrow 2$ (*C* is squared; the product is multiplied by *B*; *A* is then added to the product)

$A + B/C * D$ (*B* is divided by *C*; the result is multiplied by *D*; *A* is then added to the product)

On lines 30, 35, 50, and 55, we find BASIC *arithmetic assignment* statements. The word LET is used to introduce this type of statement. On lines 30, the variable *S* is assigned a value of 2; on line 35, the variable *A* is assigned a value of 2; on line 50, the product of 2 times *A* is assigned to *A*; and on line 55, the value of *A* is added to the variable *S*.

That briefly is how to write programs in BASIC.

Lines 40, 45, 50, 55, and 60 put the program into a looping or iterative process. The FOR/NEXT statements are always used together and have the general form

line number FOR $v = n_1$ to n_2 STEP n_3
_____ BASIC statement _____
_____ BASIC statement _____
_____ BASIC statement _____
_____ BASIC statement _____
_____ BASIC statement _____
line number NEXT v

where v is a variable name acting as an index, n_1 is the initial value given to the index, n_2 is the value of the index when the looping is completed, and n_3 is the amount by which the index should be increased after each iteration through the loop (if the increment is 1, this portion of the statement may be omitted as it is on line 40). In our example, the index (D) is initially set at 1 and the program steps called for in lines 45, 50, and 55 are executed. The end of the loop is reached in line 60. If a test shows that D (in this case 32) has not been reached, the index is increased by 1 and the next pass through the loop occurs. When the looping has been completed and the height of 32 additions of paper has been computed and totaled, program control moves to line 65.

The word PRINT is used in output operations to display program results. A statement that reads

100 PRINT X, Y, Z

would cause the values of the three variable names to be printed across the page, with X beginning at the left margin, Y beginning 15 spaces to the right, and Z beginning 30 spaces to the right. The width of many terminal printers (such as the teletypewriter) is 75 characters, and the use of commas in the PRINT statement automatically establishes a format of 5 columns of 15 characters each. This implicit format specification feature of BASIC is especially appreciated by problem-solvers who are not professional programmers. The statement in the program

45 PRINT S, S * .5

would cause the value of S to be printed 15 paces to the right.

If you wish to have the output data printed in a more compact form, use a *semicolon* instead of a comma. In other words, the semicolon serves a function similar to that of the comma, but also specifies that different spacing is to be used between printed values.

So far we have discussed the printing of values only, that is, data represented in the program by variables. It is also possible to print *messages* exactly as they are written in the program. Quotation marks serve a special purpose in statements used to print messages.

A PRINT statement containing quotation marks is the only statement in the BASIC language in which blanks are counted, and the computer will print the exact message enclosed in quotation marks. For exmaple, the statement

200 PRINT "COMPUTERS IN BUSINESS"

will cause the message

COMPUTERS IN BUSINESS

to be printed. Statements 15 and 20 in the "Mountain of Paper" program will cause the heading

NUMBER   HEIGHT
OF SHEETS   IN MILLIMETERS

to be printed.

Messages and variables can also be mixed in the same PRINT statement. For example, when the statement

100 PRINT "INVESTMENT = $ ", N

is processed by the computer, the *message* INVESTMENT = $ will be printed at the left margin of the paper, and the *value* of N will be printed to the right. Commas (or semicolons) must be inserted between items to be printed. If N represented a value of 174, then the printed message would appear as

INVESTMENT = $ 174

On line 65, we find an END statement. Every BASIC program must be terminated with this statement to which the highest numbered line number in the program is assigned. This statement identifies the end of the program and consequently terminates computer processing. Figure 14–2 is the flowchart for this BASIC program.

Review Questions

1. What are some advantages to using a programming language such as BASIC?
2. What types of problems can best be solved in BASIC?
3. Which of the following are invalid variables in BASIC? Why?
   (a) X   (c) A3   (e) XY3
   (b) 7A   (d) Z*   (f) AY
4. What is the purpose of the REM statement? Indicate the meaning of the following symbols.
   (a) *   (d) (
   (b) ↑   (e) +
   (c) /   (f) −

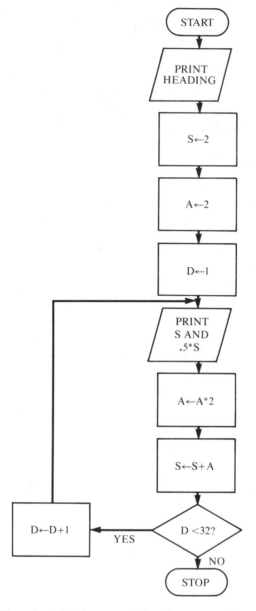

Figure   Flowchart for the mountain of paper problem.
14–2

5. Represent the following constants in E notation.
   (a) 6 321 420
   (b) .000 000 023

6. What is the function of the LET statement?

7. Convert the following mathematical expressions into BASIC notation.
   (a) $a^2 + b - 39$
   (b) $a + b/c$

8. What does the BASIC statement

    20   LET X = X + 1

accomplish?

9. Write BASIC statements to represent the following algebraic statements.
   (a) $r = a - 67 + b * 32p$
   (b) $x = 3x^2 + 4x - 27$

10. Write a BASIC statement to print the message:

    MICROCOMPUTERS ARE SMALL DIGITAL COMPUTERS

11. Write the PRINT statement to cause printing of your full name followed by the data field X.

12. What is the purpose of the comma in a PRINT statement that outputs numerical data? Of a semicolon?

13. Does the END statement have to be the last one in the BASIC program? Does it have to have the largest line number?

14. Write a program to add 631, 4210, 1167, and 36.4.

15. Have the computer compute and print a decimal value for 6/7.

16. Draw a flowchart and write a program to compute the square and cube values of the first 30 integers. The program should produce a printout in the following form.

N	Square	Cube
1	1	1
2	4	8
3	9	27
4	16	64
5	25	125
.	.	.
.	.	.
.	.	.

☐ The GO TO Statement

The simplest BASIC statement for altering the sequence of execution is the GO TO statement. This statement has the general form

        line number   GO TO   line number

Suppose, for example, that you want to print the message

    ELECT J. SMITH FOR CLASS PRESIDENT

many times.

The following program prints this message and keeps returning control to statement 10 where the message is printed again. When will this program stop printing the message? Well, let's run the program and see.

```
10      PRINT "ELECT J. SMITH FØR CLASS PRESIDENT"
20      GØ TØ 10
30      END

RUN

ELECT J. SMITH FØR CLASS PRESIDENT
ELECT J. SMITH FØR CLASS PRESIDENT
ELECT J. SMITH FØR CLASS PRESIDENT
ELECT J. SMITH FØR CLASS PRESIDENT
ELECT J. SMITH FØR CLASS PRESIDENT
ELECT J. SMITH FØR CLASS PRESIDENT
ELECT J. SMITH FØR CLASS PRESIDENT
```

As you might guess, the program would continue printing the message until the printing device was worn out. In the next section, you will find a statement that will allow us to repeat a statement and stop the process at some predetermined point.

☐ The IF-THEN Statement

The general form of the IF-THEN statement is

> *line number*   IF   *expression relation expression*
> THEN   *line number*

Both *expressions* are evaluated and compared by the *relation* in the statement. If the condition is *true,* program control is transferred to the line number given after THEN. If the condition is *false,* program control continues to the next statement following the IF-THEN statement.

In the IF-THEN statement, the following six relations symbols are used to compare values.

Symbol	Relation
$<$	less than
$<=$	less than or equal to
$>$	greater than
$>=$	greater than or equal to
$=$	equal to
$<>$	not equal to

The line number following the word THEN may be the line number of any executable statement (not DATA or REM) in the program.

Consider the BASIC program shown in Figure 14–3. This program illustrates program control using the IF-THEN and GO TO statements and three FOR-NEXT loops.

```
10    FØR N = 1 TØ 50
20    FØR A = 1 TØ 7
30    FØR B = 1 TØ 7
40    IF A ↑ 2 + B ↑ 2 < > N THEN 70
50    PRINT N; " = " ; A ↑ 2 ; " + " ; B ↑ 2
60    GØ TØ 90
70    NEXT B
80    NEXT A
90    NEXT N
99    END

RUN

2  = 1  + 1
5  = 1  + 4
8  = 4  + 4
10 = 1  + 9
13 = 4  + 9
17 = 1  + 16
18 = 9  + 9
20 = 4  + 16
25 = 9  + 16
26 = 1  + 25
29 = 4  + 25
32 = 16 + 16
34 = 9  + 25
37 = 1  + 36
40 = 4  + 36
41 = 16 + 25
45 = 9  + 36
50 = 1  + 49
```

Figure 14–3   Program to find all numbers less than 50 that can be written as the sum of two squares.

The program finds all numbers less than 50 that can be written as the sum of two squares. For example,

$$13 = 2^2 + 3^2$$

In the fourth statement in the program, the relation of "not equal to" was used in the IF-THEN statement to determine whether $A^2 + B^2$ was not equal to N. If the conditional part of this statement was satisfied ($A^2 + B^2$ not equal to N), then program control will be transferred to the statement at line number 70. If the condition was not satisfied (i.e., $2^2 + B^2$ equal to N), program control will continue with the next in-line statement (line number 50). The GO TO statement at line number 60 transfers program control to the statement at line number 90, thus by-passing the statements at line numbers 70 and 80.

☐ READ and DATA Statements

Look at the following program.

```
10     READ A, B, C
20     LET Y = A * B * C
30     PRINT "Y = " ; Y
40     DATA 60, 37, 14
50     END
```

How did that work? The READ statement tells the computer that some variables follow which have not yet been assigned values. To find their values, the computer searches for a DATA statement where the values are listed.

In this example, at line number 10 the computer "sees" the READ instruction and then the A; it searches for a DATA statement, finds it, and stores the first value in the DATA statement in the storage location for variable A.

```
10     READ  Ⓐ , . . .
20                 ↑
30                 |
40     DATA  ⑫
50
```

Values for B and C are found in the same way.

```
10     READ      Ⓐ    Ⓑ    Ⓒ
20                ↑    ↑    ↑
30                |    |    |
40     DATA     ⑥⓪  ③⑦  ⑫
```

When finished with the statement at line number 10, the computer has given A the value 60, B the value 37, and C the value 12. At line number 20, using A, B, and C, the value of Y is calculated in the following statement, the value of Y is printed.

The general form of READ and DATA statements is

> *line number*   READ   *list of variable names*
> *line number*   DATA   *list of data values*

where the values to be assigned to the variable names identified in a READ statement are found in a DATA statement.

▢ Review Exercises

17. What is the basic purpose of the GO TO statement?
18. Write a statement that will transfer program control to line number 100.
19. List the general form of the IF-THEN statement.
20. In the following program, what is the final value of S?

```
10      LET  S = 3
20      FØR  J = 1  TØ  4
30      IF  S < J  THEN  50
40      LET  S = S + 1
50      NEXT  J
60      END
```

21. Write a BASIC program to determine whether Y is between — 30 and + 30. If Y falls within these limits, print out TRUE; if not, FALSE.
22. Draw a flowchart and write a BASIC program to sum the numbers less than 100 that are divisible by 8.
23. Why are READ and DATA statements always linked together?
24. How many values will read by the follow statement?

```
200      READ A, B, C, X1, X2, X3
```

25. Draw a flowchart that could be used to write the following BASIC program.

```
10      READ  A
20      LET  B = 3
30      LET  C = 14 / B
40      LET  X = A + B + C
50      PRINT  X
60      DATA  6
70      END
```

26. Write a program that will read values for X, Y, and Z and print them, first in the order read and then in reverse order.

▢ The INPUT Statement

In the last section, we saw how data were assigned to variables using the READ and DATA statements. A more flexible way of assigning data values to variables is by using the INPUT statement. This statement allows data values to be entered while the computer is executing the program. Here is another version of the program shown on page 362.

```
10      INPUT  A
20      INPUT  B
30      INPUT  C
40      LET  Y = A * B * C
50      PRINT  "Y = " ; Y
```

```
60      END
RUN
?60
?37
?14
Y = 31080
```

The INPUT statement causes the computer to print a ? and then *wait* for you to type a number. In the preceding program, 60 was typed after the first ?, and the computer assigned this number to A because the corresponding INPUT statement was:

```
10      INPUT  A
```

Similarly, 37 was assigned to B, and 14 was assigned to C.

The three INPUT statments in the previous program could have been represented by one INPUT statement.

```
10      INPUT A, B, C
20      LET Y = A * B * C
30      PRINT "Y = " ; Y
40      END
RUN
?60, 37, 14
Y = 31080
```

In this example, the INPUT statement causes the computer to print a ? and then wait for you to type three numbers, separated by commas. A 60 was typed after the ? followed by a comma, the number 37, a comma, and the number 14.

It is often desirable to print a message identifying what variables are to be typed.

```
10      PRINT "TYPE VALUES FØR A, B AND C"
20      INPUT A, B, C
30      LET Y = A * B * C
40      PRINT "Y = " ; Y
50      END
RUN
TYPE VALUES FØR A, B AND C
?60, 37, 14
Y = 31080
```

If you use a semicolon at the end of the PRINT statement preceding the INPUT statement, it will cause the ? to appear on the same line.

Here is an example of this point.

```
10      PRINT "I AM THINKING ØF A NUMBER BETWEEN"
20      PRINT "1 AND 10. WHAT IS THE NUMBER";
```

```
30      INPUT N
40      IF N < > 6 THEN 70
50      PRINT "HURRAY—YØU GUESSED THE NUMBER"
60      GØ TØ 80
70      PRINT "WRØNG NUMBER"
80      END
RUN
I AM THINKING ØF A NUMBER BETWEEN
1 AND 10. WHAT IS THE NUMBER? 3
WRØNG NUMBER
```

Using Library Functions

The computer is frequently used in applications that require the use of a mathematical function, such as square root, absolute value, or sine. The following mathematical functions are supplied as part of the BASIC programming language.

Function	Description
SQR(X)	Square root of $|X|$
SIN(X)	Sine of X (X is in radian measure)
COS(X)	Cosine of X (X is in radian measure)
TAN(X)	Tangent of X (X is in radian measure)
ATN(X)	Arctangent of X (result is in radian measure)
EXP(X)	Exponential in base e (e^x)
LOG(X)	Natural logarithm of $|X|$
RND(X)	Random number between 0 and 1
INT(X)	Greatest integer less than or equal to X
SGN(X)	Sign of X ($+1$ if $X > 0$, 0 if $X = 0$, -1 if $X < 0$)
ABS(X)	Absolute value of X

The following list gives some mathematical expressions that include functions and their equivalent representation in BASIC:

Mathematical Expression	BASIC Expression
$|x|$	ABS(X)
$\sqrt{a^2 - b^2}$	SQR(A ↑ 2 − B ↑ 2)
$\cos 30°$	COS(30*(3.14159/180))
$\sqrt{1 - \sin^2 x}$	SQR(1 − SIN(X) ↑ 2)

The *integer part* function INT associates with its argument (whatever number lies within the parentheses) the greatest integer that is less than or equal to that argument. For example,

$$INT(10.3) = 10$$
$$INT(36) = 36$$
$$INT(-6.8) = -7$$
$$INT(.0006) = 0$$

The general form of the INT function is INT(X), where INT is the *name* of the function, and X is the *argument* of the function.

The *random number* function RND causes the computer to select a *surprise* number between 0 and 1, such as .032614, .532610, or .931667.

The general form of the function is RND(X), where RND is the name of the function, and X is the argument of the function. On some computers, the value of the argument is not important; on other computers, it makes a difference. The program in Figure 14–4 produces 120 random numbers between 0 and 1.

```
10    FØR R = 1 TØ 120
20    LET X = RND (1)
30    PRINT X,
40    NEXT R
50    END

RUN
```

.714538	.136021	.634909	.611097	.995399
.767829	.52238	.431631	.189791	.880298
.965662	.827365	.998011	.292369	.462316
.707134	.476298	.181421	.390138	.269247
.131316	.588899	.873123	5.15131E-03	.854478
.531386	.456029	.402311	.383618	.654666
.775026	.783806	.979504	.368235	.411953
.722154	4.69621E-03	.397803	.119648	.464844
9.22454E-02	.693242	.605894	.809092	.591741
.629522	6.34438E-02	.86332	.980199	.438101
.633641	.132843	.925294	.806297	.991141
.367288	.688433	.582114	.23722	.607218
.555182	.522052	.289177	.867488	.98052
1.93761E-02	.953336	.894808	.136456	.750354
.869134	.437032	.549475	.175967	.511809
.461668	.515332	.83659	.441179	.761094
.978695	.377135	.984013	.38201	.565124
.240167	.537501	.316594	.452897	.964487
.68131	.892887	.772182	2.66882E-02	.285746
.301889	.21905	.163173	.803492	.698881
.571832	.110148	.932459	.316459	.797319
.699078	.837215	2.67915E-02	.434311	.245117
.116518	.790594	.942001	.166004	.704437
.430321	.700708	.768928	.892572	.165082

Figure 14–4   Program that generates 120 random numbers.

Many programs require the use of random numbers in ranges other than from 0 to 1. For example, assume you want to produce the numbers than range from 2 through 6, a simulation of the roll of a die. You can accomplish this in BASIC very easily by writing the statement

20   LET S = INT(6 * RND(–1)) + 1.

The statement

30   LET S = INT(6 * RND(–1)) + 1 +
                 INT(6 * RND(–1)) + 1

will produce numbers ranging from 2 through 12, thus simulating the roll of two dice.

The *absolute value* function ABS gives the "absolute value" of the argument. The function is written ABS(X).

$$ABS(36) = 36$$
$$ABS(-36) = 36$$
$$ABS(-264) = 264$$

Let us now look at a BASIC program (see Figure 14–5) that plays a game with two players who try to guess a number that the computer randomly picked. The program prints a message indicating which player was the closer.

```
10      REM A NUMBER GUESSING GAME
15      PRINT "PLAYER 1—GUESS IS";
20      INPUT P1
25      PRINT "PLAYER 2—GUESS IS";
30      INPUT P2
35      LET C = INT (50 * RND (1)) + 1
40      PRINT "CØMPUTER SELECTED"; C
45      IF ABS (C – P1) < > ABS (C – P2) THEN 60
50      PRINT "BØTH PLAYERS WERE EQUAL"
55      GØ TØ 80
60      IF ABS (C – P1) < ABS (C – P2) THEN 75
65      PRINT "PLAYER 2 WAS CLØSEST"
70      GØ TØ 80
75      PRINT "PLAYER 1 WAS CLØSEST"
80      END
RUN

PLAYER 1—GUESS IS? 45
PLAYER 2—GUESS IS? 12
CØMPUTER SELECTED 3
PLAYER 2 WAS CLØSEST
```

Figure 14–5   Number guessing program.

This program used the functions INT, RND, and ABS. The INT and RND functions were used to determine what number the computer selected. The ABS function was used to determine the numerical distance (disregarding signs) from the number the computer picked (C) to the number the players picked (P1 and P2).

☐ Applications

This section further demonstrates how the BASIC language is used by presenting BASIC solutions to several problems.

Number Sum

The BASIC program in Figure 14–6 determines the sum of all numbers between 100 and 1000 that are divisible by 13.

```
10      REM NUMBER SUM
20      LET S = 0
30      FØR N = 100 TØ 1000 STEP 13
40      LET S = S + N
50      NEXT N
60      PRINT "NUMBER SUM = " ; S
70      END

RUN

NUMBER SUM = 38395.
```

Figure   Number sum program.
14–6

An Island of Money

King Bigfoot, leader of a wealthy South Seas island, was distributing his wealth to the one million natives who lived on the island. He gave $1 to the first native. The next 2 natives got $2 each. The next 3 natives each got $3, and so on. The BASIC program shown in Figure 14–7 determines what the millionth native received.

```
10      REM ISLAND ØF MØNEY
20      LET A = 0
30      LET B = 1
40      LET A = A + B
50      IF A > = 1.E + 06 THEN 80
60      LET B = B + 1
70      GØ TØ 40
80      PRINT "THE MILLIØNTH NATIVE GØT $ " ; B
90      END
```

RUN

THE MILLIØNTH NATIVE GØT $1414

Figure   An island of money program.
14–7

Rolling Two Dice

The BASIC program shown in Figure 14–8 simulates rolling a pair of dice. The output shows how the dice fell for 15 rolls.

```
10     REM RØLLING TWØ DICE
20     PRINT "TYPE NUMBER ØF RØLLS TØ BE MADE";
30     INPUT N
40     PRINT "FIRST DIE", "SECØND DIE", "TØTAL"
50     PRINT
60     FOR A = 1 TO N
70     LET D1 = INT (6 * RND (1) + 1)
80     LET D2 = INT (6 * RND (1) + 1)
90     LET T = D1 + D2
100    PRINT D1, D2, T
110    NEXT A
120    END
```

RUN

TYPE NUMBER ØF RØLLS TØ BE MADE? 15

FIRST DIE	SECØND DIE	TØTAL
4	1	5
6	2	8
6	3	9
2	5	7
2	4	6
2	3	5
2	5	7
3	3	6
3	1	4
3	3	6
3	4	7
3	2	5
4	2	6
4	4	8
3	4	7

Figure   Rolling two dice program.
14–8

Manhattan Island Investment

In 1627, Peter Minuet, a Dutch settler, bought Manhattan Island from the Indians for $24 worth of trinkets and beads.

The BASIC program shown in Figure 14–9 determines what that $24 would be worth in 1977 if it had been placed in a bank and earned 4% annual interest. The program uses the formula:

$$A = p(1 + r)^n$$

where r is the yearly rate of interest, n is the number of years, p is the principal, and A is the amount (principal + interest).

```
10    REM MANHATTAN ISLAND INVESTMENT
20    PRINT "$24 INVESTED AT 4% ANNUALLY"
30    PRINT "IN 1627 IS WORTH $" ;
40    LET P = 24
50    LET R = .04
60    LET N = 1977–1627
70    PRINT P * (1 + R) ↑ N ; " IN 1977"
80    END

RUN

$24 INVESTED AT 4% ANNUALLY
IN 1627 IS WORTH $2.19724E + 07      IN 1977
```

Figure   Manhattan Island investment program.
14–9

Armstrong Numbers

One hundred fifty three is an interesting number because

$$153 = 1^3 + 5^3 + 3^3$$

Numbers such as this are called *Armstrong* numbers. Any n-digit number is an Armstrong number if the sum of the nth power of the digits is equal to the original number. The BASIC program in Figure 14–10 determines three other Armstrong numbers.

```
100    REM ARMSTRØNG NUMBERS
110    FØR N = 100 TØ 999
120    LET A = INT(N/100)
130    LET B = INT(N/10) – 10*A
140    LET C = N – 100*A – 10*B
150    IF N < > A↑3+B↑3+C↑3 THEN 190
160    PRINT "ARMSTRØNG NUMBER";N
170    PRINT "EQUALS ";A↑3;"+";B↑3;"+";C↑3
180    PRINT
190    NEXT N
200    END
```

RUN

ARMSTRØNG NUMBER 153
EQUALS 1   +   125   +   27

ARMSTRØNG NUMBER 370
EQUALS 27   +   343   +   0

ARMSTRØNG NUMBER 371
EQUALS 27   +   343   +   1

ARMSTRØNG NUMBER 407
EQUALS 64   +   0   +   343

Figure   Armstrong numbers program.
14–10

Coin Tossing

The BASIC program shown in Figure 14–11 uses the RND (random number) library function to simulate heads and tails (heads if the random number is less than 0.5; tails if the random number is 0.5 or greater). The program simulates the flipping of 15 coins and prints out the number of heads and tails obtained.

```
10      REM CØIN TØSSING
20      LET T = 0
30      LET H = 0
40      FØR N = 1 TO 15
50      LET R = RND (1)
60      IF R < .5 THEN 100
70      PRINT "TAIL"
80      LET T = T + 1
90      GØ TØ 120
100     PRINT "HEAD"
110     LET H = H + 1
120     NEXT N
130     PRINT "NUMBER ØF TAILS = " ; T
140     PRINT "NUMBER ØF HEADS = " ; H
150     END
```

RUN

TAIL
HEAD
TAIL
TAIL
HEAD
HEAD
TAIL
HEAD
HEAD
TAIL
HEAD
TAIL

```
                HEAD
                HEAD
                TAIL
                NUMBER ØF TAILS = 7
                NUMBER ØF HEADS = 8
```

Figure   Coin tossing program.
14–11

The Big Robbery

A masked robber entered a New York grocery store and shouted, "Give me all your money!" The store clerk replied, "But I only have change for one dollar," and gave the robber twenty-one coins.

When the detectives arrived, the clerk could not remember exactly what coins were stolen. However, he did remember that there were no half dollars. The BASIC program shown in Figure 14–12 determines the possible combinations of coins that the robber could have taken.

```
10    REM THE BIG RØBBERY
15    PRINT "25", "10", "5", "1"
20    PRINT
25    FØR Q = 0 TO 3
30    D = 0 TO 8
35    N = 0 TO 19
40    FØR P = 0 TØ 20 STEP 5
45    LET T = 25 * Q + 10 * D + 5 * N + P
50    IF T = 100 THEN 85
55    IF T > 100 THEN 65
60    NEXT P
65    NEXT N
70    NEXT D
75    NEXT Q
80    GØ TØ 99
85    IF Q + D + N + P < > 21 THEN 65
90    PRINT Q, D, N, P
95    GØ TO 65
99    END
RUN
```

25	10	5	1
0	3	13	5
0	7	4	10
1	3	7	10
2	3	1	15

Figure   The big robbery program.
14–12

As shown in the program output, there were four possible combinations:

1. 3 dimes, 13 nickels, 5 pennies
2. 7 dimes, 4 nickels, 10 pennies
3. 1 quarter, 3 dimes, 7 nickels, 10 pennies
4. 2 quarters, 3 dimes, 1 nickel, 15 pennies

☐ Review Exercises

27. How does the INPUT statement function? What terminates the INPUT operation?

28. Show two different ways to calculate a square root.

29. Nancy Wilson sells bibles at $3.00 each plus $.65 for postage and handling. Write a BASIC program to calculate her total receipts for two weeks during which she sold 158 bibles.

30. The Western Freight Company charges the following rates on merchandise shipped from New York to Phoenix.
    $70 per ton for the first 12 tons
    $40 per ton for every ton over 12
    Write a BASIC program to determine how much it would cost to send shipments weighing 14 tons, 42 tons, 6 tons, 130 tons, 2 360 tons.

31. The student population at Western University increased by 9 percent every year. If the current student population is 2 400, how many students can this college expect in 10 years? Write a program to determine the answer.

32. Write a BASIC program to determine how many ways that change can be made for 50 cents using quarters, dimes, nickels, and pennies.

33. Write a BASIC program to compute a table of amounts that $100 will be at the end of 10, 15, 20, and 25 years at 5%, 5½% 6%, 6½%, and 7% per year compounded monthly. The program should print the years across the top and the rates in the first column of each row.

34. Simple interest is paid on $300 invested at $r\%$ for n years. Write a BASIC program to print an interest table for values of r from 0.05% to 6.5% and for integral values of n between 1 and 25.

35. You have $100. If you invest it at 6% interest compounded quarterly, how many years it will take before you have $50 000? Write a BASIC program to determine the answer.

36. A depositor banks $20 per month. Interest is 7.25% per year compounded monthly. Write a BASIC program to compute the amount the depositer has in her account after 15 years.

37. Five employees work for the XYZ Insurance Company and are paid weekly. The data on the employees is as follows:

Employee Number	Rate of Pay	Hours Worked	Deductions
11264	2.90	40	16.50
20379	3.60	46	18.75
19634	3.20	38	10.00
52370	4.10	40	20.50
36411	3.90	42	35.20

Write a BASIC program to compute and print the gross and net pay of each employee.

☐ Summary

The BASIC language is primarily designed for solving mathematic and scientific problems. The language includes input, mathematic, control, and output instructions. Input statements are READ, DATA, and INPUT. The output statement is the PRINT statement.

The BASIC arithmetic instruction is very similar to algebraic notation, using the following arithmetic operators: $+$ (addition), $-$ (subtraction), $*$ (multiplication), $/$ (division), and $\uparrow$ (exponentiation). The equal sign ($=$) is different from the algebraic sign and in BASIC means "is replaced by." For example, calculate the value of the expression to the right of the "is replaced by" symbol and store that value in the storage area named by the variable to the left of the symbol. Parentheses are used in the same way as in algebra.

BASIC control commands include unconditional and conditional branching statements as well as a pair of looping statements. The unconditional branch is the GO TO statement, which causes the computer to branch to the statement specified by the line number included in the GO TO command. The conditional branch is the IF-THEN statement, which causes the computer to branch, depending upon whether the condition tests true or false. The condition tests discussed in this chapter include greater than ($>$), greater than or equal to ($>=$), less than ($<$), less than or equal to ($<=$), equal ($=$), and not equal ($<>$). The FOR-NEXT statement combination provides a convenient method for program looping.

The END statement is used to terminate every BASIC program. Comments can be added to a BASIC program by using the REM statement.

BASIC includes several mathematical functions to perform such operations as square root, absolute value, sine, or cosine. An advance feature of the language also includes a set of matrix statements that allows matrix operations, such as the addition of two matrices or the inverse of a matrix.

Key Terms

BASIC	REM
statements	LET
line number	READ
system command	DATA
comment	IF-THEN
arithmetic statement	FOR
expression	NEXT
relation symbol	INPUT
variable name	END
library function	PRINT
argument	GO TO
random number	
absolute value	

15

FORTRAN

As stated in Chapter 14, FORTRAN (acronym for FORmula TRANslation) is a higher-level language that was originally designed as a scientific and mathematical language to allow scientists, engineers, and mathematicians to use the computer to solve their problems. However, for the past decade, management scientists and business programmers have found FORTRAN to be extremely valuable for solving a wide variety of business problems: queuing models, statistical studies, inventory management, sales forecasting, class scheduling, etc.

The material in this chapter consists only of carefully selected FORTRAN statements. After studying this chapter, you will be able to write FORTRAN programs which will instruct the computer to solve simple business problems dealing with interest, statistics, inventory, sales, etc.

☐ The FORTRAN System

A FORTRAN program consists of a series of *statements*. These statements represent the solution to a specific problem. FORTRAN statements may be classified into four types:

1. *Arithmetic Statements.* These statements describe computations that are to be performed ($X = 3 + Y ** 2, K = K + 1$).

2. *Control Statements.* These statements specify the sequence in which other statements are to be executed. (GO TO 20, DO 20 $N = 1$ TO 10).

3. *Input/Output Statements.* These statements provide communication between the computer and other system equipment, such as card readers, printers, and magnetic-tape units. (READ (2,10) A, B, C).

4. *Specification Statements.* These statements provide information to the FORTRAN compiler (100 FORMAT (F10.6), DIMENSION M (10,20)).

In order to aid the user in handling the various statements, there is a standard FORTRAN coding form (Figure 15–1). FORTRAN state-

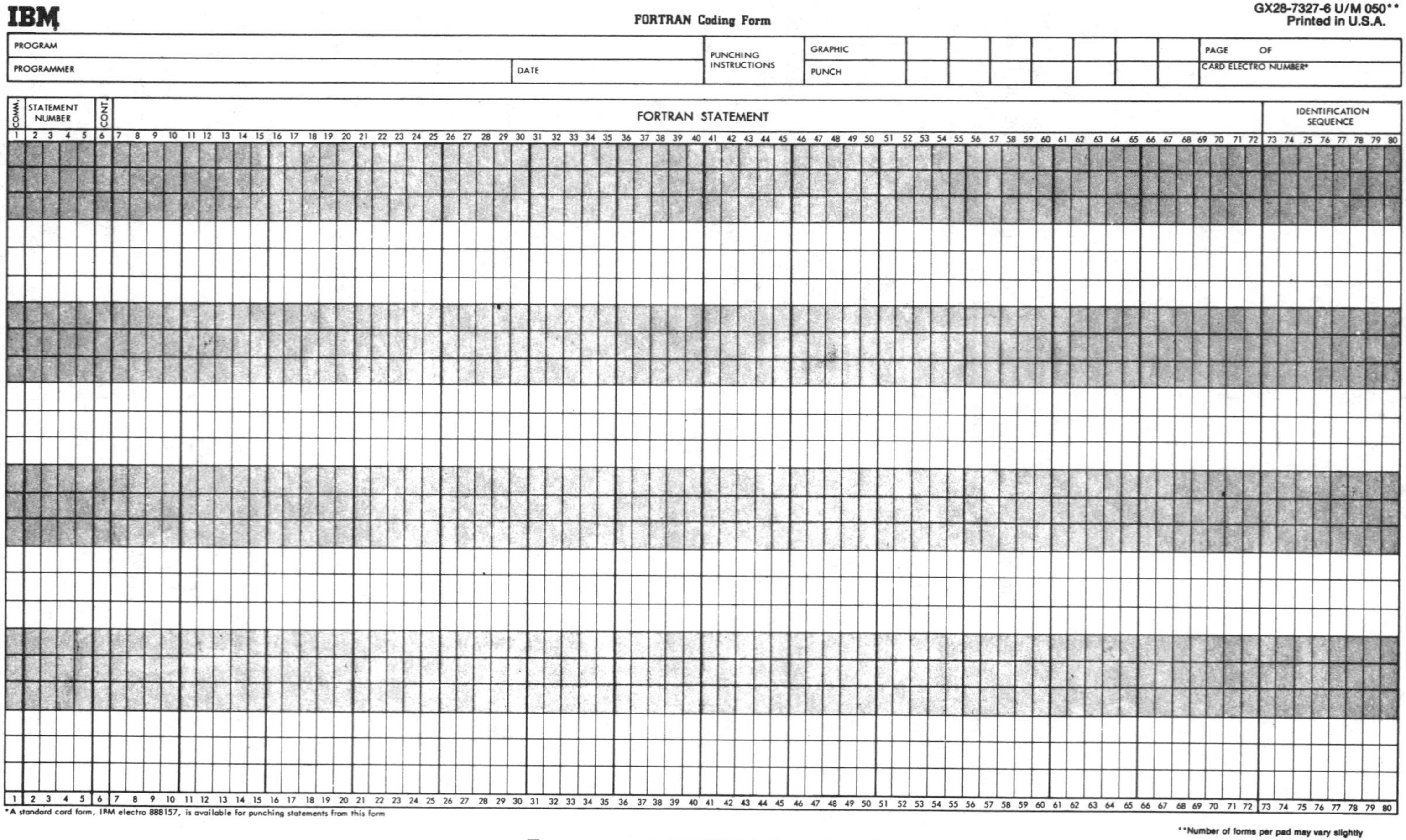

Figure 15-1 A FORTRAN coding form.

ments are written one to a line in the spaces marked 7–72. Spaces are numbered to correspond to the columns in a standard punched card (Figure 15–2). Columns 1–5 may be used to write numbers by which the statements may be subsequently referenced. A statement number may vary from 1 to 9999. You may also insert comments into a FORTRAN program by placing the letter C in column 1, followed by the comment itself. Comments do not affect the execution of the object program but will be printed on the compilation listing. Comments are user aids, and one should use them freely in order to clarify or explain a program (see Figure 15–3).

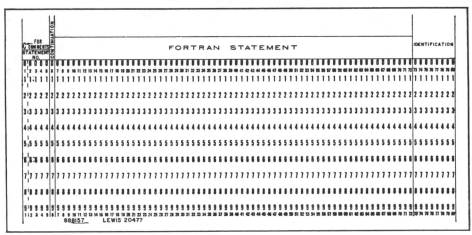

Figure 15–2 A FORTRAN statement card.

If a statement is too long for one line on the coding form, column 6 can be used to indicate the order of the lines to follow. If a statement is contained on one line, column 6 should remain blank.

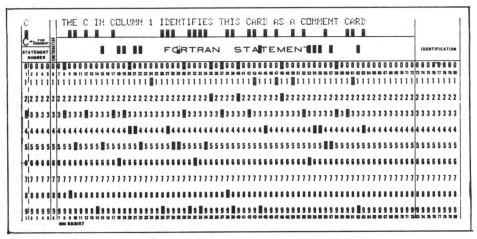

Figure 15–3 A FORTRAN comment card.

Columns 73–80 are for program identification purposes; they may include both a program code name and a card sequence number. For example, the first card of an inventory program may have INV00001 punched in columns 73–80; the second card, INV00002, and so forth. If the cards are dropped (heaven forbid!) or the sequence of cards is disturbed in some way, these columns could be used to restore the proper sequence.

A *FORTRAN program* consists of a set of statements constructed from the FORTRAN language elements described herein. In the compilation process, the source statements are translated into machine code (object program). In addition, when the FORTRAN compiler detects mistakes in the source program, it produces appropriate diagnostic messages (Figure 15–4).

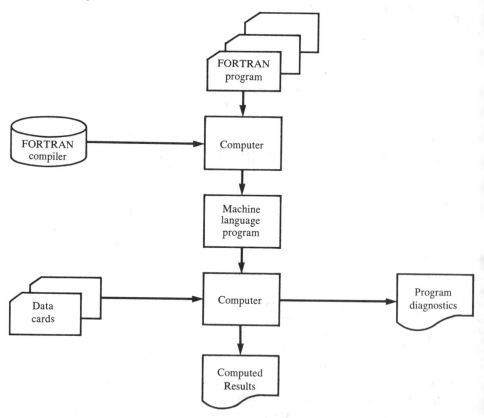

Figure 15–4   General FORTRAN translation process.

Figure 15–5 is a complete FORTRAN program represented on a coding form. The purpose of the program is to find the average of four test scores. The program reads four test scores from a punched card, adds

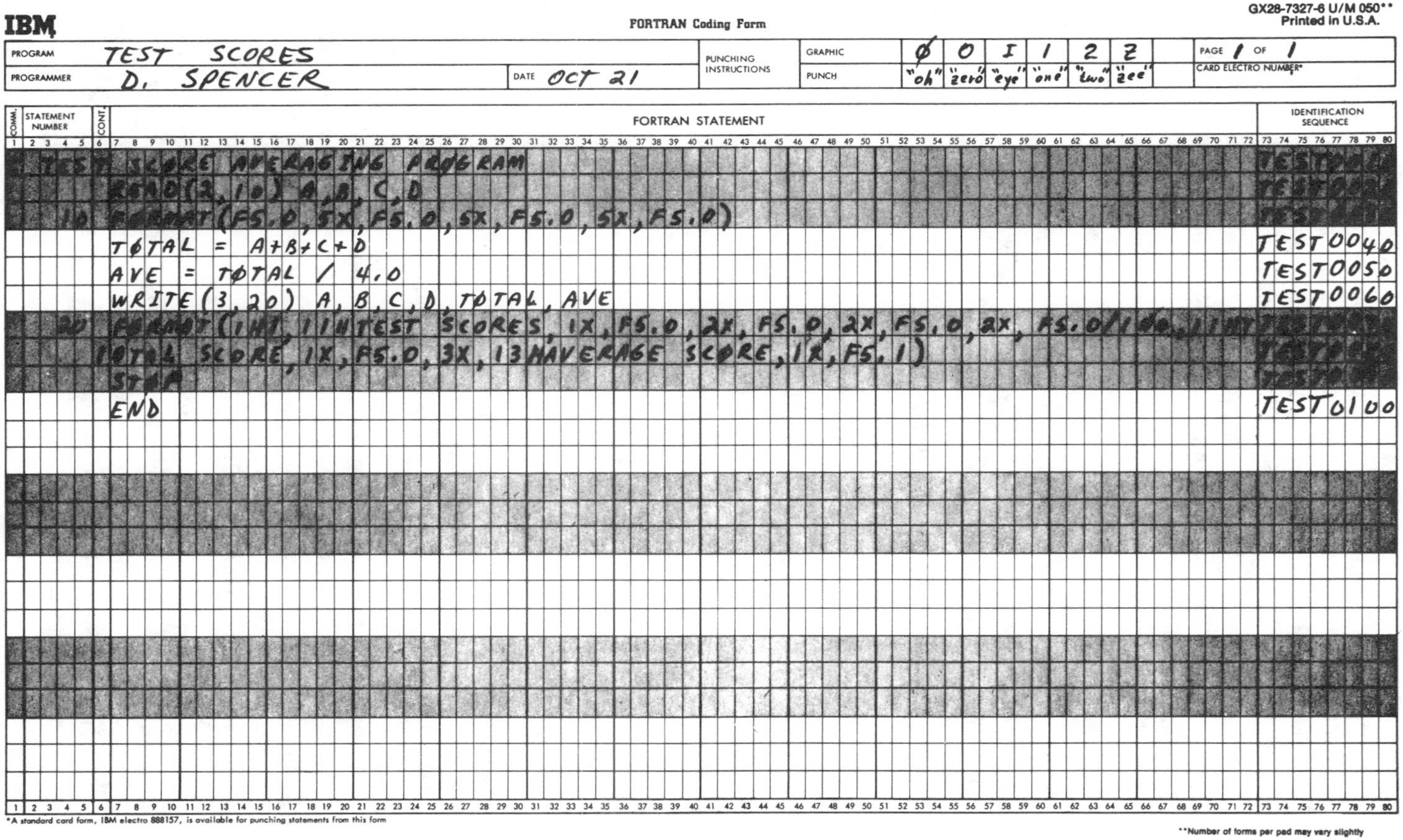
IBM FORTRAN Coding Form GX28-7327-6 U/M 050** Printed in U.S.A.

PROGRAM TEST SCORES

PROGRAMMER D. SPENCER DATE OCT 21

PUNCHING INSTRUCTIONS

GRAPHIC	Ø	O	I	1	2	Z
PUNCH	"oh"	"zero"	"eye"	"one"	"two"	"zee"

PAGE 1 OF 1

CARD ELECTRO NUMBER*

```
TEST SCORE AVERAGING PROGRAM
      READ(2,10) A,B,C,D
   10 FORMAT(F5.0,5X,F5.0,5X,F5.0,5X,F5.0)
      TØTAL = A+B+C+D                                                   TEST0040
      AVE = TØTAL / 4.0                                                 TEST0050
      WRITE(3,20) A,B,C,D,TØTAL,AVE                                     TEST0060
   20 FORMAT(1H1,11HTEST SCORES,1X,F5.0,2X,F5.0,2X,F5.0,2X,F5.0/1H0,11H
     1OTAL SCORE,1X,F5.0,3X,13HAVERAGE SCORE,1X,F5.1)
      STOP
      END                                                               TEST0100
```

*A standard card form, IBM electro 888157, is available for punching statements from this form

**Number of forms per pad may vary slightly

Figure 15–5 Coding for a sample FORTRAN program.

the scores to get their total, calculates the average of the scores by dividing their total by four, and writes the test scores and the results of the calculations on the printer. Although the program is quite simple, it illustrates a complete program. You should not at this time try to determine how the FORTRAN program works. This example is given only to show how a complete program is represented on a FORTRAN Coding Form.

⬚ The Character Set

The FORTRAN character set consists of decimal digits 0 to 9, letters A through Z (uppercase), and the following symbolic characters.

Period (decimal point)	.
Comma	,
Left parentheses	(
Right parentheses	)
Apostrophe	'
Currency symbol	$
Space	(blank)
Plus	+
Minus	—
Asterisk	*
Slash	/
Equal	=

⬚ Constants and Variables

In FORTRAN, there are two types of constants and variables—integer and real. *Integers* (sometimes called *fixed-point numbers*) are values that contain no decimal point; e.g., 643, 22, or 42 678. An *integer variable* is identified by the variable name beginning with an I, J, K, L, M, or N; e.g., INK, L27, or JACK.

Real numbers (also called *floating-point numbers*) contain a decimal point, and *real variables* can begin with any letter except I, J, K, L, M, or N; e.g., A27, SPEED, or T. All variable names must begin with a letter. Most FORTRAN systems allow five or six letters and/or numbers to appear in a variable name.

There are two forms for real numbers. One form contains a number with a decimal point; e.g., 46.3, 176.9, 0.001. The other form is expressed in an exponent notation; e.g., 6.3E2, which represents 6.3×10^2, or 630.

Am I familiar with FORTRAN? I may be. What's his first name?

Review Exercises

1. List the four types of FORTRAN statements.
2. What is the purpose of the FORTRAN coding form?
3. How are comments placed in a program?
4. What type of information is written in columns 1–6 of a FORTRAN coding form?
5. When a program is punched from the coding on a coding form, how many cards are punched for each line on the coding form?
6. How is a statement that is longer than one line coded in FORTRAN?
7. What is the purpose of columns 73 to 80 on the coding form?
8. Of what is the FORTRAN character set composed?
9. What is the difference between an integer and a real constant? An integer and a real variable? Give an example of each.
10. Which of the following are valid names for integer variables? Real variables? Why? MAGIC, TI, IT, ABC, SPEED, K2, FORD.
11. Which of the following numbers are valid integer constants? Why? 263, 21.4, 6E02, 76231, 0, 0.0, +264, −3.14, −6666, .0241, −.06.

FORTRAN Operators

There are five basic *arithmetic operators* in FORTRAN:

+	Addition
−	Subtraction
*	Multiplication
/	Division
**	Exponentiation

In addition to the five basic arithmetic operators, FORTRAN includes six *relational operators*—.LT. (less than), .LE. (less than or equal to), .GT. (greater than), .GE. (greater than or equal to), .EQ. (equal to), and .NE. (not equal to). FORTRAN also includes *several elementary functions*—sine, cosine, logarithm, square root, arctangent, exponential, absolute value, hyperbolic tangent, etc.

☐ FORTRAN Expressions

An *expression* in FORTRAN consists of a series of constants, variables, and functions, separated by parentheses, commas, and/or operating symbols so as to form a mathematical expression. Expressions in their simplest form consist of a single constant or variable.

In a FORTRAN expression, such as

$$8 * 6 + 4/2 - 2 ** 4$$

the computer is being instructed to follow a specific procedure. Exponentiation will be performed first, then multiplication and division, followed by addition and subtraction. Following this order in the previous expression, the computer would evaluate $2 ** 4 = 2^4 = 16$. Then $8 \times 6 = 48$. Then $4/2 = 2$. Now the computer has three numbers in its memory: 16, 48, and 2. In its next operation it will add 48 and 2, obtaining the sum of 50 $(48 + 2 = 50)$, and then subtract 16 from the sum, resulting in a final answer of 34 $(50 - 16 = 34)$. Thus

$$8 * 6 + 4/2 - 2 ** 4 = 34$$

When parentheses are used, the quantities in parentheses are evaluated first. In the expression $(5 * 2) * * 3$, the multiplication, $5 * 2$, would be performed first, and then the product 10, would be cubed, giving $10^3 = 1\ 000$. If parentheses were not used here and the expression were written as $5 * 2 ** 3$, then the normal rules would apply; exponentiation $(2 ** 3 = 2^3 = 8)$ would be performed first, and this quantity would then be multiplied by 5, giving a result of 40 $(8 * 5 = 40)$. Likewise, the expression $2 * * (3 ** 4)$ will result in a value of 2^{81}. If parentheses had not been used, $2 ** 3 * * 4$, the expression would have a resulting value of 8^4, or 4096.

The expression

$$A * X ** 2 - B * X + SUM/F$$

would cause the FORTRAN compiler to generate instructions to perform the following sequences of operations:

1. Calculate X^2
2. Multiply X^2 by A

3. Multiply B by X
4. Divide SUM by F
5. Subtract the product BX from AX^2
6. Add result of SUM/F to the difference of $AX^2 - BX$

Some examples of expressions appear in the following list.

Mathematical Expression	FORTRAN Expression
$a + b$	A + B
$ab - c + 17$	A * B − C + 17
$c - df$	C − D/F
$(a + b)^2$	(A + B) * * 2
$x^{a + 3}$	X ** (A + 3)
$\dfrac{a + b}{c - d}$	(A + B) / (C − D)
$a + cb^x$	A + C * B ** X

Parentheses can be freely used within FORTRAN expressions and should be used whenever any question as to the precise meaning of the statement might arise. Spaces may be used almost anywhere within an expression to make an expression easier to understand.

The modes of constants and variables should be the same; that is, one should not mix integer and real quantities in the same expression. An exception is a real quantity raised to an integer power.

Some examples of mixed mode arithmetic follow:

Mixed Mode	Correct
X + 3	X + 3.0
A + B + 63 − 20.0	A + B + 63.0 − 20.0
N + 4.0	N + 4
N/2 − A/7	N/2 − IA/7

There are, however, many FORTRAN compilers that will allow mixed mode arithmetic.

Review Exercises

12. The symbols for arithmetic operations used in FORTRAN are:
    (a) Addition
    (b) Subtraction
    (c) Multiplication
    (d) Division
    (e) Exponentiation
13. What does an expression do?
14. Explain the order of priority of evaluating an arithmetic expression.
15. Explain how mathematical calculations are performed in FORTRAN. Give an example.

16. Represent the following mathematical expression as FORTRAN expressions.
    (a) $a + 3$
    (b) $ab - bc$
    (c) $\dfrac{a + b}{c - d}$
    (d) $\dfrac{c + d + 10}{c}$
    (e) a^{b^c}

17. Rewrite any of the following expressions that would be incorrect in FORTRAN.

    (a) A + B²   (c) A + BC + D
    (b) A * 2 + −6   (d) A * B + C × D

18. Identify the following expressions as integer mode, real mode, or mixed mode:
    (a) 42.6
    (b) MAGIC * * 4
    (c) PI * R * * 2 * LENGT
    (d) 9.0 * * 3 + A / B
    (e) 9 * * 3 + J/K
    (f) 9.0 * * 3 + N/L

☐ Arithmetic Statements

In algebra, a statement is of the form $c^2 = a^2 + b^2$ and represents a mathematical equation. In FORTRAN, an arithmetic statement is quite similar to the conventional algebraic equation. It consists of the variable to be computed on the left side of the statement, followed by a *replaced by* symbol, and an arithmetic expression on the right side of the statement. The general form of the arithmetic statement is

$$v = e$$

where e represents the expressison to be evaluated, the = (replaced by) symbol, and v is the variable that is set to the value of the expression. If the mode of the expression is different from that of the variable on the left of the "replaced by" symbol, then it is converted to the mode of the variable.

The statement

$$K = K + 1$$

is an arithmetic statement and is interpreted as follows:

1. The expression $K + 1$ is evaluated by adding 1 to the current value of K.
2. K is then set equal to the value of the expression.

Several other examples of FORTRAN statements follow.

```
A = 3
Y = A
X = A + C + D
AMT = UNITS * RATE
ANS = ((A + B) / (C − D)) ** 2
X = (A + B) / C + 2.0
```

One must not confuse mixed-mode arithmetic with different modes on opposite sides of the "replaced by" symbol. Mixed mode applies only to the mixing of variable modes of an *expression*. It is often desirable to perform some computation in one mode (e.g., real mode) and store the result in an integer variable. For example, in the statement

$$K = 46.3 + 12.2$$

the value of the expressison is first determined as 58.5, then truncated (not rounded) to 58, and then assigned to the variable K.

I'd like to see you code that in FORTRAN.

☐ Library Functions

The FORTRAN library contains a large number of mathematical functions. These routines are so frequently required that instructions for their evaluation have been programmed previously and are permanently stored where they are always available to the FORTRAN compiler.

A few commonly used functions which are available in FORTRAN are:

Function Name	Mathematical Expression
SQRT(X)	$\sqrt{X}$
SIN(X)	sin X
COS(X)	cos X
TAN(X)	tan X
EXP(X)	e^x
ARCOS(X)	arcos x($\cos^{-1}$)
ARSIN(X)	arcsin x($\sin^{-1}$)
ATAN(X)	arctan x($\tan^{-1}$)
ABS(X)	$|X|$
FLOAT(K)	Convert K to real
FIX(X)	Convert X to integer

A library function may be used in an arithmetic expression in the same way that a variable is used. The following three examples of arithmetic statements use library routines:

FORTRAN Statement	Mathematical Statement
Y = SQRT(B**2-4.0*A*C)	$y = \sqrt{b^2 - 4ac}$
K = FIX(A) + N + FIX(X)	$k = a + n + y$
Z = ABS(A) + ABS(B)	$z = |a| + |b|$

☐ **Review Exercises**

19. What is the meaning of the symbol = as used in FORTRAN? How does this differ from that in mathematics?

20. Write each algebraic statement as a FORTRAN arithmetic statement.
    (a) $x = 4y$
    (b) $y = a - b + c - d$
    (c) $r = x^3$
    (d) $p = y^3 - c + 32$
    (e) $x = \dfrac{y}{2}$

21. In the following statements, indicate which operation is to be carried out first.
    (a) X = 2.0 + 4.0 * 6.0
    (b) A = 2.0 * 3.0 * * 3
    (c) Y = 6.0/2.0 − 2.0
    (d) C = 3.0 * * 3/3.0
    (e) T = B * * 2 + C
    (f) R = A * B * * C
    (g) X = A * (B + C)
    (h) Z = A / (B − C)

22. Write FORTRAN statements for each of the following algebraic expressions.

(a) $c = (a + b)^{1/2}$
(b) $c = \sqrt{a^2 + b^2}$
(c) $x = |a| + 10.0$
(d) $r = \sqrt{25} + |n| - 36$

23. What would be the value of S after executing the following sequence of FORTRAN statements?

$A = 4.0$
$B = 3.0$
$C = 3.0$
$X = A + B + 3.0$
$Y = X + 2$
$S = Y - A + 6.0$

Control Statements

Rules, rules, and more rules. When are we ever going to get down to writing some FORTRAN programs? Well, we are just about there. Now that we are familiar with the elements of the language, we can examine some of the control statements that make up FORTRAN programs.

Unconditional GO TO

The unconditional branching statement is of the form GO TO n, where n is the number of some other statement in the program. The GO TO statement causes program control to be transferred to statement n, thus providing a way of breading the linear sequence of commands.

Examples

GO TO 70
GO TO 200

Here is a coding example.

———————
———————

———————

$X = 3.0$
$Y = 10.7$
GO TO 30
20 $Z = X + 10.0$
30 $Z = Y + 10.0$

———————

———————

Statement 20 will not be executed. Statement 30 will be evaluated, and Z will be assigned the value of 20.7.

Computed GO TO

The *computed GO TO* statement permits transfer of control to one of a group of statements, the particular statement being chosen at the time of the computer run.

The statement is of the form

$$\text{GO TO } (k_1, k_2, k_3, \ldots, k_n), i$$

where k^1, k^2, k^3, ..., k^n are statement labels, and i is an integer variable reference. Execution of this statement causes the statement identified by the statement label k_j to be executed next, where j is the value of i at the time of the execution. The value of i must be in the range of 1 to n, where n denotes the number of statement labels contained between the parentheses. If i is not in the range, the results are unpredictable.

Examples

$$\text{GO TO } (6, 7, 8, 9, 10), K$$
$$\text{GO TO } (10, 20, 30, 40), N$$

When you write

$$\text{GO TO } (10, 20, 30, 40), K2,$$

the computer transfers program control to statement number 10 if K2 equals 1 at execution time, to 20 if K2 equals 2, to 30 if K2 equals 3, and to 40 if K2 equals 4 at execution time.

Arithmetic IF

The *arithmetic IF* statement has the form IF (e) a, b, c, where e is an expression and a, b, c are statement numbers where program control will be transferred to, depending on whether the expression is negative, zero, or positive. If the expression is negative, control is transferred to statement number a; if the expression is zero, control is transferred to statement number b; and if the expressison is positive, control is transferred to statement number c. The statement numbers a, b, and c may be the same or may all be different. The arithmetic IF statement is called a *conditional branching statement*.

Examples

$$\text{IF } (X - Y) \ 10, 20, 30$$
$$\text{IF } (K) \ 20, 100, 100$$

Consider the following example. Suppose a value, A, is being computed. Whenever this value is positive, it is desired to proceed with the program. Whenever the value of A is negative, an alternate route starting at statement 40 is to be followed. If A is zero, an error routine at statement 100 is to be followed. This may be coded as

```
    _____
    _____

    _____
A = (X + Y - Z) / (X ** 2 + 20 * Y)
IF (A) 40, 100, 20
```

```
20   _____
     _____
     _____
     _____
40   _____
     _____
     _____
     _____
100  _____
     _____
```

Logical IF

The *logical IF* statement has the form IF (*e*) *a*, where *e* is a logical expression, such as A .GT. B .OR. 63.0, and *a* is an executable statement, such as K = K + 4. If the value of the logical expression is *true*, statement *a* will be executed. If the value of the expression is *false*, the statement following the IF will be executed next.

The logical expression in this statement uses the following relational operators, which are preceded and followed by a period.

Relational Operator	Definition
.GT.	Greater than (>)
.LT.	Less than (<)
.EQ.	Equal to (=)
.NE.	Not equal to (≠)
.GE.	Greater than or equal to (≥)
.LE.	Less than or equal to (≤)

Examples

```
            IF(A .LE.  5.0) GO TO 100
            IF(X .EQ. 10.0) ANS = Y + 2 * A
```

In the following example, if Z is greater than 100, program control is transferred to statement number 20. If Z is less than or equal to 100, control goes to statement number 10.

```
      _____
      _____

      IF (Z .GT. 100.0) GO TO 20
10    _____
      _____

20    _____
      _____
```

DO

The *DO statement* is the most powerful statement in the FORTRAN language. It has the form DO n i = m_1, m_2, m_3, where n is a statement number, i is a nonsubscripted variable, and m_1, m_2, and m_3 are unsigned integer constants or integer variables.

We can illustrate the operation of the DO statement by using the following example: DO 100 K = 4, 10, 2. When this statement is encountered in a program, the integer K is set equal to the initial value of 4. This initial value has to exceed 1 to be 1. All statements following the DO statement are executed until statement number 100 is reached. At this point, the DO variable K is increased by 2 and control returns to the statement following the DO statement. The program keeps repeating this loop until the variable K is greater than 10, at which point control is directed to the statement following the DO loop terminating statement.

Examples

```
DO 100 K = 1, 30
DO 250 N = 2, 200, 2
```

The DO statement

```
DO 150 J = 1, 15, 2
           _____
           _____
           _____
150        _____
           _____
           _____
```

says "execute the statements immediately following the DO statement up to and including statement number 150." The first time through the loop, J will have a value of 1; the second time, a value of 3; the third time, a value of 5; and so on, until the last time, when J will have a value of 15. The variable J is increased by 2 each time through the loop.

CONTINUE

The *CONTINUE statement* is a "do-nothing" statement and is often used as the terminating statement in a DO loop.

Example

```
       DO 20 K = 1, 30, 2
       IF (X  .EQ.   100.0) Y = X + 20.0
20     CONTINUE
```

STOP

The *STOP statement* causes the execution of the program to halt.

END

The *END statement* informs the FORTRAN compiler where the end of a source program is located. The END statement must be the last statement in a program.

Example

```
                    A = 10.0
                    B = 36.0
                    C = A + B * 2
                    WRITE (6, 10) C
          10        FORMAT (F10.0)
                    STOP
                    END
```

☐ **Input-Output Statements**

READ

The *READ statement* is of the form READ (i, n) list, where i is an integer constant or variable that identifies the input device (card reader, typewriter, paper-tape reader, etc.), n is the statement number of an associated FORMAT statement, and *list* is the names of variables whose values are to be transmitted. The READ statement provides us with a way of getting information into the computer.

Examples

```
                    READ (2, 10) A, B, C
                    READ (3, 200) JOBNO,EMPNO
```

When you write

```
                    READ (5,20)A,B,C,
```

the program will read from a punched card the values for the variables A, B, and C. The number 20 identifies the FORMAT statement used. The data on the cards must be in the same order as the variables in the input list.

WRITE

The *WRITE statement* is of the form WRITE (i, n) *list*, where i is an integer constant or variable that represents the output device (printer, typewriter, card punch, etc.), n is the statement number of an associated

FORMAT statement, and *list* is the name of the variables whose values are to be transmitted.

The WRITE statement provides us with a way of getting information out of the computer.

An example of a WRITE statement is

WRITE(6,400) A,B,X,SUM

which would direct the computer to output to the printer the values of A, B, X, and SUM according to the specifications of FORMAT statement 400.

It is possible to use the WRITE statement without an output list. A statement such as

WRITE(6,30),

would inform the computer to produce output on the printer using FORMAT 20. This FORMAT statement would contain the actual information to be printed.

FORMAT

The *FORMAT statement* specifies the arrangement of data on the input or output medium and also the type of conversion that is to be made between the internal and the external format.

The form of the FORMAT statement is—FORMAT (field specifications)—where several field specifications are used to describe the data structure which may take any of the following forms:

Alphanumeric Data—Alphanumeric messages may be read or printed by using the letter H, preceded by the number of characters in the message itself. Some FORTRAN compilers allow the use of *quotes* to specify a message.

Floating-Point Data—The specification F$w.d$ is used for floating-point data transfer, where w is the entire length of the number, including decimal point and sign, and d specifies the number of figures to the right of the decimal point. If a data value contains a decimal point upon input, the F specification is overridden.

The floating-point exponential notation can be specified by using the form E$w.d$, where w and d have meanings similar to their F specification meanings.

Integer Data—The format Iw is used for integer values, where w is the number of places needed.

Slash—A slash (/) is used to inform the computer to return the carriage on the typewriter, to go to the next line on the printer, or to read the next card on the card reader.

Skip Spaces—To skip spaces between data on a card or printout, one can use the X specification. The general form of this specification is *w*X, where *w* is the number of spaces to be skipped.

Maybe we shouldn't let the FORTRAN programmers check out this COBOL training lesson?

Examples

```
10    FORMAT (18H THIS IS A MESSAGE)
70    FORMAT (F10.8, F6.3)
20    FORMAT (I10, I6, I3)
      FORMAT (I15, /, I15, /, F5.2)
60    FORMAT (F10.5, 10X, F5.1)
```

The statements

```
      WRITE (6,100) X, Y, Z
100   FORMAT (F10.2, /, F10.2, /, F10.2)
```

would result in the value of X being printed on one line, the value of Y on the next line, and the value of C on the third line.

Figure 15–6 shows three data cards. Each card contains a data value punched in columns 6 through 10. The statements

```
      READ (5,1000) I, J, K
1000  FORMAT (5X, I5, /, 5X, I5, /, 5X, I5),
```

or the statements

```
      READ (5,1000) I, J, K
1000  FORMAT (I10, /, I10, /, I10),
```

or the statements

```
      READ (5,1000) I, J, K
1000  FORMAT (I10, /, I10, / , 5X, I5),
```

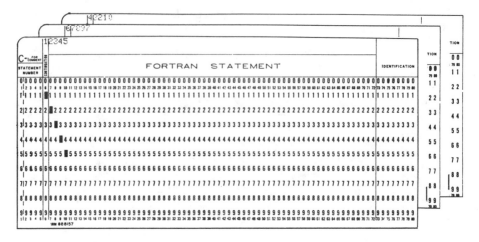

Figure 15–6 Data cards for example.

or the statements

        READ (5,1000) I, J, K
1000   FORMAT (I10),

or the statements

        READ (5,1000) I, J, K
1000   FORMAT (I10, /, 5X, I5, /, I10)

would cause the three cards to be read and the data values contained on the cards to be assigned to I, J, and K in computer memory.

If you wanted to print the values of A, B, and C on one line, skip three lines, and then print a line containing the values of D, E, and F, the statements

        WRITE (6,40) A,B,C,D,E,F
40   FORMAT (1H1,3F5.0,////,3F5.0)

would create this printout.

☐ Arrays and the DIMENSION Statement

Consider the arrangement of a tic-tac-toe board on the following page. The board is divided into nine cells, consisting of three rows and three columns. In FORTRAN, we can give the board a variable name such as BOARD, and can designate an arbitrary location on the board by— BOARD (I,J)—where I and J are fixed-point variables that assume the values 1, 2, and 3. I and J are called *subscripts,* and BOARD (I,J) is called *a subscripted* variable. I in the above expression represents a

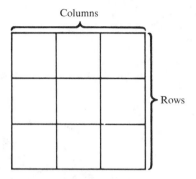

row, and J represents a column. A variable of this type is called an *array* in FORTRAN. If I represented 2 and J represented 3, then BOARD (I,J) refers to the array item in the second row and third column of Array BOARD. Subscripts need not be integer variables; they may also be integers. Thus, BOARD (2,1) would refer to the item in the second row and first column of Array BOARD.

Before arrays can be used in FORTRAN programs, the storage requirements must be specified. This is accomplished by using a statement of the form—DIMENSION BOARD (3,3)—where the DIMENSION statement contains the name of the array, the maximum number of rows in the array, and the maximum number of columns in the array. Any number of array storage specifications may be contained in one statement by simply separating the variables by a comma. Thus, the statement—DIMENSION A(2, 3), B(16, 6) C(27)—would cause the FORTRAN compiler to reserve storage for a 2 by 3 array named A, a 16 by 6 array named B, and an array named C which has 27 items. This last array, called a *one-dimensional array,* has only one subscript. This type of array is often called a *list.* Arrays with two subscripts are *two-dimensional* and are often called *tables* or *matrices.*

Examples

```
DIMENSION  COSTS(20)
DIMENSION  TIC(30), TAC(30), TOE(30)
DIMENSION  MAGIC(15,15)
```

☐ Examples of Simple Problems

Interest Calculation

Mary Wilson borrowed $3 000 from a banker to buy a late model car. She pays 12 percent interest on her four-year loan, compounded annually. Figure 15–7 shows the program Mary used to compute the total amount she paid for the car.

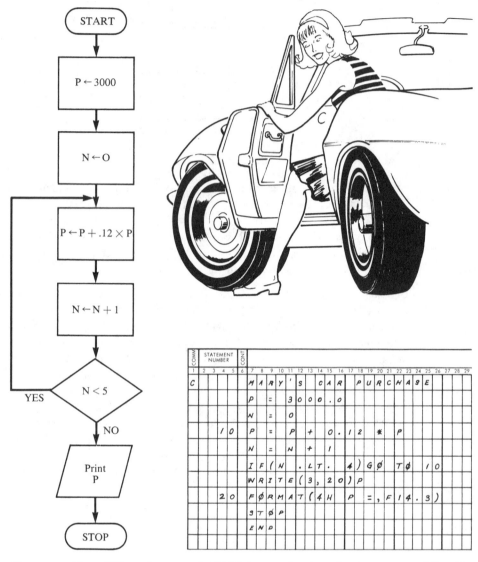

C					M A R Y ' S C A R P U R C H A S E
					P = 3 0 0 0 . 0
					N = 0
		1 0			P = P + 0 . 1 2 * P
					N = N + 1
					I F (N . L T . 4) G Ø T Ø 1 0
					W R I T E (3 , 2 0) P
		2 0			F Ø R M A T (4 H P =, F 1 4 . 3)
					S T Ø P
					E N D

Figure 15–7   Mary Wilson borrowed $3000 from a bank to buy an automobile. She used this program to determine the total amount she paid for the car.

Let us trace through the program to see how the compounding is accomplished. The first statement is a comment statement. In the next two commands, P is set equal to $3 000, and N is set equal to 0. The first time that statement 10 is reached, P equals 3 000; so $P = P + 0.12 * P$ equals 3 360. In the next statement, $N = N + 1$, so N equals 1. Thus, N is less than 5, and program control loops back to statement 10. At this point, P = $3 360. Thus, the value of $P = P + 0.12 * P$ is 3 763.20. This procedure is repeated until the looping is terminated ($N \geq 5$) and the final value of P is printed.

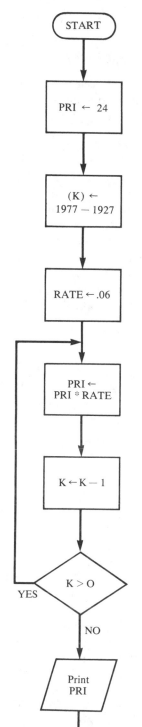

START

PRI ← 24

(K) ← 1977 − 1927

RATE ← .06

PRI ← PRI * RATE

K ← K − 1

K > 0

YES

NO

Print PRI

STOP

Figure 15–8
The Manhattan Island problem. Manhattan Island was sold by the Indians to the settlers in 1627 for $24 worth of beads and trinkets. This program computes what the investment would be worth today if it had been invested at 6 percent interest, compounded annually.

```
C        THE MANHATTAN ISLAND PROBLEM
         PRI = 24.0
         RATE = .06
         DØ 10 K = 1627, 1977
   10    PRI = PRI + PRI * RATE
         WRITE(3, 20) PRI
   20    FØRMAT(//H  PR VALUE =, F14.2)
         STØP
         END
```

Manhattan Island Problem

In 1627, Peter Minuet purchased Manhattan Island from the Indians for $24 worth of beads and trinkets. If this money had been invested at 6 percent interest and the interest had been compounded annually, what would the investment be worth in 1977?

The program for solving this problem is fairly straightforward and is shown in Figure 15–8. The first statement is a comment statement. The next three statements initialize the variables PRI, K, and RATE. The variable K is a counter used to control the number of program iterations, which, in this problem, is 350(1977-1627). The interest for a given year is computed as PRI * RATE, and the principal at the end of a given year is computed as PRI + PRI * RATE. Statements 10 through 20 constitute a program loop; the principal is recomputed as K decreases from 350 to 0. After the loop is completed (that is, the number of iterations specified by K has been satisfied), the resulting principal (PRI) is printed in statement 30. Statement 50 terminates execution of the program.

Statistics

Richard Weddy, a race car driver from Louisville, Kentucky, won 17 NASCAR races last year. With the help of his friend, a programmer at one of the local banks, he was able to write a FORTRAN program to determine the mean speed of last year's races. The average speeds of his races are as follows:

DAYTONA RACETRACK	156 MPH
ATLANTA RACTRACK	201 MPH
NEW ORLEANS RACETRACK	147 MPH
MIAMI RACETRACK	176 MHP
HOUSTON RACETRACK	182 MPH
DALLAS RACETRACK	196 MPH
BARBERSVILLE RACETRACK	190 MPH
TAMPA RACETRACK	200 MPH
WASHINGTON RACETRACK	153 MPH
LOUISVILLE RACETRACK	183 MPH
HUNTSVILLE RACETRACK	204 MPH
LITTLE ROCK RACETRACK	177 MPH
ASHVILLE RACETRACK	171 MPH
ORLANDO RACETRACK	159 MPH
NEW YORK RACETRACK	169 MPH
BOSTON RACETRACK	170 MPH
CHICAGO RACETRACK	168 MPH

Richard used the following equations in his program.

The *mean* (or average), which is a measure of the central tendency of a statistical distribution, is determined by

$$X = \frac{1}{n} \sum_{i=1}^{n} X_i$$

where X_i for i = 1, 2, 3, 4, 5, . . . , with n representing the value of X at the ith race. The variance, which is a measure of the dispersion or spread of a statistical distribution, is determined by

$$V = \frac{1}{n-1} \left[\sum X_i^2 - \frac{(\sum X_i)^2}{n} \right]$$

where X_i = 1, 2, 3, 4, 5, . . . , n represents the value of X at the ith race.

The standard deviation is also a measure of the dispersion of a statistical distribution and is defined as the positive value of the square root of the variance (V).

$$\sigma_x = \sqrt{V} = \sqrt{\frac{1}{n-1} \left[\sum X_i^2 - \frac{(\sum X_i)^2}{n} \right]}$$

For this problem, Richard used an n of 17 and the following values of X:

X_i = 156	X_9 = 153
X_2 = 201	X_{10} = 183
X_3 = 147	X_{11} = 204
X_4 = 176	X_{12} = 177
X_5 = 182	X_{13} = 171
X_6 = 196	X_{14} = 159
X_7 = 190	X_{15} = 169
X_8 = 200	X_{16} = 170
	X_{17} = 168

Richard's program is shown in Figure 15–9.

The program caused the following message to be printed.

```
WEDDY'S CAR SPEEDS
NUMBER OF RACES = 17
STANDARD DEVIATION = 17.4894
VARIANCE = 305.8824
MEAN = 176.5882
```

Gas Station Robbery

This problem involves a knowledge of the Pythagorean theorem. Before we continue with the problem, let us review the elementary trigonometry involved.

The Pythagorean thorem is one of the most basic theorems we have today. It concerns, in particular, so-called right triangles, i.e., triangles containing a 90° angle. These right triangles have a unique property.

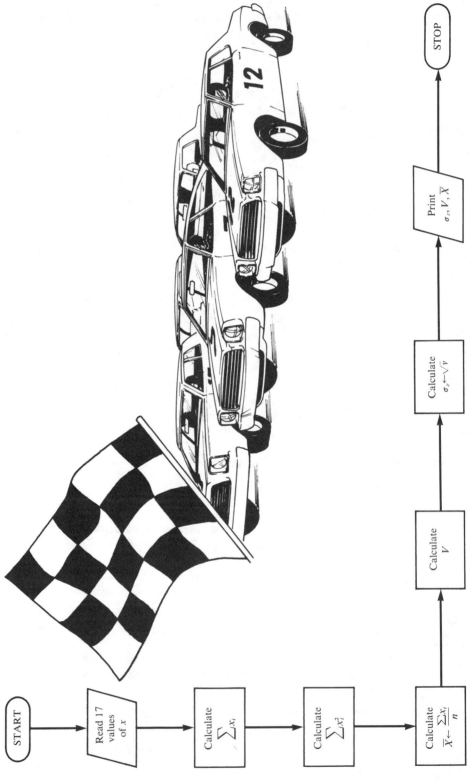

FORTRAN STATEMENT

```
C     RICHARD WEDDY'S AUTO RACES
C     COMPUTES THE MEAN, VARIANCE, AND SD. DEV.
      DIMENSION X(17)
      SUMX = 0.0
      SUMSQ = 0.0
C     READ 17 VALUES OF X
      DO 20 N=1,17
      READ(2,10)X(N)
10    FORMAT(F5.0)
      SUMX = SUMX + X(N)
      SUMSQ = SUMSQ + X(N)*X(N)
20    CONTINUE
C     COMPUTE THE MEAN
      XBAR = SUMX/17.0
C     COMPUTE VARIANCE
      VAR = (SUMSQ-(SUMX**2/17.0))/17.0-1.0
C     COMPUTE STANDARD DEVIATION
      STDEV = SQRT(VAR)
C     PRINT STANDARD DEVIATION, VARIANCE, AND MEAN
      WRITE(3,30)STDEV,VAR,XBAR
30    FORMAT(19H WEDDY'S CAR SPEEDS,/,20HNUMBER OF RACES = 17,/,
     2 20HVARIANCE = F16.4,/,16HMEAN = F16.4)
      STOP
      END
```

Figure 15-9 This program computes the mean, variance, and standard deviation of the speed of Richard Weddy's auto races last year.

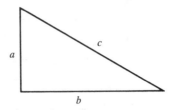

In any triangle containing a right (90°) angle, the square of the hypotenuse is equal to the sum of the squares of the other two sides. (The longest side—the side opposite the right angle—is called the *hypotenuse.*) Thus, if the triangle *abc* shown contains a right angle, then

$$c^2 = a^2 + b^2$$

An infinite number of integer triplets conform to this pattern. Such a Pythagorean triplet is 3, 4, 5, where $5^2 = 3^2 + 4^2$. Another is 5, 12, 13, where $13^2 = 5^2 + 12^2$.

Now let us examine the problem. In a small western state, the automobile license numbers are of the form:

XX-XX-XX

where X can be any digit from 0 to 0.

For every license plate issued, there is a punched card containing the number of the plate. The format of the card is (I2, 1X, I2, 1X, I2). A typical batch of such cards would look like the following:

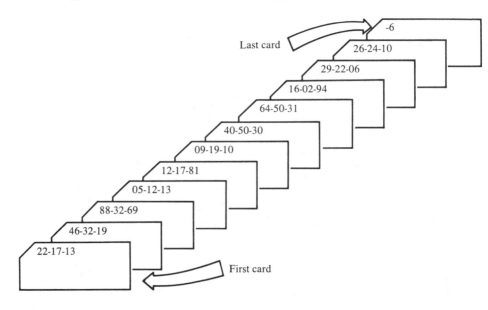

The exact number of cards is not known, but a special card (called a *trailer card*) with -6 punched in columns 1 and 2 is placed behind the last card.

Following a robbery of his gas station, the owner, a former mathematics teacher, gave chase while the robbers were making their getaway in a truck. As he approached the truck, they shot him just as he managed to catch a glimpse of the license plate. The sheriff soon arrived and immediately questioned the wounded gas station attendant about the license plate number. His last words before dying were, ". . . *the sides of a right triangle.*"

The sheriff, who had been using computers for years, quickly wrote the FORTRAN program shown in Figure 15–10. This program examined all the license plate numbers in the state and determined what automobiles were possible "suspects".

The program output produced the following license plate numbers.

A short time after watching the owners of the automobiles with these license plates, the sheriff caught the man who performed the robbery and murder. The murderer is now spending time in a penitentiary—thanks to a modern-day sheriff.

Review Exercises

24. What is the purpose of control statements?

25. Distinguish the difference between a conditional and an unconditional branching statement. Give an example of each.

26. Distinguish the difference between an arithmetic IF and a logical IF statement. Give an example of each.

27. Explain the function of the DO statement.

28. What is the main function of input/output statements?

29. What are the primary functions of the READ and WRITE statements? Give examples.

30. Define an array, and discuss the usefulness of arrays in FORTRAN.

31. For what is the DIMENSION statement used?

32. Write a program to calculate and print a table of numbers from 1 to 20 with their squares.

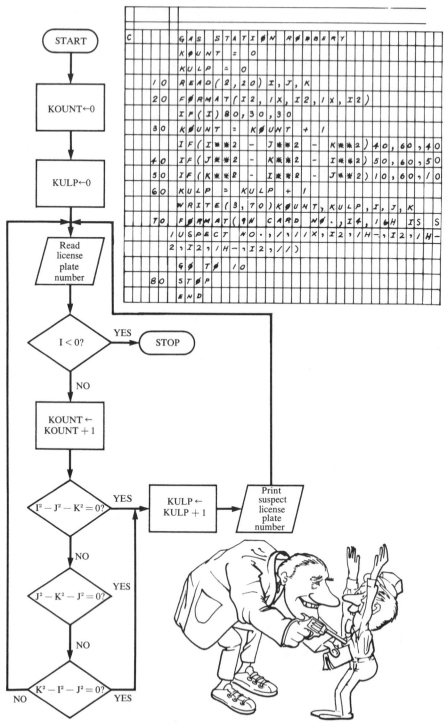

```
C           GAS STATION ROBBERY
            KOUNT = 0
            KULP = 0
10          READ (2,20) I, J, K
20          FORMAT (I2, 1X, I2, 1X, I2)
            IF (I) 80, 30, 30
30          KOUNT = KOUNT + 1
            IF (I**2 - J**2 - K**2) 40, 60, 40
40          IF (J**2 - K**2 - I**2) 50, 60, 50
50          IF (K**2 - I**2 - J**2) 10, 60, 10
60          KULP = KULP + 1
            WRITE (3,70) KOUNT, KULP, I, J, K
70          FORMAT (9H  CARD NO. , I4, 16H IS S
           1USPECT NO. , , / , 11X, I2, 1H-, I2, 1H-
           2, I2, 1H-, I2, //)
            GO TO 10
80          STOP
            END
```

Flowchart labels:

START

KOUNT←0

KULP←0

Read license plate number

I < 0? —YES→ STOP

NO

KOUNT ← KOUNT + 1

I² − J² − K² = 0? —YES→ KULP ← KULP + 1 → Print suspect license plate number

NO

J² − K² − J² = 0? —YES→

NO

K² − I² − J² = 0? —YES

NO

Figure 15–10   This program examines all the license plate numbers of a western state to determine "suspects" in a robbery and murder case.

```
        XXXX
       X    VX
      X  VV   X
     X  Ø   Ø  X
      X   )   X
     X    -    X
       XXXXX
       XXXX
      XX - -XX
      XXX - -X
      XXXX - - )
      XXXX - - )
       XXXXXX
         VVV
       VV VV
        Ø )Ø )
```

33. Here is Charlie Brown! The picture shown was generated by a BASIC program on a teletype-writer. Write a FORTRAN program that will produce this "piece of art". The characters and symbols to use in your program are: X, V, O, — (minus sign), and the right parentheses,).

34. Write a program that reads time in seconds, then converts it to hours, minutes, and seconds.

35. Write a FORTRAN program to determine the perimeter of the pentagon shown.

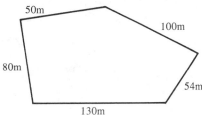

36. Bill purchased a television set that was advertised at a 25% discount in price. Write a FORTRAN program to determine what Bill paid for the TV, given that the regular price of the TV was $364.

37. Nancy Sweetface receives a wage of $3.40 per hour. Write a program to determine what Nancy earns in one week if she works 38.5 hours.

38. Three values are punched in a card. The first and second values are integers punched in columns 10 and 11, and 20 and 21 respectively. The third value is real, with one place to the right of the decimal point. It is punched in columns 30 through 34.

    Write a FORTRAN program to read the values and then to print them with 10 spaces between the output fields. To test the program, let the three values be 67, 21, 364.2.

39. Write a program to calculate the final balance of a 30-day savings account where the amount deposited each day is twice the amount of the previous day. Start the account with $1 on day 1, then add $2 on day 2, $4 the next day, etc.

40. The annual depreciation of an asset by the straight-line method is cal-culated by the following formula:

$$\text{depreciation} = \frac{\text{cost} - \text{salvage value}}{\text{service life}}$$

41. Write a FORTRAN program that reads the cost, salvage value, and service life in format (F10.2, F8.2, F2.0). Then calculate the depreciation and write the result in the following format (x's represent digits):

ANNUAL DEPRECIATION IS $xxxxxx.xx$

Test the program, using $14,200 for the cost, $1,200 for the salvage value, and 9 years for the service life.

42. The telephone company charge for long-distance calls is based not only on distance but on the length of time of a call. Let us assume that between two cities the rate is $1.10 for the first three minutes or fraction thereof and $0.40 for each additional minute. Data for a number of customers who made calls between these two cities is punched in the following format:

Card Columns	Field
1–5	Customer ID number
10–11	Length of call (minutes)

Write a FORTRAN program to calculate the charge for each call. Print the customers' ID number, the length of the call, and the charge.

Use the following data to test the program:

Customer ID Number	Length of Call
12630	10
16438	3
26107	22
46623	1
51210	6
10622	12
36107	2
71927	3
10037	9
21100	2
56274	3
37552	1
99999	

Note that the data includes a trailer card that can be used to terminate processing.

☐ Summary

FORTRAN is a higher-level programming language primarily designed for solving mathematical problems. It is used widely throughout the computer-using community. It is undoubtedly the most used higher-level language for nonbusiness applications.

The FORTRAN arithmetic command, which is very similar to common algebraic notation, uses the following arithmetic operators: + (addition), − (subtraction), * (multiplication), / (division), and ** (exponentiation). The equal sign (=) is different from the algebraic equal sign and in FORTRAN means: calculate the value of the expression to the right of the equal sign and store that value in the variable named to the left of the sign. Parentheses are used in the same way as in algebra.

The FORTRAN input command is the READ statement, which specifies an input device, refers to a FORMAT statement, and gives variable names for input data. The FORMAT statement specifies the type of data, the size of the fields in the input record, and the location of any necessary decimal positions. The FORTRAN output command is the WRITE statement, which specifies an output device, refers to a FORMAT statement, and lists the variable names of the data to be included in the output record.

FORTRAN control statements consist of the unconditional GO TO, arithmetic IF, logical IF, computed GO TO, and DO statement. Every FORTRAN program must physically end with an END statement.

This brief introduction to FORTRAN should enable you to write FORTRAN programs that will solve elementary business and statistical problems.

Key Terms

variable	statements
integer variable	coding form
real variable	library functions
constant	comments
integer constant	program
real constant	character set
expression	operators
FORTRAN expression	control statements
mathematical expression	unconditional GO TO
mixed mode	computed GO TO
array	arithmetic IF
subscript	logical IF
subscripted variable	DO
one-dimensional array	CONTINUE
two-dimensional array	STOP
list	END
table	READ
matrices	WRITE
	FORMAT
	DIMENSION

16

COBOL

Courtesy of Montgomery Ward

COBOL is an acronym for COmmon Business Oriented Language. It is a higher-level programming language that has been implemented on a large number of medium- and large-scale computer systems. As the name implies, it is a language well suited to solving business data-processing problems. The language itself and the techniques for using it are, for the most part, conceived in terms of the problem to be solved and the results to be obtained rather than in terms of the specific features of the computer.

COBOL is a language that enables a user to: (1) describe files, (2) sort files, (3) update files, (4) obtain reports from files, and (5) make calculations, using various numeric values found in its file.

COBOL is widely used in business, since it permits the easy programming of complex business applications and can act as its own documentation.

In Chapter 13, you were introduced to programming concepts that applied to all programming languages. In Chapter 14, you were introduced to the easy-to-learn and easy-to-use BASIC language. Chapter 15 contained a description of the scientific programming language, FORTRAN. In this chapter, you will be introduced to the language most widely used to solve business problems. The presentation has been extremely simplified so that you may obtain a quicker grasp of the COBOL language. By simplifying the material, we have had to omit many of the features which make COBOL an excellent language for processing business applications.

☐ History of the COBOL Language

When computers designed to handle business applications were first commercially produced, each computer manufacturer developed its own business-oriented programming language, each essentially a version of COBOL. Although there were some similarities among these languages, there were many differences. In an attempt to standardize the rules governing the coding of COBOL programs, the Conference on Data Systems

Languages (CODASYL) regularly maintains the revision and updating of COBOL specifications. The recommendations of CODASYL are endorsed by the American National Standards Institute (ANSI) and the National Bureau of Standards (NBS).

I'd like to help you with your computer homework, but I don't understand COBOL.

☐ Pro's and Con's of COBOL

Like all other programming languages, COBOL has rules for grammar and punctuation. Because of the standardization of these rules, a COBOL program written for one computer could be compiled and run (this sometimes requires minor changes) on some other computer. Not only is the language machine independent, it is also vendor independent; that is, a program written in IBM 360 COBOL can be compiled on a Burroughs 6700 COBOL.

Programs written in COBOL make for easier communication between decision-making management, the systems analyst, the programmer, and the computer operator.

COBOL is a self-documenting language, which facilitates program analysis and simplifies any future modifications to the program. Programs produced by the COBOL compiler are free from clerical errors.

Because COBOL is easy to code, it is possible to write COBOL programs quickly. Corrections and modifications in program logic are easy to make.

New programming personnel can be trained to write productive programs with COBOL in substantially less time than it takes to train them in assembly language coding (such as the IBM 370 assembly language).

Because programming time is reduced, so are programming costs. COBOL will undoubtedly gain in popularity in the years to come, primarily because it is the only business programming language with sufficient versatility. RPG is a more limited language, primarily designed for the production of reports. PL/I is not available on a great number of machines. The Department of Defense, a large user of COBOL, has essentially closed the door on the development of other business data-processing languages by computer vendors or software service firms.

COBOL does have disadvantages. It is verbose; programs often contain a large number of statements. Due to the large size of the programs and the complexity of the language, COBOL programs typically require lengthy compilation times. Since the checkout phase of a program may require several compilations of the program before it is completely "debugged", the lengthy compilation time is a factor to consider.

Some users feel that the large amount of writing required to achieve documentation in COBOL is too great and prefer to use other programming languages.

COBOL Characters and Words

The character set for COBOL consists of the fifty-one following characters. Some COBOL implementations allow the use of other characters not shown.

Alphabetical Characters

A B C D E F G H I J K L M N
O P Q R S T U V W X Y Z

Numerals

1 2 3 4 5 6 7 8 9 0

Special Characters

$ * , . " ( ) ; > <
= + − / and space

A COBOL word is composed of a combination of characters chosen from the COBOL character set. The word cannot begin or end with a hyphen. The space is not an allowable character in a word. There are two types of COBOL words: *user-defined words* and *reserved words* (or names). User-supplied words or names, such as EMPLOYEE-NUMBER, PART-NUM, LAST-NAME, VENDOR, GRADE-CARDS, and SALES-FILE, are assigned by the user. Reserved words, such as RANDOM, ACCEPT, MULTIPLY, and TALLY, have special meaning to the COBOL compiler and must be used according to COBOL language rules. These words are an inherent part of the COBOL system, and users should avoid using them for data or procedure names. Examples of some reserved words and their special purpose are:

ACCEPT—This word causes data to be read from an appropriate input/output device.

ADD—This word causes two or more numeric operands to be summed and the result to be stored.

ALTER—This word modifies a predetermined sequence of operations.

CLOSE—This word terminates the processing of input and output files.

COMPUTE—This word assigns to one or more data items the value of a numeric data item, literal, or arithmetic expression.

DEFINE—This word allows new statements to be defined in terms of standard COBOL statements.

DISPLAY—This word causes data to be written on an appropriate input/output device.

DIVIDE—This word divides one numeric data item into others and sets the values of data items equal to the results.

EXAMINE—This word replaces or counts the number of occurrences of a given character in a data item.

EXIT—This word provides a common end point for a series of procedures.

GO TO—This word causes program control to be transferred from one part of the PROCEDURE DIVISION to another.

HOLD—This word provides, in an asynchronous environment, a delay point that causes synchronous processing to be resumed.

IF—This word causes a condition to be evaluated. The subsequent action of the object program depends on whether the value of the condition is *true* or *false*.

INCLUDE—This word incorporates library routines into the PROCEDURE DIVISION of the source program.

INITIATE—This word begins processing a report.

MOVE—This word transfers data to one or more data areas.

MULTIPLY—This word causes numeric data items to be multiplied and sets the values of data items equal to the results.

NOTE—This word allows the user to write commentary which will be produced on the listing, but not compiled.

OPEN—This word initiates the processing of both input and output files. It performs checking and/or writing of labels and other input/output operations.

PERFORM—This word is used to depart from the normal sequence of execution in order to execute one or more procedures either a specified number of times or until a specified condition is satisfied and to return control to the normal sequence.

READ—This word makes available the next logical record from an input file (for sequential file processing); and, for random file processing, the READ statement makes available a specified record from a mass storage file.

RELEASE—This word transfers records to the initial phase of a sort operation.

RETURN—This word obtains sorted records from the final phase of a sort operation.

SEARCH—This word is used to search a table for a table-element that satisfies the specified condition and to adjust the associated index-name to indicate that table-element.

SEEK—This word initiates the accessing of a mass storage data record for subsequent reading or writing.

SET—This word establishes reference points for table-handling operations by setting index-names associated with table elements.

SORT—This word creates a sort-file by executing input procedures or by transferring records from another file, sorts the records in the sort-file on a set of specified keys, and in the final phase of the sort operation, makes available each record from the sort-file, in sorted order, to some output procedures or to an output file.

STOP—This word halts the object program permanently or temporarily.

SUBTRACT—This word is used to subtract one, or the sum of two or more, numeric data items from one or more items, and to set the values of one or more items equal to the results.

TERMINATE—This word terminates the processing of a report.

WRITE—This word releases a logical record for an output file.

A list of COBOL reserved words is shown in Figure 16–1. ANSI COBOL has additional reserved words. Also, each manufacturer's COBOL compiler may include some additional words. It is always wise to check the manufacturer's COBOL Reference Manual for the system being used.

In Chapters 15 and 16, we learned that BASIC and FORTRAN had about 20 or 30 reserved words (or statement names) respectively. In contrast to these languages, COBOL has over 250 reserved words (some systems have over 300 reserved words).

☐ Literals

A *literal* is an actual value that remains unchanged during the execution of the program. The two main types are numeric and nonnumeric literals.

ACCEPT	DE	INDICATE	PAGE	SELECT
ACCESS	DECIMAL-POINT	INITIATE	PAGE-COUNTER	SENTENCE
ACTUAL	DECLARATIVES	INPUT	PERFORM	SEQUENTIAL
ADD	DEPENDING	INPUT-OUTPUT	PF	SIZE
ADVANCING	DESCENDING	INSTALLATION	PH	SORT
AFTER	DETAIL	INTO	PICTURE	SOURCE
ALL	DIRECT	INVALID	PLUS	SOURCE-COMPUTER
ALPHABETIC	DIRECT-ACCESS	I-O	POSITIVE	SPACE
ALTER	DISPLAY	I-O-CONTROL	PRINT-SWITCH	SPACES
ALTERNATIVE	DISPLAY-ST	IS	PROCEDURE	SPECIAL-NAMES
AND	DIVIDE		PROCEED	STANDARD
APPLY	DIVISION	JUSTIFIED	PROCESS	STOP
ARE			PROCESSING	SUBTRACT
AREA	ELSE	KEY	PROGRAM-ID	SUM
AREAS	END		PROTECTION	SYMBOLIC
ASCENDING	ENDING	LABEL		SYSIN
ASSIGN	ENTER	LABELS	QUOTE	SYSOUT
AT	ENTRY	LAST	QUOTES	SYSPUNCH
AUTHOR	ENVIRONMENT	LEADING		
	EQUAL	LESS		TALLY
BEFORE	ERROR	LINE	RANDOM	TALLYING
BEGINNING	EVERY	LINE-COUNTER	RD	TERMINATE
BLANK	EXAMINE	LINES	READ	THAN
BLOCK	EXHIBIT	LINKAGE	READY	THEN
BY	EXIT	LOCK	RECORD	THRU
		LOW-VALUE	RECORDING	TIMES
CALL	FD	LOW-VALUES	RECORDS	TO
CF	FILE		REDEFINES	TRACE
CH	FILES		REEL	TRACK-AREA
CHANGED	FILE-CONTROL	MODE	RELATIVE	TRACKS
CHARACTERS	FILE-LIMIT	MORE-LABELS	RELEASE	TRANSFORM
CHECKING	FILLER	MOVE	REMARKS	TRY
CLOCK-UNITS	FINAL	MULTIPLY	REPLACING	TYPE
CLOSE	FIRST		REPORT	
COBOL	FOOTING		REPORTING	UNIT
CODE	FOR	NAMED	REPORTS	UNIT-RECORD
COLUMN	FORM-OVERFLOW	NEGATIVE	RERUN	UNITS
COMMA	FROM	NEXT	RESERVE	UNTIL
COMPUTATIONAL		NO	RESET	UPON
COMPUTATIONAL-1	GENERATE	NOT	RESTRICTED	USAGE
COMPUTATIONAL-2	GIVING	NOTE	RETURN	USE
COMPUTATIONAL-3	GO	NUMERIC	REVERSED	USING
COMPUTE	GREATER		REWIND	UTILITY
CONFIGURATION	GROUP	OBJECT-COMPUTER	REWRITE	
CONSOLE		OCCURS	RF	VALUE
CONTAINS	HEADING	OF	RH	VARYING
CONTROL	HIGH-VALUE	OH	RIGHT	
CONTROLS	HIGH-VALUES	OMITTED	ROUNDED	WHEN
COPY	HOLD	ON	RUN	WITH
CORRESPONDING		OPEN		WORKING-STORAGE
CREATING		OR	SA	WRITE
CYCLES	IDENTIFICATION	ORGANIZATION	SAME	WRITE-ONLY
	IF	OTHERWISE	SD	
DATA	IN	OUTPUT	SEARCH	ZERO
DATE-COMPILED	INCLUDE	OV	SECTION	ZEROES
DATE-WRITTEN	INDEXED	OVERFLOW	SECURITY	ZEROS

Figure   COBOL reserved words.
16-1

A *numeric literal* is a string of characters chosen from the digits 0–9, the plus or minus sign, and the decimal point. The value of the literal is implicit in the character itself. Thus, 457 is both the literal and the value itself. The primary use of numeric literals is in arithmetic computations.

A *nonnumeric literal* is a string of characters enclosed by quotation marks. Nonnumeric literals are used mainly for displaying messages and printing headings for reports.

Examples

COMPUTE TAX = RATE * AMOUNT + 210.   The numbers
ADD SALES TO 1000 TO OBTAIN TOTAL.   210, 1000, and
MULTIPLY SALES BY .05 GIVING BONUS.   .05 are *numeric*
                                         literals.

77 LOWER-LIMIT, PICTURE XXX.X, VALUE '76'.   Characters enclosed
DISPLAY 'GUEST NAME SAM BIGFOOT'.   by quotation
                                              marks are *non-
                                              numeric* literals.

A numeric literal cannot be represented in exponential form (such as $0.230E+02$) as can be done in BASIC, FORTRAN, and other scientific-oriented languages.

Operators

Operators are used in COBOL to specify some type of action or relationship between two items in a program. Symbols are special items in a program. Symbols are special characters that have a specific meaning in COBOL programs. The type of operators and their symbolic forms are as follows:

Arithmetic Expression Operators are used in expressions.

Arithmetic Operator	Name	Meaning
+	Plus	Addition
−	Minus	Subtraction
*	Asterisk	Multiplication
/	Slash	Division
**	Double Asterisk	Exponentiation
=	Make equivalent to	Equal

Relational Expression Operators are used to make comparisons between data values.

Symbol	Name	Meaning
>	Greater than	$6 > 2$
<	Less than	$4 < 10$
=	Equal	$12 = 12$

Logical Expresssion Operators are used to combine simple statements in the same expression for the purpose of testing the condition of the expression, e.g.,

IF X = Y or X > Z AND W IS NEGATIVE, GO TO AAA.

The logical operators are:

Logical Operator	Meaning
AND	Used to evaluate both statements
OR	Used to evaluate either or both statements
NOT	Used to negate a positive condition

Punctuation Symbols are used in special ways in a COBOL program.

Symbol	Name	Meaning
.	Period	Used to terminate entries
,	Comma	Used to separate operands or clauses in a series of entries
;	Semicolon	Used to separate clauses and statements
/	Quotation mark	Used to enclose nonnumeric literals

Parentheses Symbols, ( ), are used to enclose subscripts, to control the sequence of calculations, and to control the sequence of statements to be evaluated.

Welcome aboard. This is your captain, IBM 370, speaking.

☐ Pictures

A *picture* is a string of specific alphabetic, numeric, or alphanumeric characters which give certain characteristics of data items. It may describe the number (size) and type (alphabetic, numeric, or alphanumeric) of characters in a data item, the location of a decimal point, if any, and the extent of editing needed to form a data item. This information often is necessary before the computer is able to process certain files.

The specific characters which constitute a picture are

0 9 A B CR DB E K P S V X Z + − ( ) , . * $

Examples

02   UNIT-PRICE PICTURE $$,$$$.99.
03   MONTH PICTURE 99.
03   DAY PICTURE 99.
03   YEAR PICTURE 9999.
02   XYZ PICTURE AAA.
02   MEN AVAILABLE, PICTURE 9999.

A picture may also use an unsigned numeric literal enclosed in parentheses to indicate a repetition of picture characteristics. For example, the following statement

02   CREDIT-FILE, PICTURE A(11).

means the same as

02   CREDIT-FILE, PICTURE AAAAAAAAAAA.

☐ COBOL Coding Form

To write programs in COBOL, the user must pay attention to punctuation, spacing, and indentions. A special COBOL coding form is usually used as an aid to the programmer. Although not necessary, its use simplifies writing the format required by COBOL. Figure 16–2 shows a sample COBOL coding form. In compiling, only columns 7 to 72 are used; columns 1 to 6 and 73 to 80 are for identification and reference purposes. The positions on the coding form have the following meaning:

COLUMN	USE
1–3	Recording the page number
4–6	Recording the line number
7	Signaling the continuation of a command, indicated by a hyphen
8–72	Program coding. Column 8 is also called the A margin and column 12 the B margin.
73–80	Program identification

Each line on the coding form corresponds to a single punched card. Division, section, and paragraph names begin at the A margin (column 8), while paragraph contents are written starting at the B margin (column 12). Most of the program coding, except significant names, starts at the B margin.

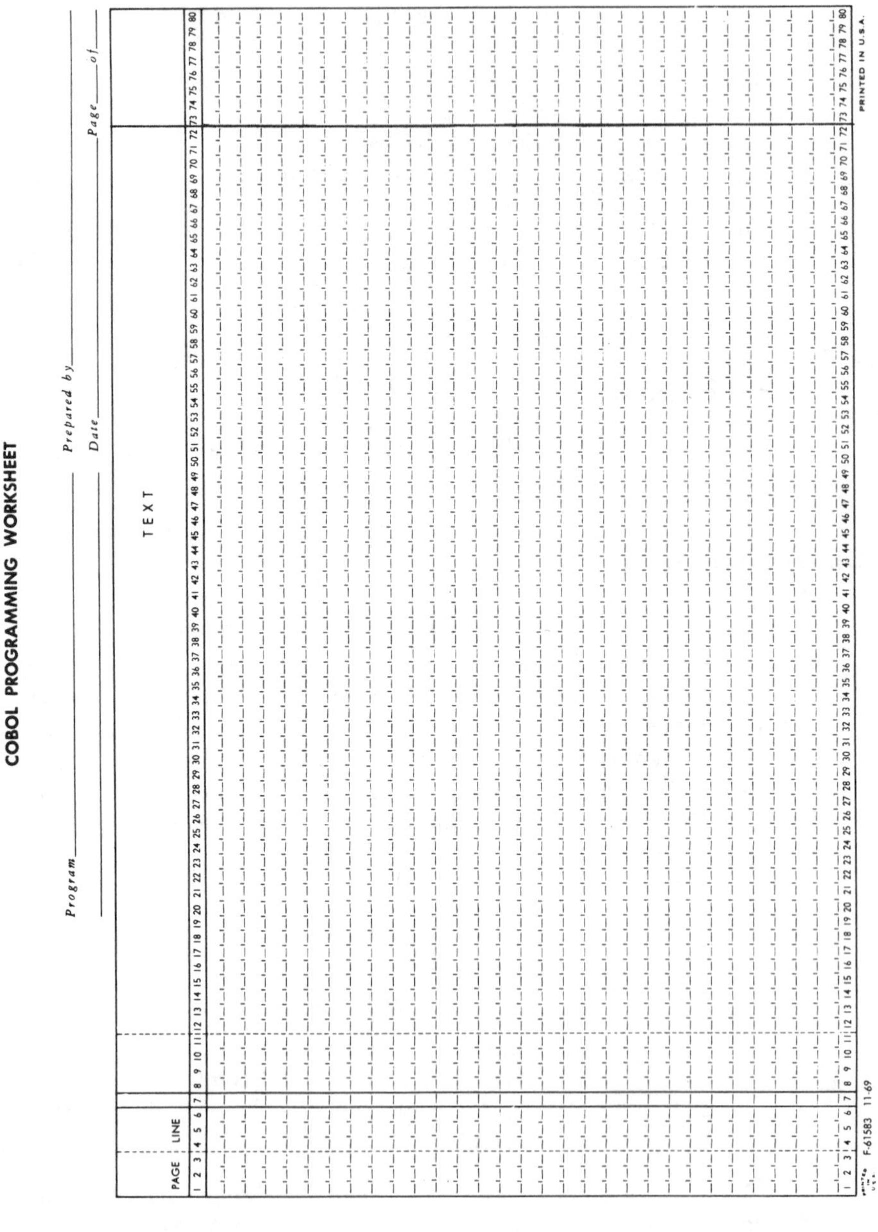

COBOL PROGRAMMING WORKSHEET

Figure 16-2 COBOL coding form.

420

☐ Structure of a COBOL Program

A COBOL program consists of four parts, called divisions:

1. The *identification division* is used to attach a unique identification, such as program name, program number, program version, programmer's name, and installation, to the program.
2. The *environment division* is used to specify the computer on which the program is to be compiled and executed.
3. The *data division* is used to define the characteristics and format of data to be processed.
4. The *procedure division* is used to describe the internal processing that is to be performed. All input/output operations, computational operations, logical decisions, and data movement must be defined in this section.

All four divisions must be present in the order specified in Figure 16–3. In summary, the four divisions of a COBOL program provide identification, a description of the equipment being used, a description of the data being processed, and a set of procedures specifying how the data is to be processed. A more detailed description of each division follows.

Identification Division

The IDENTIFICATION DIVISION identifies a program and the output from a compilation. It is the shortest of the major COBOL divisions.

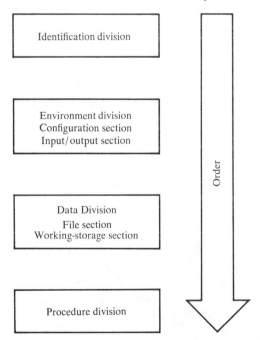

Figure 16–3   Major divisions of a COBOL program.

It allows the programmer to assign the program a name and to supply other information serving to identify the program, such as the author, the date the program is written, the date the program was compiled, and other information as desired under the paragraphs in the General Format. This division is similar to the COMMENT statement in FORTRAN and the REM (remark) statement in BASIC.

The following format shows the structure of the IDENTIFICATION DIVISION. It consists of seven paragraphs, of which only the first is required; the others are all optional and may appear in any order.

```
IDENTIFICATION DIVISION.
PROGRAM-ID. Name.
AUTHOR. Name.
DATE-WRITTEN. Date
DATE-COMPILED. Date
REMARKS. Remarks.
INSTALLATION. Remarks
SECURITY. Remarks
```

The program name may be any word meeting regular COBOL requirements. This name is associated with the program during compilation and serves to identify the compiled program with diagnostic printouts and computer-oriented comments. Each entry starts in column 8 (A margin), and both the specified COBOL words and programmer-supplied names, dates, and remarks must end with a period.

An example of an IDENTIFICATION DIVISION follows.

```
IDENTIFICATION DIVISION.
PROGRAM-ID. PAYROLL
AUTHOR. NANCY ROSEDALE.
INSTALLATION. ACCOUNTING DEPARTMENT.
DATE-WRITTEN. MARCH 4.
DATE-COMPILED. MARCH 8.
REMARKS. THIS PROGRAM PROCESSES THE
         COMPANY PAYROLL. THE PROGRAM
         IS USED ON THE 20TH DAY OF
         EACH MONTH.
```

Environment Division

The ENVIRONMENT DIVISION specifies a standard method of expressing those aspects of a data-processing problem that depend on the physical characteristics of a specific computer. This division allows specification of the configuration of the compiling computer and the computer on which the program is to be executed. In addition, information relating to input/output control, special hardware characteristics, and control techniques can be specified. In other words, the environment division indicates what hardware is to be used for compilation, input/output, and program execution (see Figure 16–4).

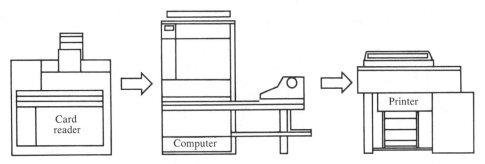

Figure The environment division is used to specify the hardware to be used.
16–4

The ENVIRONMENT DIVISION is divided into two sections—the Configuration Section and the Input/Output Section.

The *Configuration Section* specifies the computer that is used to compile the source program and to execute the machine-language program. This section is divided into three paragraphs: the SOURCE-COMPUTER paragraph, which describes the computer configuration on which the source program is compiled; the OBJECT-COMPUTER paragraph, which describes the computer configuration that will be used to execute the program; and the SPECIAL-NAMES paragraph, which relates the implementor-names used by the compiler to the mnemonic-names used in the source program.

Following is the general structure of the configuration section of the ENVIRONMENT DIVISION. All paragraphs except SPECIAL-NAMES are always required.

```
ENVIRONMENT DIVISION.
CONFIGURATION SECTION.
SOURCE COMPUTER. Computer name.
OBJECT COMPUTER. Computer name.
SPECIAL-NAMES. Compiler name IS mnemonic name.
```

Having identified the configuration, the programmer must then define input/output techniques, files, and associated files with external media. This is accomplished by the *input/output section,* which is divided into two paragraphs: the FILE-CONTROL paragraph, which names and associates the files with external media; and the I/O-CONTROL paragraph, which defines special control techniques to be used in the object program. The general structure of this section follows:

```
INPUT/OUTPUT SECTION.
FILE-CONTROL.
   SELECT file-name ASSIGN TO hardware-name.
I/O-CONTROL.
   APPLY input/output techniques ON file-name.
```

An example of an **ENVIRONMENT DIVISION** follows.

```
ENVIRONMENT DIVISION.
CONFIGURATION SECTION.
SOURCE-COMPUTER. IBM-370.
OBJECT-COMPUTER. IBM-370.
INPUT-OUTPUT SECTION.
FILE-CONTROL.
     SELECT CARD-FILE ASSIGN TO
     UR − 3641 − S − TAPE1.
     SELECT PRINT-FILE ASSIGN TO
     UR − 6412 − S − TAPE2.
```

Data Division

The **DATA DIVISION** describes the files and records that will serve as input to and output from the program. It has two parts—the file section and the working-storage section

```
DATA DIVISION.
FILE SECTION.
     • file description entry
     • record description entry

WORKING STORAGE SECTION.
     • data item description entry
     • record description entry
```

The file section defines the contents of data files stored on an external medium. Each file is defined by a file description followed by a record description or a series of record descriptions. At this point, we should review the terms *file* and *record*. A file is a collection of related information about some subject that is directed toward some purpose. Two types of files are usually needed to maintain most recorded business information—master files and transaction files. A *master file* is a permanent recording that shows the status of any segment of information. With manual bookkeeping, a ledger book is an example of a master file and may include inventory, payroll earnings, and accounts receivable. *Transaction files* are made up of daily or periodic transactions that are assembled and then recorded into the permanent file of master records. Transaction files may be made up of invoices of sales to customers, records of goods received for inventory, etc. A file consists of a collection of *records* providing information about a group of stock items, related accounts, etc. A file, then, is composed of a collection of many records as shown in Figure 16–5.

Because a variety of files may be used by a program, each with a different format, the user must describe each of these to the computer, using the following format:

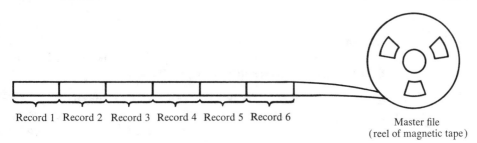

Record 1   Record 2   Record 3   Record 4   Record 5   Record 6   Master file
                                                                                (reel of magnetic tape)

Figure   A master file showing the breakdown into many records.
16–5

FD file name . . .
01 record name . . .
02 description of record item . . .

The FD stands for file description.

The working-storage section describes records and noncontiguous data items which are not part of external files but are developed and processed internally. The skeleton format for the working-storage section is as follows:

WORKING-STORAGE SECTION.
77 field name.

.
.
.

01 record name.

.
.
.

```
DATA  DIVISION.
FILE  SECTION.
FD      PAY-FILE
01      PAY-REC.
        02          EMP-NUMB            PICTURE 999999.
        02          PAY-RATE            PICTURE 99V99.
        02          HOURS-WORKED        PICTURE 99V99.
        02          FILLER              PICTURE X(20).
FD      GROSS-FILE
        TOTAL-REC.
01      GROSS-REC.
        02          EMP-NO              PICTURE 999999.
        02          GROSS-PAY           PICTURE 9999V99.
        02          FILLER              PICTURE X(50).
01      TOTAL-REC.
        02          TOTAL-PAY           PICTURE 9(6)V99.
        02          FILLER              PICTURE X(50).
WORKING-STORAGE SECTION.
77 TOTAL-GROSS                          PICTURE 9(6)V99 VALUE ZERO.
```

Considerable care must be taken in developing the DATA DIVISION of a program. It provides a standard technique to describe files and data within files; however, careful planning of file structure and precision in the item descriptions is still required of the user.

The ENVIRONMENT DIVISION describes the computer upon which the source program will be compiled and the computer that will be used to execute the object program; the DATA DIVISION describes the characteristics of the data; and the PROCEDURE DIVISION describes the logical steps necessary to process the data.

Procedure Division

The last part of a COBOL program is the PROCEDURE DIVISION, where step-by-step instructions for computer operation are written in meaningful English with verbs denoting actions, sentences describing procedures, and conditional statements specifying alternate paths of action.

The principal subdivision of the PROCEDURE DIVISION is the *paragraph* (or section). This is a program segment of at least one sentence, introduced by a name, called a paragraph or *procedure* name. *Sentences* exist within paragraphs. A sentence consists of one or more statements. Sentences are composed of words and symbols beginning with a COBOL verb.

Examples

```
ADD X TO Y.
SUBTRACT ERROR FROM SALES-TOTAL.
MULTIPLY A BY B GIVING C.
DIVIDE YEARLY-PAY BY X.
COMPUTE X = W + Y / A + V * U.
COMPUTE Y = Y + 1.
MOVE 274 TO ALPHA.
GO TO INCOME-TAX.
STOP RUN.
DIVIDE A INTO B, GIVING C, ROUNDED.
SUBTRACT DEDUCTIONS FROM GROSS, GIVING NET-PAY.
IF RESULT IS POSITIVE, GO TO FINAL-RUN.
```

The preceding three divisions (IDENTIFICATION, ENVIRONMENT, and DATA) are passive, since they contain only information for documentation and description of files, records, hardware, and work areas where intermediate results are to be stored. However, the procedure division is active in the sense that it contains verbs that tell the computer what to do with the files and records described in other divisions.

The **PROCEDURE DIVISION** contains instructions for the transfer of data between input/output devices and the computer. It also carries instructions informing the computer just what to do with the data. Still other instructions in the procedure division tell the computer in what sequence to execute the operations. A sample procedure division follows:

```
PROCEDURE DIVISION.
START.
  OPEN INPUT PAY-FILE OUTPUT GROSS-FILE.
  MOVE SPACES TO GROSS-REC.
MAIN-JOB
  READ PAY-FILE AT END GO TO JOB-END.
  MOVE EMP-NUMBER TO EMP-NO.
  IF HOURS-WORKED GREATER THAN 40.0 GO TO OVER-TIME.
  COMPUTE GROSS-PAY = PAY-RATE * HOURS-WORKED.
  GO TO WRITE-RTN.
OVER-TIME.
  COMPUTE GROSS-PAY = PAY-RATE * 40.0 + (HOURS-WORKED − 40.0)
  * PAY-RATE * 1.5.
WRITE-RTN.
  WRITE GROSS-REC.
  COMPUTE TOTAL-GROSS = TOTAL-GROSS + GROSS-PAY
  GO TO MAIN-JOB.
JOB-END.
  MOVE SPACES TO TOTAL-REC.
  MOVE TOTAL-GROSS TO TOTAL-PAY.
  WRITE TOTAL-REC.
  CLOSE PAY-FILE GROSS-FILE.
  STOP RUN.
```

☐ A Sample Program

Before we look at a sample COBOL program, let us examine the
skeleton format of a complete program shown in Figure 16–6. This
format shows the four divisions of a COBOL program and the relative
order that each division appears in the program. All four divisions must
be present in the program in the indicated order.

COBOL PROGRAM SHEET

SEQUENCE		A	B		ID/UPDATE SEQ.
00101 0		IDENTIFICATION DIVISION.			
00102 0		PROGRAM-ID. name.			
00103 0		AUTHOR. name.			
00104 0		DATE-WRITTEN. date.			
00105 0		DATE-COMPILED. date.			
00106 0		REMARKS. remarks.			
00107 0		INSTALLATION. remarks.			
00108 0		SECURITY. remarks.			
00201 0		ENVIRONMENT DIVISION.			
00202 0		CONFIGURATION SECTION.			
00203 0		SOURCE-COMPUTER. name.			
00204 0		OBJECT-COMPUTER. name.			
00205 0		SPECIAL-NAMES.			
00206 0		hardware name IS mnemonic name.			
00207 0		INPUT-OUTPUT SECTION.			
00208 0		FILE CONTROL.			
00209 0		SELECT file ASSIGN TO hardware name.			
00210 0		I-O-CONTROL.			
00211 0		APPLY input-output-techniques ON file-name.			
00301 0		DATA DIVISION.			
00302 0		FILE SECTION.			
00303 0		FD file name RECORDING MODE IS mode BLOCK CONTAINS integer RECORD			
00304 0		S RECORD CONTAINS integer CHARACTERS LABEL RECORDS ARE			
00305 0		record-name -1, record-name -2 SEQUENCED ON data name.			
00306 0		01 record-name-1 descriptive clauses.			
00307 0		WORKING STORAGE SECTION.			
00308 0		nn data-name descriptive clauses.			
00401 0		PROCEDURE DIVISION.			
00402 0		section name SECTION pn.			
00403 0		paragraph-name.			
00404 0		procedural statements.			
00405 0		paragraph-name.			
00406 0		procedural statements.			

**Figure
16–6**   Skeleton format of a source program written in COBOL.

The sample program in Figure 16–7 shows the COBOL language. Normally, the program is prepared on a COBOL Coding Form and then transferred to 80-column punched cards. The sequence numbers appear in the first six columns, followed by position for continuation. The remainder of the line to column 72 contains the COBOL statement.

This sample program calculates the product of the values 643 and 761 and causes the product to be printed on the printer. This program is extremely simple and is used only to show how the different divisions go together to form a complete COBOL program.

The IDENTIFICATION DIVISION is simple and has six entries. Each entry starts in column 8. The first entry gives the program a name consisting of six characters. The next entry gives the programmer's name. Lines 001040 and 001050 supply information about when the program was written and compiled. The remarks at line 001060 describe the purpose of the program.

The ENVIRONMENT DIVISION consists of only four entries and describes the specific hardware to be used to compile and later to run this program. The first two entries are the standard division and section titles. The *source computer* paragraph starts at line 001100 and indicates the source computer is an IBM System/370. The *object computer* paragraph specifies on line 001110 that an IBM System/370 is also to be used to run the program.

The DATA DIVISION consists of five paragraphs, starting on line 001120 with the standard title for this division. In this division, we have identified names for the values used in the program. The first name is NUMBER-ONE and has been assigned the value of 643. The second name is NUMBER-TWO and has been given the value of 762. In this division, we also reserved an area in which to store the product. This area is given the name TOTAL and is a large enough storage area to contain any six-digit number. The names defined in the DATA DIVISION will be used in the following division.

The last division in our sample COBOL program is the PROCEDURE DIVISION. This division starts on line 001170 and consists of four paragraphs. In this division, the actual calculation of 643 and 762 takes place. Line 001180 causes the values contained in NUMBER-ONE and NUMBER-TWO to be multiplied together and the value of the product to be assigned to TOTAL. Line 001190 causes the computer product to be printed on the printer and then to stop the execution of the program. The last statement in the program is used to inform the COBOL compiler that this is the last paragraph in the program.

Figure 16–8 shows the sample program as it appears on punched cards. Observe that each line of information on the COBOL Coding Form resulted in a card being punched.

COBOL PROGRAM SHEET

| Program Name | MULTIPLICATION PROGRAM | Program No. | | Ext. | | Graphic | | Sheet 1 of 1 |
| Programmer D. SPENCER | | Pay No. | Charge No. | | | Punch | | Date JAN 5 |

SEQUENCE (Page)(Serial)	A	B						ID/UPDATE SEQ. Key / Serial
010	IDENTIFICATION DIVISION.							
020	PROGRAM-ID. SAMPLE.							
030	AUTHOR. D. D. SPENCER.							
040	DATE-WRITTEN. JANUARY 5.							
050	DATE-COMPILED. JANUARY 7.							
060	REMARKS. PROGRAM COMPUTES AND PRINTS THE							
070	PRODUCT OF 643 AND 762.							
080	ENVIRONMENT DIVISION.							
090	CONFIGURATION SECTION.							
100	SOURCE-COMPUTER. IBM-370.							
110	OBJECT-COMPUTER. IBM-370.							
120	DATA DIVISION.							
130	WORKING-STORAGE SECTION.							
140	77 TOTAL PICTURE 9(6).							
150	77 NUMBER-ONE PICTURE 999 VALUE IS 643.							
160	77 NUMBER-TWO PICTURE 999 VALUE IS 762.							
170	PROCEDURE DIVISION.							
180	CALCULATION. COMPUTE TOTAL = NUMBER-ONE * NUMBER-TWO							
190	DISPLAY TOTAL. STOP RUN.							
200	END PROGRAM.							

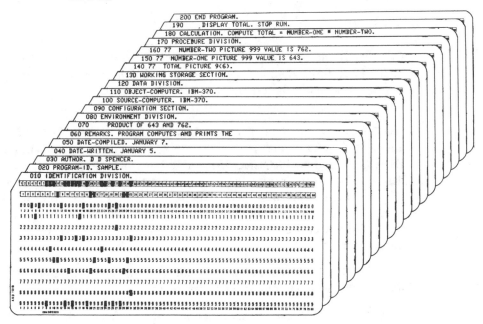

The cards read, from back to front:

```
200  END PROGRAM.
190       DISPLAY TOTAL. STOP RUN.
180  CALCULATION. COMPUTE TOTAL = NUMBER-ONE * NUMBER-TWO.
170  PROCEDURE DIVISION.
160  77  NUMBER-TWO PICTURE 999 VALUE IS 762.
150  77  NUMBER-ONE PICTURE 999 VALUE IS 643.
140  77  TOTAL PICTURE 9(6).
130  WORKING STORAGE SECTION.
120  DATA DIVISION.
110  OBJECT-COMPUTER. IBM-370.
100  SOURCE-COMPUTER. IBM-370.
090  CONFIGURATION SECTION.
080  ENVIRONMENT DIVISION.
070       PRODUCT OF 643 AND 762.
060  REMARKS. PROGRAM COMPUTES AND PRINTS THE
050  DATE-COMPILED. JANUARY 7.
040  DATE-WRITTEN. JANUARY 5.
030  AUTHOR. D D SPENCER.
020  PROGRAM-ID. SAMPLE.
010  IDENTIFICATION DIVISION.
```

Figure 16–8   Source deck of the sample COBOL program.

[] **Review Exercises**

1. Explain the main purpose of COBOL.

2. What are the important advantages of COBOL as a programming language?

3. What are some of the actions that COBOL may perform in connection with files?

4. What is the difference between the source computer and the object computer in a COBOL program?

5. What types of symbols are used in COBOL programs?

6. Describe the program structure of a COBOL program.

7. Discuss the difference between COBOL source and object decks. How do they differ from FORTRAN source and object decks?

8. What are the divisions of COBOL, and what are their main purposes?

9. What is the only entry required in the IDENTIFICATION DIVISION?

10. What is the purpose of the ENVIRONMENT DIVISION?

11. Can you compile a COBOL program on one computer and run it on another computer? Explain.

12. What are the primary functions of the DATA division?

13. Flowchart and code a program to compare X to Y. If X is greater than 100, the program is to transfer control to ABC-1. Otherwise, it should transfer control to ABC-2.

☐ Summary

COBOL is an acronym for *common business-oriented language,* a higher-level programming language. The COBOL language was developed to simplify the programming of business applications, such as payroll, inventory, and accounts receivable problems.

A COBOL program is divided into four divisions—the IDENTIFICATION DIVISION, the ENVIRONMENT DIVISION, the DATA DIVISION, and the PROCEDURE DIVISION. In these divisions, users describe data items in records, then instruct the computer what to do with the data items described. The IDENTIFICATION DIVISION names the program, names the author, specifies the date the program was written, identifies the problem, and indicates any other pertinent information about the program.

The ENVIRONMENT DIVISION indicates what hardware is used for compilation, input/output, and execution.

The DATA DIVISION provides for the explicit description of a program's data files and contents of the file records. The DATA division is divided into two sections. The FILE and WORKING-STORAGE section describes data records and fields that are necessary for processing but are not part of any input or output file.

The PROCEDURE DIVISION includes the commands needed by the computer to solve the problem, including logic, arithmetic, data movement, control, input and output instructions.

COBOL uses over 250 reserved words. Users can also define their own words or names.

This chapter could not begin to describe all COBOL features thoroughly. The interested reader is advised to select one of many excellent COBOL texts available on the market for further study.

Key Terms

COBOL	picture
Identification Division	CODASYL
Data Division	ANSI
Environment Division	NBS
Procedure Division	literal
reserved word	numeric literal
user-defined word	non-numeric literal
file	operators

master file

transaction file

record

paragraph

sentence

statement

coding form

source computer

object computer

compiler

17

PL/I

Courtesy of IBM Corporation

The preceding three chapters introduced two programming languages (BASIC and FORTRAN) designed to simplify the programming of scientific problems and a programming language (COBOL) designed to simplify the writing of business problems. This chapter presents the overview of a general-purpose programming language called *PL/I*.

PL/I contains many of the desired features of both FORTRAN and COBOL and even advances beyond their capabilities in many respects. One of the advantages of PL/I is that the user can write programs for both scientific and business applications.

Many people working in computer programming feel that PL/I is becoming increasingly important as a programming tool. As a result, it is attracting widespread interest.

☐ PL/I Fundamentals

Before we can even begin to write a PL/I program, we need to have some understanding of the elements that go into making up a program. Let us examine these elements to see how they are combined to form PL/I programs.

In Chapter 13, we defined a program as a series of statements that direct the computer to perform a specific operation or a series of operations. The sequence in which the statements are written in the program also defines, to some extent, the sequence in which the problem is to be solved.

PL/I Character Set

There are 60 characters in the PL/I language. These characters are English language alphabetic characters, decimal digits, and special characters.

- Alphabetic characters—the capital letters A through Z
- Numeric characters—the decimal digits 0 through 9
- Special characters—

Name	Character
Blank	
Equal or assignment symbol	=
Plus sign	+
Minus sign	−
Asterisk or multiply symbol	*
Slash or divide symbol	/
Left parentheses	(
Right parentheses	)
Comma	,
Period or point	.
Single quotation mark or apostrophe	,
Percent symbol	%
Semicolon	;
Currency symbol	$
Commercial "at" sign	@
Number sign	#
Colon	:
NOT symbol (logical operator)	⌐
AND symbol (logical operator)	&
OR symbol (logical operator)	|
"Greater than" symbol	>
"Less than" symbol	<
Break character	—
Question mark	?

Some of these characters are combined for special meanings; others have meanings different from what their symbol would imply normally. The combination ** denotes exponentiation. The symbols $>$, $<$, and $=$ are used as PL/I comparison operators:

Operator	Meaning
>	denoting greater than
> =	denoting greater than or equal to
⌐ =	denoting not greater than
=	denoting equal to
⌐ =	denoting not equal to
<	denoting less than
< =	denoting less than or equal to
⌐ <	denoting not less than

Format

The PL/I language allows the user many options and greater freedom in constructing the program than are available in either COBOL or FORTRAN. Similar to COBOL, though, the programs are made up of

Cartoon from "Computer Science Mathematics"

statements very much like sentences in the English language. Each statement either states a property of the program or tells the computer to perform some operation or sequence of operations.

Every PL/I statement ends with a semicolon rather than a period. In examples in this chapter, each statement will take a separate line, although this format is not necessary and does not affect the meaning of the program. A long statement might take several lines, while several short statements might be placed on one line together. The free format of PL/I eliminates the need for coding on special forms or for punching items in particular columns of a punched card.

Comments

Program authors frequently insert *comments* into their programs to clarify the action that occurs at a given point. These comments enable someone unfamiliar with the program to follow the author's line of thought and are helpful to the author when looking back over program sections that were written earlier.

The general form of a comment is

/ * *comment* * /

Examples

/ * THIS IS A COMMENT * /
/ * SO IS THIS *#?#8%*+#@ * /
/ * PROGRAM NAME—ACCOUNTING PAYROLL * /

As indicated, any legal PL/I character may be used in comments. Note that the comment *is not* a statement and, therefore, does not end with a semicolon.

Identifiers

An *identifier* is a combination of alphanumeric characters and break characters used in a program as names of data items, files, and special conditions, and as labels for statements. The actual words of the language, such as READ, GET, GO TO, PUT, DO, LIST, and WRITE, are also identifiers (called *keywords*). When used in proper context, these keywords have a specific meaning to the PL/I compiler; they specify such things as the action to be taken, the nature of the data, and the purpose of a name. Blanks are not permitted in identifiers.

Examples

SUM2	X
GROSS__SALES	ABC123
SALESPERSON	DECIMAL
INCOME__$	READ
AREA	#SALES
COMPUTER	$2ABC
PAY__NUMBER	AB@CD

The last three examples (#SALES, $2ABC, and AB@CD) illustrate the use of the characters #, $, and @. In the PL/I language, these characters are considered to be alphabetic characters so they can be used in PL/I identifiers. The first character of a word must be an alphabetic character.

The following examples cannot be used as identifiers:

GROSS SALES	(because it contains a blank)
7Y	(because it starts with a number)
AV*CD	(because * is not an alphameric character)

Variables

A *variable* may have different values during the execution of a program. For example, the variable EMPLOYEE_NUMBER is an identifier that can have a different value for each employee. Therefore, variables must be assigned identifiers to label or identify them. The identifier should be selected to suggest the use of the variable. For example, A could be used rather than EMPLOYEE_NUMBER but is more difficult to remember when writing the program.

Examples

CHECK	A	TEMP
SPEED	MASS	ID

PI	PAYROL	S123
UNIT	WAGE	INVENTORY

Constants

A *constant* is a specific value or number that does not change during the execution of the program. In PL/I, there are several different kinds of constants; the only ones we will use are decimal numbers. A constant can be written as an integer with or without a sign, such as:

6   47   0 -632

A constant may be written as a real number, which is a number with a decimal point. Examples are:

2.140 -63.7 .002

These examples represent a fixed format. Another format for real constants is the floating point format. It is similar to the scientific notation frequently used in scientific work. In scientific notation, the number is written as a decimal value usually lower than 10, followed by 10 to the appropriate power. For example:

9000 in scientific notation is 9.0×10^3
.000444 in scientific notation is 4.44×10^{-4}

The power of 10 indicates the number of places the decimal point must be moved to the right ($-$) or the left ($+$) in the original number to equal its scientific notation. Converting scientific notation to PL/I floating point notation is accomplished by using the letter E in place of the times sign and the number 10 in the scientific notation and writing the power as a regular number since PL/I has no raised numbers. For example:

9.0×10^3 is 9.0E3
4.44×10^{-4} is 4.44E-4

Expressions

Arithmetic expressions in PL/I differ somewhat from the way they are written in algebra. These differences are primarily due to limitations in the computer input/output media. For example, exponents cannot be raised, the square root sign cannot be used, and fractions have to be written with the numerator and denominator on the same line separated by the diagonal.

Arithmetic expressions consist of operators, operands, and parentheses. The operators indicate the operations to be performed and consist of $+$, $-$, *, /, **, in PL/I. The * for multiply cannot be omitted as it frequently is in algebra; for example, XY must be written X * Y.

Examples

Mathematical Notation	PL/I Notation
$a + b$	A + B
$4\pi r$	4 * PI * R
$\dfrac{a + b}{c}$	(A + B) / C
y^4	Y ** 4

The order in which the operations are performed is determined by their strength, which is:

strongest	exponentiation
next strongest	multiplication and division
weakest	addition and subtraction

Multiplication and division have equal strength, and the order does not matter within these two operations. Therefore, the leftmost operation is done first. The same is true with addition and subtraction. This order may be changed with the use of parentheses. When changing algebraic expressions into PL/I, it is frequently necessary to use parentheses; for example, A ** B + C implies (A ** B) + C; this may be modified to A ** (B + C) by inserting parentheses.

Examples

Mathematical Notation	PL/I Notation
a^{n+1}	A ** (N + 1)
$\dfrac{x + y}{a + \dfrac{b}{c}}$	(X + Y) / (A + B / C)
$\dfrac{abc}{2 + d}$	A * B * C / (2 + D)
a^{b^c}	A ** (B ** C)

When in doubt as to whether you need parentheses, remember that too many are better than not enough.

Le us examine exactly how the PL/I compiler examines an arithmetic expression. The expression

$$A * (B + C) / D + E * (F + G)$$

would result in the following evaluation:

B + C
F + G
A * (B + C)
(A * (B + C)) / D

$$E * (F + G)$$
$$(A * (B + C_Q / D) + (E * (F + G)))$$

Built-in Functions

Built-in functions are operations that are automatically provided by the PL/I compiler. They perform standard operations that would be difficult and time consuming for the user to write. One such function is square root, indicated by SQRT in this form:

SQRT (*expression*);

The *expression* may be one or more variables and/or constants. The PL/I system contains several functions.

The expression

SQRT(X)

finds the square root of the present value of X.

Our computer shows no record of you. We hereby declare you a non-person.

The Assignment Statement

An *Assignment statement* gives the value that is indicated on the right side of the equal sign to the variable name on the left side of the equal sign. The general form of the Assignment is:

variable name = expression;

Although the equal sign is used, this statement does not mean that the two sides of the statement are equal; it means that the value of the *expression* to the right should be assigned to the *variable name* on the left. Therefore, it states an action to be performed, not a condition of equality. The equal sign is called the *assignment operator* for this reason. The computer interprets the expression, performs any necessary calculations, and assigns the resulting value to the variable name. The expression may be a single number or an arithmetic operation.

Examples

```
X = A + B - C ;
INTER = PRINC * RATE ;
BAL = PRINC + INTER - PAY ;
ARRAY = ARRAY + MATRIX ;
PI = 2.14159 ;
C = SQRT(A ** 2 + B ** 2) ;
```

A multiple assignment statement can assign the same value to more than one variable, as is frequently necessary. The general form of a multiple assignment statement is:

$$variable_1 = variable_2 = \ldots variable_n = expression ;$$

Examples

$$TRUE = A = 1 ;$$
$$A = B = C = D = E = 100 ;$$

In the first example, the value of 1 is assigned to both TRUE and A. In the second example, 100 is assigned to the variables A, B, C, D, and E.

The Assignment statement is the fundamental operation statement in PL/I, as it is with other programming languages. It is the only way a computation can be made with its value saved for future use. All that may be to the left of the Assignment operator is the name of the variable, or the names of the variables in a multiple assignment statement.

☐ Review Questions

1. What is the main purpose of PL/I as a programming language?
2. What advantages does PL/I have over FORTRAN and COBOL?
3. What is a *keyword?* Give examples.
4. What special symbol is used to end a PL/I statement?
5. Write a comment statement.
6. Explain the use of identifiers and constants in a PL/I program.
7. Which of the following are valid PL/I constants:
   (a) 26   (c) π (e) A
   (b) .007   (d) 2.4623   (f) −63
8. Explain the use of expressions in PL/I programs. Give several examples.
9. List and identify the arithmetic operators that can be used in PL/I arithmetic expressions.

10. List the order of priority of executing a PL/I arithmetic expression.

11. Which is the correct expression for $x + y$?

$$\frac{b}{c} - d$$

   (a) X + Y / (B / C − D)
   (b) (X + Y) / (B / (C − D))
   (c) (X + Y) / (B / C − D)

12. Convert the following mathematical expression into PL/I expressions.
   (a) $a + b + c$
   (b) $x + y + 10$
   (c) $a/b + c/d$
   (d) $2a + 3$
   (e) $ab + ed + ef$
   (f) a^4
   (g) $\sqrt{x^2 + y^2}$

13. What is an assignment statement? Give an example.

14. Convert the following mathematical formulas into PL/I statements.

   (a) $A = p(1 + ni)$ (*simple interest*)

   (b) $p = \theta \dfrac{n}{v}$ (*Boyle's law*)

   (c) $\dfrac{1}{U} = \dfrac{X}{K} = \dfrac{1}{h}$ (Heat of convection)

   (d) $\dfrac{1}{4r^2} - \dfrac{h}{2r^3 l}$ (Protrusion of a floating sphere)

☐ Procedures

In PL/I, a program may consist of a single procedure or several procedures. During execution of the program, control can go from one procedure to another and can return to a previously executed or partly executed procedure.

A procedure is headed by a PROCEDURE statement and is ended by an END statement as follows:

NAME: PROCEDURE ;

----------------------   Statements in the
----------------------   procedure

END NAME   ;

Each procedure must have a name; that is, each PROCEDURE statement must be labeled. A procedure name denotes an entry point through which control can be transferred to the procedure.

The different procedures in a program may be entirely separate from one another, or some may be nested within other procedures. Consider the following two examples:

Example 1

```
FIRST:   PROCEDURE OPTIONS (MAIN);
         ....................
         ....................
         ....................
         ....................

         ....................
         END FIRST  ;
UPDATE:  PROCEDURE;
         ....................
         ....................
         ....................
         END UPDATE;
```

The two procedures shown are separate from one another; they are *external* procedures. All of the text of a procedure, except its entry name, is said to be connected in that procedure. The first procedure of a program must have the OPTIONS(MAIN) attribute specified for it in its PROCEDURE statement. At execution time, then, this procedure is called automatically to begin execution of the program.

Example 2

```
FIRST:   PROCEDURE
         ........1.........
         ........2.........
         ........3.........
         ........4.........
         ........5.........
         UPDATE:   PROCEDURE;
                   ........a.........
                   ........b.........
                   ........c.........
                   ........d.........
                   END UPDATE;
         ........6.........
         ........7.........
         ........8.........
         CALL UPDATE;
         ........10.........
         ........11.........
         ........12.........
         END FIRST;
```

In this example, UPDATE is nested within—or contained in—FIRST. FIRST is an external procedure; UPDATE is an *internal* procedure. The execution of the CALL UPDATE statement causes program control to be transferred to the entry point of the procedure named UPDATE.

Execution starts with the FIRST: PROCEDURE statement. When control reaches the UPDATE: PROCEDURE statement, that statement is ignored and execution continues with statement 6. Upon execution of the ninth statement, CALL UPDATE, control is transferred to UPDATE. Statements a, b, c, and d are executed. When the END statement in UPDATE is executed, control is transferred back to the procedure, FIRST, to execute the statement immediately following the CALL UPDATE statement; that is, program control is transferred to statement 10.

As shown in Example 2, more than one procedure may be contained in a single procedure, either as separate internal procedures or as nested internal procedures:

```
PROC_1:   PROCEDURE;
               ...........1..........
               ...........2..........
          CALL PROC_A;
                    PROC_A:   PROCEDURE;
                              ..........1a.........
                              ..........2a.........
                              CALL PROC_B;
                                        PROC_B:   PROCEDURE;
                                                  .........1b.........
                                                  .........2b.........
                                                  .........3b.........
                                        END PROC_B;
                              .........4a.........
                              .........5a.........
                              .........6a.........
                    END PROC_A;
               ...........4..........
               ...........5..........
          CALL PROC_C;
                    PROC_C:   PROCEDURE;
                              .........1c.........
                              .........2c.........
                              .........3c.........
                    END PROC_C;
               ...........7..........
               ...........8..........
               ...........9..........
END PROC_1;
```

PROC_A, PROC_B, and PROC_C are all contained in PROC_1.
PROC_B is also contained in PROC_A.

A contained procedure must be wholly within its containing procedure;
all the statements of a contained procedure must appear between the
PROCEDURE and the END statement of the procedure in which it
is contained.

This one suggests we replace you with a computer.

☐ Statements

The basic unit of a PL/I program is the statement. It tells the computer
what to do, how to do it, and, by its relationship to other statements,
when to do it. A semicolon terminates a statement.

It is often necessary that a statement contain a label. As stated in the
preceding section, a PROCEDURE statement must have a label. A
statement label is an identifier written as a prefix to a statement so
that, during execution, program control can be transferred to that
statement through a reference to its label. A colon separates the label
from the statement.

$$XYZ : TOTAL\_PAY = HOURS * RATE;$$

In the preceding example, XYZ is the statement label. This statement
can be executed either by normal sequential execution of instructions
or by transferring control to this statement from some other point in
the program by means of a statement such as GO TO XYZ.

This section describes the following statements:

- DECLARE
- GO TO
- IF
- STOP
- DO
- END
- GET LIST
- PUT LIST

The DECLARE Statement

Attributes are the characteristics of data; for arithmetic data, this refers to the range of values it can assume and the form it maintains. *Constants* are specified by writing their values directly in the program so that the form in which they are written determines their attributes. *Variables* are referred to by writing their names or identifiers so that their attributes are described in the DECLARE statement. Then their attributes remain the same throughout the program. The form of the DECLARE statement is:

DECLARE (*name*) *attributes*;

If several identifiers have the same *attributes,* they can all be listed in one DECLARE statement:

DECLARE (*name*$_1$, *name*$_2$, . . .) *attributes;*

For *fixed numeric data,* the statement is:

DECLARE (*name*) FIXED (*n,d*);

The *n* refers to the number of digits in the entire item, and the *d* refers to the number of decimal places. For example, (10,4) means that the entire number can consist of 10 digits, with 4 of these being decimal places. Therefore, the range of the number is 0 through 999999.9999.

For floating point numeric data, the statement has the form

DECLARE (*name*) FLOAT;

Examples

DECLARE (UNITS, PRICE) FLOAT;
DECLARE (WAGES, RATE) FLOAT;
DECLARE (COUNTER) FIXED (7,2);
DECLARE (SALARY) FIXED (5,2);

In the last two examples, the keyword FIXED specifies that the data items are represented in fixed point format. In the last example, FIXED (5,2) specifies that no data item assigned to SALARY should contain more than five digits and that each data item is assumed to have a decimal point immediately preceding the last two digits.

The *PICTURE attribute* (a statement borrowed from COBOL) defines the form of arithmetic items by a symbolic representation of their contents, or a *picture*. It is not frequently necessary to do this, and rules concerning its necessity are rather complex. It is generally a part of a special DECLARE statement, and its form is:

DECLARE (*name*) PICTURE *specifications*;

Its *specifications* are written similarly to the COBOL statement and have a similar function.

The GO TO Statement

In PL/I, the GO TO statement consists of the words "GO TO" followed by a label identifier. It can be used to alter the sequence of program execution. The general form of the GO TO statement is:

GO TO *label*;

The *label* must be the same identifier that was used to identify the statement which the computer is to transfer its processing. For example, the following GO TO statement

GO TO JAIL;

JAIL: IF PAID < $300 THEN PASS = 1;

causes program control to be transferred to the statement labeled JAIL.

The keyword GO TO may be written as either GO TO or GOTO. The PL/I compiler recognizes both words as a keyword.

The IF Statement

The IF statement allows the computer to decide what path to follow by testing a condition. The general form of the IF statement is:

IF *condition* THEN *statement*;

The *condition* is specified by two expressions separated by a comparison operator ($<$, $=$, $<$ $=$, etc.). The *statement* is what is to be done if the comparison is true. If the comparison is not true, then the rest of this statement is ignored and the next statement in sequence is executed.

An example of the IF statement is

IF A = O THEN GO TO PRINT;

In this example, the computer tests whether A $=$ 0 is *true* or *false*.

If A *is* equal to zero (true), the computer goes directly to the statement with the label PRINT, which appears elsewhere within the program. In establishing the test condition, the computer ignores any statements appearing before the statement labeled PRINT. The following program segment illustrates this;

IF A = O THEN GO TO PRINT;

X = P * W — A;

PRINT: ----------------------

However, if, in the previous example, the value of A is *not* equal to zero, the computer goes to the very next statement in the program (X = P * W — A;).

Frequently, several conditions are possible, and the next sequence to follow is different for each possible condition. In this case, several IF statements follow each other. This can best be explained by an example. When an employee has produced exactly his quota of items for the week, his pay is calculated based on one set of figures; when he has produced less than his quota, his pay is calculated based on another set of figures; and when he has produced more than his quota, his pay is calculated based on still another set of figures. Follow the partial flowchart in Figure 17–1 and following statements.

IF ITEMS = 100 THEN GO TO PROC_1;

IF ITEMS > 100 THEN GO TO PROC_2;

IF ITEMS < 100 THEN GO TO PROC_3;

It is best to state the condition that exists or is expected to exist most frequently first and the condition that is expected to exist least frequently last so that the computer does not have to go through an unnecessary amount of statements.

In addition to the IF-THEN statement, we can also use an IF-THEN-ELSE statement. Used in the ELSE form, the IF-THEN clause enables us to be explicit about the alternatives we take in the program.

The general form is:

IF *condition* THEN *statement–1*; ELSE *statement–2*;

It means that if the *condition is* met, the computer follows *statement–1* which is immediately after the word THEN; and if the condition *is not* met, the computer follows *statement–2* which is immediately after the word ELSE. An example of this type of statement is:

IF A THEN STOP; ELSE GO TO LOOP;

In this example, the value A is tested to see whether the magnitude of the expression A is greater than one (*true condition*); if it is, the com-

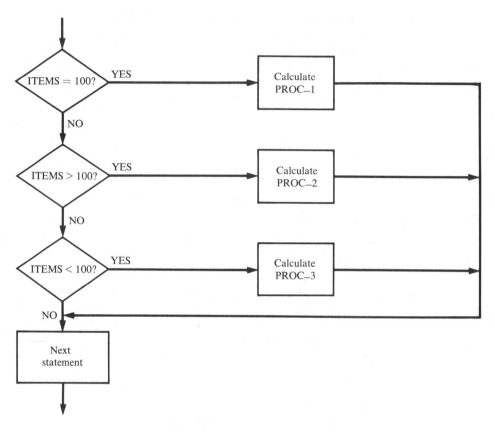

Figure 17–1   Flowchart for decision example.

puter stops. However, if the magnitude of A is less than one, then the statement is *false* and the portion following the ELSE is executed, causing the computer to go to a statement labeled LOOP.

The STOP Statement

As in all computer programs, the computer must be told to stop the program upon execution of all its instructions. The PL/I STOP statement has the form:

STOP;

indicating the last instruction to be executed by the computer. In many programs, the STOP statement is placed just before the END statement.

The DO Statement

The IF statements we have used so far indicate whether a single statement is to be executed or which one of several alternative single statements should be executed. Even the GO TO statement is a single statement, although it refers to other statements. Often it is convenient or necessary for an IF statement to indicate the execution of a group of statements rather than just one statement. The DO statement, used together with an END statement, provides a means of grouping a set of statements. It also provides for the repeated execution of a sequence of statements and permits modification and testing of data items to control the repetition. Consider the following example:

$$DO\ X = 1\ TO\ 20;$$
..............2............
..............3............
..............4............
..............5............
END;
..............7............

The DO and END statements specify that statements 2, 3, 4, and 5, whatever they may be, are a *DO group*. The DO statement further specifies that these statements are to be executed, as a group, twenty times before control is transferred to statement 7. The variable X is used to control the number of times the group is executed. When the DO statement is executed for the first time, X is assigned a value 1. Statements 2, 3, 4, and 5 are then executed. When the END statement is reached, X is incremented by one, and control is transferred back to the beginning of the group, where X is tested to see that it is no larger than 20. This *looping* continues until the value of X exceeds 20, when control passes on to statement 7. The previous example is exactly equivalent to the following:

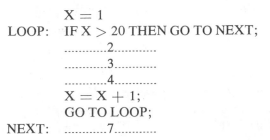

Note that since the test is made *after* X is incremented, its value at the end of the loop will be one incrementation larger than the number of times the loop is executed. In this case, the value of X will be 21 when execution of the loop is complete.

In the preceding DO statement, the value of X is increased by one each time the DO statement is executed. Since the variable usually serves as a counter, an increment of one is assumed. However, any increment can be stipulated. For example:

$$\text{DO X} = 2 \text{ TO } 20 \text{ BY } 2;$$

This DO statement causes the initial value of X to be set to two. Each time the DO statement is executed thereafter, the value is increased by two. Thus, the statements of the DO group would be executed ten times, and the final value of X would be 22.

The GET LIST Statement

The GET statement provides the program with the input data. It contains the names of the identifiers whose values are read into the computer from the input data.

Its form is:

$$\text{GET LIST } (identifier, \ldots , identifier) ;$$

The *identifiers* are separated by commas. The GET statement may contain one or more identifiers.

Consider an example where UNITS = 36 and PRICE = 20. The statement

$$\text{GET LIST(UNITS, PRICE)};$$

would cause 36 to be assigned to the variable UNITS and 20 to be assigned to PRICE. This statement has the same effect as would the following two assignment statements:

$$\text{UNITS} = 36;$$
$$\text{PRICE} = 20;$$

The PUT LIST Statement

The PUT LIST statement is the output statement used for printing the results of the computations required in the program. The general form of the PUT LIST statement is:

$$\text{PUT LIST } (identifier, \ldots , identifier);$$

This statement provides a printout of all the values represented by *identifiers* inside the parentheses. The identifiers are separated by commas. This form of the PUT LIST statement prints as many decimal places in the result as were used in the computer for the computation.

Examples

$$\text{PUT LIST(UNITS, PRICE)};$$
$$\text{PUT LIST(EMPID, DATE, WAGES)};$$
$$\text{PUT LIST(HEIGHT, BASE, AREA)};$$

There are several special PUT LIST statements. One used for controlling the line of print has the form:

$$\text{PUT LIST } (identifier, \ldots , identifier) \text{ SKIP(N)};$$

The letter *n* in parentheses refers to a number. If *n* is 1 or is omitted, the printer skips to the next line, giving single-spaced printing. If the number is 0 or negative, the printer goes back to the beginning of the current line; this means that it might print over data previously printed on the line. If *n* is 2, the printer will go down 2 lines, giving double-spaced printing. Another form of the same statement is:

PUT SKIP (*n*) (*identifier*, . . . , *identifier*);

Another special PUT LIST statement for controlling the page of print is:

PUT LIST (*identifier*, . . . , *identifier*) LINE (*n*);

The letter *n* refers to the specific line on the page, and the print begins at the left margin on that line. It does not indicate how many lines to go down, as does the PUT SKIP LIST form. Another form of this statement type is:

PUT LINE (N) (*identifier*, . . . , *identifier*)

The put statement that indicates to print on line 1 of the next page is:

PUT PAGE (*identifier*, . . . , *identifier*) ;

or

PUT (*identifier*, . . . , *identifier*) PAGE ;

The previous PUT statements specify some action to be taken by the printing device before any data is transmitted.

Another special PUT statement is required when it is necessary to specify the format of the output. The general form of this statement is:

PUT EDIT (*list*) (format) ;

The *list* refers to the identifiers, and the *format* indicates the desired form of the data on the printed page. The format may consist of the following (the capital letters are standard in the statement):

A (*n*)   Place the data in output with the length indicated by the number. If *n* is greater than the length of the data, it will be left-justified and followed by blanks. Data that is left-justified is usually alphabetic data.

E (*n,d*)   Place the data in output as a floating point number written in scientific notation. The number is right-justified if it requires fewer characters than indicated by *n*. The *d* indicates the number of decimal places.

F (*n,d*)   Place the data in output as a fixed-point number with a total of *n* digits and *d* digits to the right of the decimal point. The number is right-justified with leading zeros omitted.

X(*n*)   Leave *n* blanks.

The X(n) notation may be omitted if you allow more spaces than necessary in an E or F phrase. For example, F(9) is the same as X(3) F(6) if it is known that the largest number occupies 6 spaces.

⬚ Review Exercises

15. Explain the purpose of the PROCEDURE statement.
16. What is the difference between an external and an internal procedure?
17. For what purpose is a DECLARE statement used?
18. Distinguish between the GO TO and IF statements.
19. How does the DO statement work? Give an example.
20. Identify the statements that can be used for program looping.
21. What is the function of the GET LIST statement?
22. What is the STOP statement used for?
23. Explain how the PUT LIST statement works. Give an example.
24. Correct the following PL/I statements:
    (a) LET A = B + C;
    (b) GO TO STOP
    (c) Y = (A + B) (C + D);
    (d) IF A = B OR C = D THEN 12;
    (e) RETURN;
25. Write equivalent PL/I statements for the following BASIC statements:
    (a) LET X = Y + 1
    (b) GO TO 20
    (c) IF X <> 10 THEN 30
    (d) LET X = A ↑ 2 + B ↑ 2
26. Write equivalent PL/I statements for the following FORTRAN statements:
    (a) IF(A .EQ. B) X = X + 3.0
    (b) DO 30 K = 1, 100, 5
    (c) READ(2,20) A, B, C
    (d) A = B ** 2 − 32.0

⬚ Sample PL/I Programs

In this section are three simple problems with PL/I solutions and flowcharts.

Powers of Two

The following PL/I program will compute and print out a table of powers of 2 which are less than 1 000.

```
POWERS:    PROCEDURE OPTIONS (MAIN);
           / * POWERS OF TWO PROGRAM * /
```

```
          DECLARE (A) FIXED;
          A = 1;
LOOP:     IF A > 1000 THEN STOP;
          PUT SKIP LIST (A);
          A = A * 2;
          GO TO LOOP;
          END POWERS;
```

A flowchart for this program is shown in Figure 17–2. The program caused the following output to be printed.

$$1$$
$$2$$
$$4$$
$$8$$
$$16$$
$$32$$
$$64$$
$$128$$
$$256$$
$$512$$

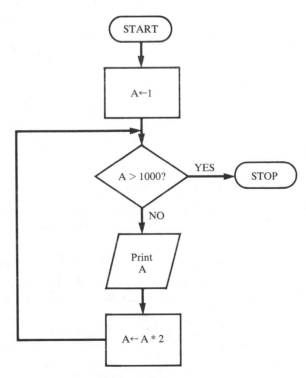

Figure   Flowchart for "Powers of Two" problem.
17–2

Inches to Centimeters

The following PL/I program converts 12 numerical integers (in inches) to their equivalent values in metric measurement (centimeters).

```
METRIC:   PROCEDURE OPTIONS (MAIN);
          / * INCHES TO CENTIMETERS PROGRAM * /
          DECLARE (INCH) FIXED, (CENT) FIXED (10,2);
          DO INCH = 1 BY 1 TO 12;
          CENT = 2.54 * INCH ;
          PUT SKIP LIST (INCH, CENT);
          END;
          STOP;
          END METRIC;
```

A flowchart for this program is shown in Figure 17–3. The program produced the following output.

1	2.54
2	5.08
3	7.62
4	10.16
5	12.70
6	15.24
7	17.78
8	20.32
9	22.86
10	25.40
11	27.94
12	30.48

Area of Circle

The following PL/I program computes and prints the area of a circle. The program uses the identifiers RADIUS and AREA and the formula Area = πr^2.

```
CIRCLE:   PROCEDURE OPTIONS (MAIN);
          / * AREA OF CIRCLE PROGRAM * /
          DECLARE (RADIUS, AREA) FLOAT;
          GET LIST (RADIUS);
          AREA = 3.14159 * RADIUS ** 2;
          PUT SKIP LIST (RADIUS, AREA);
          STOP;
          END CIRCLE;
```

A flowchart of this program appears in Figure 17–4.

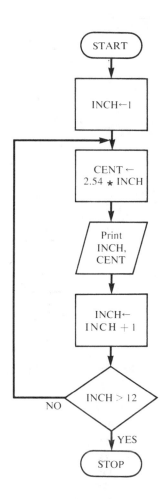

Figure 17-3   Flowchart for "Inches to Centimeters" program.

☐ Review Exercises

27. Write a PL/I program to compute the hypotenuse of a right triangle based on the formula

$$c = \sqrt{a^2 + b^2}$$

28. Given the formula $C = 5/9(F - 32)$, write a PL/I program to convert any Fahrenheit temperature into Celsius temperature.

29. Job X lasts 30 days and pays $10 per day; Job Y lasts 30 days and pays as follows: $1 first day, $2 second day, $3 third day, and so forth. Write a PL/I program to determine which job pays more.

30. A formula for computing the property tax on a piece of real estate is

$$T = (A \,/\, 100)R$$

where T = tax, A = assessed value, and R = rate per $100. Write a PL/I program to calculate the tax on a house worth $36 000 with a tax rate of $6.50 per $100.

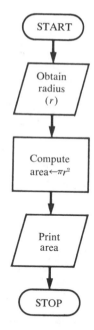

**Figure
17–4**   Flowchart for "Area of Circle" program.

31. Write a PL/I program to compare $300 compounded monthly at 6½%, quarterly at 6¼%, and daily at 5%.

32. Explain what the following PL/I program does.

```
XYZ:   PROCEDURE OPTIONS (MAIN);
       DECLARE (RADIUS, AREA) FLOAT;
       GET LIST (RADIUS);
       PI = 3.14159;
       AREA = PI * RADIUS ** 2;
       PUT LIST (RADIUS, AREA) SKIP;
       END XYZ;
```

☐ **Summary**

PL/I is a higher-level programming language that may be used for scientific and business applications. It has more capabilities than COBOL or FORTRAN; therefore, it is more extensive and contains more options in its programming statements that are available. Because of these possibilities, PL/I has more potential and is considered more powerful than the other programming languages. Like the other languages, though, it requires a user who understands all the details to properly utilize these options in the language.

PL/I provides for structured programming, a new technique for writing programs with fewer errors.

Key Terms

PL/I

comment

identifier

keyword

variable

constant

scientific notation

arithmetic expression

built-in function

assignment statement

attributes

PROCEDURE

END

internal procedure

external procedure

DECLARE

GO TO

IF

STOP

DO

GET LIST

PUT LIST

DO group

18

RPG

Courtesy of Braniff International

RPG (Report Program Generator) is a higher-level, limited-purpose programming language designed to process business data and to provide business reports.

There are two versions of RPG. RPG I is a system used widely on IBM System/360 computer systems. RPG II is used widely on System 3 and System 32 computer systems. Both versions of the language are available on other IBM computers as well as on machines manufactured by other companies (NCR Corporation, UNIVAC, Burroughs, Varian, etc.). The differences between RPG I and RPG II are minor for the vast majority of applications, particularly those involving punched card processing. In this chapter, we will cover RPG in general terms.

The RPG language has been designed to facilitate preparation of computer programs by those who wish to concentrate more upon the problem to be treated by the computer system than upon details of computer system operation or the specific procedure by which the computer will solve the problem.

RPG programs are written on a set of *specification sheets*. The RPG compiler reads the program specifications written in the RPG symbolic language and produces an object program in machine language that can be used to perform a particular application. RPG provides the capability for writing programs that can:

1. Obtain data records from single or multiple-input files.
2. Produce printed reports.
3. Perform calculations on data taken from input records.
4. Use table hookup.
5. Branch within calculations.
6. Sequence-check input records.
7. Create disk and card files.
8. Maintain disk and card files.

The primary purpose of this chapter is to provide you with an elementary knowledge of RPG. The material in this chapter will consist of only selected RPG instructions and will in no way provide a complete understanding of RPG programming.

☐ Getting Started

Preparing an RPG program is not really much like preparing a program using BASIC, FORTRAN, COBOL, or other similar programming language. The logic of an RPG program is predetermined. The user is concerned with only four basic considerations: (1) the general nature of the data files to be processed by the programs; (2) the specific nature of the input data; (3) the specific nature of the output data, and (4) the calculations that must be performed on the input data to produce the output results.

You can easily see why RPG is called a *limited-purpose* programming language. Because the user does not write the statements that represent the sequence of steps to be followed in the program, the application use is rather limited. Of course, it is not suitable for scientific applications; but commercial users who process business applications on small scale computers (such as the IBM System/32, IBM System/3, IBM System 7, and IBM System 360 Model 20) have found it to be an extremely valuable language.

The RPG user uses four different forms*, called *specification sheets,* to code the RPG program. They are:

- File Description Specifications
- Input Specifications
- Calculation Specifications
- Output-Format Specifications

---

* Some RPG systems use additional forms.

RPG programming consists of correctly filling out the forms. The specification sheets are shown in Figure 18–1.

Each specification sheet is divided into 80 spaces and vertical columns for convenient punching into cards. Eighty columns are available because RPG was first developed for 80-column card input/output equipment. For System/3, the data are punched into 96-column cards, leaving the last 16 columns blank.

Certain information is common to all forms, as follows:

Columns 75–80 (top right corner) are reserved for program identification.

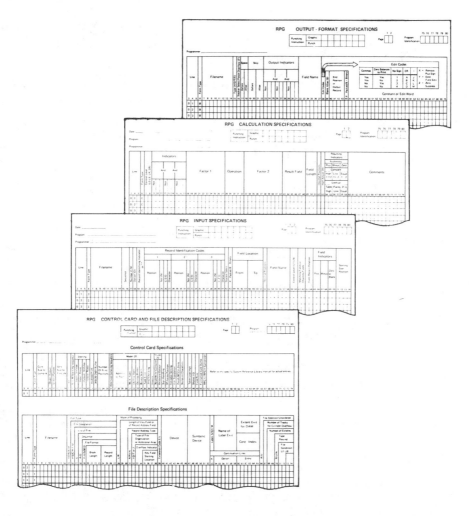

Figure 18–1   RPG specification sheets.

Columns 1 and *2* (just to the left of the program identification) are used to number the pages.

Columns 3–5 are used to number the lines of coding.

Column 6 indicates the type of form so that this information will also be punched in the source deck: H for control card, F for File Specifications, I for input specifications, and so on. All type codes are printed on the forms.

Column 7 may contain an asterisk to identify written comments.

☐ Using RPG to Prepare a Report

Figure 18–2 depicts the general operations involved when using RPG to prepare a report. The circled numbers in Figure 18–2 refer to the numbers in the following text.

1. The user evaluates the report requirements to determine the format of the input files and the layout of the finished report. For example, he or she determines what fields in the input records are to be used, what calculations are to take place, where the data is to be located in the output records, and how many and what kind of totals must be accumulated.

2. After the user has evaluated the requirements of the report, he or she provides the RPG program with information about these requirements as follows:

   a. He or she describes all files used by the object program (input files, output files, table files, etc.) by making entries on the *Control Card and File Description Specifications* form.

   b. He or she describes the input (record layout, fields used, etc.) by making entries on the *Input Specifications* form.

   c. He or she states what processing is to be done (add, subtract, multiply, divide, etc.) by making entries on the *Calculation Specifications* form.

   d. He or she defines the layout of the desired report (print positions, carriage control, etc.) by making entries on the Output-Format Specifications form.

3. After the specifications have been written on the appropriate forms, cards are punched with the data from the forms. Each line on the form is punched into a separate card.

4. These punched cards (called a *source deck*) are combined with the RPG control card. The source deck and the control card are placed into a card reader and processed by the RPG compiler. At the end of this processing run (known as the *compilation run*), a program capa-

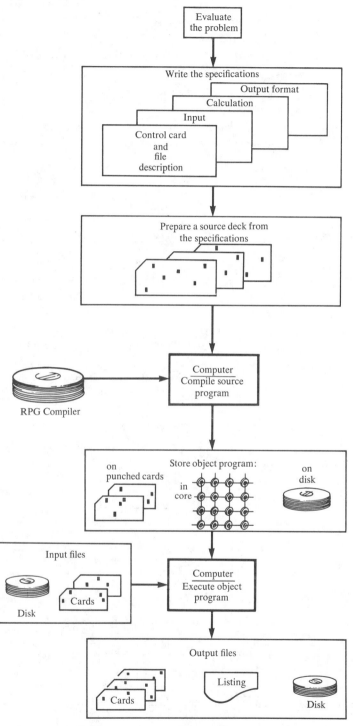

Figure 18–2   Producing reports using the RPG system.

ble of preparing the report specified by the user has been produced and stored in the working storage area of the disk. This program, known as the *object program,* contains all the machine instructions required to prepare the desired report.

The user may have the object program:
(a) executed immediately.
(b) punched into cards for storage.
(c) stored on disk for later execution.

5. The input files are then read into the system, and production of the report begins. This is known as the *object run.*

☐ File Description

The File Description form shown in Figure 18–3 furnishes information about the files used in a job. In this example, the first line provides information about the detail labor file. The name DETLABOR identifies this file. The letter C in file type indicates that the file is a combined file, that is, a file that contains both cards read into the system and cards used for punching. The P in file designation is required to define the

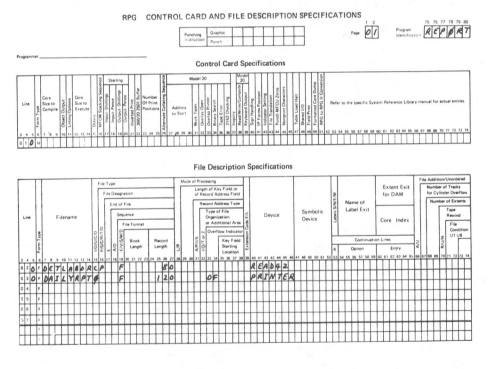

Figure 18–3　File description specifications.

primary or only input file. The particular input/output device that is to be used with this file is specified in Device. In this example, the card read/punch is used.

The second line describes the output file. The letter O in file-type indicates that the file is an output file. PRINTER in the device column indicates that the file is to be printed on the printer.

The term *file* as used in conjunction with RPG programming has a meaning slightly different from its usual definition. It *does* mean a collection of logical records, which is the usual meaning of the term. However, in RPG usage, it *also* can mean the type of input-output device which is processing the file. Thus, in RPG, we discuss a deck of cards as a file, a reel of tape as a file, a disk pack as a file, and a line printer as a file. Clearly, the first three of these can easily be interpreted as files, since cards, tape, and disk packs are used to store records. Referring to a line printer as a *file,* however, seems a little more obscure. But, considering that records are indeed being stored—on paper—by the printer just as records are stored on disk packs by a disk drive unit, this use begins to appear less bizarre.

☐ Control Card

One form is used to define the RPG *control card* and the characteristics of all files in the user's program (see Figure 18–3). The form is divided into two parts. The top portion is used for the RPG control card; the bottom part is used for File Description Specifications.

One RPG control card is needed for each source program. The program will not compile unless the card is present. The card specifies items of information that apply to both the compilation process and the entire application.

Columns 1–5 identify the page and line number assigned to this control card.

Column 6 identifies this card as an RPG control card.

Columns 7–14 are used for the file name.

Column 15 indicates what kind of file is named (I, input file; O, output file; C, combined file).

Column 16 is used to describe further an input or combined file.

Column 17 applies only to combined files.

Column 18 is used to describe the sequence of an input or combined file.

Columns 24–27 are used to indicate the length in bytes (characters) of both input and output file records.

Column 32 may be used to assign two input or output areas to input/output files.

Columns 33–34 are used to assign an overflow indicator to the printer.

Columns 40–46 are used to assign a specific input or output device to the file names in columns 7–14.

Computer, computer against the wall, who is the fairest . . . ?

☐ Input Specifications

Entries on the *Input Specifications* form describe the data to be read into the system.

The detail labor file (DETLABOR) contains card records as shown in Figure 18–4. Three fields from each card are to be read into storage. Field A is contained in Columns 46–50; field B is contained in columns 56–60; and field C is contained in columns 66–70 of each record.

Each card that contains fields A, B, and C is identified by two distinct attributes. It must contain a digit 5 in column 35 and no 11-punch in column 80. When these two conditions exist in the card record, the record is valid; that is, it contains fields A, B, and C.

In Figure 18–5, the entries on the Input Specifications form that apply to this example are circled and identified by numbers referring to the items in the text that follows.

1. Each file must be given a name. Each file name can be used to identify one file only. This file name must be the same as specified on the File Description Specifications form.

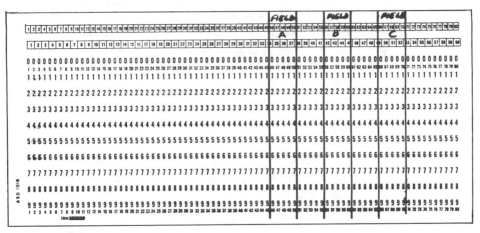

Figure 18-4   Input card from a detail labor file.

2. If several card types exist in a file, each card type must be identified by its particular card code. The identifying codes must be entered into the Record Identification Codes (columns 21–41) of the Input Specifications form.

In this example, the card codes desired are a 5 punch in column 35 without an 11 zone in column 80. They are specified by writing a 5 in Character (column 27) and a 35 in Position (columns 21–24) for the first code; and by writing an 80 in Position, a minus in Character, and an N in Not (column 32) for the second code. The fields C/Z/D (columns 26 and 33) on the form indicate how the card code is to be compared:

D = digit portion only
Z = zone portion only
C = zone and digit portions

After all the identification codes are established, the user assigns a two-digit number (from 01–99) to the card type identified. This code, known as a Record Identifying Indicator (columns 19–20), is used as a switch or selector. Whenever a card of the specified type is being read, the associated indicator is turned on. If the card read is not one of the type specified, the indicator is turned off or remains off. The Record Identifying Indicator is used wherever it is necessary to refer to the specific card type on other RPG specification forms.

3. If the input card is to be placed into a stacker other than the one into which it would normally be selected, the stacker number is written in Stacker Select (column 42).

4. Each field of the card to be read must be defined as shown on the lines following the record identification line (line 010 using columns

7–42). The specifications shown in this example obtain the data from the input record and place it in fields A, B, and C in three separate locations in storage (named FLDA, FLDB, and FLDC). The entries in Decimal Position (column 52) define the associated fields as numeric.

The user need not know the actual location of these fields in the computer's memory. To refer to these fields on other RPG forms, the user writes only the appropriate field name.

A field name may consist of six or fewer alphanumeric characters. The first character must be alphabetic. No blanks or special characters can be used in a name.

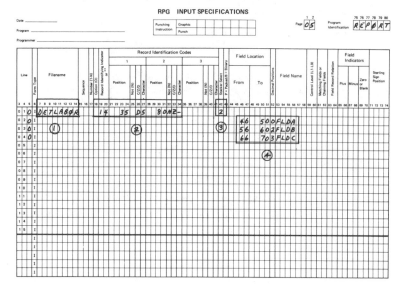

Figure 18–5   Input specifications form.

☐ Calculation Specifications

Once input data has been described on the Input Specifications form, calculations to be performed with that data can be defined on the *Calculation Specification* form.

In our example, the contents of fields A, B, and C are used to calculate the contents of a new field D. The calculation A + B − C = D is to be performed. Figure 18–6 shows the entries necessary on the Calculation Specifications form.

The first line of the Calculation Specifications form causes the contents of field B (FLDB) to be added to the contents of field A(FLDA) and

RPG CALCULATION SPECIFICATIONS

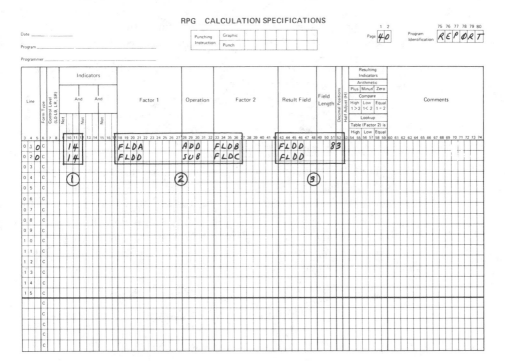

Figure 18-6 Calculation Specification Form.

the result of this arithmetic operation to be placed in field D(FLDD), thus replacing any previous information in this field.

The second line on the form causes the object program to subtract the contents of FLDC from the contents of FLDD, and to replace the contents of FLDD by the result of this subtraction.

The numbers in the following text refer to the items circled in Figure 18-6.

1. The 14 in Indicator (columns 9-11) specifies the condition under which the calculations are to be performed. This number was assigned as the Record Identifying Indicator on the Input Specifications form (see Figure 18-5).

2. The card columns for FLDA, FLDB, and FLDC were defined on the Input Specifications form. These fields are referred to on the Calculation Specifications form by their names.

3. The result field FLDD is defined for the program by writing the name FLDD in Result Field (columns 43-48) and indicating in Field Length (columns 49-51) the number of positions that must be reserved for this field in core storage. Just as in the case of FLDA and

FLDB, which were defined on the input form, the name FLDD can now be used in other calculation operations or in output specifications.

If an entry is made in *Decimal Positions,* the field is considered to be a numeric field. In operations involving quantities that have decimal positions, the number of decimal positions in each of the fields is frequently not the same. When the number of decimal positions is not the same in both factors of an arithmetic operation, the factors usually require shifting to align the decimal point.

The RPG system automatically shifts factors and aligns decimal points. The user need only indicate the number of decimal positions required in the result field in column 52. If a field is to be used in arithmetic operations, the number of decimal positions must be specified. If there are no decimal fractions, a 0 must be entered in column 52. The fields in Figure 18–5 have decimal positions as indicated in column 52 of the Input Specifications form.

A set of values for these fields might appear in the programs as follows:

Field	Decimal Positions	Contained in Card	Actual Value
FLDA	0	00126	126.
FLDB	2	01123	11.23
FLDC	3	04264	4.264

If, as in Figure 18–6, the user had specified three decimal positions for the result field in Decimal Positions (column 52), the calculation $A + B - C$ would result in a shifting of the values as follows, (result field has three decimal positions):

$$
\begin{array}{rl}
00126.000 = & \text{FLDA} \\
\underline{+011.230} = & \text{FLDB} \\
00137.230 & \text{FLDD} \\
\underline{-\ 04.264} = & \text{FLDC} \\
00132.966 = & \text{FLDD}
\end{array}
$$

The result 00132.966 is stored as the value of FLDD.

☐ Output Specifications

The printing of information obtained from each record as it is read is called *detail printing.*

Our example shows how the input fields FLDA, FLDB, and FLDC and the calculated result (FLDD) can be specified for listing.

Figure 18–7 shows the output specifications required. The numbers in the following text refer to the numbers circled in Figure 18–7.

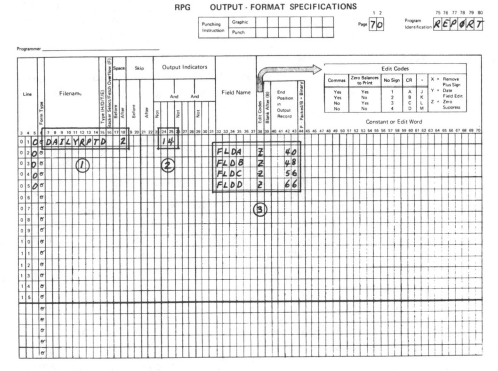

RPG   OUTPUT - FORMAT SPECIFICATIONS

Figure 18–7   Output—Format Specification Form.

1. A filename must be assigned to the output listing. In this example, it is named DAILYRPT. This is the same name used on the File Description Specifications in Figure 18–3.

   The D in Type H/D/T/E (column 15) indicates that the line to be printed is a detail line. (The other possible entries, H, T, and E are described later.).

   Space After (column 18) contains a 2 and provides a double-spaced listing. (Each printed line is followed by one blank line).

2. The 14 in Output Indicator (columns 24–25) governs the printing of the line.

3. Each field to be printed must be specified in Field Name (columns 32–37). The Z in column 38 means that all zeros to the left of significant digits and the sign are not printed (suppressed). For example, if the value 00126 is stored in FLDA, it is printed as 126.

The positions where the data is to be printed on the output report are specified in End Position in Output Record (columns 40–43). All specifications in these columns must be right justified. The user indicates only the last (or right-most) print position of each field. The length of each field has been established either as part of the input specifications or in the Result Field of the Calculation Specifications form.

When preparing a simple listing such as the one in this example, the programmer would probably mentally select print positions based upon the number of positions in each field plus a number of positions for spaces between two fields.

More elaborate reports are laid out before the pertinent program is written. Usually, this indicates both the location on the form where data is to be printed and the source of the data (the card columns of the input data or the name of data fields developed in the program).

Figures 18–3 through 18–7 show how to read data into the system, how calculations can be performed upon the data, and how the original data and the data developed in the program can be printed. The example shows the items required to prepare a report.

☐ Review Exercises

1. What is the main reason one might want to use RPG?
2. What specification sheets or coding forms are involved in RPG programming?
3. Briefly explain how RPG differs from programming languages such as BASIC, FORTRAN, or COBOL.
4. Briefly describe the steps required to produce an RPG object program deck.
5. What four types of files does the RPG system handle?
6. Name the four specification forms used in RPG programming.
7. Explain the primary use of the File Description Specifications form.
8. What is the purpose of the RPG control card?
9. Explain the use of the Input Specifications form.
10. Explain and illustrate the use of the Calculation Specifications form.
11. What is the primary function of the Output-Format Specifications form?

☐ Summary

RPG (Report Program Generator) is specifically designed to prepare business-type reports and is best suited for applications that require printed reports. There are two versions of RPG. RPG I is used primarily on the smaller IBM System/360 models. RPG II is used on smaller machines, such as the System 3.

RPG programs are written using four different forms called specification sheets: *Control Card and File Description, Input, Calculation,* and *Output-Format.*

The *Control Card and File Description Specification* form is used to prepare the RPG Control Card and to identify each file to be used in the program and to specify the input and output device to be used to process each file.

Entries on the *Input Specifications* form describe the data that is to be read into the system.

The *Calculation Specifications* form designates the arithmetic and logic processes that are to occur in the solution to the problem.

The *Output-Format Specifications* form designates the arrangement of headings and detail lines of the report, as well as editing that is to occur.

Key Terms

RPG	Control Card and File
RPG I	Description Specifications form
RPG II	Input Specifications form
specification sheets	Calculation Specifications form
RPG control card	Output-Format Specifications form
RPG source deck	file
RPG object program	detail printing

19

APL

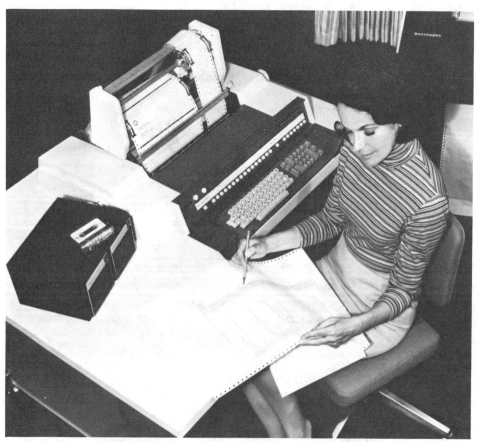

Courtesy of Burroughs Corporation

As was the case with RPG, APL (A Programming Language) is quite different from the languages presented in Chapters 14 through 17 (BASIC, FORTRAN, COBOL, and PL/I). Invented by Dr. Kenneth E. Iverson of the IBM Corporation, the language is based on a system of mathematical notation originally described in Dr. Iverson's book, *A Programming Language* (published by John Wiley, New York, 1962). APL, being quite flexible, can be used on large-scale, time-sharing computer systems like the IBM System/370 computers, or smaller, more specialized computers like the IBM 5100 Portable computer.

APL is commonly thought of as a scientific language and, for a variety of reasons, has tended to be regarded more as an intellectual curiosity than as a viable production tool. More recently, however, the introduction of enhancements to the language—notably proprietary file-handling systems and fast formatting routines—has led to an increasing awareness of its potential for a broad class of management information problems.

In general, APL is not advocated for a large class of applications where routine operations involving massive volumes of input and output are the rule, and where on-line requirements are a minimum. These applications are best handled in a batch environment.

On the other hand, APL is much more at home in a less-structured setting where I/O is modest and where user interaction and feedback are among the most important requirements. Such applications might include business simulation, financial planning, and performance analysis, as well as many types of management information systems.

Another class of problems where APL can be used effectively is in business analysis, characterized by wearisome and laborious manual calculations, often numbering in the hundreds. These applications may lack structure or may be one-time efforts, which usually precludes computerization in the conventional way. APL, in the hands of an analyst, lends itself admirably to this type of problem.

APL is best learned at the terminal. This chapter introduces the terminal and the APL language and gives several APL solutions to common business problems.

☐ Using APL

As stated earlier, APL is a terminal-oriented language. The terminal can be in the computer room, a classroom, or an office. At the terminal keyboard, you type input data and problem-solving statements, transmitting them (over telephone lines) to the computer. The computer works out the problem's solution and sends the results back over the telephone line to the terminal, where they are printed.

In the case of portable computers, such as the IBM 5100 or Microcomputer Machine's MCM/700, the keyboard and computer are located in the same unit.

It's a disposable computer; you solve one problem and throw it away.

Problem-solving statements are typed in the APL language and are essentially the same as ordinary mathematical notation. To make A the sum of B and C, you type:

$$A \leftarrow B + C$$

APL statements may be typed on the terminal for immediate answers or, for specific problems requiring lengthy or repetitive computations (in physics, mathematics, finance, statistics, or any field), may be combined to form programs.

You may carry on your "conversation" with the APL system either on a line-by-line basis or by writing programs and getting results on an extended series of operations.

On a line-by-line basis, the APL system is as a powerful deck calculator. For example, to total a shopping list,

STEAK←1.50
POUNDS←2.5
LETTUCE←.19
HEADS←1
SODA←.15
CANS←7
MILK←.25
QUARTS←4
+ / (*STEAK, LETTUCE, SODA, MILK*) × (*POUNDS, HEADS,*
  CANS, QUARTS)

5.99

Programs are used when a long task is to be performed or when a special output format is required. The following APL program computes the average summer and winter temperatures in Computerville, U.S.A.

▽ *AVERAGES*
(1)*SUMMER*←(÷3) × + / 59.1, 58.8, 59.4
(2)*WINTER*←(÷3) × + / 52.6, 50.7, 53.3
(3)*'AVERAGE SUMMER TEMPERATURE IS'* ; *SUMMER*
(4)*'AVERAGE WINTER TEMPERATURE IS'* ; *WINTER*
(5) ▽

The ▽ signifies the beginning and ending of a program. After you type in the first ▽ followed by the name of the program (in this case AVERAGES), the computer responds with the line numbers and you supply it with statements.

Line 1 (+ /) sums the three sample temperatures for June, July, and August (59.1, 58.8, 59.4), multiplies the sum by one-third, and names the result of this calculation SUMMER. The second line averages 52.6, 50.7, and 53.3 for December, January, and February and names this result WINTER.

Lines 3 and 4 tell the computer to print a message followed by the appropriate answer. Line 5 indicates that you have finished writing the program.

Once you have typed the program, you can tell the computer to run it by typing the program's name:

AVERAGES

AVERAGE SUMMER TEMPERATURE IS 59.1
AVERAGE WINTER TEMPERATURE IS 52.2

☐ The APL Symbols and Keyboard

The APL typeface was chosen to end confusion between the letter O and the number 0, or between the letter I and the number 1, or between the letter X and the sign that means multiplication. Three different styles of lettering distinguish letters, numerals, and operation signs, as follows:

Alphabetics: * always capitalized
              * always italic
              * always condensed (higher than wide)
              * always with serifs

$$A\ B\ C\ D\ E\ F\ G\ H\ I\ J\ K\ L\ M\ N\ O\ P\ Q\ R\ S\ T\ U\ V\ W\ X\ Y\ Z$$

Numerals: * always upright
           * always condensed

$$1\ 2\ 3\ 4\ 5\ 6\ 7\ 8\ 9\ 0$$

Operators: * not condensed
            * upright (except for Greek letters)

$$+ - \times \div \ \lfloor\ \lceil\ \top\ \perp\ \vee\ \wedge = \neq\ <\ >\ |\ \leftarrow \rightarrow \iota\ \rho\ \epsilon\ \alpha\ \omega$$

This typeface makes it quite clear whether any character is a letter, a numeral, or an operator sign. For instance, the phrase that indicates "the letter O times the letter X plus the letter I minus ten" can be typed

$$O \times X + I - 10$$

which leaves no doubt about which are the letters, which the numerals, and which the operator signs.

Figure 19–1 shows the APL keyboard. The letters and numbers all appear in their usual places on a typewriter, except that the capital letters are in the lowercase positions (the lowercase letters do not appear). The up-shift positions on the keyboard are occupied by symbols used to represent the powerful set of APL operators.

Figure 19–1   APL keyboard.

Besides $+$, $-$, $\times$, $\div$, (the familiar symbols for addition, subtraction, multiplication, and division located in the two right-most keys on the top row), there are distinct single character notations for the operations of negation; signum; reciprocal; logarithms (to both natural and arbitrary base); combinations and factorials; any base raised to a power; the residue of a number modulo any divisor. There are characters which represent taking PI times a number; sines; cosines; tangents; hyperbolic sines, cosines, and tangents; and the inverse functions for the six preceding functions. Available too are: floor (truncating a number to the largest integer less than or equal to the number), ceiling (rounding up to the smallest integer greater than or equal to the number), and maximum of minimum of a pair of numbers.

APL also provides the relations which test whether two numbers are: less than, less than or equal to, greater than or equal to, greater then, equal, or not equal. The last two relations are also applicable to characters. These relations check to see, for example, if a relation is true and produce 1 (representing TRUE) or 0 (FALSE); these binary quantities may be operated upon by the logical functions of: OR, AND, NOT, NOR, and NAND. All these are available as standard functions in APL and are designated by a single character graphic. These operations are all listed in Figure 19–2.

−	minus (as part of the specification of a negative number)
<	less than
≤	less than or equal to
=	equal to
≥	greater than or equal to
>	greater than
≠	not equal to
∨	or
∧	and
−	minus (as arithmetic operator)
+	plus
÷	divided by (dyadic); reciprocal of (monadic)
×	times (dyadic); sign of (monadic)
?	random choice (dyadic or monadic)
ε	membership of
ρ	structure from (dyadic); size of (monadic)
∼	not
↑	take
↓	drop
⍳	index of (dyadic); integers up to (monadic)
O	trigonometric or hyperbolic functions (dyadic); pi times (monadic)
*	to the power (dyadic); e to the power (monadic)
→	branch to command
←	specified as
⌈	the greater one of (dyadic); integer just above (monadic)
⌊	the lesser one of (dyadic); integer just below (monadic)
∇	del (opening or closing of function definition)
△	delta (in trace and stop control)
○	small circle (see *comment* and *outer product*)
′	quote (to enclose character data)
▯	quad calling for output (▯ ←) or input (← ▯)
( )	parentheses (grouping of terms in expressions)

[ ]   brackets (enclosing indices of arrays)
⊥   decode
⊤   encode
| remainder of (dyadic); absolute value of (monadic)
;   semicolon (to separate indices of a matrix or an array of higher
       dimensionality)
,   catenate with (dyadic); unravel (monadic)
:   colon (to separate label from command)
.   decimal point
\   expand
/   compress
⍱   nor
⍲   nand
⌽   rotate (dyadic); reverse (monadic)
⍟   logarithm for any base (dyadic); base *e* (monadic)
⍉   transpose (dyadic or monadic)
⍒   grade down
⍋   grade up
!   number of combinations (dyadic); factorial (monadic)
⍞   quote-quad (calling for character input ← ⍞)
⍝   comment
I   system information
d/   reduction with respect to last index
d/   reduction with respect to first index
d.*D* inner product
○.*d* outer product

Figure   List of APL symbols.
19–2

⬜ APL Arithmetic

In APL, constants can be signed or unsigned. The following numbers
are all valid as constants:

      674   .00000000000000001
     ⁻1234567891   ⁻298.26
      0.0   42017

Notice that the negative sign ($^-$) is used to specify a negative value.
The minus sign ($-$) cannot be used. To illustrate, suppose you wanted
to write a negative 7:

      ⁻7

This is different from the negation of plus seven which is written as

      $-$7

From this example, the differences between the two symbols are quite
apparent. The minus sign (or negation operator) tells us that the opera-

tion to be performed is one of subtraction. The negative sign is part of the number itself and applies only to a single number. It does not apply to any numbers other than the one immediately following it, nor does it indicate that an arithmetic operation is to be performed.

In APL we can generate fairly large numbers by using *scientific notation,* or E notation.

For example, the mass of the earth, about 6.6 sextillion tons, would be written in full as:

$$6\ 600\ 000\ 000\ 000\ 000\ 000\ 000$$

This figure is normally expressed in scientific notation as 6.6×10^{21} and in APL would be expressed in the following comparable format.

$$6.6E21$$

Very small numbers are treated similarly. The mass of a proton (1.7×10^{24} grams) would be expressed in E format as:

$$1.7E^{-}24$$

E format can be used for input values or for constants, within the program (your choice is dictated strictly by your own preferences). Using E notation, the system can handle very large or very small numbers.

With APL, you can work with a set of constants as easily as with a single number. For use on the terminal, these *sets* are always typed with a space between the numbers or elements.

Examples

```
3 6 4 2 1 7 0 8
26 94 22 86 27 73
6 ‾14 12 ‾11 ‾9 21
1 2 3 4 5 6 7
9 8 7 6 5 4 3
```

These sets are called *vectors.* A single number is called a *scalar.*

The operator ⍳ (Iota, found above the I on the keyboard) produces a vector of integers between 1 and the last element of the vector. The vector

$$⍳8$$

is the same as the vector

$$1\ 2\ 3\ 4\ 5\ 6\ 7\ 8$$

The arithmetic operating symbols can be used to apply to all of the elements of a vector in a single command.

Example

$$2 + 1\ 2\ 3\ 4\ 5$$

directs the computer to perform

$$2 + 1$$
$$2 + 2$$
$$2 + 3$$
$$2 + 4$$
$$2 + 5$$

The result will appear in vector form

$$3\ 4\ 5\ 6\ 7$$

The arithmetic operators can also be used with two vectors as long as they have the same number of elements or one of them has a single element (as the preceding example did).

Evaluating Expressions

In a compound expression, such as

$$3 \times 4 + 6 \div 2,$$

the functions are executed (evaluated) from rightmost to leftmost, regardless of the particular functions appearing in the expression. (The foregoing expression evaluates to 21.) When parentheses are used, as in the expression

$$(3 \ulcorner Q) \div X \times Y - Z,$$

the same rule applies, but, as usual, an enclosed expression must be completely evaluated before its results can be used. Thus, the foregoing expression is equivalent to

$$(3 \ulcorner Q) \div (X \times (Y - Z)).$$

In general, the rule is as follows: every function takes as its righthand argument the entire expression to its right, up to the right parenthesis of the pair that encloses it.

Spaces are not required between operators and constants or variables, or between a succession of operators, but they may be used if desired. Spaces are needed to separate names of adjacent defined functions, constants, and variables. For example, the expression $3 + 4$ may be entered with no spaces, but if F is a defined function, then the expression $3\ F\ 4$

---

* Defined functions are discussed in a later section.

must be entered with the indicated spaces. The exact number of spaces used in succession is of no importance, and extra spaces may be used freely.

Modes of Operation

The APL system has two modes of operation, called *execution mode* and *definition mode*. When the computer is in execution mode, it carries out any instruction immediately as soon as you enter it. If you enter an arithmetic expression, the computer immediately responds with the result.

$$7 \times 12$$
$$84$$

Ordinarily, the computer is in the execution mode. It stays in this mode unless you specifically direct it to switch to definition mode. When the computer is in definition mode, it does not execute the instruction that you enter, but stores it as part of the definition of a program. The instructions that make up the program are not executed until (at some later time, when you are back in execution mode) you call for execution of this program.

To indicate that you wish to change from the *execution mode* to the *definition mode,* you begin the *headline* of a program by typing the character ▽ (called "del"). This character is followed by the name of the program.

Examples

$\qquad$ ▽ *PAYROLL*
$\qquad$ ▽ *QUADRATIC*

The *header* of a program is the name of the program. The name used in the header is entirely arbitrary; however, it *must* be alphabetic. To return to the execution mode, you simply type another ▽ as will be illustrated in a future example.

You can store data or the results of calculations. A stored item is called a *variable*. Every variable has a name and a value; the computer associates the value with the name and preserves that association in its memory. Whenever you refer to a variable by its name, the computer automatically supplies the value that has been associated with that name.

Variable Names

You indicate *variable names* as either a single letter of the alphabet or a letter followed by a combination of characters (letters, numbers, or both). Blanks may not be used within a variable name. Usually, names are chosen which have some relationship to the equation to be solved. Following are examples of variable names:

A	*KILOGRAM*
LENGTH	*Y*10
*TAX*80	*MASS*

The symbol for assigning a value to a variable is the left-pointing arrow. If you enter the instruction

$$SPEED \leftarrow 107.5$$

you cause the value 107.5 to be associated with the name *SPEED*.

The left-pointing arrow causes the value of the expression to the right of the arrow to be stored under the name that appears immediately to the left of the arrow. This instruction may be read in several ways. You can read it as "*SPEED* is specified as 107.5," or "*SPEED* is assigned the value 107.5," or even "*SPEED* is 107.5."

Once you have assigned a value to a variable, from then on whenever you refer to that variable's name, the computer supplies the associated value. If you simply type the name of a variable, the computer responds by printing its value:

$$SPEED$$
$$107.5$$

If you use the name of a variable in an instruction, the computer carries out the instruction, substituting the associated value wherever the name appears in the instruction. For instance, the value of *SPEED* is the average speed of an automobile in kilometers per hour. If you need to know how far the car travels in 12 hours, you can find out by the following instruction:

$$12 \times SPEED$$
$$1290.$$

Or, since multiplication is commutative (i.e., order doesn't matter) you could just as well enter:

$$SPEED \times 12$$
$$1290.$$

If you prefer to have the result stored, the following instruction assigns the result as the value of a variable named *DIST*:

$$DIST \leftarrow SPEED \times 12$$

You could display the value of *DIST* like this:

$$DIST$$
$$1290.$$

Suppose that at one point you type:

$$X \leftarrow SPEED \times 8$$

and then later you type:

$$X \leftarrow SPEED \div 8$$

Each of these instructions calls for a result to be stored under the name X. What happens? The first time you use the name X to the left of a specification arrow, a variable is introduced, with the name X, and whatever value results when the value of $SPEED$ is multiplied by 8.

The next time you specify a value for X, that new value replaces the former one. The value of $SPEED$ is divided by 8, and the result of that division becomes the value of X. The old value is erased.

Clearly, this would be the wrong way to write the instructions if you really wanted to preserve both of those results. To keep both, you must give them distinct names. However, there are many situations in which it is convenient to be able to replace one value of a variable by another value stored under the same name. Suppose you want to count how many times a task has been done. If, for example, you have a variable called $COUNT$, you might have use for an instruction which updates the counter, perhaps something like this:

$$COUNT \leftarrow COUNT + 1$$

Each time this instruction is executed, the computer adds 1 to whatever value it finds already associated with the name $COUNT$ and then stores the resulting value back under the name $COUNT$. (Note that $COUNT$ must have received its very first value in some other instruction: it cannot *always* have been specified by referring to its own earlier value.).

The instruction

$$A \times B$$

means that the operation of multiplication is to be performed on the value of A and the value of B. When the computer executes that instruction, it finds in the memory the values of the variables A and B and then performs the operation, using those values. (The values associated with A and B in the memory are not changed unless you specify that they should be.)

Suppose that A and B have been assigned the following values:

$$A \leftarrow 6.25$$
$$B \leftarrow 144$$

Then you can use those values in simple instructions, and the computer types results, like this.

$$A + B$$
150.25
$$A + 1$$
7.25
$$B \div A$$
23.04
$$B - A$$
137.75
$$A \times B$$
900
$$900 \div B$$
6.25
$$Z \leftarrow 1 \div A$$
$$1 \div Z$$
6.25
$$A - A$$
0
$$B \div B$$
1

Since APL statements must be written on a keyboard terminal, they must be typed on a single line. The equation:

$$f = G\, \frac{m_1\, m_2}{d^2}$$

would be typed as:

$$F \leftarrow G \times M1 \times M2 \div D * 2$$

When you type an equation, you must make sure to include *all* multiplication symbols. The computer would not have understood the preceding equation if the expression had been typed as $GM1M2 \div D2$.

IF... YOU DON'T UNDERSTAND WHAT YOU ARE DOING.

TRY... DOING IT ANYWAY.

WHY? YOU'LL NEVER LEARN UNLESS YOU DO.

☐ **Functions**

Primitive and Defined Functions

An APL program consists of a combination of *functions* and their *arguments*. The arguments may be numbers or variables and/or any combination of these and must be combined with functions in a manner acceptable to the system. Let's pause for a moment to find out what functions are. Mathematically, when one thing depends on another, we say that one is a *function* of the other. Thus, if y is a condition, magnitude, or decision that depends on one or more other conditions, magnitudes, or decisions of x, then y is called a function of x. When x is given, y is determined.

In this respect, we say that a correspondence exists between x and y and that this correspondence is based on the relationship various numbers or variables may have to each other. In APL, certain functions (which establish correspondence) are built into the system.

In APL, the fundamental arithmetic operations (e.g., $+$, $-$, $\times$, $\div$) are called *primitive functions* and are provided by the system. Primitive functions are differentiated from *defined functions,* which are a sequence of statements created by the user in the course of defining a particular function to serve a specific need. The user can discard defined functions when no longer needed, but the primitive functions are always available, since they are built into the system. For this reason, primitive functions are also called *standard functions* and are available to all users of the APL system.

Monadic and Dyadic Functions

The ordinary operations of arithmetic, such as addition and multiplication, require two operands (e.g., $x + y$) and are classed as *dyadic operators*. Dyadic operators are further characterized by the fact that the operator separates the operands, as in $x + y$. For example, if $\lceil$ denotes the dyadic maximum operator, then max (x,y) would be expressed as $x \lceil y$.

On the other hand, it is possible to define operators, such as negation, which require only one operand. For example, if B has the value -36, then you get the negation of B like this,

$$-B$$
$$36$$

Negation is an example of an *monadic operator*. Thus, in APL, dyadic operators are always placed between their arguments.

Examples

$$6 + 7 \qquad \text{addition}$$
$$43 - 8 \qquad \text{subtraction}$$
$$8 \times 7 \qquad \text{multiplication}$$
$$30 \div 5 \qquad \text{division.}$$

Monadic operators always precede their arguments.

Examples

$$-9 \qquad \text{negation}$$
$$\div 4 \qquad \text{reciprocal}$$
$$|4 \qquad \text{absolute value}$$

Many of the same symbols are used for both monadic and dyadic functions (see Figure 19–3). A rule to remember is "If there is an argu-

SYMBOL	MONADIC USAGE	DYADIC USAGE
$+$		Addition
$-$	Negation	Subtraction
$\times$		Multiplication
$\div$	Reciprocal	Division
$*$	Exponential	Exponentiation
$\lceil$	Ceiling	Maximum
$\lfloor$	Floor	Minimum
$\mid$	Absolute value	Residue
$\circledast$	Natural logarithm	Logarithm to a base
$<$		Less
$\leq$		Not less
$\geq$		Not greater
$>$		Greater
$=$		Equal
$\neq$		Not equal
$\triangle$		Grade up
$\triangledown$		Grade down
$!$	Factorial	Combination
$,$	Revel	Catenation
ρ	Dimension	Restructuring
ι	Index generator	Inverse indexing
$/$		compression
$[\,]$		Indexing
$\square$	Quad	

Figure 19–3   Standard functions.

ment immediately preceding the operator, the function is dyadic; otherwise, it is monadic."

The factorial function !N is defined in the usual way as the product of the first N positive integers. For example, if we have

$$!7$$
$$5040$$

this would be the same as if we had written

$$1 \times 2 \times 3 \times 4 \times 5 \times 6 \times 7$$

The function $A!B$ (pronounced A out of B) is defined as $(!B) \div (!A) \times !B - A$ and is the number of combinations of B things taken A at a time.

The symbols $< \leq = \geq >$ and $\neq$ denote the relations *less than, less than or equal,* etc., in the usual manner. However, an expression of the form $A < B$ is treated not as an assertion, but as a function which yields a 1 if the proposition is true, and 0 if it is false. For example:

$$4 \leq 9$$
$$1$$
$$8 \leq 2$$
$$0$$

Let us now look at a few of the operators in Figure 19–3. However, it is not essential that you grasp all of these functions in order to understand APL programming. Treatment of the functions is readily available in standard texts.

Exponentiation (Raising to a Power)

In conventional arithmetic, exponentiation is indicated by writing the power to which a number is to be raised in a smaller typeface and placing it above the line. For instance, 2 raised to the 3rd power is written:

$$2^3$$

APL uses a special symbol for exponentiation, placed between the number (or variable, expression, etc.) and the power to which it must be raised. The sign is $*$ and is located on the keyboard above the P (P for Power). For example:

$$2 * 3$$
$$8$$

Here is an example of a calculation that uses exponentiation. It is based upon the familiar rules of compound interest. The names chosen for the variables should be self-explanatory.

$$PRINC \leftarrow 1045.28$$
$$INT \leftarrow .03$$
$$YEARS \leftarrow 17$$
$$RATE \leftarrow 1 + INT$$
$$MULT \leftarrow RATE * YEARS$$
$$TOTAL \leftarrow PRINC \times MULT$$
$$TOTAL$$
1727.69

This sequence of instructions estimates the total to which $1045.28 would grow if invested for 17 years at 3 percent, compounded annually.

Taking Roots

APL does not have a special sign for the extraction of a root. It does not need one. Taking the square root of a number is exactly the same as raising it to the one-half power. That is the way you write it in APL. If *A* has the value 144, you find the square root of *A* like this:

$$A * 0.5$$
12

The designers of musical instruments that are tuned to the "even-tempered" scale (such as pianos) face the problem of dividing an octave into 12 equal parts. The frequency of any note must be in a constant ratio to the note one semitone below it. Since it takes twelve semitones to make an octave, the ratio between one semitone and the next must be picked so that the product of all twelve of them will just make an octave. The semitone ratio is therefore the twelfth root of the octave ratio. Knowing that the octave ratio is exactly 2, you could find the size of an even-tempered semitone by the following two instructions.

$$POWER \leftarrow \div 12$$
$$2 * POWER$$
1.05946

Larger of Two Numbers

It is often convenient to be able to pick the larger of two numbers. APL includes an operation which does this. When the sign $\lceil$ is typed between two numbers (or variables that have numerical values), the computer selects whichever value is greater. If you type

$$A \lceil B$$

the computer examines what has been stored under those names. Then it takes whichever value is greater.

Suppose that earlier calculations resulted in the following values for the variables *ABC* and *XYZ:*

ABC has the value of 5678, and
XYZ has the value of 5679.

Then your dialogue with the computer might look like this:

$$ABC \lceil XYZ$$
$$5679$$

Consider an example in which this operation might be useful. Suppose you work for a department store. Each month, the store calculates for each of its customers how much he or she charged and how much was paid that month. You have a program that handles the billing. You calculate for each customer the value of a variable you call *BALDUE*, which is the difference between the total of the accumulated charges and the total of the accumulated payments for that customer.

The store charges each customer a service charge of 1.5% of the unpaid balance each month. You might find this charge by the following instruction:

$$CHARGE \leftarrow BALDUE \times .015$$

However, for some reason, some of the customers have overpaid their bills. For them *BALDUE* is a negative number and shows as a credit on their monthly statements. If you calculate the service charge by the instruction just shown, you will be paying them interest at 1.5% of either the balance due or zero, whichever is greater. You can do this by using the following instructions:

$$TRUBAL \leftarrow \lceil BALDUE$$
$$CHARGE \leftarrow TRUBAL \times .015$$

Smaller of Two Numbers

Similarly, another primitive APL operator selects whichever is the smaller of the two values on either side of it. If *ABC* and *XYZ* have the same values as before, the lesser is selected by this instruction:

$$ABC \lfloor XYZ$$

$$5678$$

Rounding Numbers

It is common practice to round numbers to the nearest integer. When the fractional part is less than .5, the number is rounded down, but if the fraction is .5 or greater, the number is rounded up. This effect is produced if you first add .5 and then take the *floor*. Suppose *A* has the value 3.14159 and *B* has the value 3.5:

$$X \leftarrow .5 + A$$
$$\lfloor X$$

$$3$$

$$X \leftarrow .5 + B$$
$$\lfloor X$$

$$4$$

Absolute Value

In conventional arithmetic, the absolute value of a number is indicated by placing the number within a pair of vertical bars:

$$|X|$$

In APL, we can find the absolute value by using a single bar with the argument of the function appearing to the right of the bar:

$$|A$$

Thus, to find the absolute value of ⁻4326.07, we write:

$$|\ ^{-}4326.07$$

$$4326.07$$

and, since absolute value is concerned with the magnitude of a value, APL responds with our unsigned answer.

☐ System Commands

We have discussed the operators of the APL language. In addition to these operators, you also need to be able to give instructions directly to the computer. The APL system has a family of instructions, called *system commands,* by which instructions to the computer are given. System commands are easily differentiated from APL program statements by the presence of a *right parenthesis* preceding the command.

Examples

>)1234567   (sign-on user number)
>)*OFF*   (sign-off command).

A system command can never occur as part of an APL program. Whenever you enter a system command, it is always executed at once, even if you enter it in the midst of a program definition.

Signing On

The Signing-On command consists of the right parenthesis and your user number.

Signing Off

When you are finished working, you should sign off. The standard sign-off is simply to enter the command

$$)OFF$$

to which the system responds like this

>)*OFF*
> *SIGNED OFF*

Workspaces and Libraries

A *workspace* is a block of space in the computer's memory. This work-space is essentially a "saved" area within the computer's memory which allows a particular user to access programs as they are written. It is also the area in which calculations take place. Within this area are stored program definitions, the names and values of variables used in the calcu-lations, the intermediate steps or partial results of the calculation, in-formation on the progress of a particular program, and information relating to the editing or disposition of the computer output. All this information is held in the area called the *active* workspace, which is that area of computer storage being used at a particular moment by a given user. The size of the active workspace will vary from system to system.

A user may have more than one workspace at a given time (see Figure 19–4). In active workspaces are stores in *libraries,* where they are identi-

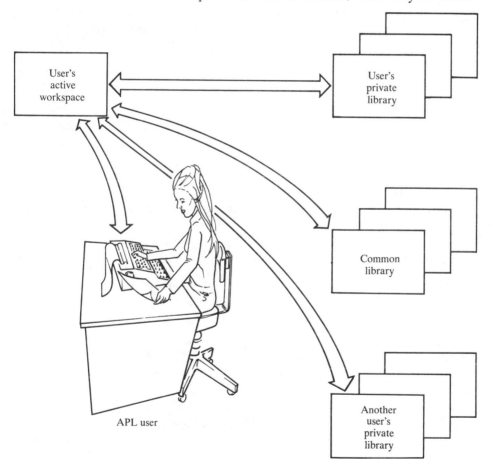

Figure   Data flow in computer memory.
19–4

fied by arbitrary names. These workspaces occupy space in the computer's secondary storage facilities (usually a magnetic disk unit) and cannot be worked with directly.

Libraries are associated with individual users of the system and are identified by the user's account number. Access to them by other users is restricted in that one user may not store workspaces in another person's library. However, one user may activate a copy of another user's workspace if he knows the library number and workspace name.

You may visualize the APL system as a series of notebooks (called libraries) and a blackboard. When you sign on, your terminal gives you access to the "blackboard". You may choose to use a clean slate (the condition of the blackboard when you first sign on), or you might want to have one of the workspaces duplicated on the blackboard.

To use a workspace, you type:

)*LOAD*   (LIBRARY NUMBER)   WORKSPACE NAME

The workspace in the common library contains a program named DESCRIBE, which guides you in the use of the programs in that workspace. For example, to learn how to perform a depreciation analysis, you would type:

)*LOAD*   4   *DEPRE*
   DESCRIBE

To save the contents of your blackboard in your workspace, you would type:

)*SAVE* WORKSPACE NAME

Branching

The ordinary order of execution of the lines of a program is to start at line 1, then do line 2, then line 3, and so on until you reach the last line for which there is a definition. Inside each workspace is a line counter that tells the computer which line of the program it should execute next. When you call for a fresh execution of a program, it always starts out with line 1. In the usual course of events, in order to decide which line to do next, the computer simply adds 1 to the last value of the line counter.

In the programs which have been used as examples thus far, work always ended because the line counter moved up in the usual sequence until it came to a line that had not been defined. If a program has four lines, after the computer executes line 4, it sets its line counter to 5 and looks for line 5. When it finds that there is not any line 5, it concludes that it has reached the end.

There are many situations in which you want to be able to tell the computer to go to some other line of the program instead of to the one that it would ordinarily do next. For instance, after the computer has executed a particular sequence of lines, you might want to have the computer go back and do them again with a different set of values. If the sequence that you want to have repeated starts at line 3, you might want to be able to tell the computer, "Go back to line 8." Or, if you want to repeat the sequence starting at line 8 only if a counter has not reached a particular value, you might want to say, "Go back to line 8 if $COUNT$ is less than $VALUE$, otherwise stop."

An instruction which explicitly tells the computer which line to go to next is written with a *right-pointing arrow,* followed by an expression whose value is the number of the line that is to be executed next. Such an instruction is called a *branch.* The two examples mentioned in the last paragraph would be written like this:

$$\rightarrow 8$$
$$\rightarrow 8 \times COUNT < VALUE$$

The second example, which depends for its effect on some condition that is tested, is often called a *conditional branch.*

Examples

$\rightarrow 0$	means "terminate the program"
$\rightarrow 5 \times N < A$	means "go to line 5 if $N < A$; go to 0 otherwise."
$\rightarrow (N \neq A) / 4$	means "go to line 4 if $N \neq A$; to the next instruction otherwise."
$\rightarrow 6$	means "go to line number 6"

Instead of writing $\rightarrow 6$ (last example, above) you could just as well use this

$$\rightarrow 2 \times 3$$

The "go to" arrow means that the calculation on the right is to be performed and that the result of that calculation is to be used to reset the line counter for the current program.

Now, suppose you give the instruction:

$$\rightarrow 8 \times COUNT < VALUE$$

This instruction calls for a test to see whether it is true that $COUNT$ is less than $VALUE$. If it is true, then the expression $COUNT < VALUE$ has the value 1; otherwise, 0. Thus, this instruction either means "Go to 8" or "Go to 0; that is, exit from the program." Which of those meanings prevails depends in any instance upon whether it is true that $COUNT$ is less than $VALUE$.

Suppose you want a program to compute factorials. The factorial of (n!) n is the product of the consecutive integers from 1 to n.

$$n! = 1 \times 2 \times 3 \times \cdots \times n$$

You will need a counter; call it X. You will also need another variable, F, to hold the result as it is developed. Start with X set equal to 1 and F also set equal to 1. (It is all right to write both of them in the same line.)

$$\nabla \ FACTL$$
$$(1) \quad F \leftarrow X \leftarrow 1$$

Next increase X by 1. Then respecify F as the product of F and X.

$$\nabla \ FACTL$$

[1] $F \leftarrow X \leftarrow 1$
[2] $X \leftarrow X + 1$
[3] $F \leftarrow F \times X$

If N is the number whose factorial is to be computed, you now need an instruction that says "Go back to line 2 if it is true that X is less than $N;$ otherwise, go to 0."

$$\nabla \ FACTL$$

[1] $F \leftarrow X \leftarrow 1$
[2] $X \leftarrow X + 1$
[3] $F \leftarrow F \times X$
[4] $\rightarrow 2 \times X < N$
[5] ∇

Here is a sample execution of the program called $FACTL$. First, you set a value of N; then, you call for execution of the program; finally, you ask for display of the latest value of F.

$$N \leftarrow 6$$
$$FACTL$$
$$F$$

In the *FACTL* program, the sequence of lines 2 to 4 is repeated as many times as required. A repeated segment of a program is called a *loop*. Whenever you write a program with a loop, there is some danger that a mistake in the program will cause the loop to be executed endlessly. For example, if the instruction on line 4 had requested a return to line 3 instead of to line 2, X would never be increased. The computer would return to line 3 indefinitely, because X would always be smaller than N. In this example, F would get larger and larger, being doubled at each repetition of line 3. Eventually, the program would stop when the size of F exceeded the capacity of the computer.

Any time the computer seems to be taking longer to execute a program than you think it should, it is possible that it is in an endless loop.

☐ Writing the APL Program

Finally, we are ready to write a program in the APL language. In this section, we will show how to construct an APL program, using the compound interest formula:

$$A = P \left(1 + \frac{i}{100}\right)^n$$

P is the amount originally invested or deposited; i is the period interest rate in percent; and n is the number of periods involved. A, the amount available at the end of N years, is to be determined.

$$\nabla \ INVEST$$

[1]	$P \leftarrow 1000$
[2]	$I \leftarrow 5$
[3]	$N \leftarrow 10$
[4]	$A \leftarrow P \times (1 + I \div 100) * N$
[5]	A
[6]	∇

$$INVEST$$
1628.894627

The preceding program solves for A when $1 000 has been invested at 5% for 10 periods. Statements 1, 2, and 3 set P to $1 000, I to 5%, and N to 10 periods (note that dollar signs, commas, and percent signs are omitted; decimal points, if any, are included). Statement 4 is the formula, and statement 5 tells the computer to print its answer.

As shown in this example, the first line of the program was the program *header,*

$$\nabla INVEST$$

and the last line of the program is a second ∇ that terminates the program.

Often, it is helpful to have the computer format your output (this step may include rounding off numbers and creating columns). Let us assume that the APL system that we are using contains a program named *DFT* in a common workspace named *PLOTFORMAT*.

Now let us rewrite our program.

```
     ) ERASE INVEST
     ) COPY 1 PLOTFORMAT DFT
SAVED      8.39.56   02 / 03 / 70
     8   2   DFT   1628.894627
1628.89
        ∇ INVEST
[1]   P ← 1000
[2]   I ← 5
[3]   N ← 10
[4]   A ← P × (1 + I ÷ 100) * N
[5]   ' IN TEN PERIODS, THE AMOUNT WILL BE ' ; 8 2 DFT A
[6]   ∇
     INVEST
IN TEN PERIODS, THE AMOUNT WILL BE 1628.89
```

The typed entry 8 2 *DFT* 1628.894627 is an example of the use of *DFT*. The quantity 1628.894627 is the number to be formatted, and the number pair 8 2 is the format (8 columns to be used 2 places to the right of the decimal). The result of the formatting is 1628.89, with a blank filling the unused column. It is often desirable to have a qualifying message printed out during execution as shown in line 5 in the preceding program.

Single quotes enclose the character string to be printed, and this is separated by a semicolon from the next item to be outputted (which is the formatted quantity *A*). The last two lines in the previous program show the instruction to run the program (*INVEST*) and the result.

Rewriting the program is one way, though awkward at best, of varying the data handled by the program. Requesting input is a much easier technique. In Figure 19–5, input is requested by the use of a ⎕, which gives the computer a "window" on the outside world. Lines 1, 3, and 5 print out character strings. When the computer runs across the ⎕, it prints out ⎕: during execution to signify it is waiting for data. Lines 2, 4, and 6 request data and assign the quantities typed in to *P, I,* and *N*. Line 8, the output statement, prints out three character strings, two variables (*N, I*), and the formatted result. All of these items have been separated by semicolons.

Figure 19–5 shows two runnings of the program with different sets of data.

```
∇ INVEST
' WHAT IS THE PRINCIPLE? '
P ← □
'WHAT IS THE INTEREST PER PERIOD?'
I ← □
'WHAT IS THE NUMBER OF PERIODS?'
N ← □
A ← P × (1 + I ÷ 100) * N
' IN ' ;N; ' PERIODS AT ' ;I; ' PERCENT, THE AMOUNT WILL
   BE' ; 8 2 DFT A
∇
        INVEST
WHAT IS THE PRINCIPLE?
□:
        100
WHAT IS THE INTEREST PER PERIOD?
□:
        4
WHAT IS THE NUMBER OF PERIODS?
□:
        6
IN 6 PERIODS AT 4 PERCENT, THE AMOUNT WILL BE 126.53
        INVEST
WHAT IS THE PRINCIPLE?
□:
        100
WHAT IS THE INTEREST PER PERIOD?
□:
        5
WHAT IS THE NUMBER OF PERIODS?
□:
        4
IN 4 PERIODS AT 5 PERCENT, THE AMOUNT WILL BE 121.55
```

**Figure
19–5**   APL program.

Let us now consider a simple interest problem.

An interest table shows the amount to which an initial sum will grow
at various rates after each of the intervals at which interest is compounded. Suppose that the columns of the table are the various rates
of interest, while the rows are the successive compoundings. If *PRINC*
is a scalar, containing the principal sum, and *RATES* is a vector of
interest rates, while *YEARS* is the number of years for which interest

is annually compounded, a simple program to generate the table might be as follows:

$$\nabla \ INT1$$
$$I \leftarrow 0$$
$$\rightarrow (YEARS < I \leftarrow I + 1)/0$$
$$PRINC \times (1 + RATES) * I$$
$$\rightarrow 2$$
$$\nabla$$

Here is an execution of INT1 for five years and three different rates of interest:

$$PRINC \leftarrow 100$$
$$YEARS \leftarrow 5$$
$$RATES \leftarrow .05 \quad .06 \quad .07$$

105	106	107
110.25	112.36	114.49
115.762	119.102	122.504
121.551	126.248	131.08
127.628	133.823	140.255

☐ Review Exercises

1. What does the acronym APL represent?

2. Who invented APL?

3. APL is available only on very large-scale computers. True or False?

4. APL is a _____ oriented language.

5. In APL, what is the symbol for multiplication? Division? Exponentiation?

6. Are all of the following valid APL constants?
   .0000000023   0.0   −26401.01

7. The value
   26 000 000 000 000
   is represented in E notation as
   (a) $2.6E13$
   (b) $2.6E12$
   (c) $2.6E26$

8. Define the following terms:
   (a) vector
   (b) scalar
   (c) header
   (d) variable
   (e) constant

9. Explain "execution mode" and "definition mode".

10. What are the two types of functions in APL?

11. Write APL expressions that would give the result:
    (a) 2 to the fourth power
    (b) 10 factorial
    (c) the square root of 25
    (d) larger of X and Y
    (e) smaller of A and B

12. Evaluate these compound expressions.
    (a) $6 - 3 \times 12$
    (b) $^-4 \times 6.3$
    (c) $4 + (2 - 6) \div 2 \lceil 3$
    (d) $23 \times 4 - 5$

13. Convert the following formulas into APL notation:
    (a) $h = \sqrt{r - r^2 - (1/2w)^2}$ length of a segment of a chord

    (b) $pv^{1.37} = c$ law of expansion

    (c) $D = d\left(.94 + \dfrac{\sqrt{N - 37}}{.907}\right)$ numbers of wires that can be contained in a conduit

14. Identify each of the following as monadic or dyadic functions:
    (a) $\div A$
    (b) $A \div B$
    (c) XC
    (d) $R \times Y$
    (e) $!B$

15. Write an APL statement that will compute the absolute value of variable R.

16. What are system commands? Give two examples.

17. Identify a workspace.

18. Write a branching statement that will transfer program control to line 10 if X < A, otherwise go to the next statement.

19. Write an APL program to compute the average of a set of 20 numbers.

20. A savings bank gives 6.25% interest, compounded quarterly. If you have P dollars in your account, your funds will increase to

$$P \times 1 + .0625 \div 4$$

at the end of the quarter. If you were to leave your money for n quarters, you would get

$$P \times (1 + .0625 \div 4) * n$$

After 15 years (60 quarters), how much would you have if you started with $200?

☐ Summary

APL, which began as a mathematical notation in 1962 and was first made available as a programming language by the IBM Corporation in 1968, has begun to attract a rapidly growing group of dedicated enthusiasts. APL's advantages over many other programming languages and the emergence of new, more powerful versions should lead to an epidemic growth in its use. Although originally used exclusively for scientific programming, APL is now finding use in the business area.

Key Terms

APL	function
constants	primitive function
variable	defined function
scientific notation	monadic function
sets	dyadic function
vectors	system commands
scalar	workspace
operators	active workspace
execution mode	libraries
definition mode	
headline	
header	
arguments	

seven

Processing Methods and Applications

20

Information Processing Methods

Courtesy of IBM Corporation

The majority of present computer applications fall into the category of *information systems*. In these applications (Table 20–1 lists a few of them), the computer is used as a massive filing system. The files are updated and analyzed by the computer; information is retrieved rapidly; and individual documents or reports are prepared automatically from information in the files. Since the 1950s, computers have been the central controlling element of such systems. Today, computers handle information processing in a variety of different ways: by allowing time-sharing between several users, by providing data processing in real-time, etc. A few of the newer methods for processing information will be discussed in this chapter.

Table 20–1   Information systems applications.

Accounting	Election returns
Inventory control	Income tax return processing
Reservation control	Language translation
Sales analysis	Hospital administration
Billing & invoicing	Economic analysis
Actuarial research	Census data analysis
Library search & retrieval	Medical data bank
Personnel files	Patent search
Credit card processing	Newspaper printing
Record keeping	Menu planning
Book publishing	Law data bank
Movie production	Stock market analysis
School administration	Test grading
Production control	Report preparation
Scheduling	Market research

☐ Time-Sharing Systems

Time-sharing is the simultaneous utilization of a computer system from multiple terminals. The purpose of time-sharing is to reduce the time required to solve problems on a computer system and to allow users to economize by sharing computer costs.

Time-sharing, oriented toward general problem solving, is particularly suitable for use in scientific, engineering, and educational environments. In the field of education, time-sharing makes computers available to many students in college, secondary, and elementary schools. Information systems will eventually be the largest user of time-sharing systems—for example, doctors will retrieve information from a large medical data bank, lawyers will be able to retrieve exact information from a similar centrally located data bank, etc. The field of accounting is another area which can benefit from time-sharing, since many functions of a desk calculator can be performed more quickly and accurately by the computer.

The time-sharing concept is based on the principle that there is enough capacity in a computer system for multiple users, providing that each user terminal is active only a fraction of the time. Each user of a time-sharing system has the illusion that he is the only person using the system. Each user can execute his program on-line as he would with a conventional computer. How does a time-sharing computer system take care of several users simultaneously? By loose analogy, the computer can be compared to the distributor in an automobile ignition system. The distributor head rotates, connecting each spark plug in turn for a brief moment. This momentary contact provides the electricity for the spark that ignites the compressed mixture of air and gasoline in the cylinders. In computer time-sharing, the system allots each user a tiny slice of time, and gives full attention for that brief moment to each user in turn.

Consider a time-sharing system with twenty terminals. (Actually, many systems can accommodate several hundred terminals.) The computer picks up orders from one user, works on his problem—say, for one-twentieth of a second—and stores the partial answer. It then moves to the next user, receives his orders, works on the second problem for one-twentieth of a second, and moves to the third user, and so on. When a user's problem is completed, the result is printed on the user's terminal. The computer system accomplishes this work so fast that the user feels the system is working for him full-time.

In a typical time-sharing system, the users communicate with a central computing facility (such as the one shown in Figure 20–1) by means of remote terminals. These terminals may be located only a few feet from the computer, or they may be several miles away. Data communication between the computer and the terminals is via a common communication network, such as telephone lines or microwave links.

A terminal is usually a typewriter, a teletypewriter (Figure 20–2), or a display/keyboard device. Shown in Figure 20–3 are cadets at the

(Courtesy of General Electric Company Information Systems)

Figure 20–1 Over 100 users can use this computer facility at essentially the same time.

(Courtesy of General Electric Company Information Systems)

Figure 20–2 A teletypewriter with paper tape input and output facilities. This device is the most common terminal used in time-sharing computer systems.

U.S.A.F. Academy using teletypewriters to communicate with the computer. Figure 20–4 shows a businessman using a display/keyboard terminal.

The time-sharing computer system includes the same equipment that is found in many conventional computer systems with the addition of a *communications processor,* a direct-access storage device,* and user *terminals.* The communications processor is used to gather and route all

---

* Also called a *communications controller.*

(Courtesy of USAF Academy)

**Figure
20–3**   Cadets at the U.S. Air Force Academy all communicating with the same computer system.

(Courtesy of Control Data Corp.)

**Figure
20–4**   Business manager using a display system in his office. This terminal is connected to a computer system located several miles away.

data communications between the computer and the user terminals. The communications processor is usually a separate smaller digital computer, such as that shown in Figure 20–5.

(Courtesy of Sanders Associates, Inc.)

Figure 20–5 A communications processor that can be used to connect 250 user terminals to a central computer facility. This device gathers and routes all data communications between the computer and the terminals.

A direct-access storage device is required in a time-sharing system to store the user's programs and to be used as intermediate storage. This data must be available to the computer system as rapidly as possible. Inadequate magnetic drum or disk storage will dilute performance to the point where system response is low. The equipment used in a time-sharing system is diagrammed in Figure 20–6.

The use of time-sharing systems will vary with the system; however, they all follow a similar pattern. First, the user dials the computer using a telephone dialing system connected to the terminal. This call goes through the normal telephone exchange network and establishes contact with the computer system. When contact is made, the user will be asked to identify himself (usually some special code or identification number) and to select the programming system he will be using. If the user is using a program that is already written and stored in the time-sharing system program library, he simply requests to execute the program. If, however, the user is developing a new program, he will type the program in some conversational programming language (such as BASIC); and, once the program is entered, he will inform the computer that the program is to be executed. The computer will then execute the program and transmit the program results to the user's terminal. The user also has the option of storing this newly created program in the time-sharing system program library for use at some future time.

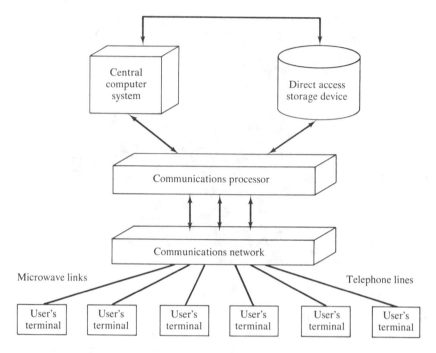

Figure   Basic Time-Sharing Network.
20–6

Perhaps the greatest advantage of time-sharing is that the user can run a program, write a program, or change a program while at the terminal; and he gets his results back immediately.

☐ Review Questions

1. Indicate which of the following complete(s) the statement correctly. Time-sharing

   (a) is the simultaneous use of a computer system by a number of different persons

   (b) is the use of a computer at different times by different people

   (c) consists of stacking jobs in order to enable the computer to process them at one time

   (d) always involves the use of two or more digital computers.

2. List three devices that are commonly maintained as user terminals in a time-sharing system.

3. How is a communications processor used in a time-sharing system?

4. Why is it necessary to have a large direct access storage device in a time-sharing system?

☐ Real-Time Information Processing

Real-time is a term used to describe a system that controls an ongoing process and delivers its outputs not later than the time when these are needed for effective control. An example of a real-time system is an airline reservation system, in which each reservation must be processed by the system immediately after it is made so that a complete, up-to-date picture of available seating is maintained by the computer at all times. With a real-time airline reservation system, a customer can request space for a specific date between cities. A reservation agent would insert a flight card in the computer, querying it on seat availability. Instantaneously, the computer searches for the appropriate flight record and transmits back to the agent the latest availability information. This information is then displayed for the agent on a cathode ray tube viewing screen. If the agent sells a seat by pressing a different button, the computer center can then update the seat inventory for that flight. Figure 20–7 illustrates the computer-controlled terminals used with Delta Air Lines' reservation system.

A real-time system network is also being used in the railroad industry where, in a matter of seconds, recording of and access to freight car

(Courtesy of Delta Air Lines, Inc.)

Figure 20–7   In this reservation center in Atlanta, Georgia, Delta Air Lines ticket agents take bookings at CRT terminals. When an agent types a customer's travel inquiry to this center, a computer flashes back flight schedules, seating availability, and other information. The passenger makes his selection, and the computer subtracts a seat from Delta's availability list. With this system, Delta keeps track of millions of reservations simultaneously.

location and movement information can be accomplished. The system enables a railroad to supply shippers with freight car location, as well as approximate time of freight car arrival within seconds after an inquiry is received. The system also makes it possible to eliminate many hand-written daily reports that have been a burden on operating personnel since the inception of railroads.

Real-time systems are also used to control complex space systems. Shown in Figure 20–8 are computer systems used to route telemetry and command information between sites located around the world. The data communications network is capable of sending thousands of characters of information each second.

Many department stores, insurance companies, and banks use real-time systems. Banks and other financial establishments use these systems to send transactions from branches to a central computer installation. Real-time terminals are being used on bank counters to check customers' balances and sometimes to produce statements or to process the customer transactions on-line (see Figure 1–9 on page 17).

Boston's State Street Bank, the country's largest custodian/transfer agent for mutual funds, uses a real-time computer system to maintain up-to-the-minute records for its customers. Using displays, such as the one shown in Figure 20–9, personnel can enter information directly into the computer and receive instantaneous answers to questions.

Real-time data processing equipment also controls dissemination of the New York Stock Exchange trading data, runs stock tickers and even "speaks" to member subscribers over the Exchange's Telephone Quotation service. Trading information, which was previously transmitted by pneumatic tubes and voice, is now sped to a computer center in the Exchange via direct electronic signals from *data readers* on the trading floor. The system prints sales on exchange tickers across the United States in as little time as a half-second after a special reporting card is "read" on the floor.

Common elements of all these applications of real-time systems include a file to store information, a computer to process it, and communications lines and terminals to provide access to/for someone remotely located.

The impetus for acquiring a real-time operation is the need for immediate information. With a real-time system, information managers have the capability of making human judgments based on the most recent data.

Real-time systems normally require the use of data communication equipment to feed data into the system from remote terminals, direct-access storage devices to store incoming data in large volumes, and computers capable of executing the programs needed to validate data and

a

b

(Courtesy of NASA)

**Figure
20–8**   During Apollo space missions, Univac 494 computers at NASA's Space
Flight Center in Maryland route telemetry and command information
streaming between this center (a), a similar computer system in Texas,
and Univac 1230 computer systems at worldwide tracking sites (b).

(Courtesy of Sanders Associates, Inc.)

Figure 20–9   Customer transactions being processed on-line in Boston's State Street Bank. Keyboard displays like these are part of the bank's real-time computer system.

control the input data at the same time as this data is being used for the particular application.

Real-time systems have definite advantages over more conventional methods of processing data. These systems provide immediate interaction between man and machine or between machine and machine (computer to computer, terminal to computer, etc.).

Real-time Computer

A *real-time computer* is one that has an interrupt capability which will permit I-O components, such as interrogating keyboards and random access devices, to signal the processor when they are ready to enter a message. The computer can then interrupt its current program and issue appropriate instructions to receive the incoming message before the message is destroyed in the line buffers by the arrival of subsequent messages.

For example, using a real-time system in an airline reservation system, the computer would interrupt its current operation to input and store a reservation request message, whenever one occurred. This capability would eliminate the possibility of the message being lost in a waiting position. Here the important distinction is the ability to respond to the stimuli in a time period which will permit servicing of the stimuli before the reason for the stimulus is no longer valid. The computer must be capable of servicing multiple interrupts so that an interrupt signal is not lost because of servicing of prior interrupt signals.

The computer must have an expandable internal core storage. Accurate core requirements for real-time programs are often very difficult to estimate when a system is originally designed. Thus, the ability to add additional core memory to the computer (if required) can prevent the possible reprogramming of parts of the system.

The real-time computer must have an asynchronous input-output capability. The computer must be able to perform input-output operations and processing functions simultaneously. Other features, such as a built-in clock, methods to protect information in storage, and methods to automatically relocate computer programs in storage, are desirable on many real-time computers.

☐ Designing a Real-Time System

In designing a real-time system, it is possible to break down the process into various steps and examine each in detail: system design, hardware selection, program design, testing, and integration.

System Design

It is generally agreed that problems in real-time systems to date have not been those of hardware or even of generalized software, but rather problems of systems design and programming—notably problems of communication between the people involved. Because of the inherent complexity of real-time programs, the systems design work, the foundation for the programming itself, is exceedingly important. The makeup of the design team, the documentation and communications standards adopted, and the feedback system are all critical.

The use of an interdisciplinary team for system design is strongly recommended. The team should include programmers with intimate knowledge of the hardware and accompanying software being considered, the customer who will be serviced by the system, and representatives of the advanced planning section. The team should be supervised by an individual who is familiar with management's plans and objectives, both immediate and far-reaching.

This team must be responsible for problem definition and the operational specifications of the system. They will also be responsible for the broad system which includes a functional breakdown, a diagram of the main information flow, the initial sequencing of functions and transaction types, and the general allocation of computer capacity among the many required tasks indicated by the various parties involved.

Because programming for large systems costs more per instruction than does programming of less complex jobs, and because real-time programming is normally accomplished (because of its size and complexity) by concurrently writing separate segments of the program, great emphasis must be placed on systems design. The key is to ensure adequate design controls while the system is still in the formative stages.

The design team must also consider costing. At this juncture, the programming manager must be consulted. Estimates must be made as to memory and file requirements and educated guesses ventured as to computer running times. The cost of a particular program feature must be compared to the operational value of its result or to its effect on the available computer capacity and features deleted or added in an attempt to balance the system to acceptable requirements.

Another part of the initial systems design is to identify how all programs will work together as a system. Too often this is left to develop during the coding process, and experience has shown that this leads to extensive and costly reprogramming at late stages in development.

The system design team should not be disbanded after preliminary development of the system, but should continue to operate even into the implementation phase. The later work of this team will include the design of operational procedures, the investigation of message format options, the evaluation of alternative computational methods, and the design and specification of testing procedures. The team operates as a control and coordination group. Their work and its documentation is of the utmost importance to the success of any real-time system.

Hardware Selection

After systems requirements have been determined, the selection of hardware must be made. Basically there are three criteria for the choice. The size of the computer must be considered with special attention to the potential modularity of the hardware. Because real-time subsystems— e.g., shop order location and inventory control—cross functional lines, real-time systems have a marked tendency to grow. It is, therefore, very important that the computer system selected can expand in terms of number of communication channels, size of internal memory, and capacity of auxiliary storage.

The operating speed of the computer must be taken into account. The internal and input-output speeds of the hardware must be such that the rather complex programs typical of a real-time system can operate, with a safety factor for scanning or switchover, at the necessary speeds. The requirements of the system under development must be considered. Often system response time on the order of several seconds or even minutes is sufficient to fulfill requirements.

There is no more important criteria for hardware selection than that of reliability. The reliability of not only the central computer, but of the communication channels and of the auxiliary storage devices must be carefully evaluated. Usually the question of reliability centers around cost versus system requirements.

Programming

Real-time programs are usually composed of many separate segments written concurrently by many different programmers. All of these segments are linked through both independent overlays and access to the executive routine. The programs are large and very complex and yet must be very fast. They must provide for a validity check of all input data and proper disposition of errors; and the programming system must recognize hardware failure and provide for alternative handling at microsecond speed. It must be stressed that program segments must "fit" each other exactly under all circumstances.

There are many constraints imposed on programs by the real-time system. The real-time program must sample data from input devices at prescribed intervals, thereby placing a constraint on the time spent in performing computations and other processing functions. This time limitation and the complexity of program interfaces mean that real-time computer programs cannot be organized in as simple and logical a manner as in batch processing—i.e., they must be time-conscious. A system may consist of scores of tables, 50 to 100 program segments, and hundreds of data items all interacting in real-time with the sequence of execution dependent upon the content of the incoming data. Yet, no matter how the above factors may vary, the system must continue to operate within the time constraint imposed by input volume. In addition, real-time programs must deal successfully with a great variety of input-output devices of disparate speeds. The problem of equipment malfunction and programming or data errors in a real-time system places additional burdens on the people developing the system. Data errors must be dealt with in such a way that the system is protected against the broadening ripples of false information that are the effect of erroneous data being admitted to the system. Yet, the program must keep pace with the ever-present time requirements.

The *executive program* is the keystone of any real-time program. It functions as a scheduler and housekeeper accomplishing the handling of all inputs and outputs, including the construction of queues and the determination of individual transaction priority. It is responsible for supplying to the operational programs all subroutines and data necessary. In addition to these duties, the executive routine provides the accounting for the system in terms of message volumes, controls program allocation in the computer's internal memory, and performs the necessary recovery procedures in case of equipment malfunction.

With all of these functions to perform, the executive program has a tendency to become very large and complex. A better procedure is to design separate subroutines for each major function and have the executive program simply reference these subroutines whenever it is time for them to be executed. In this way, the executive program can be fully debugged and ready for use when the first program segments are to be tested. Further, changes can be made in any of the individual functions performed by the executive program without having to change the executive itself.

Programming Standards

The need for complete programming standards is obvious. As part of these standards, a formal system of documentation plays a large part in determining the relative success of the effort. These standards must include strict rules for the use of the selected programming language, a functional description of the executive program (including entrance and exit locations), detailed data formats, locations of logical program interfaces, design of major subroutines (input-output, standard computations, etc.), and explicit rules for programming procedures.

Program Testing and Integration

Program testing involves a verification that all of the permissible inputs to the system are received properly, processed properly, and the results returned correctly to the proper destination. This is usually an obvious and simple task for non-real-time programs, and it is often performed only after the programmer is fairly confident that his program works. In a real-time system, however, the magnitude of the testing effort precludes such an approach. Test programs should be used whenever possible to avoid the use of human *guinea pigs*. The danger in using human guinea pigs is that they tend to lose confidence in the system extremely quickly, and then regain that confidence at an agonizingly slow rate. In many cases, a shaky system tends to aggravate a user's basic distrust of computers.

From the programmer's point of view, the most annoying characteristic of *guinea pig* testing is that it may take months or years to uncover some problems, and it is often nearly impossible to re-create the conditions that caused the problem. A good test program, on the other hand, can check all of the features of the system in an organized manner. If an error should occur in the system, the programmer usually has a good idea of the cause of the error—simply because he knows what the test program was doing at the time of the error. A test program also has the advantage that it can be repeated indefinitely, thus giving the programmer the opportunity to try the test again several times while searching for the error, and also allowing him to retest it at periodic intervals in the future to guarantee that new errors have not crept into the system.

The process of testing a real-time system must be very well organized and very carefully controlled if it is to be effective. The manner in which components of the system are to be tested, the order in which they are to be tested, and the manner in which the results of test runs are to be saved and compared with other runs of the same test—all of these are important for a good testing environment.

Probably the most agonizing task a programmer faces is the elimination of "bugs" from his program. The simple bugs may be found by extensive desk-checking, but the more obscure bugs have traditionally required the use of selective dumps, test programs, and other procedures which attempt to catch a program in the act of performing some incorrect action.

Program testing is an area that deserves the closest scrutiny. This function is much more important in real-time than in batch processing systems. Each program segment must be individually tested for logic and clerical errors, run in conjunction with the executive routine to check linkage, and then incorporated into the system and tested once again. Experience has shown that the errors most difficult to detect show up when the program segment is incorporated into the system.

This phase of testing, called *system integration,* should be carried out over as long a period of time as possible. The entire system should be retested with the addition of each program segment or subroutine. Throughout the testing procedure, extensive test tools must be used. Test data generators are invaluable. Simulators must be sophisticated enough to manipulate all of the variables present in the real environment. Because errrors many times refuse to repeat themselves during debugging, sampling programs which monitor the running system and print out the contents of certain storage areas should be used throughout the testing of a program segment. Equipment failure must be introduced in order to test switchover and recovery procedures.

The programming package for a real-time system generally consists of an executive program and a package of *operational programs.* In most cases, a different group of programmers is assigned to each project, and their testing needs are quite different.

While the executive program is being tested, another group of programmers is often working on a package of operational programs. In a real-time system, this involves many different subroutines. The operational programs tend to be more *logic-oriented* and less *I-O oriented* than the executive system. A large part of an operational program might thus be tested with the standard procedures of dumps and test programs.

Operational programs can be partially tested in a *stand-alone environment;* however, there comes a time when all further work must be done under the executive system. It would be nice at this point to have a program-testing tool under the control of the executive system. This tool would allow the programmer to maintain control over the running of his program from a terminal.

It must be stressed that program-testing aids and test programs can never act as a substitute for careful design procedures. The most sophisticated testing program in the world cannot correct design errors: it can only help the programmer find them and their subsequent coding consequences.

Real-Time Software

Real-time software requirements differ from those associated with general-purpose data processing in several aspects. These differences have made many vendor-supplied standard software packages unsuitable or only partly usable in real-time work.

One of the most basic and important requirements of real-time software is that it operates in a real-time environment. For example, signals and control lines between input-output interface equipment and the computer must be serviced on demand. Furthermore, accurate time synchronization to initiate data conversions and other events must also be handled on an interrupt basis. Thus, the executive program must be capable of processing both synchronous and asynchronous priority interrupt requests initiated by an arbitrary number of external sources.

The real-time user requires general software control over interrupt hardware. In some cases, it is important to disable interrupts during program execution to assure immediate completion of the associated function. In such a case, it is important that the interrupt signals not be lost during the period of disablement.

An implicit software requirement for real-time systems is the generation of efficient object programs. The user can frequently trade accuracy for execution speed in certain areas, since there are many programming techniques for accomplishing this tradeoff. Thus, computer programs designed for maximum accuracy and capable of full-word precision are not always needed or desirable. Most standard software, however, is so characterized.

On-line problem debugging and optimization are commonplace in real-time systems. Moreover, the ability to monitor problem solutions on benchboards and consoles and then adjust the program structure on-line is typical of the man-machine relationship that exists in real-time systems. Although it is not a strict software requirement, this direct communication between man and machine should be emphasized in the software design.

The previous paragraphs indicate some of the more important considerations in the development of real-time software. These factors, however, are in no way intended to minimize the necessity for software features usually associated with general-purpose computation. For example, the capability for batch assemblies and compilations is also a requirement in a well-organized real-time computing system. This feature is important, not only for multiple assemblies and compilations of computer programs, but also for off-line debugging. More simply stated, the automatic processing features that are commonplace in the digital computation system should be equally available to the real-time system user.

□ Review Questions

5. Define the following terms:
   (a) real-time
   (b) real-time computer
6. List four applications where real-time systems are used.
7. Describe the system design process used in developing real-time systems.
8. Is computing equipment selected before or after the system is initially designed? Why?
9. Why is developing real-time programs more difficult than developing programs for a batch processing environment?
10. What is an executive program?
11. What is the difference between program testing and system integration?
12. What is meant by "on-line program debugging"?
13. Explain how a bank might use a real-time computer system? a department store? an airline company?

□ Batch Processing

Batch processing is a method of processing data in which transactions are accumulated for a predetermined period of time and prepared for input to the computer for processing as a single unit. Input is collected in batches and sorted in the same sequence as it is to be processed. For example, all memos of transactions (invoices, sales slips, etc.) are collected. The batch of memos is then sorted numerically or alphabetically for posting to accounts. The indicated time period may be any length: an hour, a day, a week, or a month. In batch processing, however, there is often some delay between the occurrence of original events and the eventual processing of the transactions. This type of processing is contrasted with real-time processing in which transactions are dealt with as they arise and are automatically applied to files held in a direct-access storage device.

Batch processing has several important advantages. It makes mechanization of processing operations more feasible by assuring that a large number of items will be processed at one time. Preparation time for processing data is reduced since a few large processing runs are made instead of numerous smaller processing runs.

☐ **Review Questions**

14. Compare batch processing with real-time processing.

☐ **Multiprogramming**

There is an extreme difference in the speeds at which a computer is able to perform calculations and the speeds at which even the fastest input-output devices operate. In the time taken to print one line on a line printer working at 1 200 lines a minute, a computer could perform 10 000 additions. Multiprogramming is a technique developed to relieve this imbalance and to further increase the utilization of the computer.

Multiprogramming is the concurrent execution of two or more programs simultaneously residing in the internal storage unit of a computer* (See Figure 20–10a). The basic principle of multiprogramming is that the programs in internal storage share the available central processing unit's time and input-output units. Each program is written as a completely independent program. While input-output operations of one program are being handled, the CPU is essentially idle and can handle some non-input-output processing of another program at the same time. For example, a program to read data from punched cards and transcribe it to magnetic tape will only require the use of the computer for a small fraction of the program running time. The remainder of the time represents input-output transfer time during which other programs can use the central processing unit.

Benefits to be gained from multiprogramming include the elimination of *off-line* equipment normally used to transcribe data onto a faster medium for input. While this activity is proceeding, using limited numbers of input-output devices and little processing time, other more productive

---

* In the IBM System/370 under MFT (Multiprogramming with a Fixed number of Tasks), as many as 15 programs can be executed concurrently. Under MVT (Multiprogramming with a Variable number of Tasks), the number of programs is limited primarily by the amount of available storage.

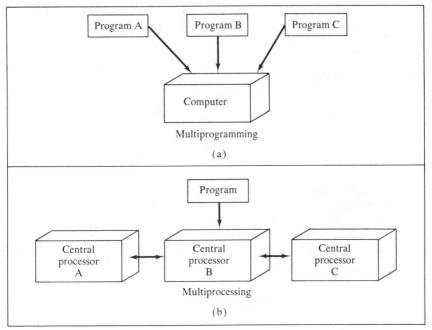

Figure   Multiprogramming and multiprocessing configurations.
20–10

programs can use the remaining input-output devices and central process-ing unit time.

⬜ Multiprocessing

A multiprocessing computer system is one which contains two or more interconnected central processing units, each with its own arithmetic and logic units and each capable of independent operation (See Figure 20–10b). A computer system operating in a multiprocessing configuration must be able to interpret and execute its own programmed instructions. In addition, facilities must be available to transfer data from one CPU to another, to transfer data and instructions to and from internal storage, and to transfer data and instructions to and from a common auxiliary storage device.

The requirements for multiprocessing, in terms of both equipment and programs, are extensive. One of the first multiprocessors was the Control Data 6600. This system consisted of 10 small computers, each capable of performing input, output, and processing, while connected to a main cen-tral processing unit. The main CPU included many multiply, add, shift, and test units which could operate at the same time to improve process-ing speed.

Multiprocessing offers data processing capabilities that are not available when only one central processing unit is used. Many complex operations can be performed at the same time.

☐ Review Questions

15. What is meant by "multiprocessing"?
16. Define "multiprocessing" and give an example.

☐ Operating Systems

When computers were first developed, they were usually put to work solving jobs that had required a great deal of routine human activity. Basic accounting, record keeping, and problem solving were a few of these early applications (Figure 20–11). By and large, the automatic processing of such jobs proved the speed, economy, and reliability of electronic data processing.

A few years later, computer users began to use computers for applications that went far beyond the mere mechanization of manual operations.

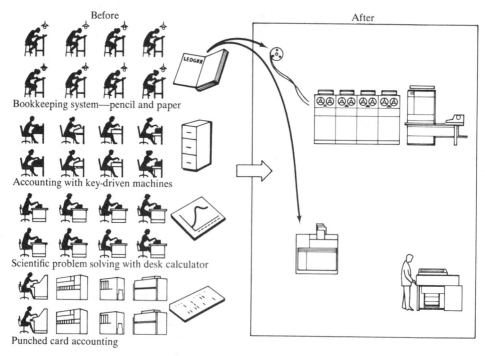

Before   After

Bookkeeping system—pencil and paper

Accounting with key-driven machines

Scientific problem solving with desk calculator

Punched card accounting

(Courtesy of IBM Corporation)

Figure 20–11   Mechanizing routine human activities.

Process control systems, medical diagnosis systems, management information systems, computer-assisted instruction (CAI) systems, and storage and retrieval systems are a few recent examples (Figure 20–12).

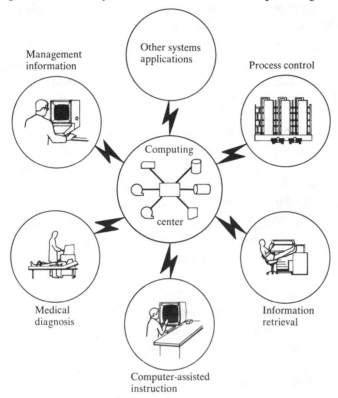

Management information

Other systems applications

Process control

Computing

center

Medical diagnosis

Computer-assisted instruction

Information retrieval

(Courtesy of IBM Corporation)

Figure 20–12   System applications.

Today, as a result of this rapid progress, most data processing installations are facing an increase in the number of conventional applications as well as an increase in the scope and complexity of new system applications. To cope with these problems, a data processing system must efficiently apply all of its resources: hardware, information, and human. These resources represent a considerable investment and must be used efficiently.

Hardware and information resources must be readily available, so that the CPU can be kept busy processing data. Human resources must be relieved of tasks that the computing system can perform.

An *operating system* is an organized collection of programs and data that are specifically designed to manage the resources of a computer system and to facilitate the creation of computer programs and control their execution in that system. The primary purpose of operating systems is to reduce the cost of running problems (production programs) by increasing the use of the various computer system components and by avoiding lost time. Through the use of operating systems, the computer user delegates part of the burden of improved information processing efficiency to the computer itself.

For an operating system to achieve the high efficiencies of which present information processing systems are capable, it should be able to handle the following functions:

1. Scheduling and performing input-output and related functions for programs
2. Interpreting human operator commands and/or control cards which describe to it the work to be done
3. Handling requests for the allocation of system resources
4. Controlling the stacking of jobs for continuous processing
5. Allocating space for external storage devices
6. Governing the operation of compilers, assemblers, and other manufacturer-provided software
7. Readying programs for execution
8. Monitoring the execution of processing programs
9. Protecting the various programs from one another
10. Providing a variety of user services

Operating systems range in complexity from simple systems that manage only simple functions to quite complex ones. In general, the more sophisticated the computer system, the more complex the operating system required to manage its use. The philosophy underlying the operating system is that the computer should perform those operator tasks that it can do faster and more accurately and that the computer should be kept operating as continuously and as effectively as possible.

A small scale computer system may have a very minimal operating system which deals primarily with input/output activities. Minicomputers and microcomputers may not have operating systems, since they may be dedicated to particular tasks. In most medium and large scale systems, however, the operating system controls the total computer environment. Perhaps the most complex operating system in existence is that used in the IBM System/370 computer. Operating System/370 (OS/370) is designed to be used with the largest and most powerful configurations of IBM System/370 computers. OS/370 spans a range from the medium scale computers using sequential scheduling up to the very largest computers operating with multiprogramming.

One of the major features of an operating system is that the computer operator can stack the jobs for continuous processing (batch processing), which, of course, greatly reduces the setup time between jobs. The system will then take advantage of all the facilities offered in the system by calling special programs, routines, and data as needed. The operator uses a *job control language* to give instructions to the computer. The job control language statements permit the computer operator to communicate wishes to the computer in a language that both parties can understand. The user may, for instance, use job control language to request that a COBOL or PL/I program be compiled or that a program that has been stored in the computer's auxiliary memory be executed. No matter what the request is, the operating system software processes job control language statements. After checking the job control statements to be sure that valid requests have been made, the operating system software locates, in auxiliary storage, needed programs and brings (loads) them into the computer's internal memory.

Other operating system software is responsible for initiating input/output operations, checking and creating file labels, processing interrupt signals, responding to end-of-file conditions, error recovery, printing control messages for the computer operator, and a variety of other tasks.

The utility system component of an operating system assists the computer user by performing library maintenance, diagnostics, sorting and merging, and job reporting. Library maintenance routines consist of software that can add, delete, or copy programs into or from the various program libraries located in auxiliary storage. Diagnostic software provides the computer user with error messages when conditions exist that make it difficult or impossible for the computer to continue processing a job.

The sort and merge programs are designed to reorder data files. Job reporting software records information that will be used to evaluate the efficiency with which the computer system is run and to bill computer users. This software stores the name of every program run on the computer, when the program was run and how much time it took, and the name of the person or department responsible for having the program run.

The operating system functions mentioned in this section are merely an indication of the type of programs that are included in operating systems. Additional operating system software is required for computer systems that support such features as time-sharing, multiprogramming, virtual memory, or remote processing. In all cases, operating system software exists to provide the computer user with a workable system.

☐ Structured Programming

Structured programming is concerned with improving the programming process through better organization of programs and better programming notation to facilitate correct and clear descriptions of data and control structures.

Improved programming languages and organized programming techniques should help one produce programs that are: (1) more understandable and therefore more easily modified and documented, (2) more economical to run because good organization and notation makes it easier for a compiler to "understand" the program's logic, and (3) more correct and therefore more easily debugged.

The physical structure of a well-organized program corresponds to the sequence of steps in the algorithm being implemented. At a lower level, all parts of the implementation of one idea are grouped in a structure that clearly indicates how the various parts are selected and sequenced, and the relation of this idea to neighboring ideas.

The program should be expressed in the most natural and appropriate representation. The program should not contain a GOTO statement when a better representation is available. A program designer should, however, use a GOTO statement when the alternates are worse. Whenever a GOTO statement is used in a program, it should be accompanied by enough comments to make its purpose perfectly clear.

Some program designers limit their conception of structured programs to programs with structured control, and ignore the equally important factor of structured data. When the data has to be manipulated to fit the available data structure representations, the program becomes less readable. The program designer should inform the reader and the computer how to represent his data structure representations into the computer's representations, and then go about using his representations in his program.

A good language for structured programming has a carefully thought-out assortment of control structures and data-structure definition facilities. If a language provides one kind of iterative control statement for counter-controlled loops and others for loops controlled by a decision value of an expression, then the former should be used when the loop is expected to terminate as a result of the counter's reaching its terminal value, and the others should be used when some other condition is expected to terminate the loop. This makes it easier for a reader to distinguish between the "nature" of the control being exercised by the loop.

When a line of code is a continuation of a previous line or a subsidiary idea, it should be indented from the left margin established by the principal statement. When an indented code might be so complex or long as to obscure the principal level of control, then one should consider making this code into a procedure. A good rule of thumb is to try to get each principal idea to fit on a single page.

Structured programming is often associated with "top-down programming." Although this technique is a useful tool for explaining a program and illustrates how much nicer it is to explain a structured program than a haphazardly written one, it is unlikely that the art of programming can be restricted to the use of a single technique.

☐ Review Questions

17. What is the purpose of an operating system?
18. List several functions that are performed by an operating system.
19. What is a job control language?

☐ Summary

Today, computers handle information processing in a variety of ways: by sharing the computer with several users, by processing data as it is obtained (real-time processing), by collecting many jobs in batches and executing the batches at one time, and by processing several programs simultaneously (multiprogramming). Sophisticated operating systems, which are basically control programs, are used to get the maximum amount of processing from a specific computer system.

Time-sharing is the simultaneous utilization of a computer system from multiple terminals. A time-sharing system makes computer facilities available to many users, all at essentially the same time.

A *real-time system* controls an ongoing process and delivers its output not later than the time when these are needed for effective control. Real-time systems are used in many businesses to control events in essentially real-time. An airline uses a real-time system to provide seat reservations immediately for passengers. Banks use real-time systems to send transactions from one branch to another. NASA uses real-time systems to control space vehicles and missions.

Batch processing is a method of processing data in which transactions are accumulated for a predetermined period of time and prepared for input to the computer to be processed as a single unit.

Multiprogramming is the concurrent execution of two or more programs simultaneously residing in the internal storage of the computer. *Multiprocessing* is the simultaneous operation of two or more interconnected CPUs to perform many complex operations that must be performed at the same time.

An *operating system* is a set of programs to manage the running of the computer system. Operating systems range in complexity from simple systems which manage only basic functions to very complex ones. In general, the more sophisticated the computer system, the more complex the operating system required to manage its use.

Structured programming is concerned with improving the programming process through better organization of programs and better programming notation.

Key Terms

information systems	executive program
time sharing	programming standards
communications processor	system integration
terminal	batch processing
real-time	multiprogramming
real-time computer	multiprocessing
system design	operating systems
job control language	structured programming

21

Computer Applications in Business

Courtesy of National Cash Register Company

Assuming now some knowledge of computing equipment and programming techniques, this chapter will explore in some detail how computers are used in actual business applications.

☐ System Flowchart

Before this discussion starts, however, the concept of the *system flowchart* should be explained. In chapter 12, the *program flowchart* was described as a method of showing the steps required in the solution of a problem. The *system flowchart* is a picture showing the interrelationships of equipment and processes (or programs) in an electronic data processing system.

Basically, the system flowchart is a graphic representation of an entire system or portion of a system consisting of one or more computer operations. It is composed of interconnected flowcharting symbols arranged in the sequence in which the various system operations are performed. The system flowchart is essentially an overall planning, control, and operational description of a specific application.

The symbols described in chapter 12 and the symbols shown in Figure 21–1, 21–2, and 21–3 may be used on system flowcharts. Most of these symbols are represented on a standard programming template (see Figure 12–4). The missing symbols can easily be constructed by using parts of other symbols on the template.

The use of these symbols is illustrated in the accompanying two examples. Figure 21–4 on page 539 shows a system flowchart of an inventory updating process, in which old inventory item balances are adjusted by receipts and issues that bring about current item inventory balances. As shown in this example, system flowcharts are not as formalized as program flowcharts, and are more flexible.

Figure 21–5 on page 540 illustrates the use of the communication link symbol representing the transmission of information from one location to another over communication channels (telephone lines, microwave links).

Symbol	Name	Symbol Use
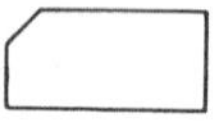	Punched Card	Represents punched card input and output.
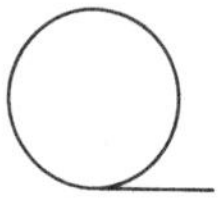	Magnetic Tape	Represents magnetic tape input and output.
	Paper Tape	Represents punched paper tape input and output.
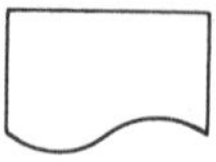	Document	Represents paper document input and output.
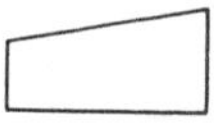	Manual Input	Represents inputs from keyboards, switches, console buttons, etc.
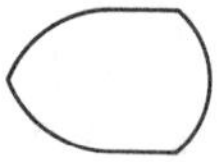	Display	Represents display input and output.
	Communication Link	Connects remote locations via a transmitting link.
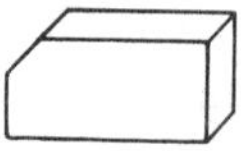	Card Deck	Represents a collection of cards.
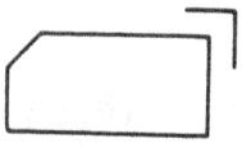	Card File	Represents a file of related punched card records.

Figure 21–1   Input-output symbols for system flowcharts.

Figure 21–6 on page 540 shows a system flowchart which illustrates the use of the sort, magnetic tape, card deck, process, and document symbols. There is also a broken line to indicate that an output tape produced as a result of today's operation will be the input tape for processing when this job is run again.

Symbol	Name	Symbol Use
	On-line Storage	Represents an on-line storage device.
	Off-line Storage	Represents off-line storage of information.
	Magnetic Drum	Represents information stored on a magnetic drum.
	Magnetic Disk	Represents information stored on a magnetic disk.
	Core Storage	Represents information stored in a magnetic core device, other than the internal core storage of the computer.

Figure 21–2   Storage symbols for system flowcharts.

☐ **Review Questions**

1. What is a system flowchart? How is it used?
2. Identify the following system flowchart symbols.

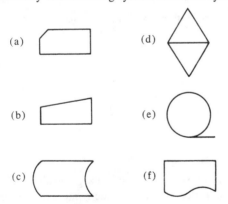

(a) (d)

(b) (e)

(c) (f)

3. How does the system flowchart differ from a program flowchart?
4. Draw a system flowchart of a simple process.
5. What flowchart symbols are common to both system and program flowcharts?

Symbol	Name	Symbol Use
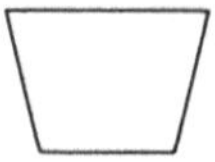 ⏢	Manual Operation	Represents a process that is performed manually.
▢	Auxiliary Operation	Represents an operation not under the control of the central processing unit.
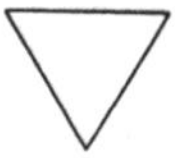 ▽	Merge	Represents the creation of one set of items from two or more sets of items arranged in the same sequence.
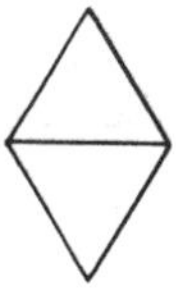 ⧓	Sort	Represents the arrangement of a set of items into a sequence on the basis of some key, which is generally the data value in a specified control field.
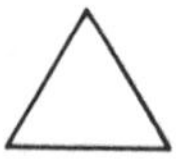 △	Extract	Represents the creation of two or more sets of items arranged in the same sequence as one original set.
 ⧖	Collate	Represents a combined merge and extract operation.

Figure 21–3   Process symbols for system flowcharts.

☐ Payroll Preparation

Payroll is one of the most widely used and generally useful business applications for a computer. In many electronic data processing payroll systems, punched cards are used to contain the weekly time card information and magnetic tape is used to store the master payroll records. To illustrate how a payroll procedure works, Figure 21–7 shows a system flowchart for processing a typical hourly-rate payroll. This procedure is set up to use punched cards containing hours worked for each employee.

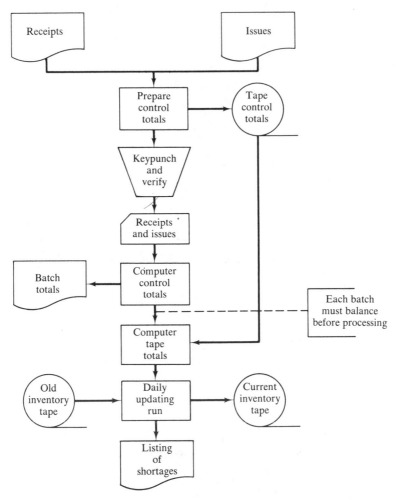

Figure   System flowchart of an inventory update process.
21–4

The flowchart in Figure 21–7 shows the Master payroll records and weekly time cards being input to the computer. The computer, as indicated by flowchart symbol #1, computes the gross pay, tax, and insurance deductions for each employee and produces this information on a temporary file. This temporary file, which is ordered by employee identification number, is then used as input to a sort program (flowchart symbol #2) which produces a file in order by employee name. This second temporary file is used as input to the final step (flowchart symbol #3). Finally, this program computes the net pay and produces a printed listing of each employee's name and net pay.

Figure 21–8 (page 542) is a program flowchart of the procedure for the computation indicated by flowchart symbol #1 in Figure 21–7. Inputs

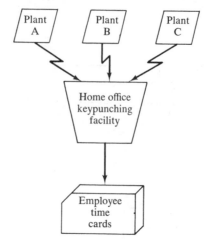

**Figure
21–5**   System flowchart indicating data transmission over communication lines.

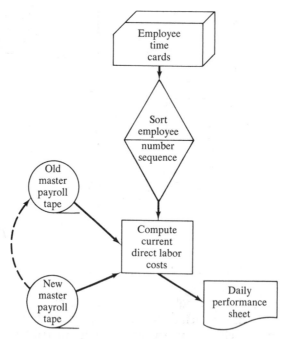

**Figure
21–6**   System flowchart of a direct labor cost updating procedure.

to this program are the master payroll records and weekly time cards. Information from both files is required to perform the primary function of the program, computing the gross pay and the two deductions. The first step in the program is to read records from both files until a record from each file indicates the same employee. Using information for that

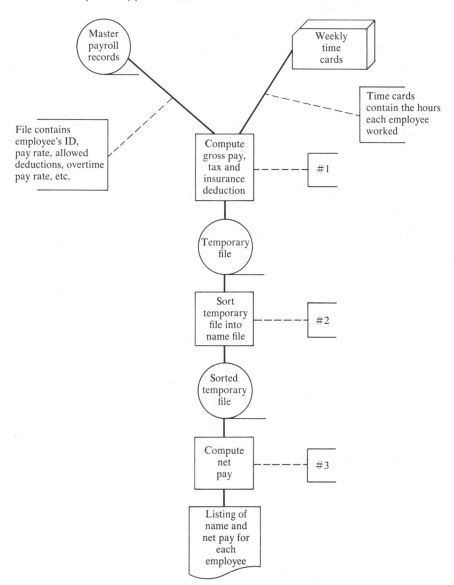

Figure 21–7 System flowchart of payroll procedure.

employee from both files, the necessary computations can be performed. The results of the computations are then written on a temporary file.

The contrast between this program and the system flowchart illustrates the major differences in the system and program flowcharts. Where a system flowchart is a broad, general picture of the flow of data, a program flowchart is a detailed picture of the flow of data. Another way of saying this is: one symbol in a system flowchart may represent many

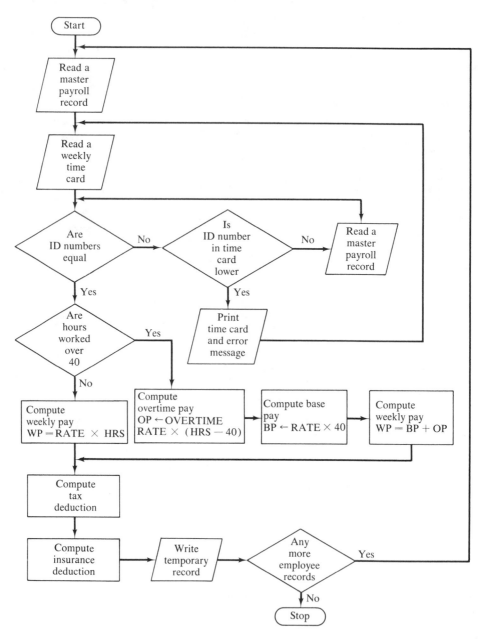

**Figure
21–8**   Program flowchart of payroll computation.

operations, while one symbol in a program flowchart often represents only one operation. An entire system can be shown on one or two sheets of a system flowchart. The same system in the much more detailed program flowchart may require many sheets.

☐ Retail Cash Sales

Another typical business application for the computer is a system used when several retail stores are controlled by a single headquarters office. Figure 21–9 shows the sales-audit data flow of such a system. This appli-

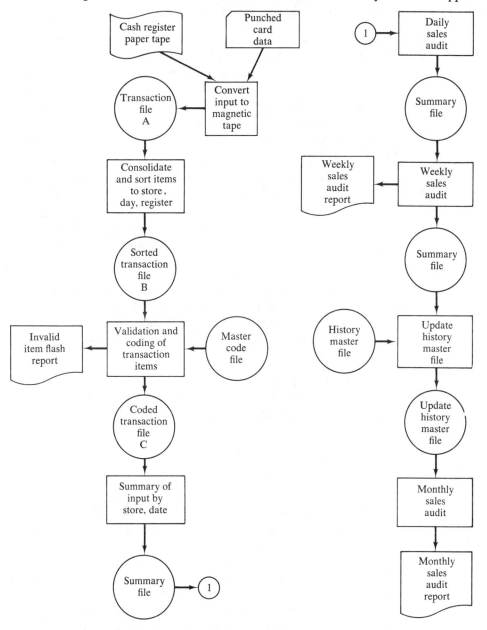

Figure 21–9 System flowchart of sales-audit data flow.

cation consists of recording and reporting on all cash received and sales completed, maintaining accurate inventory records, and developing statistical and analytical reports on buying trends. The output includes flash sales reports, daily sales-audit reports, monthly sales-audit reports, weekly purchase orders, weekly update of master detail file exception listings, weekly style history reports and weekly class/price reports.

The majority of the input information used in sales-audit processing is generated at each cash register in each store. As a sales clerk rings up a sale on a cash register, the data relating to that sale are punched automatically into paper tape. This tape-recorded data may include the transaction number, a merchandise code, the amount of the sale, and the cash register identification number. The punched paper tape for each register shows beginning and ending dollar accumulation for all sales data registered for the day.

As a second input, all additional information required for sales auditing is keypunched into cards. This includes the sales data from stores using print-punch price tickets, clerical data developed by cashiers when they balance out their cash registers each day, and accounting control data for adjusting sales and distributing dollars to proper amounts.

The punched paper tape and punched cards from all stores are sent daily to the computer system, where they are recorded on magnetic tape. This tape, created by the input information, includes regular cash item sales, refund items, lay-away items, federal tax, state tax items, and voids for each type of item. This information is then used to produce the required reports and updated tapes.

Figure 21–10 shows part of a class/price report. This report accumulates totals by class and price line for each store and for the entire chain. Such a report gives management a clear picture of unit sales by class.

☐ Accounts Receivable

The flowchart in Figure 21–11 illustrates how a department store uses a computer to bill overdue accounts. If payment for an account is more than 30 days late, a special late charge fee is added to the customer's account. The fee is determined by the customer's balance. If the balance is less than or equal to $300, the late charge is three percent of the balance; if the balance is over $300, the late charge is four percent of the balance. After the late charge is computed, it is added to the customer's account. A customer statement is then printed indicating the amount that is currently due. A special "payment overdue" message is printed on the statement if the account has been due for 60 days or longer.

Class/Price Line Report

Dept.	Class	Price	Store	Sales This Week	Sales This Month	Sales This Month Last Year	Sales Next Month Last Year	On Hand	On Order
230	104	3.27	1	6	27	31	41	22	60
			2	12	46	39	48	52	30
			3	10	32	34	38	12	40
			4	8	39	48	32	15	15
		4.50	1	4	21	25	30	40	20
			2	10	18	20	22	14	15
			3	16	32	34	42	32	20
231	6	10.95	1	26	104	110	160	172	50
			2	36	123	136	119	93	40
			3	42	162	150	104	122	75

Figure 21–10 Management report produced by computerized retail system.

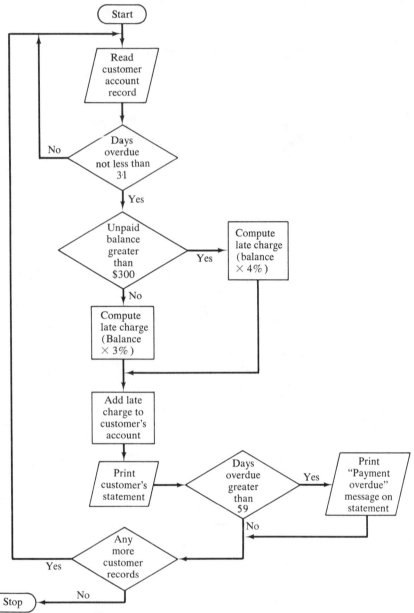

Figure 21–11   Program flowchart of accounts receivable procedure.

☐ Compound Interest Computation

In 1627, Peter Minuet purchased Manhattan Island from the Indians for $24.00 worth of beads and trinkets. If this money had been invested at a four percent interest and the interest had been compounded annually, what would the investment be worth in 1980? A flowchart for this procedure is shown in Figure 16–12. This procedure uses the formula

$$a = p \left(1 + \frac{i}{100}\right)^n$$

where p is the principal ($24.00), i is the yearly rate of interest (4%), n is the number of years, and a is the total amount of the investment (principal plus interest).

The procedure in Figure 21–12 illustrates a simple loop. Each time the computer executes the loop, the year and amount are printed. At the

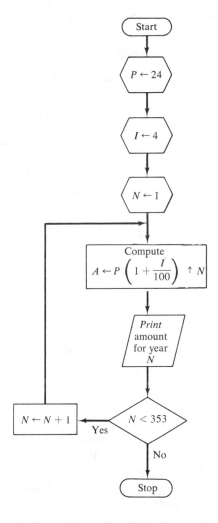

Figure 21–12 Program flowchart to compute compound interest.

termination of the procedure, 353 lines of information will be printed, the number of years between the year 1627 and the year 1980.

☐ Investment Simulation Problem

Steven Spencer has set aside $200,000 for investing in gold mines. Understandably, he does not want to invest his money without first examining closely the probabilities for success. Steve knows that

(1) it costs about $100 000 to dig a mine
(2) a mine with some gold will provide a net profit, after taxes, of about $1 000 000
(3) a mine without gold will result in a loss of $100 000
(4) one out of every four mines contains gold.

Steve also wants to retire when he has made $2 000 000.

Prior to digging the mines, Steve decides to simulate the histories of several investments identical to the one he is considering. To do so, he uses the information given above to construct a flowchart. A program flowchart for the simulation is shown in Figure 21–13. As shown in the flowchart, the indicated logic will permit Steve to evaluate his probability of success by simply "flipping a coin." The "flipping a coin" procedure is accomplished by having the program calculate a binary number (0 or 1) at random. The number 0 represents "tails" while the number 1 represents "heads." Whenever two ones appear at random, the procedure assumes that a mine with some gold has been found. The other combinations of two random numbers (two 0s, one 0 and one 1, and one 1 and one 0) are used to indicate that a mine was dug without finding gold. After the procedure produces and checks two random numbers, either $100 000 is subtracted or $1 000 000 is added to M (M was originally set to $200 000). Whenever M reaches $2 000 000 the procedure causes the message "RETIRE—MONEY EXCEEDS $2,000,000" to be printed. If M reaches zero, the message "MONEY IS GONE" will be printed. To see how Steve fared with his hypothetical investment, use a coin to work through the simulation.

☐ Summary

In chapter 12 the *program flowchart* was discussed in detail. In this chapter the *system flowchart* is contrasted with the more detailed program flowchart. The system flowchart is a pictorial representation of the interrelationships of equipment and processes (or programs) in an information processing system. Basically, the system flowchart is a graphic representation of an entire system or portion of a system consisting of one or more computer operations. Flowcharting symbols for system flowcharts are illustrated early in the chapter.

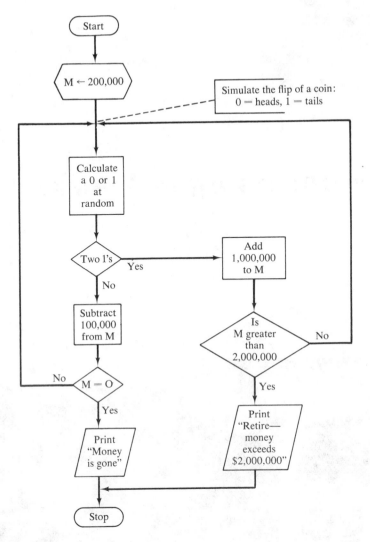

**Figure
21–13**   Program flowchart of a simulation problem.

Included in this chapter are program descriptions and flowcharts for
the following business problems: payroll preparation, retail cash sales,
accounts receivable, compound interest computation, and investment
simulation.

Key Terms

system flowchart   flowcharting symbol

22

Teleprocessing Networks

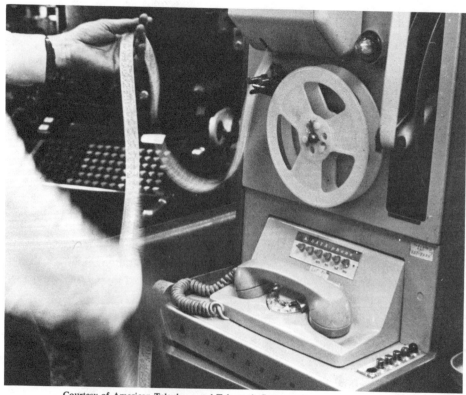

Courtesy of American Telephone and Telegraph Company

Teleprocessing* is a term formed by a combination of the words *tele-communications* and *data processing*. The process it describes is a form of information handling in which a data processing system utilizes communication facilities. The communication network permits processing of data at a point remote from its origin. Figure 22–1 illustrates a system that has five remote locations. As illustrated in this figure, data communications between the central processing facility and remote locations is accomplished by such data communication facilities as telephone lines,

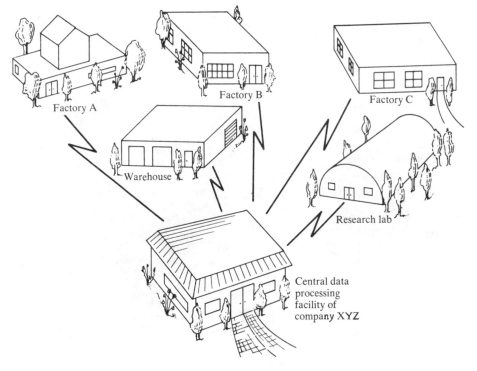

Figure 22–1 A Teleprocessing Network.

---

* Originally, but no longer, an IBM Trademark.

electric cables, and microwave systems. The source or destination points of data are called *terminals*.

A terminal can have one or a combination of I-O devices. A large variety of such devices are available for use at remote terminals. These include special keyboards, TV-like graphic display devices, printers, card read-punch units, and telephones. In addition, a terminal may include a remote processing system, in which case the application is not only a teleprocessing application but a *multiprocessing* application as well.

Teleprocessing applications range from those in which data is received by a central processing system and merely stored for later processing, to large complex system applications in which the hardware and information resources of the central system are shared among a great many users at remote locations. Teleprocessing capabilities are particularly useful in situations where a central computer can coordinate several facilities remote from one another. Figure 22–2 shows the telecommunications center at McDonnell Automation Company. Operators use this center to connect computers to many remotely located users.

(Courtesy of McDonnell Automation Company)

Figure 22–2   Telecommunications operators using equipment to connect remotely located users to several computer systems.

The three major areas of teleprocessing are *data collection, data communication,* and *data transmission.* A single teleprocessing system may include any combination of these three. These three aspects are described in the following sections.

☐ Data Collection

Data collection implies that data are received by a central processing system from one or more remote terminals and are stored for later processing. Depending on the specific application, the transfer of data may be initiated either at the terminal or by the central processing system.

An example of a data collection application would be one in which data is received intermittently during the day (as it is generated) and then is processed when convenient during the second or third shift, perhaps taking advantage of lower data processing rates for the shift. This could be an application in which production workers, upon completion of their jobs, transmit by means of special input devices such data as their ID numbers, the number of work units they completed, and other pertinent data. The central system, after all the data for the day have been collected and stored, could then process it for accounting and production control purposes.

In other applications, data may be accumulated during the day and then placed on an input device, such as a punched card reader. The data could be collected by the central computing system during off-peak hours in order to take advantage of lower communication line rates.

☐ Data Communication

Data communication is the movement of data by means of electrical transmission systems. Data can be sorted out, compiled in many ways, and subjected to arithmetic operations. The machine for handling these operations, the computer, is frequently called a *data processing machine,* although it may also be responsible for the conveyance of information from one place to another—for the *data communication* itself. The importance of data communication cannot be stressed enough. A static society can exchange its small store of knowledge with little effort, but a large, rapidly-changing society has to organize its vast daily flood of communications.

Thus, systems that used data communications grew along with other computer systems. As communications needs grew more complex in the 1920s and 1930s, telephone engineers began developing many of the concepts that later were carried over into the computer field. Bell Telephone Laboratories' engineers and scientists, recognizing the need for a better way to carry out the laborious mathematics of their own problems, completed a large digital computer in 1940. It was built from electromechanical parts normally used in dial switching systems.

This and similar computers that followed were used to solve scientific and defense problems during World War II. But these computers were limited by their large numbers of electron tubes that consumed tremendous amounts of power and space. Then, in 1948, Bell Laboratories solved this problem with the transistor—with its smaller size, lower power consumption, and greater dependability, an ideal solution.

By the 1950s, rapid communications and improved transportation encouraged business and government to decentralize—to spread their operations across the country. To use their computers efficiently, however, it was necessary to funnel information from far-flung locations into a data processing center. At first, people mailed packages of cards. But it soon became obvious that better methods were needed to send data faster and more conveniently.

Today, machines communicate with one another with *lines*. These lines may be wires, cables, or microwave circuits (see Figure 22–3). A wide

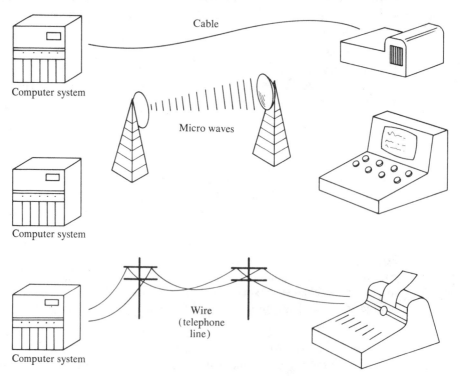

Figure 22–3   Types of data communication lines that are used to connect terminals to computer systems.

range of transmission services is available from such firms as American Telephone and Telegraph (A. T. & T.), General Telephone and Electronics (G. T. & E.), and Western Union (W. U.). *Telephone lines* permit data to be sent at speeds of up to 9 600 bits per second. *Teletype lines* transmit data at a much slower speed, about 150 bits per second; although teletype line speed is often adequate for input conveyed by manual keying or punched paper tape.

A. T. & T. offers the following communication services:

WATS (Wide Area Telephone Service) permits a user to place an unlimited or metered amount of outgoing calls at a flat rate within a geographical area of specified radius.

Data-Phone Services provides for the transmission of data using the regular dial-up telephone network (see Figure 22–4). This is done by the use of *modems* (devices that modulate and demodulate signals) and the same dial telephone network used for local and long distance voice communication. The modem, which is connected electrically to the line, converts binary information available from digital equipment into tones, making it suitable for transmission over voice grade lines. In a

(Courtesy of American Telephone and Telegraph Company)

Figure 22–4   Data-phone service lets the user plug computers into the regular Bell telephone lines that are used for talking—so information can be sent just about anywhere.

similar manner, the modem converts tones received on the voice grade line into binary data and makes them available to digital equipment.

Telpak is a pricing arrangement that permits a wide-band communication channel between two points. This wide band can be broken down into many voice grade lines or used as one high-speed data line. There are four basic Telpak services available: A,B,C, and D corresponding to 12, 24, 60, and 240 voice grade lines respectively. Channel capacities similar to that of Telpak are also available with private microwave systems.

Private Line Voice Service provides a private voice grade line for the exclusive use of a particular user. This service can be used for either voice communication or data transmission using a modem.

Private Line Teleprinter Service furnishes circuits for the exclusive use of particular users. Keyboard printers, paper tape punches, and paper tape readers are used with these services. One circuit can connect two or more teleprinter machines.

Teletypewriter Exchange Service provides direct-dial-point-to-point connections using teleprinter equipment, such as keyboard printers and paper tape readers and punches. Facilities are also available to permit digital computers to be connected to this service.

G. T. & E. offers most of the services available from A. T. & T. Western Union furnishes communication services by wire and microwave radio throughout the United States and also offers leased-line services for data transmission as well as teletypewriter service.

☐ Data Transmission

Data transmission is the sending of data. Magnetic tape-to-computer communications is an example of data transmission. This form of transmission is desirable wherever large amounts of data must be conveyed at high speeds from one location to another. For example, in Figure 22–1 a design modification to some electrical apparatus might be sent from the research lab to the central data processing facility. Likewise, new circuit diagrams resulting from the modification might be sent to Factory A.

☐ Data Communication Terminals

Terminals range from a simple send-only teleprinter to a complicated terminal computer with considerable data manipulation power. The common denominators of these terminals are the capability to transmit and/or receive data over communication lines, and an input and/or output medium.

In terms of function, terminals can be divided into transmitters, receivers, and transceivers. They communicate with computers and other terminals equipped with appropriate connecting devices. The type of communications circuit required is most often a voice grade telephone line; however, other networks such as microwave links and telegraph lines are sometimes used.

The transmitters accept as input media the keyboard, punched card, voice message, magnetic tape, magnetic disk, plastic card, punched paper tape, pencil-marked card, edge-punched card, etc. Receivers output data in the form of printed hard copy, punched card voice message, magnetic tape, magnetic disk, punched paper tape, cathode ray tube, or direct signals to the computer's memory.

Figure 22–5 shows two students using Model 33 ASR Teletype terminals. These terminals are used in many teleprocessing systems, especially as user terminals in general time-sharing systems.

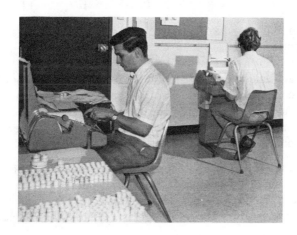

Figure 22–5 Hamilton College students using terminals to communicate with a computer located many miles away.

☐ Modems and Acoustic Couplers

Modems and acoustic couplers are essential in data communications, because common carrier phone lines cannot carry signals as they are emitted from computers or other digital machines, nor can they input signals directly into the machines. Either a *modem* or *acoustic coupler* is required to convert the signals to *phone line language* for data transmission.* Often called a *data set,* a modem is used between the communication line and the digital machine in a position to convert digital output signals from machines to analog signals for transmission, and vice versa on the receiving end, as shown in Figure 22–6 Modems are made by the telephone companies and computer manufacturers.

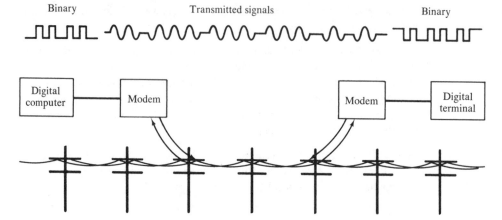

Figure 22–6   Modems are used to interface digital equipment with standard communication facilities.

The acoustic coupler is an alternate way of connecting digital terminals to a computer system. It accepts a conventional telephone hand set and does not require special wiring. To use the coupler, the operator merely uses an ordinary telephone, dials the telephone number, and places the telephone cradle into the acoustic coupler.

There are differences in the performance capabilities of the two devices. One is speed. Most couplers have a maximum transmission rate of 300 bits per second, though a few can handle rates as high as 1 800. Modem transmission rates can go as high as 1 000 000 bits per second.

The speed, of course, is largely dependent on the type of communications line used. A teletypewriter line operates at about 150 bits per second, or less. A voice grade telephone line will carry up to about 9 600 bits per second, depending on whether the line is upgraded through conditioning and whether it is a private line, a leased line, or a part of a high-speed communications network. Some data communication networks can transmit up to 500 000 bits per second.

Although both devices operate with equal efficiency, the acoustic coupler offers a portable feature and is thus preferred in many systems. The

* Before 1968, A.T.&T. could legally restrict the use of "foreign" attachments on its phone lines. In 1968, the Federal Communications Commission made a decision that allowed modems to be used without such restrictions.

coupler utilizes the data tone which is transmitted by the computer to the terminal. Any standard telephone can be used without requiring the special installation necessary for the data set. Thus, the user can go wherever a telephone is available, dial the computer, and start processing his data.

Most of the modems and acoustic couplers employ serial transmission, which can be synchronous (in which the sending and receiving terminals are synchronized bit for bit) or asynchronous (in which the start and end of each character is indicated by signal elements).

Another characteristic to be considered is the directionality of the unit. Simplex units operate in one direction only; half duplex indicates two-way alternate transmission; and full duplex indicates two-way simultaneous transmission. A modem or acoustic coupler may also have numerous interchange circuits.

☐ Digital Communication Codes

There are many codes used in communications today. Some of the more popular ones are the Baudot Code, ASCII Code, Hollerith Code, BCD, EBCDIC, and Four of Eight Code.

The *Baudot Code* is used only for telegraphs, printers, readers, punches, and keyboards. This five-bit code can accommodate only 32 unique codes. The *ASCII* (American Standard Code for Information Interchange) code is a seven-level code that provides several control characters and permits double-shift printing. This code, mentioned in chapter three, has been established by computer manufacturers, computer users, and terminal manufacturers. Most communication terminals are designed to conform to ASCII format; however, due to the wide range of terminal usage, some manufacturers have made minor changes in the code to make it more applicable to their particular terminals.

The *Hollerith Code* is used almost exclusively for punched card applications. It is a 12-level code, designed to represent the alphabet, the digits, and several special characters. This code lends itself to easy error detection. When data on a card are transmitted, they are usually first converted to BCD (binary coded decimal) code. BCD code is merely a compression of the Hollerith Code: two bits in the BCD code replace the three-zone bits in the Hollerith code, and four bits replace nine-data bits.

The EBCDIC (Extended Binary Coded Decimal Interchange Code) is merely the BCD code extended to eight bits (see chapter three). This expansion allows many graphic and control codes to be added. The Four of Eight Code represents data with a fixed number of one bits and a fixed number of zero bits. Four of the eight bits are always ones, and four are always zeros. This eight-bit code is less efficient than many of the other codes; however it is useful in applications where high accuracy and easy error detection are required—i.e., credit card verification systems and Bell System touch-tone inquiry systems.

Many data communication codes use an extra bit, called a *parity bit,* in each code for checking purposes. This bit indicates whether the total number of binary "1" digits in a code is odd or even. If a "1" parity bit indicates an odd number of "1" digits, then a "0" bit indicates an even number. If the total number of "1" bits, including the parity bit, is always even, the system is called an *even parity* system. In an *odd parity* system, the total number of "1" bits, including the parity bit, is always odd.

Teleprocessing Applications

Message switching is a type of teleprocessing application in which a message received by the central computing system from one remote terminal is sent to one or more other remote terminals. Message switching can be used in a nationwide or worldwide telegraph system or it can be used by a geographically dispersed business or scientific enterprise to provide instantaneous communication within the enterprise.

Remote job processing is a type of application in which data processing jobs, like those that are entered into the system locally, are received from one or more remote terminals and processed by the operating system.

On-line problem solving is a teleprocessing application in which a number of users at remote terminals can concurrently use a central computing system in solving problems. In this type of application, each user at a terminal has the impression that he is the sole user of the computing system. In reality, however, the resources of the system are shared among several users. Accordingly, such applications are often referred to broadly as *time sharing* (see chapter 20) applications. Because of its speed, the computing system can respond to the needs of all the users within a few seconds or less. Thus, when the use of the computing system is momentarily not required by one user, it is available to satisfy the needs of others.

Often, in this type of application, a dialogue or conversation is carried on between the user at a remote terminal and a program within the central computing system. The program may be designed to interrogate the user and immediately respond to his replies or requests, or even his mistakes.

On-line problem solving has a great many potential applications in the fields of education, engineering, and research. Because the system can respond immediately to the needs of the user, it can directly participate in, and speed up the problem-solving process as well as other similar processes, such as program design and learning. Thus, if a user, in the course of designing a program, makes a mistake, he may be immediately alerted by a program in the central computing system to take corrective action. Therefore, he need not wait until the complete program is compiled and tested before the mistake is detected. Similarly, in a *computer-assisted instruction* (CAI) system (an important variation of this type of application) a student is immediately informed of his mistakes and learns from them as they occur.

☐ Review Questions

1. The term "teleprocessing" was formed from what two terms?
2. What is a terminal?
3. What are the three major types of teleprocessing?
4. Describe the following:
   (a) data collection
   (b) data communication
   (c) data transmission
5. Describe the process whereby a machine located in Miami, Florida can communicate with a machine in Houston, Texas.
6. List some of the common communication services that are available for data communication.
7. Distinguish between modems and acoustic couplers.
8. List some of the codes that are used with data communication systems.
9. Describe a teleprocessing activity that you are familiar with.

☐ Summary

Teleprocessing is a term formed by a combination of the words telecommunication and data processing. It is a form of information handling in which a data processing system utilizes communication facilities. The three major types of teleprocessing are data collection, data communication, and data transmission.

Data collection implies that data is received by a central processing system from one or more remote terminals and is stored for later processing.

Data communication is the movement of data by means of electrical transmission systems, i.e. telephone lines, teletype lines. Communication services covered in this chapter include WATS, Data-Phone, Telpak, Private Line Voice, and Private Line Teleprinter.

Data transmission is the sending of data. Magnetic tape-to-computer communications is an example of data transmisson.

Modems and *acoustic couplers* are used in data communication systems to convert the signals to phone-line language for data transmission. These devices are ways of connecting computing equipment to telephone facilities.

Codes used in data communications include Baudot Code, ASCII code, and EBCDIC code. Most data communication codes use an extra bit, called a *parity bit,* in each code for checking purposes.

Teleprocessing systems are widely used for message switching, remote job processing, and on-line problem solving.

Key Terms

teleprocessing
terminal
data collection
data communication
data transmission
telephone lines
teletype lines
Wide Area Telephone Service
 (WATS)
modem
Telpak
acoustic coupler

data set
Baudot code
ASCII
Hollerith code
parity bit
odd parity
even parity
message switching
remote job processing
on-line problem solving
computer assisted instruction (CAI)

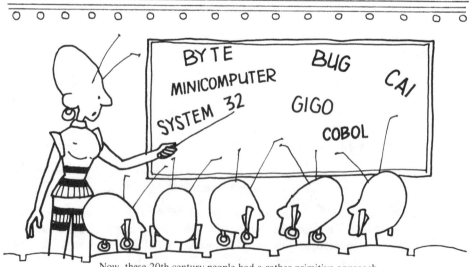

Now, these 20th-century people had a rather primitive approach to computing.

23

System Design

Courtesy of American Airlines

A *systems study* is the investigation made in a business to determine and develop needed informational improvements in specified areas. In some cases, the needed improvements will involve using a computer to achieve specific objectives. There are at least three reasons for making a system study. First, substantial investment may be involved in using a computer, and a proper study reduces the risk of loss. Second, many of the common pitfalls associated with inadequate planning may be avoided. Finally, the study may point the way to substantial benefits.

Let us now look at an approach to follow in conducting such a study.

☐ Systems Analysis and Design

Systems analysis and design is the evaluation and creation of computer-based information systems. Its relationship with computer programming is shown in Figure 23–1.

The process begins with the recognition of a problem or an opportunity (Step 1). The problem may be specific, such as payroll for 260 employees, or the general idea that control could be enhanced by a more effective computer-based information system. In either case, the next step is *system analysis* (Step 2), which is to learn enough about the present system to design a better one.

This step involves collecting, organizing, and evaluating facts about a system and the environment in which it operates. The system analysis step is intended to evaluate the necessity and the economic and technological feasibility of a solution to the problem. The written report produced in the systems analysis step is the *feasibility study*.

The third step is *systems design*. Once it is determined that the project is feasible, a general outline of the proposed solution (feasibility study) is used to produce a detailed design. This detailed design is literally the specifications that are supplied to programming (Step 5).

The fourth step is equipment selection and acquisition. The object of this step is to select and acquire the computer system which will do the job effectively at the lowest possible cost. This step is accomplished by converting the feasibility study to a nonhardware oriented specification. To obtain the lowest price, computer vendors are invited to submit bids based on the specifications. The user evaluates the bids and selects the vendor from which to buy or lease equipment.

What makes you think I'm lying about the capabilities of our system?

The first four steps—problem recognition, systems analysis, systems design, and equipment selection and acquisition—constitute systems analysis and design.

The remaining three steps are: programming, implementation, and evaluation. The objectives of the programming and implementation steps (Steps 5 and 6) are to write, test, and check-out (debug) the programs for the new system. The manpower resources expended to do the programming and implementing in these steps are the most used for any other tasks in the development cycle. The evaluation step (Step 7) involves reviewing and checking the effectiveness of the process and the finished product.

The role of the *systems analyst* in these last three steps varies from organization to organization. In some businesses, the systems analyst has no control or authority over the programming, implementing or evaluating. However, in other instances, he or she has total responsibility for and control of these functions. In this book we will consider the systems analyst in the latter role.

Systems analysts accumulate a great deal of data as they work. Initially, the data are objective and appear as grid charts, flowcharts, or on data sheets. Systems analysts also obtain much subjective information, however. They draw conclusions about the present system. First, they acquire a complete understanding of the system's data flow. Second, they know the actions taken by each work center in the system. Third, they

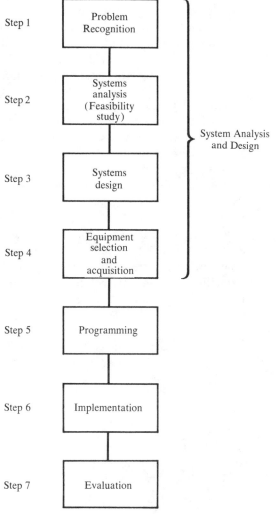

Step 1 — Problem Recognition

Step 2 — Systems analysis (Feasibility study)

Step 3 — Systems design

Step 4 — Equipment selection and acquisition

} System Analysis and Design

Step 5 — Programming

Step 6 — Implementation

Step 7 — Evaluation

Figure 23–1 Steps in the process of developing a computer-based information system.

know the total activity of the system from data organization to product delivery. Fourth, they identify the possible areas for integration of functional areas. This step is important when the work progresses to systems design. Fifth, they produce a written report, the feasibility study.

☐ The Systems Analyst

Although there is no generally accepted job description for the position of *systems analyst,* the job basically consists of (1) determining company information needs; (2) gathering facts about and analyzing the basic methods and procedures of current business systems; and (3) modifying, redesigning, and integrating these existing procedures into new systems specifications as required to provide the needed information. In addition to making the most effective use of existing information processing equipment, the systems analyst may also recommend (during the equipment selection and acquisition step) justifiable equipment changes.

Systems analysts are aptly characterized as generalists. They must be familiar with the specific firm—they must know its objectives, its personnel, its products and services, its industry, and its special problems. Systems analysts must have a thorough grasp of programming and programs. They must also know the uses and limitations of computers as well as other types of information processing equipment, for they are the interpreters between managers and data processing specialists. They must be able to determine which jobs are candidates for computer processing. They must be able to organize the complete set of tasks for a given system into a series of interrelated programs, estimating the time and hardware resource requirements for these programs, and estimating the time it will take to design, write, and check-out the programs. They must have logical reasoning ability. They must be able to plan and organize their work, since they will frequently be working on their own without much direct supervision. They must be able to communicate with, and secure the cooperation of, operating employees and managers. Most systems analysts are programmers who have been

But I'm sure you'll all agree that what our new systems analyst lacks in ability and experience, he more than compensates for by being my son.

promoted; however, some come from particular application areas, and others are trained as systems analysts in college educational programs.

Educational backgrounds vary, but a college degree (often an advanced degree) or the equivalent is generally desired.

☐ The Feasibility Study

The *feasibility study* analyzes the practicality and economics of installing a new system in one or more application areas within an organization. It is a familiar technique used for years by systems personnel. Its name describes its function—a study to determine the feasibility of a request for a change from one method to another in accomplishing certain processing functions. The request normally involves a major system change. Performing a study has the effect of averting certain problems because it:

- Forces the requestor to examine in detail the system under consideration and to reduce the proposal to writing.
- Induces a broader look at the system under study. Many related functions must be examined, such as the data conversion and input, audit and control function, and the interrelationship with other departments and system functions.
- Includes the participation and contribution of members of the user department. Too often, the request for a new system technique comes from a source outside of the department most directly affected.
- Prohibits a one-sided proposition from being adopted. Public acknowledgement that a study is in progress alerts other interested parties and gives them a chance to participate.
- Enables the study to be reviewed in terms of other studies being performed and allows corporate management to properly forecast potential future expenditures.

A feasibility study should be as factual as possible and all-inclusive in examining the many factors that affect system selection. The study results in a document of a few pages or a substantial report of many pages, depending on the magnitude of the system investigated. The study should outline the scope of the system, the objectives that such implementation hopes to accomplish, and the desired results as far as its contribution to overall corporate processing is concerned. In addition, it should be a vehicle to obtain approval from the user department manager and any other responsible individuals. Included with the goals must be an estimate of systems man-hours required, a general assignment of personnel, and a plan for integration of this request with other current and future projects.

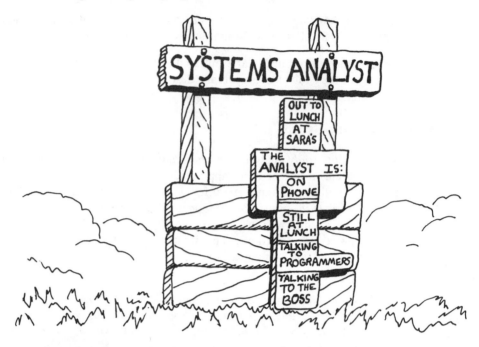

Frequently, the study can deteriorate into a one-sided attempt to place an application on the computer, so it is important to outline both advantages and disadvantages. Such seemingly incidental factors as user training, user department documentation, program maintenance, and forms design and cost should be included. The finished study should allow management to make an unbiased decision.

As the systems analyst or the systems team approaches a feasibility study, there are four basic solutions to the request for computer system implementation.

(1) *Develop a Computer System as a Solution.*   In these days of microcomputers, minicomputers, large disk storage units, virtual storage, multiprogramming, time-sharing, and improved programming techniques, a computer may be the most obvious (although not necessarily the best) solution. Generally, the request for a system is proposed on the assumption that a computer system would be designed and implemented.

(2) *Develop a Manual System as a Solution.*   If a new system must be designed, then often it is less expensive and simpler to develop a manual system and operate it at least until it is error free. In addition, performing the job manually allows the user to develop a better understanding of what the system entails. Historical information can be accumulated, and the initial data base can be developed under the manual system.

Later, automation of the system as experience and volume grow may offer the most efficient solution. Systems people should not be blinded by the computer. Sometimes, modifications to a manual system can accomplish corporate purposes.

(3) *Develop an Integrated Manual and Computer System as a Solution.* With any computer system, there is some manual effort in its initial processes, but it may be determined that other intermediate steps or validation techniques could be performed more economically.

Occasionally when computerizing a system, one small part may require an inordinate amount of time for programming and testing, or it may require a large amount of hardware resources. To do this manually would be the best solution.

(4) *Do Not Change the Current Method.* Frequently, a manual system or a manual-computer system cannot be improved enough to justify the expense involved in the change. Do not change something for the sake of change. It is important, if the information processing manager is to fulfill his or her responsibility, that he or she select or recommend the method that is most beneficial to the company, whether it be computer, manual, or combination. This selection cannot be done by viewing only cost savings as the determiner, but by evaluating all factors.

User department participation in feasibility studies is important to success. This participation not only provides a better and more comprehensive study and system but also makes the user department feel that the system is its own.

Participation should be by a designated individual or individuals to provide continuity. On major projects it is important, if not imperative, that a member of the user department be assigned to work full-time on the study. This lets the user staff member identify with the system from the beginning, understand why certain things are done or are not done, and have a say about how and what should be done. It also dispel any feelings among user department personnel that a system is being imposed upon them. In addition, the participation promotes cooperation during the design, training, conversion, and implementation phases of the project.

A system must be designed for the user, not for convenience of the computer. The best computer system can fail without user department cooperation.

How can I relax, knowing that J.B. may be thinking of replacing me with a computer?

Several important steps need to be taken before actually starting a feasibility study. First, the systems analyst together with the requestor and appropriate systems and user department personnel should:

(1) Define, review, and confirm the study scope, objectives, and desired results in a preliminary form that includes the purpose, extent, and limitation of the study. This phase should point out the possible effects of the proposed system on other systems, sections, and departments. It may also result in dropping the project or significantly widening its scope.

(2) Develop a preliminary study approach, timetable, and manpower requirements. This step will document a proposed study approach and estimate the following requirements of the study: total man months, total elapsed time, number of systems personnel, number of user department personnel, and number of other personnel.

(3) Review the previous steps with management. The scope, objectives, desired results, study approach, timetable, and estimated manning requirements should be reviewed with the user department head and head of the systems department. The objective of this review is to obtain approval for making the study, the scope and desired results of the study, and commitment of manning and projected start date.

When time and manning requirements are significant, a cost estimate for the feasibility study may be required. In many companies, and rightly so, for any significant project it is necessary to obtain high management approval and an assignment of project priority from the total company view.

Staffing the Feasibility Study. All full-time team members should be selected and be given any necessary education or orientation. It is helpful to give nonsystems team members a course in information processing systems or at least a short course covering flowcharts, vocabulary, and methods of documentation. It is also a good idea to have a member of the user department spend some time outlining the department work that the study will affect.

Once the team has been formed, the study plan can be reviewed, modified if necessary, and made formal. From this an outline of the various steps to be followed can be produced, including the company areas and/or departments to be contacted and external visits or contacts to be made to avoid duplication of work already done.

A timetable should be set up. It will either reinforce the original estimates or allow them to be modified prior to the actual start of the study.

One of the most important steps to include in the outline and timetable is periodic review and reporting. This should not be just a frequency; it should be specific dates and times, for instance, the first and third Monday of each month at 10:00 a.m. in the conference room. A set time will ensure that meetings occur; whereas a vague "once a month" may never come. Without reporting and review by the whole team and the respective section or department heads, a study may go off on an unwanted tangent or the timetable may become so warped that it cannot be fulfilled.

Conducting the Study. After establishing goals and objectives, the study team begins to collect information about the current system and its environment.

All information gathered, including minutes of meetings, should be documented, categorized, indexed, and copied so that each member of the team has a complete set. Included in this documentation should be any suggestions or comments on the design of the system that have been made during the fact-finding phase.

In most cases, some of the information will need expansion. This additional information should be documented and indexed, and, if appropriate, cross-keyed to previous documentation. As in all systems work, "documentation" is the byword.

Using the facts and documentation developed in earlier steps and any additional information needed, begin to develop possible solutions. Identify the areas of difficulty and examine their implications. This step helps determine the requirements of the system. A good system does not have to be automatic from beginning to end. Manual intervention may easily overcome some of the problem areas at certain points.

Develop as many alternative solutions and approaches as possible. Weed out those that are obviously unworkable. Then evaluate the remaining solutions from the standpoint of technical, economic, administrative, and implementation feasibility.

Be sure to project the volumes for the current system and for the proposed systems 3 to 5 years in advance. A system that is marginal now may be a real money-saver at the increased volumes. In addition, it may show the total inability of the current system to cope with future volumes.

After this preliminary evaluation, select the preferred solutions for further evaluation.

And there will be no major conversion problems with your new System/390.

Develop the Project approach and schedule. For the chosen solutions, you must next design approaches to the overall design, a systems approach, programming implementation, and evaluation.

First, develop the manning requirement for analysts, programmers, training and followup, and user department personnel. Second, using the estimated manning requirement, develop a detailed schedule for the completion of the system. Actually, both the first and second points are handled together, as one depends on the other. Do not forget vacations and allowances for sick time, meetings, and any other factor that may require time of the project personnel. If left out, these items can quickly wreck the best schedule.

Develop an economic evaluation. Develop all costs for the system, both recurring and nonrecurring. Costs deriving from the implementation of system include:

- Cost of the computer hardware system
- Cost of the software system
- Additions to the programming and systems staff
- Site preparation

- Staff training
- Systems analysis and design
- Software development and checkout
- User training
- Security
- Physical facilities (floor space, lighting, heating, and air conditioning)
- Conversion
- Printed forms

The final report on the feasibility of a system should be produced professionally. A hastily typed, slapped-together document with sloppy handwritten material makes poor backup and starts readers off with a negative attitude. A good feasibility report contains at least the following:

- A *summary* that states the recommended solution to the request or problem. This summary should be the first page of the report.
- List of any *new equipment* necessary with details why the particular equipment was chosen.
- Estimated *cost* of the system, including a future projection of the costs and savings for the next 3 to 5 years.
- List of *intangible benefits*.
- If new jobs have been created, then new *job descriptions* should be written. Identify old jobs that are no longer necessary.
- A recommended *schedule* for design, programming, system check-out, training, conversion, implementation, and documentation.
- Estimate of the *useful life* of the system.
- Indicate the future growth pattern and the *ease of system expansion*.
- List of the *advantages* and *disadvantages* of the system.
- A conclusion which provides some detail.
- An *index* if the report is large enough to warrant it.

During the preparation phases of a system feasibility study, the systems analyst's greatest assets are an *open mind* and a *willingness to be convinced*. One should avoid tunnel vision by looking at all solutions.

☐ Review Exercises

1. What is a systems study?
2. List the steps required in the process of developing a computer-based information system.
3. Distinguish between systems analysis and systems design. Discuss the importance of each function.
4. What is a feasibility study?
5. List several qualifications of the systems analyst.
6. What is the difference between a manual system and a computer system?

7. Why should we spend time studying the current system when we are planning another system to replace it?

8. Discuss some of the information that must be collected in a systems study.

9. Why are costs important when one is designing a new system?

10. List several of the items that should be contained in the feasibility report.

11. When conducting a systems study, why is it important that the systems analysts or system team keep an "open mind"?

12. Develop a plan for the redesign of a system with which you are familiar.

☐ Summary

In this chapter, we have looked at the steps required to conduct a system study. In developing a system, a systems analyst or systems team must marshall all the factors at their disposal and form the most effective combination of those factors as possible. No two systems are alike. The analysts must, therefore, make sure that they understand the problem, the assets at their disposal, and the feasibility of combining them efficiently.

The seven steps in the process of developing a computer-based information system are:

1. Problem recognition
2. Systems analysis
3. Systems design
4. Equipment selection and acquisition
5. Programming
6. Implementation
7. Evaluation

Systems analysis and design (the first four steps) is the evaluation and creation of computer-based information systems. The remaining three steps involve developing the necessary software system, implementing (putting the system into operation), and evaluating (checking the effectiveness of the process and of the finished product).

The *systems analyst* (usually a college graduate) must have many unique qualifications to be able to perform all the tasks needed in evaluating and designing a computer-based information system.

A *feasibility study* is of prime importance in developing a computer-based information system. The analyst has to determine the objectives of the system, to understand the operation of the current system, and to plan the new system with respect to what is to be done, how it is to be done, who will do the work, and when the work will be done. The feasibility study provides a path for producing a new system.

Key Terms

systems study	feasibility study
systems analysis	programming
systems design	implementation
systems analyst	evaluation

eight

Computer System Management

24

Management and the Computer

Courtesy of IBM Corporation

Several years ago, a cartoon appeared in *The Wall Street Journal.* It showed a computer being moved out of a building by some lads who were working very hard to pull it through the doors and push it onto a truck. Running alongside the computer were two gentlemen who obviously were members of the management of the business. One of them was saying to the other: "I tell you, we are ruined; it's the only one that really understood the business."

One of the peculiar things about that particular cartoon is that, in one form or another, it has appeared before—not just last year, not just 5 years ago, not just 10 years ago, but some 20 years ago. I think this says something about the field of computers. There was then, and there is today, widespread use of computers in business.

The computer is used widely in engineering, manufacturing, finance, and marketing. From the point of view of the general management of a business, however, computer usage is only on the threshold of really significant use. What is the reason for this slow progress? I think there is probably a basic mismatch between the computer and the manager. Computers over the past two decades have changed unbelievably. But let's face it, business managers have not changed their circuitry very much during that time. Every manager is a product of his or her background, education, and experience. Computers have been in broad use for only a few years, and the present generation of top business executives was formed somewhat earlier. Hopefully, business managers of the future will be "raised" with computers and will have a better understanding of how to use them in a business environment.

The purpose of this chapter is to focus on the impact that computers are having (and have had) on business managers and on the environment in which managers work. Included in this chapter is a broad orientation to the managerial implications of computer use.

☐ Effect on Management

Computers have made important changes in management techniques, giving executives closer contact with the activities under their control.

It is essential that significant facts be made available to executives if they are to make decisions and give instructions to persons working under them.

What is management? For our purposes, *management* is defined as the process of achieving organizational objectives through the efforts of other people. Management levels are often classified in three categories: *top management,* the company officials who have overall responsibility, which includes such offices as Chairman of the Board, President, and Executive Vice-President; *middle management* or department heads, frequently with the title of Vice-President, who are responsible for a complete area of operations that may include the activities of several supervisors; and *operational management,* the supervisors or leaders responsible for operating details and the employees who perform them. Of course, this listing is oversimplified and subject to variations, but it provides a general picture.

The business manager is a practitioner of the art and science of management. It is his or her job to carry out the basic management functions necessary to attain company goals. Of course, the objectives pursued vary according to the manager's mission. The goal of a keypunch room supervisor may be to keypunch a certain number of punched cards in a certain time period; the goal of a sales manager may be to meet a sales quota; and the goal of the president of a company may be to see that the business returns a dividend to its stockholders. But although objectives that managers seek vary, the managerial functions that they perform in the course of their work are common to all— planning, organization, staffing, and controlling.

There has been much speculation about the role of top management in the computerized business of the future. There are many points of view, some of them predicting many changes in the management function. It is relatively easy to identify the top management responsibilities that will *not* be changed by the computer. The individual organization's identify and objectives will not be directly affected by the existence of computers in it; therefore, the people in top positions will still hold full responsibility for the accomplishments of the firm and for its successes or failures in meeting stated objectives. Nor are measurements of performance likely to change: corporate growth and financial performance will probably always be the key criteria for top management. Thus, the basic motivations of top management are unlikely to change. Top management should get summarized reports and analyses without the details needed by middle management. As a rule, top management officials do not need or want the reports that can be so useful to department heads. Many top management decisions are made on the basis of: computer forecasts of work to be done, comparative analyses of current production with relation to a previous period's production (such as First Quarter

He says he'll give you his executive decision as soon as he gets his answer from the computer.

1978 compared with First Quarter 1977), computer analyses of surveys for future planning, and computer analyses of work in progress. The computer enables management to simulate the outcomes of many alternate sets of conditions, a function often performed mainly by "best guess" and "feel".

Middle management can use a computer to prepare and transmit useful or urgent facts of operation. A real-time computer operation can inform a department head of the course of work in progress or of a critical change the moment it occurs. The immediate availability of a fact may prevent a costly or unfortunate error, or it may enable the department head to issue an order to take advantage of a newly developed opportunity. In addition to the immediate availability of facts, the computer can provide middle management with printed reports, simulations, and analyzed statistics of both production and financial operations under their control.

The computer can make the job of operational management much simpler. Men and women in the lower management category must be provided with all facts essential to their functions. They must know the functions of employees, the flow of work, schedules, employee availability, the availability of materials, and many other details. When work slows down at any work station, the supervisor must make decisions that will correct the deficiency. The computer can provide routine printed analyses and reports to inform and guide the supervisor (see Figure 24–1).

(Courtesy of Univac Division Sperry Rand Corporation)

Figure 24–1   Computer-controlled display devices offer new simplicity and efficiency wherever information is gathered or communicated. With one keystroke, for example, an important profit report can be called to the screen of the display unit. Using a display in the office, an executive can call up a variety of management reports.

It is important that each level of management be supplied with the information needed, without being burdened with unnecessary data. A department head may need a great deal of data, but may need little, if any, relating to other departments and may need little or none relating to functions controlled by a supervisor. A manager of the paint department of a retail store needs facts related to products under his control. He is not concerned with sales figures in the ladies' shoe department or with company financing and should not, ordinarily, have his attention diverted to these or other activities with which he is not concerned. A company president needs overall information summarized without distracting details. The top official of a company should not have to sift through pages and pages of computer printouts in order to find one or two data items. Each person in management should be provided with computer-analyzed data to assist him or her in performing the job, but care must be used to avoid providing him or her with data that is not needed or wanted.

We use information processing systems for inventory, advertising, and sales analysis; but we still use Miss Laura for sales forecasting.

☐ Management by Exception

A computer can save managers' time and energy by bringing to their attention only the facts of operations that have gone wrong or that for some other reason may require action. Problems not requiring manager attention should be delegated to subordinates or be forgotten entirely. This is known as *management by exception*. A busy manager is not necessarily an efficient one. When managers must examine piles of information that does not need their attention, they may have little time or energy left to solve important problems.

Many businesses are beginning to use computers to prepare manager reports which contain only vital information (see Figure 24–2). The computer is programmed to determinel "normal" and "abnormal" situations. If it is abnormal, the computer reports this fact to the proper manager.

Information prepared for management must be useful, timely, and as concise as possible.

☐ Computer Security

The rapid expansion of computer use and the vast increase in the variety of uses for computers during the past few years have created many problems for management. Today, managers recognize their responsibili-

(Courtesy of IBM Corporation)

Figure 24–2   Sometimes managers are presented with pages and pages of printer listings containing data they cannot use. Or they spend valuable time reading to sift out facts they may need. Computers should be used to present managers with concise reports containing timely and useful information.

ties to the company shareholders for protecting the company's investment in computer hardware and software. The survival of many businesses and organizations rests on the information stored in information processing media (disks, tape, punched cards, etc.). Hence, practical safeguards must be installed to assure the accuracy and protection of important programs and data files.

Every manager should ponder the following questions related to the security of the company's information processing system:

- Could the company continue to transact its business if the computer center and everything in it were suddenly destroyed?
- Does the company give its computer program and data files security and protection comparable to the security and protection it used to give its journals, ledgers, and so on B. C. (Before Computers)?
- Has the company properly protected its programs, files, and computer hardware against sabotage?

Let us briefly look at some of the things that could happen.

Environmental Disaster. Fires, explosions, national disasters, and floods can and do destroy computer centers.

Theft and Fraud. Dishonest programmers and other personnel have been "ripping off" computer systems for years. One programmer in a bank managed to steal large amounts of money simply by programming the computer to bypass his account number when reporting on overdrafts. He was then free to overdraw his checking account by any amount he pleased.

Perhaps the question that the manager ought to ask is: "What is happening that no one knows about"? The thief's opportunity is very great, and management should not be blind to the possibilities.

And somewhere tonight there's a computer that knows it meant that payroll check to be $300, not $300,000.

Mechanical Failure. A computer equipment failure can occur at any time. A general failure is almost certain to attract instant attention. However, a failure of smaller dimensions can often escape attention until a great amount of damage has already been done. For example, one company discovered a faulty magnetic tape drive in its system only after it had incorrectly processed hundreds of reels of tape. The defective equipment was not identified immediately because, although it was distorting data at random, it continuously checked its own operation and reported that it was functioning properly. This kind of error can (in this case, did) go on for months.

Sabotage. Of all the hazards that surround information processing operations, perhaps sabotage inspires the most fear. Consider the following example. One dissatisfied computer center employee used magnets to destroy virtually every file and program that his company possessed. This frightening feat took him only a few minutes, but reconstructing the data (if even possible) will take many man-years of effort. This company is not sure whether they will be able to reconstruct enough information to stay in business.

Operator Error.   Computer operators can damage equipment and inadvertently destroy valuable programs and data files. For example, one company whose prime asset is a customer file containing billing information and reorder and inventory data came very close to losing this file. After this close call, the company maintained its file in triplicate.

The following case underlies the need for careful supervision of computer personnel. The manager of a large airline noted that data losses were occurring in the company's procedures, and he found the answer one evening during a spur-of-the-moment visit to the computer facility. He discovered that the night computer operators were "speeding up" operations by by-passing an automatic safety device on the tape drives during rewind. They got away with it when they were careful, but occasionally they broke tapes and consequently lost data.

The trend toward sophisticated real-time systems implies that organizations will run greater and greater risks of sudden and complete disruptions of business as time goes on. The airlines, for example, are rapidly approaching the point where they must have their computers in operation to conduct their normal business. Risk will be compounded in the near future, as teleprocessing and multiprogrammed computer systems find a wider use. The whole purpose of many of the newer systems is to eliminate paper copy, and there will be no records that can be used to back up their operation. The lack of paper records make the job of protecting the system from hazards more difficult.

What are some of the preventive measures that management can use to minimize the various risks associated with the use of computers? First, management should measure the company's exposure to risks and hazards, estimate the cost of complete and permanent disruption, and estimate the cost of complete protection. It can then take appropriate action for security. Several preventive measures are discussed in the following paragraphs.

Location.   If choice of a building location is possible, one should consider possible catastrophes. Select or erect a strong fireproof building in a safe location. Location of the computer center within the building should be away from the regular stream of pedestrians and out of sight.

Site Construction.   Fireproof computer sites constructed in fireproof buildings provide the best protection against fire. Locked maximumsecurity doors provide the best protection against undesired intrusion. Closed-circuit television provides protection against theft, unauthorized use of the computer equipment, and sabotage during off-hours. All windows and doors should have alarm devices.

Duplicate Files. Fully updated duplicates of all important program and data files should be stored in a fireproof safe.

Computer Room Access. Access to the computer facility should be limited to those whose presence is needed. Visitors should be limited in number and always accompanied by a manager. A guard should inspect all packages to ensure against explosives or firearms being carried into the computer facility.

Production Control. Run schedules ought to be developed for all production jobs. All tapes and disk packs should have identification data, date of creation, and disposal date. All files should be checked out from the computer librarian, and after their use, returned to the librarian who will log the files in. All computer use might be monitored by a separate terminal in a secure area.

Computer Room Employees. Regardless of how complete a security system is, undependable employees can negate it. Computer room employees should be checked out carefully prior to employment.

Legal Protection. With the growth of suits by users against computer equipment manufacturers, software companies, and service bureaus, the data processing manager must pay attention to the matter of legal protection. Let the company legal department or representative look over all equipment leases, software purchases or rentals, computer purchases, etc. Particularly important are service and maintenance contracts with computer vendors.

Decentralized Computer System. The computers of a multidivision company can be decentralized. Then, if anything should put a computer installation out of working order, the complete information processing capability of the company would not be wiped out.

Business Insurance. Employees should be bonded if they are in a position to seize any asset of the company fraudulently. Fire insurance should cover not only the hardware and software, but also the additional expenses involved in restoring the system to working order.

Internal Security. A group of skilled computer-security specialists, independent of the data processing management, should design, implement, and monitor the various control procedures. This group would check for failure and sabotage and would conduct periodic tests of duplicate files to determine the availability of the operation to recover according to a planned schedule.

There are many potential hazards to a computer installation. For each hazard, there is a preventive measure. It is extremely risky for management to fail to take appropriate preventive measures. A company can implement a satisfactory security system at reasonable cost.

You beat the computer by using Roman numerals, Mr. Smarty-
pants; however. . . .

☐ Using Consultants

When a company's top management faces unresolved problems in its
information processing operation, a decision may be to seek professional
advice from a consulting firm or a professional consultant.

A company may use a consultant to help its own people solve certain
problems of systems analysis, system design, implementation, or hardware selection.

One should select a consultant or consulting firm with the same care
one would use in selecting an accountant, a physician, or a lawyer.
When a manager decides to retain a consultant, the following guidelines
are helpful.

Acquire the names of possible consulting firms or independent professional consultants. Most firms and professional consultants welcome and
expect general inquiries. Other sources are authors of literature in information processing, who may represent nonprofit or profit-making
firms.

The size of the assignment should dictate the amount of evaluation un-
dertaken. If a consulting firm is being retained to design a system encom-
passing accounting, inventory control, etc., the manager should evaluate
the proposal and the consultant's qualifications in greater depth than if
he or she merely seeking to convert a manual payroll procedure to a
computer system.

Accordingly, some of the following suggested steps for selecting and
retaining a consultant or consulting firm, depending upon the scope of
the intended study, might be incorporated in the evaluation process.

Just as it is good practice to obtain in writing more than one bid when purchasing an expensive piece of equipment, it is also good management to get a written proposal from more than one consultant or firm. The manager may request specific inclusion of the following information in the proposal prepared by the consultant:

The Scope of Study.   For a systems design study, the scope could be expressed in terms of the organizational units or offices to be included, such as controller's office, the records office, and the purchasing office, or perhaps in terms of administrative applications, such as payroll and accounting.

The Approach to be used by the Consultant During the Execution of the Study.   This approach might be outlined in several ways, but specific statements should be requested so that managers know how the consultant expects to proceed. Statements such as "All existing procedures performed by the financial office will be documented, flowcharted, and analyzed for appropriateness in light of a mechanized system" or "All existing financial reports will be evaluated to see if some can be combined or eliminated" are meaningful descriptive summaries. It is the manager's duty to make sure that he or she thoroughly understands the consultant's proposed approach before the proposal is accepted and the study commences.

The Anticipated Results.   Once again, both parties should acquire a thorough understanding of what is expected from the consultant. For example, a systems study might include such statements as "Flowcharts in sufficient detail for the company's programmers to code from will be provided for each application included within the scope of the study; sample reports formats will be developed. . . ."

The Qualifications of the Staff.   A brief resume, citing the specific staff experience related to the proposed design study, may be requested. If a computer-based system is being designed, previous experience in developing payroll applications for punched card equipment would not be as appropriate as developing the same application for a computer system.

Estimate of Cost.   Since cost usually depends on the amount of professional time actually expended, the estimate might be submitted as a range, with the maximum figure not to be exceeded unless the scope of the study is broadened. Implementation studies are an exception, because the amount of time the consultant spends with the business depends, to a large extent, on the in-house capability of the company's data processing and systems staff; here, a per diem billing arrangement may be used.

By obtaining such common information from all individual consultants and firms being considered, the manager, to assist in the evaluation, should request from the consultant a list of clients for whom he has performed similar studies. Reputable consultants and firms will be most cooperative in furnishing lists of clients whom they have served. These clients should be contacted.

☐ Summary

Managers achieve organizational objectives through the efforts of other people. To do this, they are required to perform the managerial activities of planning, organization, staffing, and controlling. These activities are interrelated; in practice, a manager may be carrying out several functions simultaneously. A computer can help. It can supply executives with the information they need in an instantly useable form.

The widespread use of computers during the past few years has created many problems for management. With large investments in computer facilities, management is concerned with the protection of equipment and information files and the accuracy of the data being processed. Among causes of alarm to computer users are theft and fraudulent use of the computer, environmental disasters, sabotage, and operating errors. Even though there are many potential hazards to a computer installation, there are preventive measures to counteract each hazard.

Guidelines for using professional consultants or consulting firms are also included in this chapter.

☐ Review Questions

1. What is management?
2. What activities or functions must managers perform?
3. What is management by exception?
4. What type of security hazards exist at computer installations?
5. Discuss how each security hazard can be guarded against.
6. What do you think management can do to ensure the proper and continuous functioning of their computer installations?
7. List some of the guidelines a manager should use when using a consultant.

Key Terms

management	security
top management	consultant
middle management	consulting firm
lower management	

25

Information Processing Center

Courtesy of Interdata

A data processing center is significant in the overall organization not only because of the expense of the equipment, software and personnel but also because of its role as a service department which accepts input data, performs processing and storage, and provides information (see Figure 25–1). If the function is not well managed, it can seriously impair the activities of the entire organization.

(Courtesy of Health, Education and Welfare)

**Figure
25–1**
An information processing center keeps track of the time it takes to solve every problem on the computer. Some problems can be completed in minutes, while others require days or even weeks.

All of the principles of good organization and management that apply to any business or organization apply to the management of information processing facilities. While information processing may be unique in the type of service that it renders and possibly in its location in the overall organizational structure, it is nevertheless composed of people, machines, responsibilities, and production deadlines.

In this chapter, we discuss the placement of the information processing function within the structure of a company and the organization of an information processing center. The following job descriptions are included in this chapter: manager of information processing, systems analyst, programmer, computer operator, and clerical jobs.

☐ Concepts of Organization

There is no universal or standard pattern for the location of the information processing center within the organization structure of a company. Individual company differences influence the nature and location of the information processing function.

Traditionally, the information processing functions were placed under the financial managers, primarily because most of the original information processing applications were related to the accounting functions (e.g., payroll, accounts receivable, and general accounting). It was therefore somewhat natural that the financial managers (usually the controller) should play a large role in the administration of information processing activities.

Today, there is a trend in the more advanced information processing functions to have a vice-president devote full time to the responsibility (see Figure 25–2).

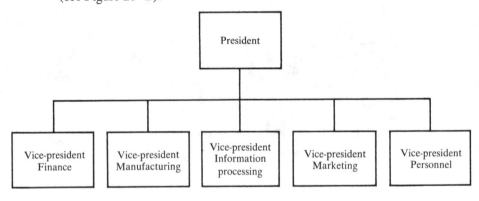

Figure 25–2   Organizational structure.

The designation of a vice-president of information processing can have a positive result because it reflects a progressive attitude toward the information processing activities. This appointment recognizes the need to be flexible and to cope with dynamic changes, new technologies, and the state of the economy. The emergence and importance of information processing activities, in many organizations, warrants suitable organizational status for the functions.

A major requirement is to develop information processing awareness in all managers and in the rank and file, so they can appreciate the role of the computer. The management of a company should be able to identify and articulate problems with the systems analysts and programmers.

Unless information processing has top management backing, the organization will be ineffective in its total systems and management information efforts and in its capability to cope with the newer technologies. A lesser reporting relationship will not have the authority and influence and knowledge of management's requirements to attain full benefit from the new technologies and to get support of affected departments of the company.

In many small businesses, the function of the vice-president of information may be combined with one or more additional responsibilities (e.g., vice-president of marketing, personnel and information).

A company or organization may either centralize or decentralize management and staff activities. When centralized, management is concentrated at one location to obtain the benefits of greater specialization and ease of coordination, communication, and top-level decision making. Generally, if management is centralized, information processing is also centralized so that it can support the staff. In fully centralized computer operations, all data to be processed are submitted or transmitted to one central location, the principal offices of the company. Information is provided to the staff agencies at the central location, and certain reports may be forwarded to field locations. Communications and data transmission costs are usually high. Centralized computer facilities ordinarily have larger scale computer systems than comparable decentralized locations. Specialized applications dealing with simulation, modeling, operations research, or other management science techniques may be in use.

On the other hand, in a decentralized operation, the authority and responsibility for results may be as far down the line as efficient management permits. Decentralization may imply that the size and volume of the organization's information processing needs are too unwieldly to control from a central point. It may take too long to send facts up the line and wait for the decision to come back down. The basic concept of decentralization is that facts are gathered and decisions are made on the scene of action. Motivation is often enhanced when personnel are allowed to participate in management decisions at the local level. Information processing is decentralized when placed with branch offices or locations to support the components of the company co-located with them. Generally, these facilities have smaller scale equipment than centralized facilities. Products are provided to local agencies, and a modest amount of data is submitted to higher echelons. Transmission and communications costs are moderate.

Some people have envisioned the role of the computer as encouraging a swing to the centralized concept because unlimited amounts of data are readily available at the home office. The lower cost and higher processing output of newer computers (especially minicomputers and microcomputers), however, encourage the decentralized concept. Communications costs are beginning to approach hardware costs for highly centralized operations. Data transmission costs are lower when decentralized units support widely separated branches or divisions.

☐ Information Processing Organization

The internal organization of the information processing function may vary, depending upon the size and nature of the business it services. Since these and other factors may influence the exact organizational structure of the information processing function, only the more general type of organization is shown (see Figure 25–3).

☐ Personnel in the Computer Center

Most companies and organizations have job descriptions which identify job titles and clearly describe all job functions required of an employee. Although titles vary between computer installations, the following general job descriptions cover the most common data processing positions.

Manager of Information Processing. At the head of most computer installations or departments is an individual who coordinates and directs the overall efforts of systems analysts, programmers, computer operators, and others involved with the use of the computer. This individual may have a title like *manager of information processing* or manager of data processing, manager of computer services or management services. He or she generally reports to a top executive of the organization.

Management of the information processing activity requires considerable experience, good management skills, and, in most companies, a college degree. Salaries vary widely, depending upon the size of the staff and the organizational level within the company.

Systems Analyst. The work of the *systems analyst* involves both the collection of facts regarding the information requirements of the computer user and the analysis of those facts. Systems analysts formulate efficient patterns of information flow from its sources to the computer, define the computer process necessary to turn the raw data into useful information, and plan the distribution and use of the resulting information.

In smaller computer installations, the functions of systems analysis and programming are frequently combined; while in the larger installations,

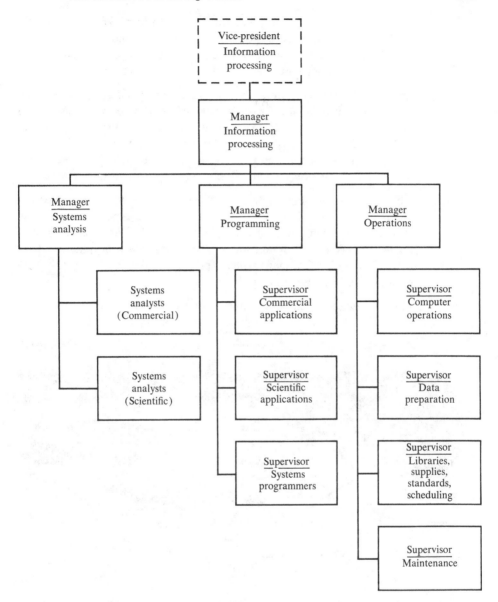

Figure 25–3   Organizational structure of the information processing function.

they are usually separate. No matter what the title, the person performing the analysis has to understand the problem and interpret it correctly and, at the same time, know how to use the computer effectively. He or she must bring to every problem a deep insight that will enable him or her to reduce it to its fundamental information-flow terms.

An engineering-scientific analyst may work on such problems as tracking a satellite or controlling a nuclear process. The analyst must consult with and understand top-level scientists and mathematicians and develop mathematical equations that describe the problem and its solution. Such an analyst, of course, must have at least one degree in mathematics, physics, or an appropriate engineering science.

On the other hand, while a formal educational background in business administration is helpful for systems analysts who specialize in business data processing, it is not always required. Business experience and the ability to reason logically are important, however. Typical of the projects that a business systems analyst may work on are the development of an integrated production, inventory control, and cost analysis system.

An area of increasing importance, as businesses grow bigger and more diversified, is operations research. This field is an especially challenging specialty, involving the analyst in the highest echelons of decision making in any business or organization. The analyst must formulate a mathematical model of a management problem and use it to provide a quantitative basis for making decisions.

Many organizations require that systems analysts have two or more years of programming experience in addition to a college degree.

Other responsibilities of a systems analyst were described in Chapter 23.

I adore programmers—they always know so many foreign languages.

Programmer. After the analysts have laid out the solution for a problem or the design of an information processing system, it goes to the *programmer.* It is the programmer's job to devise a detailed plan for solving the problem on the computer. This plan is called the *program,* and in final form it consists of a series of coded, step-by-step instructions that make the computer perform the desired operations. In most instances, the analysts or the programmer will have prepared both a flowchart which flows through the system and what actions are to be taken when a given condition is met or not met. The programmer generally employs one of several computer languages to communicate with the machine. The programmer checks the program by preparing sample data and testing it on the computer. He or she also "debugs" the program by making several trial runs with actual data from the project (see Figure 25–4).

(Courtesy of IBM Corporation)

Figure 25–4   Debugging—finding and correcting errors in computer programs—can take a large percentage of a programmer's time. There are times when programming is a lonely job.

To complete the entire programming process for a large project may take several months or a year or longer, and the program may take up several volumes of flowcharts and listings of program steps.

Programmers often work as part of a team, with different levels of responsibility (see Figure 25–5). Depending upon the size of the project, there may be a programming manager or a senior programmer leading the team, with a staff of programmers, junior programmers, coders, and trainees. The term *coder* is sometimes used instead of junior programmer. The name derives from the fact that machine instructions are often called machine codes. A coder takes detailed flowcharts and produces "coded instructions."

In some organizations, coders and programmer trainees translate the programmers' instruction into the codes understood by the particular computer being used. The junior programmers write instructions from the detailed flowcharts developed by the programmers and sometimes receive the opportunity to write specific parts of a broad program. In this way, they develop the skills and experience needed to develop programs on their own. Those who take a full range of computer courses leading to a computer science degree at a college or university can generally skip the initial training level positions in their first job and go right into full-fledged programming assignments.

The varieties of problems programmers deal with, the different computers they may work with, and the various information processing languages they must know demand a high degree of ingenuity, experience, imagination—and above all, the ability to think logically.

Well-trained and experienced programmers can write programs for many different types of problems.

PROGRAMMER WANTED
FEMALE

Bright young woman wanted. Junior College Graduate. Must be charter member of DPMA and ACM. Working knowledge of Boolean Algebra required. Background in Teleprocessing and ESP desirable. Furnish own crystal ball and template. Start at #310°°/month; work-up. Send resume to:

THIRD NATIONAL BANK, FUNNYVILLE, TENN.

Computer Operator.   Look into any busy information processing center, and you will see several men and women pushing buttons, changing magnetic tapes, flicking through punched cards, and in other ways supervising the operations of the computer (see Figure 25–6). The computer operator, the person who pushes the buttons and watches the lights, actually does much more than that. He or she reviews computer programs and instruction sheets to determine the necessary equipment set-up for the job. When the control panel lights indicate that the machine has stopped for some reason, the console operator must investigate and correct the stoppage or call in a maintenance engineer, if the cause is equipment malfunction. The console operator keeps a log of the work done by the computer and writes reports on its use.

In large installations, the console operator is assisted by tape librarians and handlers and the operators of peripheral equipment, such as sorters, collators, high speed printers, communication, and units.

(Courtesy of Control Data Corp.)

Figure   Whether working individually or in a team, programmers find that
25–5   problem solving and troubleshooting are integral part of their jobs.

Computer operators usually serve an apprenticeship, during which their
main duties are inserting punched cards in card readers and punches,
inserting forms in printers, mounting reels of magnetic tape on tape
drives, and generally readying peripheral devices for operation. More

(Courtesy of Univac Division Sperry Rand Corp.)

Figure   Computer operators controlling the equipment in an information proc-
25–6   essing center.

experienced operators are usually responsible for actually manipulating the controls that actuate the computer system. The console operator holds a position of much responsibility since mistakes can be time consuming and costly. Employers require a high school education, and many of them prefer some college. A college degree is very helpful for those who aspire to progress into programming or systems analysis.

Many computer operators have successfully advanced to positions as supervisors of operations, programmers, and managers of information processing centers.

Clerical and Keypunching Jobs.   *Clerical* jobs vary, but usually include manual coding of data verification of totals used for accounting controls, maintaining libraries of magnetic tape files (see Figure 25–7), and maintaining operating schedules and logs of operation. These tasks provide good on-the-job training for high school graduates who wish to learn something about computing. These tasks are sometimes "apprenticeship" jobs for computer operators.

(Courtesy of Health, Education, and Welfare)

**Figure
25–7**   The tape library is used in essentially the same way as a book library except that information is stored on reels of magnetic tape (or, in some installations, on disk packs) instead of on the printed page.

Keypunching of data into punched cards or paper tape and operating other key-driven data recording devices require an ability to type reasonably well (30–40 wpm) and an ability to work in a fairly noisy environment. After two or three weeks of intensive training, a high school graduate may start as a keypunch operator.

Sorry, our president is out of town, our first vice-president is out
sick, and our second vice-president is a computer.

☐ Summary

The information processing functions are rapidly growing in importance
in most large organizations, and they are beginning to loom larger in
many smaller companies. There has been much confusion and contro-
versy about where these functions fit in the organization structure. In a
number of companies, this uncertainty has intensified the unstable
character of the information processing functions; numerous costly and
disrupting reorganizations have resulted. This situation often has compounded already serious staffing and morale problems that are more or
less related to the computer.

Today, many organizations have a vice-president in charge of the information processing function. This procedure usually has a positive
result because it reflects a progressive attitude toward the information
processing activities.

The general organization of the information processing function is often
divided into the following three areas: systems analysis, programming,
and computer system operations.

The job titles found in many information processing centers are:

- Manager of Information Processing
- Systems Analyst
- Programmer

- Computer Operator
- Keypunch Operator
- Tape Librarian

☐ Review Questions

1. In the early development of information processing organizations, the manager usually reported directly to the _____.
2. What factors determine the location of the information processing function in the overall company organization?
3. What is the difference between a centralized and decentralized information processing function?
4. Describe the major operating functions of an information processing center.
5. Discuss the role of the manager of an information processing center.
6. What are the five types of information processing positions? Give examples of each.
7. A large information processing center has the employees and a large-scale computer system. Draw a chart showing a possible organizational structure for this center.

Key Terms

information processing center	programmer
manager of information processing	computer operator
systems analyst	keypunching
organizational charts	clerical jobs

nine

Computers and Automation

26

Computers and Society

Courtesy of Delta Air Lines

We discussed in Chapter 1 the many ways the computer is being used. This chapter explores the impact of computers on modern society. Although many social impacts have already been felt and others foreseen, the deepest significance of the computer may still be transparent to us and may become observable only with the passage of time. So this chapter is at best a view of the current and potential impact of computers as seen from the relatively unsteady vantage point of the mid-1970s.

◻ Impact of the Computer

The electronic computer, not yet thirty years old, has come of age, progressing from a scientific curiosity to an essential part of civilization in a remarkably short time. In many respects, computers have erased time, altered the ordinary relationships that affect our lives and our

Anything else, boss?

organizations, and accelerated the rate of change to the point that someone once entitled a speech, "The Effect of Computers on Progress, or
By the Time You've Said It, It's Happened!" As an indication of the
degree of assimilation of computers into our society, just imagine what
would happen if they were suddenly withdrawn from service. Airline
travel would be chaotically disrupted, industrial systems would grind to
a halt, banks would bulge with unprocessed paper, and much in our
lives that we now take for granted suddenly would be no more.

After each major technological development, it has possibly been true
to say, "The world will never again be the same." These products of
technology have radically altered the pattern of our private and business
lives. They have certainly increased our mobility, eliminated tedious
physical labor, and provided convenient means of communication. However, each of these products has also plagued society with ills, problems,
and frustrations.

Take as only one example the impact of the automobile. The automobile has totally changed this nation—its living standards, its housing
patterns, its work and recreation habits, and, above all, its transportation. It now causes over 20 deaths per 100 000 population per year, and
at its outset it created a moral problem of sorts by providing unmarried
young people with a privacy they had never before enjoyed.

Will the computer change society more radically than the automobile
did? There are many strong indications that it will do so in the future.
If, for example, developments in computers and communications should
enable many people to work and learn at home, there might be no need
for huge offices and crowded schools. The implications of such a change
for society are enormous.

Does the computer pose a threat or offer support to "life, liberty, and
the pursuit of happiness"? Looking to the past, few people would dis-
agree that the net impact of technological developments has been favorable. It is unfortunate to have to turn to the past and scan the present
for indications of the future, but that is all the evidence we have. This
does not mean that the future will be like the past and present. It never
has been. It only means that extension of past trends tempered by
judgments of the impact of impending developments is the scientific
substitute for the spirit of prophecy.

Technology is a tool that is neutral between good and evil. We have
used it for both, and the greater the potential for good, of course, the
greater the potential for evil. We have in our hands untested technologies
of tremendous power. It is too early to tell whether they will be used to
build or destroy. The computer's potential, of course, is not as extreme
in either direction, but many people have raised questions concerning
its value to society.

Although early computer developments were conducted in Great Britain and Germany, the computer is essentially an American invention. Today the United States uses more computers than the rest of the world combined. The United States, however, is not the only country that manufactures computers. Computer makers may be found in Japan, Germany, France, the U.S.S.R., Great Britain, Italy, The Netherlands, Israel, Norway, Sweden, Poland, and many other countries. Since the United States leads the world in computer usage, it also has a head start in some of the social problems resulting from their use. Other nations (especially Japan, West Germany, Australia, France, and Great Britain), however, are also beginning to suffer from some of the problem symptoms.

Do you realize that without computers it would be impossible to assess the impact of computers on society?

☐ Computer Attitudes

People often ask questions like the following: Are computers more clever than people? Do they have feelings of love and hate? Can they think for themselves? Can they outwit humans? Can they replace people at performing everyday jobs? Will they run the world and make slaves of human beings?

Everyone has heard at least something about computers on television, at the movies, in books, newspapers, or magazines. Probably most of the articles and pictures have been rather sensational—"Computer Makes a Mistake and Overpays XYZ Company Employees by $2 000 000,"

"Computer Causes the African Bulldogs to Lose Football Champion-ship," "Computer Causes Rocket To Go Off Target."

Cartoonists delight in giving computers robot-like stature and minds of their own that like to play tricks on ordinary mortals. Names for computers have included human analogies like *electronic brain* or *mechanical brain*.

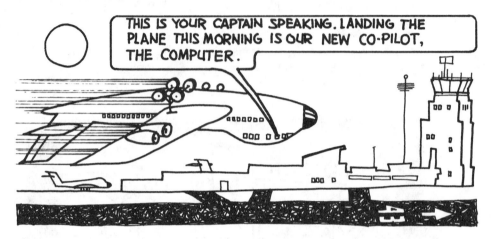

It is no wonder that the general public is often confused about computers. They don't know that many of the news items are utter nonsense or in error because of poor facts or poor understanding on the part of a journalist. Of course, the press, TV, and radio have long been ac-

"In a wild, four-hour madness, I folded, bent, stapled and mutilated 10,000 punched cards."

customed to stressing the odd or exciting elements in their news in order to capture the attention of their audiences. Only sensational stories receive widespread publicity. Consequently, much of the public blames computers (rather than the people using them) for problems that arise in data processing applications. Can you imagine blaming an automobile when an accident occurred? Or a hammer because it hit you on the thumb?

Over the past few years a number of computer centers have been demolished by misguided individuals, including even university students. Some people take delight in folding, stapling, and mutilating punched cards (utility bills, magazine subscription cards, school registration cards, and so forth) simply because they know that it will disrupt their normal computer processing. A man in London, England, went so far as to place a punched card on a drawing board and carefully cut out three or four extra holes with a razor blade in order to change the information on the card and so confound the computer altogether.

The Computer and Unemployment

Automation is the process of replacing human work with work done by a machine or system designed to perform a specific combination of actions automatically or repeatedly. For example, a machine used in the automotive industry transforms rough metal castings and other components into finished auto engines. The computer is another machine that can perform jobs automatically. Since many of these jobs have been or are still classified as human occupations, the computer poses a threat to numerous workers and their jobs.

Author L. Frank Baum shared the turn-of-the-century optimism about machines as a positive force. An admired (if not beloved) character in his famous Oz series was Tik-tok, the clockwork copper man who "was sure to do exactly what he was wound up to do, at all times and in all circumstances." That a machine "would only do the special kind of thing it had been calculated to do" was regarded as no defect by philosopher Charles S. Pierce, who observed: "We do not want it to do its own business, but ours."

It is pointless to argue whether automation destroys or creates employment. Its purpose is to reduce the costs of production or to perform tasks that could not otherwise be done. In either case, it is a substitute as well as a supplement for human labor. We might argue, as some do, that since "society" benefits from automation, "society" should provide retraining and interim support for those who are displaced by automation.

Actually, in many instances automation displaces no one. (It has been estimated that approximately one-half of the U.S. labor force would be required to staff current telephone switchboards if automatic switching and other devices had not been installed in the past.) If over the years the mechanization of physical tasks has displaced millions of people, however, most of them have been able to make the adjustment with discomfort but without great pain. The tragedies were of two types: 1) Displacements that occurred in periods of inadequate demand when alternative job opportunities were not being created rapidly enough, and 2) displacements that affected people (for example, coal miners and cotton pickers) who were unprepared and unable to compete in other fields.

Few people have been displaced by computerization. If and when computer displacement occurs, it will likely be less painful in that its impact will be primarily on managerial, clerical, and skilled workers who are better prepared for adapting themselves to other jobs. Often, whenever an employee's job is to be replaced by a computerized system, he or she is retrained to work in some other area rather than laid off. The installation of a computer, moreover, always entails the creation of new jobs. People are required to maintain, operate, and program the computer system. Displaced personnel may very well find new positions as keypunchers, computer operators, programmers, and so forth.

It's poetic justice. He was replaced by a computer that goofed and sends him a paycheck every week.

☐ The Computer and the Individual's Right to Privacy

Man has a natural aversion to becoming a statistic, a mere figure to be mulled over, like the highway death count on a July 4 weekend. Yet, for all its tremendous benefits, computerization may be doing just that: threatening the one sanctity man has left—his right to privacy.

Information concerning an individual can be represented on a tiny portion of a reel of magnetic tape. The fact that such information about ourselves (the 1's and 0's of lives) can be stored in a computerized system need not be wholly distasteful. The realization, however, that in much less than a second an entire lifetime can be translated for anyone clever enough to gain access to such a system most certainly is.

You want to take out life insurance? Sorry, but the computer says you don't qualify, you're bald.

Although privacy is not mentioned by name in the Constitution, the Bill of Rights contains guarantees against all methods to invade privacy that were prevalent in the eighteenth century. A man cannot be compelled to give up his home to quarter troops; a man cannot be forced to give testimony against himself. Perhaps most important are the words of the Fourth Amendment:

> "The right of the people to be secure in their persons, houses, papers, and effects, against unreasonable searches and seizures, shall not be violated . . ."

Congressman Cornelius E. Gallagher (Democrat, New Jersey), a strong critic of the computer's "invasion of privacy," has remarked, "The computer can be used to elevate man—as it has delivered him to the moon—or it can be used to enslave him."

One can easily pose many vital questions concerning the use of files of personal data. For example, how can society maintain the relevance of *due process of law* when reels of tape containing the intimate personal details of millions of lives can be instantly transferred from a computer in one jurisdiction to a computer in another? How can a man face his accuser when his records are submerged in an inaccessible data bank that he scarcely knows exists, much less has the technical expertise to

That's right, Mr. Cardo. According to our computer, you are nonexistent.

question? If a national data bank is formed, who will control the data?

It is now entirely feasible for a government or a private agency to construct files of personal information for interrogation by remote computer consoles. Data about an individual obtained from different sources can be matched and used without the person's knowledge by anybody with access to the system. The increasing use of the social security number as a unique identifier for each person makes this data matching possible. What safeguards do we need against the establishment of such information banks, against the accuracy of their data input and the potential use of their data? Are special congressional bills required to protect the rights of the individual against the invasion of privacy by such banks? Many people think they are.

```
                    CONFIDENTIAL
              DAILY INFORMATION SHEET
                 NATIONAL DATA BANK
                  AUGUST 22, 1987

SUBJECT        ROBERT SHIRLEY SMITH
               11036 COPLEY STREET
               ORLANDO, FLORIDA
               AGE 41
               MARRIED
               CHILDREN: JOHN, AGE 19; NANCY, AGE 14;
               WILLIAM, AGE 12; JACK, AGE 6.
               PROFESSION: PLUMBER
```

PURCHASES
BREAKFAST	2.10
GASOLINE	8.64
NEWSPAPER	.10
PHONE (867-2301)	.10
PHONE (672-4467)	.10
PHONE (772-3461)	.10
PHONE (667-8841)	.10
BANK (CASH WITHDRAWAL)	90.00
LUNCH	6.20
COCKTAILS	6.10
PHONE (772-3461)	.10
LINGERIE	35.70
CHAMPAGNE	12.60
NEWSPAPER	.10

****COMPUTER ANALYSIS****

LARGE BREAKFAST. USUALLY HAS ONLY COFFEE
BOUGHT 8.64 DOLLARS GASOLINE. OWNS ECONOMY CAR.
SO FAR THIS WEEK HE HAS BOUGHT 21.40 DOLLARS
WORTH OF GAS. BOUGHT GASOLINE IN SANFORD, FLORIDA
WHICH IS 32 MILES FROM HOME AND 37 MILES FROM
WORK. BOUGHT GASOLINE AT 7:48. SAFE TO ASSUME HE
WAS LATE TO WORK.
BOUGHT NEWSPAPER. HE ALWAYS READS THE PAPER
WHEN HE GETS TO WORK.
PHONE NUMBER 867-2301 BELONGS TO EXPENSIVE MEN'S
BARBER—SPECIALIZES IN HAIR STYLING AND BALD MEN.
PHONE NUMBER 672-4467 BELONGS TO HIS BOSS'S WIFE.
PHONE NUMBER 772-3461 BELONGS TO OLD GIRL
FRIEND NAMED LULU ROCKET.
PHONE NUMBER 667-8841 BELONGS TO ATLAS TRAVEL
AGENCY. MADE RESERVATIONS FOR MIAMI—SINGLE.
FOURTH TRIP THIS YEAR TO MIAMI WITHOUT WIFE. WILL
CHECK FILE TO SEE IF ANYONE ELSE HAS GONE TO MIAMI
AT THE SAME TIME AND COMPARE TO HIS PHONE
NUMBER CALLS.
WITHDREW 90.00 DOLLARS CASH. VERY UNUSUAL SINCE
HE USUALLY USES HIS NATIONAL DATA CREDIT CARD FOR
ALL PURCHASES AND TICKETS. CASH USUALLY USED ONLY
FOR ILLEGAL PURPOSES.
LUNCH BILL SEEMS UNUSALLY HIGH. WIFE DID NOT EAT
WITH HIM. DRINKS DURING HIS LUNCH. THIS MAY BE
POSSIBLE CAUSE OF HIS POOR PRODUCTIVITY DURING
AFTERNOON WORK DAYS.
PHONE NUMBER 772-3461 BELONGS TO LULU ROCKET.
SECOND CALL TODAY TO THIS NUMBER.

BOUGHT VERY EXPENSIVE LINGERIE AT EXCLUSIVE
WOMAN'S STORE. NOT HIS WIFE'S SIZE.
BOUGHT BOTTLE EXPENSIVE CHAMPAGNE. HE USUALLY
BUYS BOURBON OR RUM. MUST BE SPECIAL OCCASION.
LEFT WORK AT 4:10. PURCHASED CHAMPAGNE AT LIQUOR
STORE 2 MILES FROM WORK AT 4:25.
BOUGHT NEWSPAPER AT 7:25 NEAR HIS HOUSE.
UNACCOUNTABLE 3 HOURS.

**Figure
26–1**   Hypothetical computer analysis of a day in the life of Robert Smith.

Their fears are not wholly misplaced. All of us leave a trail of records behind us as we go through life, but they are widely dispersed and inaccessible in composite. The day of judgment when all our secret acts are to be revealed is remote enough to cause no discomfort. Just how would we like it to occur here and now? Consider the hypothetical "Daily Information Sheet" on Robert Smith shown in Figure 26–1. It should illustrate the need for the public's concern very well indeed.

Frankly, I'm afraid of the computer getting a look at my past
12 years of working here.

The Federal State of Hesse in West Germany has established a government data bank that will contain about 70 items of personal information on each Hesse citizen. Simultaneously, the Hesse Parliament has enacted legislation to prevent unauthorized or harmful use of the data. Safeguards include the appointment of a Data Protection Commissioner responsible to Parliament, who will have ultimate responsibility for the system; procedures for investigation and possible compensation if a citizen feels he or she has been compromised through deliberate or accidental misuse of personal information; and a requirement that state and local legislative bodies be as informed about the stored data as the executive branch. One can only wonder just how long it will take before the system is misused. Americans can look upon their past adaptability as a reassurance of their ability to devise protections as they are needed; but it is only a reassurance, not a guarantee.

☐ The Cashless-Checkless Society

The computer revolution is laying the groundwork for a future where a "universal credit card" geared to computerized data communications will be the only requirement for most financial transactions. This is the basis of the *cashless-checkless society* that government officials, bankers, and computer people foresee in the future. Their prediction is a response to the enormous challenge posed by banking's "paper tiger"— the huge and ever-increasing volume of checks generated by the nation's financial transactions.

Consider the following situation. In a hypothetical city, which we will call "Someplace, U.S.A.," a hypothetical lady, whom we will call Mrs. Cohoon, makes a trip to her shopping center where she purchases groceries for her family, shoes for her child, clothing for herself, and a case of beer for Mr. Cohoon. The only unusual aspect of this shopping trip, which is repeated daily by millions of people throughout the nation, is that Mrs. Cohoon paid for her purchases without money or check. Instead, she used a personal identification card (see Figure 26–2). The data on the lady's purchases was transmitted to the shopping center's central communications office, from which it was electronically relayed to the First National Utility of Someplace. Here, Mrs. Cohoon's purchases were debited from her account, and the various stores where she had shopped received credit for their respective share of the total bill. All of these transactions were accomplished without an exchange of cash, checks, receipts, or any other paper.

Although such an episode has never yet occurred, it may very likely do so in the near future. The concept of the cashless-checkless economy has been with us for several years. However, recent developments in computer and communications facilities, along with a favorable environment in the banking community, have made it a more feasible possibility.

A cashless-checkless society exists today for 3 000 checking account customers of a bank near New York City. The customers at the bank are able to make purchases at 35 participating shops by using a special plastic card. The card is inserted into a reading device at the shop, and an automatic credit to the merchant's account at the bank and an automatic debit to the customer's account are made. The customers can also choose to have the debits to their accounts delayed 35 days. Under this

MONEY CARD

$ $

Steven M. Spencer
1832167   0139

Good Through | Mo. | Yr. | 09 | 79 |

$ $

Figure 26–2   Cards like this one may someday allow people to purchase merchandise or services and have the cost automatically deducted from their checking accounts.

arrangement, the merchant still has his account credited immediately. After the 35 days, the customer's account is debited automatically. If an overdraft results, the amount due is automatically converted into a bank loan at 12 percent annual interest.

From a technical point of view, there is little question that it will become possible to execute, electronically, financial transactions within fractions of a second over any distance. The key problem, however, is what protection against fraud can be obtained. Even without automatic features to transfer funds, credit cards are already causing widespread concern as a result of fraudulent use. Once these cards are inserted into cash registers and the amounts are deducted electronically from the card owner's checking account, the opportunities for fraud will clearly multiply.

Criminals have begun to use stolen credit cards instead of guns—the cards are safer and produce a good return. In the New York area, a stolen card sells for $75 to $200, depending on the company that issued it, how long the card has to go, and whether it has been signed by the rightful owner. The typical loss on a card that is known to have been stolen is $500 to $7 000. Unless computer-controlled card-checking systems are implemented soon, many credit card companies may be forced out of business.

With most credit card companies, the owner's liability is limited to $50 for a lost or stolen credit card. The credit card company thus stands to lose much money whenever a card is used without authorization. In a cashless-checkless system, however, the owner himself may stand to suffer substantial loss whenever the card is used. Of course, an unauthorized transaction could be automatically stopped if the system was informed that the card had been lost or stolen and was being used without permission.

The following question still remains: Will greenbacks and checks be replaced by electronic pulses and bits? While traditionally "two bits" have been worth 25¢, in an electronic environment two bits can easily represent 2 million dollars. This consideration presents a threat to security and a temptation for fraud. Obviously, further expansion of the cashless-checkless system will be limited until antifraud measures can be effectively implemented.

☐ How Well Do We Apply Computers?

It is important to remember that computer technology is in its earliest stages. Compared with aviation, for example, we are still in the 1920s. The day will come when some of today's most advanced computers will be in museums.

The acquisition, processing, and communication of data are fundamental to continuing human progress. We will probably never reach an acceptable plateau of development. If and when computer technology levels off or begins to decline, then, inevitably, civilization will follow the same trend.

Our goal, therefore, must be constant improvement by focusing on obvious problem areas and exploiting each new technological breakthrough. Our objective is to mold computer applications to meet the needs of society. The computer will be of little value until it is used to fill human needs and to help solve human problems.

At present, we have only begun to use computers. If we have failed in some ways during the past three decades, it has been in a lack of emphasis upon the optimization of computer use and the development of more usable and understandable human-machine interfaces.

In fundamental terms, the computer is an extension of people's intellectual capacity. If a thought process can be identified, regardless of the field of endeavor, there will always be a potential benefit in following it through by the application of a computer.

☐ Review Questions

1. List the major problems the world faces today. In what ways have computers contributed to these problems? In what ways might computers contribute to the solution of these problems?
2. Prepare a list of numbers by which you are identified.
3. What difficulties would be encountered in converting to a single identification number for each individual to be used by all government and business organizations?

4. Should the individual have an absolute "right to privacy"?
5. List 10 computer applications and evaluate them as either beneficial or detrimental to society.
6. List 5 activities currently performed manually that may eventually be performed by computer.
7. Some people feel dehumanized when they are identified by "student number," "account number," or "social security number." Why do you think they feel this way? Do they have a good point?
8. Describe how you "think" one of the following would operate:
   a. Checkless-cashless society
   b. Computerized school with no teachers
   c. Computerized home
   d. Society with no books, newspapers, or magazines, in which computer terminals were used as a communications medium
9. Define two types of misuse of computers.
10. Computers will be increasingly used in business and thus will affect the nature of the business world and the consumer as an individual. Discuss the consequences of increased use of computers in business which accrue to the citizens and consumers in the United States.
11. What is the potential danger of computerized information files on private citizens? Do these files benefit or harm society when used to support law enforcement?
12. In your opinion, which area represents the greatest potential for the computer in terms of social benefit? Explain your answer.

☐ Summary

The computer has had a profound impact on our society. Some of the impact has been negative, such as harassment and loss of privacy because of misuse of personal data and unemployment for people whose jobs were computerized. These harmful uses of computers must be viewed in the total perspective by comparison with the beneficial contributions which the computer is making to a better society.

The computer, for good or bad, is here in the same way nuclear power is here. We cannot turn back the clock. People must choose to place themselves in control of the computer. They must understand the capabilities, power, and limitations of this powerful machine. They must remember to make the tool a servant and must always remain in control. The future is in people's own hands—not in the computer's.

Checkmate.

Key Terms

computer attitudes   universal credit card
automation   cashless society
privacy   checkless society
                            computerization

27

The Future

Courtesy of Digital Computer Corporation

The future is always uncertain, and predictions are necessarily inaccurate. However, one should not be paralyzed by the fear of making errors. One must study seriously the future impact of the various technological and sociological changes that occur in society. There have already been some unpleasant surprises, such as automobile pollution and soapy rivers, and the continuing rate of change in society increases the chances of more unpleasant surprises.

The purpose of this chapter is to explore some of the computer-related developments that are likely to occur within the next two or three decades.

"We heard this is the land of opportunity. Our cities are completely run by computers."

Cartoon is from "Computer Science Mathematics"

☐ Trends in Computer Hardware

Computer technology throughout the world has improved at an unbelievably fast pace during the past 20 years. In the 1960s computers were used in ways not even envisioned in the 1950s. In the next two decades, one can expect the computer to be used in many applications not envisioned today. Every few years a rapid change in computer hardware and technology occurs, thus making older systems obsolete. In this way the computer industry is quite similar to the automobile industry, which replaces its older models each year. By 1980, the value of computing equipment in use may be around 75 billion dollars.

The ENIAC (Electronic Numerical Integrator and Computer) contained 19 000 vacuum tubes, weighed about 30 tons, and filled an area of over 139.35 m² (1500 square feet) (the size of an average three-bedroom home). This enormous device, developed in 1946, could perform 5 000 additions per second. Today, computers are much smaller, much lighter, and can perform as many as 100 000 000 additions per seconds. The new machines are more reliable than the old, require less power to operate, and produce considerably less heat. All the early computers had to be placed in air-conditioned rooms. Today, computers can be placed anywhere—in an office, in one's home, in an airplane, on a ship, in a missile or spacecraft, in a bank or a hospital.

The IBM System/360 Model 195 is an example of a large computer. This machine can process instructions at a rate of one every 54 billionths of a second. In that time, light, traveling at a rate of 344 991 km (186 281 miles) a second, can move only 16.15 m (53 feet). The Model 195 can solve 15 problems simultaneously. Its capacity would allow the literary content of a library with more than 3 million books to be stored, and it would be able to locate and read any one of these books in less than one second. This multimillion dollar computer can be used in a variety of applications—airline reservations, weather predictions, space exploration, and so forth.

In contrast with the large computers are *minicomputers* and *microcomputers*. Minicomputers cost only a few thousand dollars, are about the

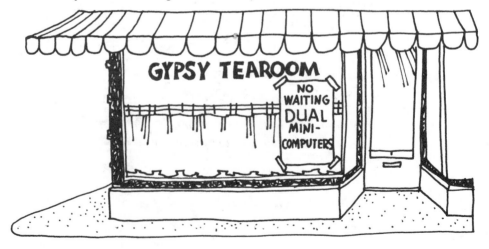

size of a small suitcase, and can perform operations similar to the large computers at rates approximating as many as 600 000 additions per second. What is the future of minicomputers and microcomputers?

The minicomputer is currently very widely used in industry, process control, and education. Continued expansion is expected in its use in industrial plants, hospitals, laboratories, secondary and elementary schools, colleges, manufacturing plants, government, military, and other areas. In business, the minicomputer will be used to a much greater extent than it is now. The small businessman will be more tempted to develop his own computer center with a minicomputer now that computer manufacturers are beginning to offer software and systems support for these machines.

Since the cost of the minicomputer, when contrasted to a larger computer, is extremely low, minicomputers will be available for use by personnel other than professional programmers. Since these machines are relatively inexpensive, management will not be concerned with idle CPU time. In elementary and secondary schools and colleges, the minicomputer will be used in many new and different ways.

Many larger businesses and governmental agencies will use a network of minicomputers, located throughout the country or world. The trend will be toward decentralization of the data processing function. Many businesses have found that a network of minicomputers can often do the job more economically than one "large" computer system. In a network, if one minicomputer becomes ill, a substitute is readily available. Due to the economy of the minicomputer, management would not be overly concerned if one was used as a "spare". When not needed in the network, the minicomputer could be assigned other tasks.

Since microcomputers are much smaller and cheaper than minicomputers, entirely new application areas are developing for their use. Although the microcomputers are often slower than the minicomputer, they are lower in cost, more flexible, and require less design time. We can expect to see several billion of these machines in use at the turn of the century. Some of the future uses of microcomputers will be to control intelligent terminals, building security systems, automobile electrical systems, medical equipment, retail cash registers, fire and burglary alarm systems, and the "home computer system".

Future computers will probably make extensive use of *firmware;* that is, special programs (called *microprograms*) within the hardware that will be able to simulate many types of machines. When this revolution occurs, it will make programming a computer and conversion from one computer to another much easier. Users will simply utilize a basic language instruction that will be interpreted through hardware (using a firmware concept) to emulate other machines.

It's the ultimate in microcomputers. I know I've got it here
someplace.

It seems reasonable to predict that future computers will be faster, more reliable, cheaper, and easier to use. In order to simplify them, one can expect computer manufacturers to develop new person/machine interface devices. Widespread employment of voice-recognition units and optical readers can be expected in the late 1970s. Devices such as the PICTUREPHONE (developed by Bell Telephone laboratories) and miniterminals will help simplify data communications with computers.

The future user of the PICTUREPHONE set can use it as a desk calculator, keying numbers into the remote computer to which it is linked with the user's TOUCH-TONE telephone buttons; the computer will then perform the calculation and display the answer on the videotelephone screen. In addition to human/computer communications, the PICTUREPHONE will also be used for normal face-to-face conversation.

Credit card readers, keyboard numbering devices, and small display terminals will undoubtedly be widely employed in future computers. A simple miniterminal consists of a display used in conjunction with a touch-tone telephone. This play might be limited to displaying 20 to 100 characters or even just ten-or twelve-digit numbers. Simple terminals like this could be used in low-cost computer communication systems, the type that might be found in homes in the 1980s.

Cathode-ray-tube displays will be much more common in future computure applications, and the cost of these devices should decrease considerly. The Plasma Tube, another type of display device, can be expected to be introduced as a low-cost terminal for computer systems during the late 1970s.

Semiconductor memories are available on many computers today. It is believed that this type of memory will find widespread use in future computer memory systems. The primary characteristic of tomorrow's computers will thus be much the same as today's: an improved price/ performance ratio.

When Christopher Columbus set foot in the New World in 1492, he did not know where he was nor how he got there. It took the world years to learn of his courageous journey. When Neil Armstrong stepped upon the surface of the moon in 1969, he knew exactly where he was, having followed a precisely preplanned route, and the entire world was watching him. In less than 500 years, people's ability to communicate has advanced from its most primitive forms to an astounding level of sophistication.

Computer centers are now being connected to one another via communication facilities. An airline reservation office in London, England, can communicate with a computer center in New York via satellite. Large companies can link facilities on opposite sides of the Pacific Ocean.

This developing relationship between computer and telecommunications technology is one of the most important events of our times. The two technologies complement each other; in combination, their power is multiplicative, not additive. Computers will one day control immense communication switching centers, and these in turn will make available the power of computers to millions of users in remote locations. The present trend toward large-scale, time-shared computers and the development of advanced, so-called "intelligent" terminals seem to indicate that, within the next decade, a large portion of the computers used will be communications-oriented.

The major computer problems of the future will be carryovers from the present. First, there is the people problem: the need to teach students the use of computer processing techniques and to train vast numbers, from minorities in particular, to become productive members of the computer industry. Then, there are the social implications of private and governmental data banks, vast nationwide information networks, and the threats they pose, if any, to the privacy of individuals. And with data traffic exceeding voice traffic in the 1970s, data communications faces the problem of overloaded and unreliable transmission lines, which could seriously hamper the growth of computer processing.

In summary, there will be dramatic progress in every important area of hardware for computers. Furthermore, the cost of any particular computation or operation will decrease steadily and significantly for the next several decades. The cost will be decreased at least by a factor of 100 and probably a factor of 1 000. A smaller decrease will occur in the cost of terminals, perhaps only a factor of 10 or 20. Even so, this means that the cost of a very powerful computer system will be well within the price range of a small business or of an average family.

☐ Future Software Systems

It is doubtful if many major software functions will be developed in the next few years. Complex operating systems for machines such as the IBM System/370 have been designed to meet user's needs for quite a time to come. In other words, the software designers have adequately specified all the major functions needed for applications foreseeable in the immediate future.

Programming languages are the primary means by which a person communicates with a computer. The use of current programming languages is not likely to change drastically for a number of years. In 1980, users will probably still be using FORTRAN, COBOL, BASIC, PL/I, RPG, and APL.

As computers become more common in schools, homes, and businesses, one can expect more people to learn computer languages. Within the next decade, BASIC will very likely have widespread use in secondary and elementary schools. For the distant future, we should expect to see the development and use of natural languages (for example, English) as well as languages designed for specific application areas (for example, languages for solving medical problems, educational problems, engineering problems, and the like).

Recently, a number of researchers have designed and implemented "two-dimensional" program languages (picture- and symbol-oriented) as opposed to the above-mentioned "one-dimensional" languages (text- and character-oriented). These may become increasingly important in human-machine communication.

In future computers, one can also expect that many functions now performed by software will be implemented by *microprograms* in a read-only computer memory (firmware).

In the future, computer manufacturers will supply more application-oriented software with their machines. Today IBM provides several application packages for the IBM System/32 computer system. These software packages allow non-data processing people to use these machines in their everyday business activities. Digital Equipment Corporation makes available hundreds of educational programs designed for use in a school environment. Programs such as these allow non-computer trained teachers in chemistry, mathematics, science, business, etc. to use the computer as an educational tool in the classroom. More manufacturers will develop and make available application-oriented software packages which will help people use their machines.

☐ Future Uses of Computers

Science fiction is rapidly evolving into fact. The computer has your number and may even be watching you. It is safe to assume that there is no aspect of human life that is not in some way affected by behind-the-scenes computers. A computerized society is no longer just a possibility: it is almost here today.

Automation will continue to grow as a way of life because people will always devote much of their efforts to finding new ways to accomplish or circumvent monotonous and laborious tasks, especially those not requiring their full abilities as human beings. Have you ever wondered what life will be like in the year 2001? This author believes that automation will play an almost unbelievable part in everyone's life.

Do you believe that unmanned ships will sail across the Atlantic and Pacific in 2001? Science fiction or logical possibility? Considering the inherent risks involved in making predictions, it might be safe to say science fiction. However, because it is stimulating to speculate about the unknown, and also because there is some security in this age of rapidly changing technology, this author calls it a logical prediction (assuming that no nuclear war occurs beforehand).

Let us now examine what life may be like in the year 2001. Many of these predictions will undoubtedly prove to be in error, but perhaps they will show us how the evolving use of computers may affect our lives.

Transportation

It was just 24 hours and a few minutes since he had left the shores of Italy; now the ship's captain saw the skyline of New York City before him. Soon, harbor control would assume control of his giant merchant ship. Automatically, the ship would be guided at high speeds through the ship channel to the docking and unloading center. Here the ship would be completely unloaded by means of a computer-controlled unloading system directly onto transportation devices for immediate shipment to various points throughout the United States. The unloading operation would take two hours. Within an additional two hours, the ship would be on its way back to Europe or some other destination, fully loaded with cargo, streaking across the ocean at better than 100 knots without a crew busy at its controls. This was the last of the manned trips. The computer would be in complete control of the ship on all future voyages. Using inputs from radars, satellites, sonars, and other navigational equipment, the computer would control ship operations as an electronic captain. The year is 2001—the age of automated transportation systems.

Ships now communicate with shore stations and other ships by using satellites in synchronous orbits (approximately 20 000 nautical miles above the earth). Each of these satellites is a view of one-third of the earth's surface. Shipowners now monitor the operations of their complete fleet. Their computer-controlled display consoles reveal at a glance the locations and status of all ships. The ship's position (latitude and longitude), speed, course, remaining fuel, engine status, electrical system status, cargo status, and weather conditions are all communicated to the computer system every few minutes. It performs a few calculations and updates the ship's position on the display console. Gone are the days when a ship is "lost at sea".

Surface transportation systems are now available that permit speeds of 250 mph through densely populated cities. Computers are used to design, test, and run these systems. Their bullet-shaped vehicles produce almost no pollutant by-products and are relatively vibration-free. Some of them are equipped with LIM (Linear Induction Motor) motors, which have no wearing parts like gears or bearings. The LIM is operated on alternating current created by electromagnetic fields.

Computers now handle most of the operating details of jetliners, allowing the captain of the ship to keep watch only for unusual occurrences. Computers switch equipment on and off, control aircraft centers of gravity, communicate with other airplane computers enroute, determine the plane's proper speed and altitude, run through preflight checklists, and perform automatic takeoffs and landings. The onboard computer takes account of winds, storms, temperature, and other aircraft. When landing, the computer automatically adjusts the speed and angle of descent of the plane so that a perfect landing can be made without any action on the pilot's part. Maintenance computers give advance notice of needed repairs or replacement of aircraft components and have practically eliminated flight delays or cancellation of flights because of mechanical problems.

Computers have made flying in the year 2001 very safe. They have minimized the possibility of mid-air collisions. They keep track of planes in the same air corridor and calculate the distance between, and direction of, all of them. If the speed and direction of any two planes indicate that a collision is likely, the computer alerts the pilots to the fact that instructions are being prepared to avoid the danger. Within seconds, the computer will advise the pilots what corrective maneuvers to take.

As the passenger stands in front of the automatic vendor, he or she is quickly guided through the necessary steps to purchase a ticket by a series of computer-controlled lighted instructions that are sequentially illuminated. During the few seconds it takes for the machine to encode, print, and bond the ticket, the instruction "Please wait for ticket" is displayed.

Medicine

In 2001 all large hospitals are using centralized computer systems to perform a large amount of patient care (see Figure 27–1). A patient entering the hospital is admitted, diagnosed, and monitored by the computer. Electroencephalogram (brain-wave recording) analysis is performed by computer. Electrocardiograms (heart waveforms) are read and interpreted accurately by computer. Phonocardiograms (heart sounds and murmurs) are processed and analyzed by computer. The timing and relative amplitudes of heart sounds are displayed on CRT display, along with the onset, duration, relative amplitudes, and relative frequency information of any systolic or diastolic murmurs which have been detected.

Most doctors have display terminals connected to medical information banks for consultation purposes.

You are able to "dial the doctor" and be connected to a medical computer system which can make a first-level medical diagnosis. This system asks questions, prescribes medication, and gives instructions on whether to go to the hospital emergency room immediately or to your family doctor or clinic tomorrow. Some medical systems even have access to your own medical history.

Computers have helped stamp out all forms of diseases so that people now enjoy healthier, more satisfying lives.

Well, uh, I think I had better consult another computer before I go ahead with the operation.

Robots

In 2001, robots will be walking, making decisions, and thinking, as it were, for themselves. Their minds are composed of programmed computers. They use television-like cameras for eyes to send inputs to the computer. For example, if a robot on an exploration trip bumps into an obstacle which it has not previously sensed, the television camera and cat-whisker antennas (wire sensors) send data to the computer that in effect ask, "What do I do now?" The computer then switches to an "I'll-walk-around-it" or a "Let-me-take-a-look" program.

Domestic robots are available to perform a variety of routine household chores. These chores include preparing some meals, mowing the lawn, cleaning up after meals, baysitting, washing clothes, and watering plants.

Robots are used to perform tasks that are boring, dangerous, or have to be performed in hostile environments, such as the floor of the ocean. When NASA sends a space vehicle to Mars, robots will be the first to

Figure 27–1 A centralized hospital computer system can receive and supply information on patients, room availability, and clinic appointments from terminals throughout the hospital. Shown here is a typical terminal that a nurse uses to enter and receive information.

explore this dangerous terrain. The temperature of the surface of Venus is about 800°; Jupiter has a poisonous atmosphere and crushing gravity; pressures on the bottom of the ocean can crush vessels with steel hulls several inches thick. People are unable to explore these areas, but robots impervious to heat, poisons, and pressure are able to.

Mobile robots are widely used in industry to perform operations in various manufacturing processes.

Computers in the Home

A typical new home in 2001 is similar to that of Mr. and Ms. Universe. This home contains three bedrooms, a family room, a kitchen, two bathrooms, and a large play room. Located in the kitchen is a family control center, the heart of which is a computer. There is a keyboard input device, a voice recognition device, and a display device. Ms. Universe (or Mr. Universe, if he's the family cook) uses the center to conjure up nutritionally balanced, tasty, eye-pleasing meal plans. She simply supplies the computer with an appropriate code for any of several major food categories. The computer then causes a printout with a full dinner menu planned around entrees such as ham, beef, chicken, trout, lobster, veal, lamb, pork, game, eggs, and cheese. For finicky or allergy-prone diners, substitutions can be obtained by entering additional costs. Ms. Universe is always free to place new menus in the computer's memory.

Ms. Universe also uses the center for typing her shopping lists, writing letters, calculating requirements for drapery material, obtaining suggestions for rearranging room furniture, keeping track of the household budget, and ordering grocery and clothing items from the computerized store.

Mr. Universe uses the computer to keep track of his investments, to prepare tax reports, to take a course in business law, to take care of his checkbook accounting, and to solve problems related to his work. For example, he can use the computer to prepare budgets and manpower forecasts for his different business projects. He, like the rest of the family, may also use the computer in his spare time to learn, say advanced psychology. The computer retrieves from its memory a teaching program for advanced psychology, remembering where the student left off at the end of the last lesson. The psychology lessons are programmed to proceed at just the pace that matches a student's learning rate.

The computer center can drive clocks throughout the house, control the air-conditioning and heating system, change television channels at predetermined times, control the stereo music center, open and close doors and windows, and perform family medical diagnoses.

The Universe children, Mars and Space, can also use the computer center. Mars is in elementary school and check all his arithmetic and language problems by computer. Space, who is in college, can use the computer as a homework aid in practically all her courses. When their lessons are done, the children can play a game of tic-tac-toe, blackjack, chess, or football with the computer.

What does the home computer cost? About $2 000, which includes all the electronic control and communication devices that are connected to the computer.

Finance

Paper money and coins are all found in "money collections." People are paid by check, and these checks are automatically deposited into checking accounts. Any amount that you owe the Internal Revenue Service in taxes will disappear out of your account before you have a chance to see it.

In making purchases, you will use a single "universal credit card." Inserting the card in a slot at a store or business will remove funds from your account and deposit them into the account of the business. Most banks also provide self-service banking. (see Figure 27–2).

(Courtesy of NCR Corp.)

Figure 27–2 Self-service, computerized banking terminals permit banking transactions to occur 24 hours a day.

(Courtesy of IBM Corp.)

Figure 27–3 Computer-assisted instruction system presents individual lessons to an elementary school child. A visual display screen and headphones allow the student to receive information and be questioned. A typewriter-like keyboard is used to communicate with the computer. With this system, each student can progress at his own individual pace.

Education

In 2001, small classroom computers are common in all schools—elementary, secondary, and college. Students learn to program computers at an early age and use them throughout their educational careers. Since most families own a home computer, students are expected to use theirs to help them with homework. Computer-Assisted Instruction (CAI), in which the computer presents tutorial and drill practice information to the student, is a feature of all schools (see Figure 27–3). For example, you may engage in the following conversation with a computer. The underlined remarks are yours:

```
HELLO
HI
HOW ARE YOU THIS MORNING.
FINE. HOW ARE YOU?
OK. ARE YOU BUSY TODAY?
FAIRLY BUSY. I AM COMMUNICATING WITH 1263 USERS
RIGHT NOW
WILL YOU HELP ME WITH A PROBLEM?
OF COURSE. TELL ME THE PROBLEM.
I HAVE AN ITEM—IN MY STORE THAT COSTS $18. TELL ME
THE SELLING PRICE I SHOULD CHARGE SO I WILL HAVE
A PROFIT OF 12% OF THE SELLING PRICE.
$20.45. DO YOU WANT TO KNOW HOW I COMPUTED
THIS ANSWER?
NO THANKS. YOU TOLD ME WHAT I WANT TO KNOW.
DO YOU HAVE ANOTHER PROBLEM?
YES. WHAT SHOULD I BUY MY MOTHER-IN-LAW FOR
HER BIRTHDAY?
SORRY. I DO NOT GET INVOLVED WITH IN-LAW PROBLEMS.
DO YOU HAVE ANOTHER PROBLEM?
NO. GOODBYE FOR NOW.
SO LONG.
```

The computer almost seems literally to understand what you want. It does not really, because the computer has been programmed to give the proper responses. Nevertheless, you are now able to have realistic conversations with the computer.

Information Systems

Computers linked to common information banks are now common in law and medicine as well as in educational institutions. Criminal justice information systems allow all allied organizations to share information, expand local data files, and analyze interdependent problems, such as manpower utilization and court docketing. Medical information systems provide doctors and hospitals with a central source of up-to-date data concerning all known diseases and medical procedures. School terminals connected to a central educational system allow access to vast amounts of general information. Book libraries have become obsolete for obtaining such information.

You can "dial the encyclopedia" and obtain rapid access to a body of factual information at least as large as a good current encyclopedia. The requests are spoken, and the response is either spoken or displayed on a visual device.

You can also "dial the store" and obtain delivery on thousands of items from peanut butter to sirloin steak (which now costs $14.50 per pound) to sandpaper to furniture. Thus, you will be able to shop by catalog and obtain the bulk of your needs without leaving your home.

Hotels use computerized systems to keep track of room reservations, hotel personnel, disposable items, and food and beverage items and to compute customer bills upon checkout (see Figure 27–4).

(Courtesy of Burroughs Corp.)

Figure 27–4   Hotels use computer-controlled reservation systems to reserve rooms and compute a customer's bill upon checking out.

Information banks are available that contain detailed information on available positions and persons seeking employment. These systems cover jobs at all levels and are a major method of the government in the analysis and control of the economy.

Law enforcement agencies use computer systems to identify criminals (by fingerprints, voiceprints, pictures, and handwriting) as well as to obtain instantaneous information on stolen items, traffic violations, and so forth (see Figure 27–5).

(Courtesy of Univac Division of Sperry Rand Corp.)

Figure 27–5   A police officer uses a computer terminal to obtain instantaneous information on wanted criminals, stolen cars, and lost children.

Entertainment

You have a wide choice over what you hear or watch on your home entertainment center. You can watch the news, a sporting event, a musical play, a travelog, an educational program, a soap opera, or a movie. You can dial programs you have missed or those you would like to see again. You can even select the commercials that you want to watch. You can also just listen to a good musical program. The cost? You pay by the program, and the computer, of course, automatically deducts the proper costs from your bank checking account.

Entertainment parks, such as Disney World in Orlando, Florida, use computers to control rides (like Space Mountain) and to move the arms, legs, ears, and eyes of all their animated characters (see Figure 27–6).

Space

In the year 2001, there will undoubtedly be a sizeable computer-controlled operation on the moon, and it is entirely possible that people

Figure 27-6 A computer-controlled elephant. Realistic artificial animals of this type may be found in entertainment centers, such as Disney World and Disneyland.

will have flown to the outer planets. A manned Mars landing may even occur by the turn of the century.

SOMEBODY PUT IN THE WRONG INPUT

Miscellaneous

Cities in 2001 are designed with the aid of computers. Mathematical models of atmospheric pollution patterns are used to predict where heavy industry and new population centers should be located to minimize environmental damage and optimize healthful living conditions. Small computers, about the size of a watch, have become available to everyone. These computers cost only about $50 (at the dollar's current value).

Computers are able to analyze a person's voice, handwriting, finger-prints, and even picture and to make a positive identification.

Computers are used to combine voice analysis and language translation into a translator device for conversations in two different natural languages. These translation devices are used primarily by tourists, business-men, and scientists.

The cause-and-effect relations of weather are now understood, and computers are used to accurately analyze and predict the weather as well as explore ways to modify weather patterns.

Supermarkets now use computer systems to keep track of the store's inventory and to speed up the food checkout process (see Figure 27–7).

(Courtesy of NCR Corp.)

Figure 27–7   Groceries are passed over the scanning window and into shopping bags in one quick motion. The scanner reads an identification symbol imprinted on each grocery item, price is linked-up in a computer memory, and the items are automatically recorded.

☐ REVIEW EXERCISES

1. Briefly explain how the future computer will differ from today's computer. From the ENIAC.
2. List 10 application areas where minicomputers will be used in the next decade.
3. In 1980, which will cost the least—the minicomputer or the microcomputer?
4. Briefly explain how the computer and telecommunication industries can be merged to help society.
5. What programming language is likely to have widespread use in elementary and secondary schools?
6. Discuss the impact that computers may have upon society in the immediate future and in the more distant future.

7. Describe a potential application of computers that is presently infeasible because of current limitations on computer hardware/software systems.
8. What do you think the computer-controlled robot of 2001 will look like? Draw a picture.
9. What unusual item can we expect to find in the home of 2001?
10. Explain what is meant by a universal credit card.

☐ **Summary**

In chapters 1 and 27, we described many current applications of computers. In this chapter, we speculated about some of the uses to which computers may be put in the future. The field of application of computers is continually increasing, and eventually there will be few kinds of endeavor that will not have some sort of computer aid. The mere existence of computers increases people's capabilities manyfold. By using these powerful machines, they may be able to solve many social and technical problems that now look almost hopeless. At the same time, we should realize that it is people themselves who will always be in control. After all, they can always turn the computer switch OFF! Assuming, of course, that people has not delegated to the computer the task of deciding when the switch should be turned off. In that case, well . . .

Key Terms

ENIAC	firmware
minicomputers	microprograms
microcomputers	PICTUREPHONE
BASIC	Large Scale Integration (LSI)
FORTRAN	robots
PL/I	universal credit card
RPG	Computer-Assisted Instruction
APL	
COBOL	

appendix

Glossary of
Information Processing Terms

Abacus: An ancient counting device used to perform arithmetic calculations. The device uses beads to represent decimal values.

ABC: Atanasoff-Berry Computer. An early electronic digital computer built in 1942 by Dr. John V. Atanasoff, and his assistant, Clifford Berry.

Absolute address: An address that is permanently assigned by the machine designer to a storage location.

Absolute coding: Coding that uses machine language instructions with absolute addresses and which the computer can execute without prior translation.

Access time: The time interval between the instant data are called out from the storage unit and the instant they are delivered to the processing unit (read time). The time interval between the instant data are requested to be stored and the instant at which storage is completed (write time).

Accounting machine: A keyboard-actuated machine used to prepare printed reports from punch card data. The machine can also perform limited arithmetic operations.

Accumulator: A register in which the result of an arithmetic or logic operation is formed.

ACM: Association for Computing Machinery. A professional computer science organization.

Acronym: A word formed from the first letter or letters of the words describing some item–for example, FORTRAN from FORmula TRANslation.

Address: A name, label, or number which identifies a location in storage.

ADP: Automatic Data Processing.

AFIPS: American Federation of Information Processing Societies.

Aiken, Howard: Headed the team of people who designed and built the first electro-mechanical computer, the Automatic Sequence Controlled Calculator (commonly called the Mark I), at Harvard University.

ALGOL: ALGOrithmic Language. A higher-level programming language designed for programming scientific problems. Used widely in Europe.

647

Algorithm: A computational procedure for solving a problem. When properly applied, an algorithm always produces a solution to the problem.

Alphanumeric: Fields containing both alphabetic and numerical characters.

Ampere: Base unit of electric current in the SI.

Analog computer: A computer that makes analogies between numbers and directly measurable quantities such as voltage, rotations, and so on.

Analysis: The investigation of a problem by some consistent, systematic procedure.

Analyst: A person skilled in the definition of and the development of techniques for the solving of a problem, especially those techniques for solutions on a computer.

Analytical Engine: A device invented about 1853 by Charles Babbage, a British mathematician, to solve mathematical problems. This machine was a forerunner of the modern digital computer.

ANSI: American National Standards Institute. An organization that acts as a national clearinghouse and coordinator for voluntary standards in the United States.

APL: A higher-level terminal-oriented programming language.

Application: The system or problem to which a computer is applied.

Arithmetic unit: The portion of the central processing unit where arithmetic and logical operations are performed.

Array: A series of related items, e.g., a table of numbers.

Artificial intelligence: Capability of a device to perform such functions as reasoning and learning usually associated with human intelligence.

ASCC: Automatic Sequence Controlled Calculator. See *Mark I.*

ASCII code: American Standard Code for Information Interchange. A seven-bit code used on many present day computers.

Assemble: To prepare a machine language program from a symbolic language program.

Assembler: A computer program used to translate a program written in a symbolic programming language into a machine language program.

Assembly language: A programming language which allows a computer user to write a program using mnemonics instead of numeric instructions. It is a low-level, symbolic programming language which closely resembles machine code language.

Assembly listing: A listing of the details of an assembly procedure.

Asynchronous: A term applied to a computer in which the execution of one operation is dependent on a signal indicating that the previous operation has been completed, rather than on a fixed time cycle.

Atanasoff, John V.: Designed an electronic digital computer in 1942.

Automation: The implementation of processes by automatic means.

Auxiliary operation: An off-line operation performed by equipment not under control of the central processing unit.

Auxiliary storage: A storage that supplements the internal storage of the central processing unit. Also called *Secondary storage*.

Availability: The ratio of the time that a hardware device is known or believed to be operating correctly to the total hours of scheduled operation.

Babbage, Charles (1792–1871): A British mathematician and inventor. He designed a *Difference Engine* for calculating logarithms to 20 decimal places and an *Analytical Engine* that was a forerunner of the digital computer. Babbage was a man ahead of his time, since engineering techniques of his day were not advanced enough to build his machines successfully.

Background processing: Processing of a low priority program that takes place only when no higher priority or real-time processing function is present.

Background program: A program that may be run on the computer when no higher priority program is being executed. It is not time-dependent.

Backspace: The process of returning a magnetic tape to the beginning of the preceding record.

Bar printer: A printing device that uses several type bars positioned side by side across the line.

Base: The radix of a number system. See *Radix*.

BASIC: Beginners All-purpose Symbolic Instruction Code. An easy-to-learn and easy-to-use programming language developed at Dartmouth College. BASIC can be used to solve business problems as well as scientific applications.

Batch: A group of records or programs that is considered a single unit for processing on a computer.

Batch processing: A technique by which items to be processed must be coded and collected into groups prior to processing.

BCD: Binary Coded Decimal Code. A decimal notation in which the individual decimal digits are each represented by a group of binary digits.

BINAC: BINary Automatic Computer. An early computer built by the Eckert-Mauchly Corporation in 1949.

Binary: (a) A condition or situation having only two possibilities. (b) A number representation system with a radix of two.

Binary digit: In binary notation, either of the digits, 0 or 1.

Binary notation: A number system written in base two notation.

Binary point: The point that separates the fractional part of a binary number from the integer part.

Bistable: Refers to a device capable of existing in one or two states—e.g., a switch is ON or OFF.

Bit: An abbreviation of "binary digit."

Bit rate: The rate at which binary digits, or pulse representations, appear on communication lines or channels.

Block: A set of things, such as digits, characters, or words, handled as a unit.

Block diagram: A graphic representation showing the logical sequence in which data is processed.

Block sorting: A technique used to break down a file into related groups.

Blocking: Combining of two or more records into one block.

Blocking factor: The number of logical records appearing within a tape record.

Bookkeeping operation: A computer operation which does not directly contribute to the result—that is, arithmetical, logical, and transfer operations used in modifying the address section of other instructions, in counting cycles, and in rearranging data.

Boole, George (1815–1864): The father of Boolean algebra. A British logician and mathematician. In 1847, he wrote a pamphlet called *Mathematical Analysis of Logic.* In 1854, he wrote a more mature statement of his logical system in a larger work, *An Investigation of the Laws of Thought,* where he set forth certain mathematical theories of logic. Boolean algebra remained just a set of interesting logical propositions until its useful application to the field of relay switching and electronic computers. It has now become indispensable to logic design in electronic computers.

Boolean algebra: The algebra of a logic which specifies that a condition may be either *true* or *false,* i.e., a logic which is concerned with binary conditions.

Branch: A technique used to transfer control from one sequence of a program to another.

Branchpoint: A point in a program where one of two or more choices is selected under program control.

Bucket: A term used to indicate a specific portion of storage.

Buffer: A storage device used to compensate for a difference in rate or sequence of data flow when transmitting data from one device to another.

Bug: A term used to denote a mistake in a computer program or a malfunction in a computer hardware component.

Burroughs, W. W.: Inventor of the first commercially successful adding machine.

Bus: A channel or path for transferring data and electrical signals.

Business data processing: Data processing for business purposes—e.g., payroll, scheduling, accounting, etc.

Byte: A grouping of adjacent binary digits operated on by the computer as a unit. The most common size of byte contains eight binary digits.

CAI: Computer Assisted Instruction. A concept that applies computers and specialized input-output display terminals directly to individualized student instruction.

Calculating: Reconstructing data or creating new data by compressing certain numeric facts.

Calculating punch: A machine designed to perform arithmetic operations with punch cards.

Call: A branch to a subroutine.

Card: A storage medium in which data is represented by means of holes punched in vertical columns in a paper card.

Card column: One of the vertical lines of punching positions on a punched card.

Card field: A fixed number of consecutive card columns assigned to a unit of information.

Card hopper: A device that holds cards and makes them available for the feeding mechanism of card handling equipment.

Card punch: An output device used to punch cards.

Card punching: See *Keypunching*.

Card reader: An input device used to transmit punch card coded data to the central processing unit of a computer.

Card reproducer: A device that reproduces a punch card by punching a similar card.

Card row: One of the horizontal lines of punching positions on a punched card.

Card stacker: The receptacle where cards are held after passing through a punch card data processing machine.

Carriage: A control mechanism for a typewriter or printer that automatically feeds, skips, spaces, or ejects paper forms.

Carriage control tape: A tape that is punched with information to control line feeding of a printing device.

Celsius: alternate of the kelvin, the base unit of temperature in the SI.

Centi: metric prefix, means one hundredth of, (10^{-2}).

Central processing unit: That portion of the hardware of a computing system containing the control unit, arithmetic unit, and internal storage unit. (abbreviated CPU).

Chad: A piece of material removed when forming a hole or notch in punched cards or punched paper tape.

Chain: A series of items linked together.

Chain printer: A printer with print characters located on a continuous steel chain.

Chaining: A process of linking a series of programs or operations together.

Character: A symbol, mark, or event which a data processing machine can read, write, or store. It is used to represent data to a machine.

Character reader: An input device which reads printed characters directly from a document.

Checkout: See *Debug*.

Chip: See *Chad*.

Circuit: A system of conductors and related electrical elements through which electrical currents flow.

Classify: To organize information into groupings based on some plan.

Classifying: Arranging data in a specific form, usually by sorting, grouping, or extracting.

Closed shop: The operation of a computer facility where actual program running service is the responsibility of a group of specialists, thereby effectively separating the phase of task formulation from that of computer implementation. The programmers are not allowed in the computer room to run or oversee the running of their programs. Contrasted with *Open shop.*

COBOL: COmmon Business Oriented Language. A higher-level programming language developed for programming business problems.

CODASYL: COnference on DAsta SYstems Languages. The conference which developed COBOL.

Code: A representation by which meaning is assigned to groups of characters or symbols.

Coder: A person who prepares instruction sequences from detailed flowcharts and other algorithmic procedures prepared by others, as contrasted with a programmer who prepares the procedures and flowcharts.

Coding: The process of translating problem logic represented by a flowchart into computer instructions and data.

Coding form: A form on which the instructions for programming a computer are written. Also called a coding sheet.

Collate: To merge two (or more) sequenced data sets to produce a resulting data set which reflects the sequencing of the original sets.

Collating sequence: An ordering assigned to the characters of a character set to be used for sequencing purposes.

Collator: A machine used to collate or merge sets of cards or other documents into a sequence.

Column: (a) The vertical members of one line of an array. (b) One of the vertical lines of punching positions on a punched card. (c) A position of information in a computer word.

COM: Computer output to microfilm. Refers to a method of converting computer output to microfilm form.

Command: See *Operation code.*

Common language: A standardized coding procedure common to several different machines—e.g., FORTRAN, COBOL, PL/I.

Compare: To examine the representation of a quantity to determine its relationship to zero or to examine two quantities usually for the purposes of determining identity or relative magnitude.

Comparison: The act of comparing. The common forms are comparison of two numbers for identity, comparison of two numbers for relative magnitude, comparison of two characters for similarity, and comparison of two numbers for sign value.

Compatible: A term applied to a computer system which implies that it is capable of handling both data and programs devised for some other type of computer system.

Compile: To generate a machine language program from a computer program written in a high-level source language.

Compiler: A computer program used to translate high-level source language programs into machine language programs suitable for execution on a particular computing system.

Compiler language: See *Higher-level Language.*

Composite Card: A multi-purpose data card, or a card that contains data needed in the processing of various applications.

Computer: A calculating device which processes data represented by a combination of discrete data (in digital computers) or continuous data (in analog computers).

Computer Classification: The three major classifications of computers are *digital, analog,* and *hybrid.*

Computer operator: A person who manipulates the controls of a computer and performs all operational functions that are required in the computing system, such as loading a tape transport, placing cards in the input hopper, removing printout from the printer rack, and so forth.

Computer program: See *Program.*

Computer programmer: A person who designs, writes, debugs, and documents computer programs.

Computer Science: The field of knowledge that involves the design and use of computer equipment, including software development.

Computer system: A central processing unit together with one or more peripheral devices.

Computer word: A fixed sequence of bits or characters treated as a unit and capable of being stored in one storage location.

Computing: The act of using computing equipment for processing data.

Console: That part of a computer used for communication between the computer operator or maintenance engineer and the computer.

Console printer An auxiliary printer used in several computer systems for communications between the computer operator and the computing system.

Constant: A number that does not change during the execution of a program.

Control console: A part of a computer system that contains manual controls.

Control punch: A specific code punched in a card to cause the machine to perform a specific operation.

Control statement: An operation that terminates the sequential execution of instructions by transferring control to a statement elsewhere in the program.

Control unit: The portion of the central processing unit that directs the step-by-step operation of the entire computing system.

Conversational mode: A mode of operation where a user is in direct contact with a computer and interaction is possible between man and machine without the user being conscious of any language or communication barrier.

Conversion: The process of changing data from one form to another.

Core: See *Magnetic core.*

Core plane: See *Magnetic core plane.*

Corner cut: A diagonal cut at the corner of a card. It is used as a means of identifying groups of related cards.

Corrective Maintenance: The activity of detecting, isolating, and correcting failures after occurrence.

Counter: A device such as a storage location or a register used to represent the number of occurrences of an event.

CPU: Central Processing Unit

CRAM: Card Random Access Memory. An auxiliary storage device that uses removable magnetic cards each of which is capable of storing data in magnetic form.

CRT: Cathode Ray Tube. An electronic vacuum tube with a screen for visual display of output information in graphical or alphanumeric form. Display is produced by means of proportionally deflected electron beams.

Cryogenics: The study and use of devices utilizing properties of materials near absolute zero in temperature.

Cycle: An interval of time in which an operation or set of events is completed.

Cylinder: As related to magnetic disks, a vertical column of tracks on a magnetic disk file unit. If the unit contained 20 recording surfaces, then a cylinder of information would consist of information from the same track on all 20 recording surfaces. Cylinder operation provides large blocks of sequential storage without the necessity of separate track-by-track addressing.

Data: A representation of facts or concepts in a formalized manner suitable for communication, interpretation, or processing by people or by automatic means.

Data base: A comprehensive data file containing information in a format applicable to a user's needs and available when needed.

Data collection: The gathering of source data to be entered into a data processing system.

Data conversion: The process of changing the form of data representation—for example, converting punched card to magnetic tape.

Data link: Equipment which permits the transmission of information in data format.

Data-phone: The name applied by A. T. & T. to the members of a family of devices used for providing data communications over telephone facilities.

Data processing: A term used in reference to operations performed by data processing equipment.

Data processing center: An installation of computer equipment which provides computing services for users.

Data processing system: A system composed of data processing hardware and software.

Data transmission: The sending of data from one part of a system to another part.

Data word: See *Word*.

Debug: To detect, locate, and remove all mistakes in a computer program and any malfunctions in the computing system hardware itself.

Debugging aids: Computer routines that are helpful in debugging programs—for example, trace, snapshot dump, or post mortem dump.

Decision: The computer operation of determining whether a certain relationship exists between words in storage or registers and then taking alternative courses of action.

Decision table: A table consisting of all decisions that are to be considered in a problem, together with the actions that are to be taken as a result of those decisions. Decision tables are often used instead of flowcharts to describe the operations of a program.

Decrement: Decreasing the value of a quantity.

Degausser: A device that is used to erase information from magnetic tape.

Delimit: To fix the limits of—for example, to establish maximum and minimum limits of a specific variable.

Density: See *Packing density*.

Desk checking: The process in which the computer user checks a program prior to executing it on a computer. It involves using sample data and working it manually ("stepping") through the program.

Detail printing: An operation where a line of printing occurs for each card read by an accounting machine (tabulator).

Diagnosis: The process of isolating malfunctions in computing equipment and detecting errors in a computer program.

Diagnostic routine: A routine designed to locate a malfunction in a computer.

Diagnostics: Statements printed by an assembler or compiler indicating mistakes detected in a source program.

Difference engine: A machine designed by Charles Babbage, in 1822, which mechanized a calculating function called the "method of differences." The machine was never built, however, because of inadequate engineering capabilities.

Digit: One of the symbols of a number system used to designate a quantity.

Digit punching position: The area on a punch card reserved to represent a decimal digit.

Digital: Pertaining to the utilization of discrete integral numbers in a given base to represent all the quantities that occur in a problem or a calculation.

Digital computer: A computer that operates on discrete data by performing arithmetic and logic processes on these data.

Digital plotter: An output unit which graphs data by an automatically controlled pen. Data is normally plotted as a series of incremental steps. Primary types of plotters are the drum plotter and the flat-bed plotter.

Direct access storage: Pertaining to the process of obtaining data from or placing data into storage where the time required for such access is independent of the location of the data most recently obtained or placed in storage. Also called random access storage.

Direct address: An address that specifies the location of an operand.

Disc: Another spelling of disk.

Disk: See *Magnetic disk*.

Disk pack: The vertical stacking of a series of magnetic disks in a removable self-contained unit.

Diskette: A floppy disk.

Display unit: A device which provides a visual representation of data. See *CRT*.

Document retrieval: Acquiring data from storage devices and, possibly, manipulating the data and subsequently preparing a report.

Documentation: The general process of logically organizing information, which will be generated in producing a computer program, into a useful file that continually reflects the current state of the program. The completeness and thoroughness of the documentation directly affects the usefulness of the program. Program documentation varies with computer installation, but often consists of the following information: program description, program flowchart, program listing, source program card deck, and operating procedures.

Downtime: A time period during which the computer system is malfunctioning.

DPMA: Data Processing Management Association. A professional data processing organization.

DPMA certificate: A certificate given by the Data Processing Management Association which indicates that a person has a certain level of competence in the field of data processing. The certificate is obtained by passing an examination that is offered yearly throughout the United States and Canada.

Drum: See *Magnetic drum*.

Drum printer: A printing device which uses a drum embossed with alphabetic and numerical characters.

Dump: Printing all or part of the contents of a storage device.

Duplicate: To reproduce data without altering the original data.

EAM: Electrical Accounting Machine.

EBCDIC: Extended Binary Coded Decimal Interchange Code. An eight-bit code used for data representation in several computers including the IBM System/360 and System/370 computers.

Eckert, J. Presper: Co-inventor of the ENIAC.

Edit: To rearrange data or information. Editing may involve the deletion of unwanted data, the selection of pertinent data, the application of format techniques, the insertion of symbols (such as page numbers and typewriter characters), the application of standard processes (such as zero suppression), and the testing of data for reasonableness and proper range.

EDP: Electronic Data Processing.

EDSAC: Electronic Delayed Storage Automatic Computer. The first digital computer to feature the stored-program concept. It was developed in Great Britain in 1949 at Cambridge University.

EDVAC: Electronic Discrete Variable Automatic Computer. Developed at the Moore School of Electrical Engineering, University of Pennsylvania in 1949. It was the first U.S.-built computer that featured a stored-program unit.

Eighty-column card: See *Hollerith punched card.*

Electrical Accounting Machine: Pertaining to data processing equipment that is predominantly electromechanical—e.g., keypunch, mechanical sorter, tabulator, or collator.

Electromechanical data processing system: A system for processing data that uses both electrical and mechanical principles.

Electronic data processing: Data processing performed largely by electronic equipment.

Electronic data processing system: The general term used to define a system for data processing by means of machines utilizing electronic circuitry at electronic speed, as opposed to electromechanical equipment.

Electrostatic printer: A high-speed printing device that prints an optical image on special paper.

Eleven-punch: A punch in the second row from the top of a Hollerith punched card. Synonymous with X-punch.

Emulate: To imitate one system with another, such that the imitating system accepts the same data, executes the same programs, and achieves the same results as the imitated system.

Emulator: A hardware device that causes a computer to behave as if it were another computer.

End of file: Termination or point of completion of a quantity of data. End-of-file marks are used to indicate this point on magnetic tape files.

ENIAC: Electronic Numerical Integrator And Calculator. An early all-electronic digital computer. It was built by J. Mauchly and J. Eckert at the Moore School of Electrical Engineering, University of Pennsylvania, in 1946.

EOF: End of File.

EOJ: End of Job.

Erase: To remove data from storage without replacing it.

Error: The general term referring to any deviation of a computed or a measured quantity from the theoretically correct or true value.

Execute: To perform the operations specified by a computer instruction (program).

Failure prediction: A technique which attempts to determine the failure schedule of specific parts or equipments so that they may be discarded and replaced before failure occurs.

Fault: A condition that causes a component, a computer, or a peripheral device to fail to perform according to its design specifications.

Feasibility study: A specialized study of data processing equipment designed to determine what equipment would best accomplish the job in what configurations.

Feed holes: Holes punched in a paper tape to enable it to be driven by a sprocket wheel.

Feedback: The part of a closed loop system which automatically brings back information about the condition under control.

Fetch: To obtain data from a location in storage.

Field: A column or group of columns in a punch card allocated for punching a particular category of data.

File: An organized collection of related data. For example, the entire set of inventory master data records make up the Inventory Master File.

File maintenance: The activity of keeping a file up to date by adding, changing, or deleting data.

First generation computers: A class of computers which utilized vacuum tubes in their electronic circuitry.

Fixed-word length: The condition in which a machine word always contains a fixed number of bits, characters, bytes, or digits. Contrasted with *Variable-field length*.

Flat-bed plotter: See *Digital plotter*.

Floppy disk: A flexible disk (diskette) of oxide-coated mylar that is stored in paper or plastic envelopes. The entire envelope is inserted in the disk unit. Floppy disks are a low-cost storage that is used widely with minicomputers and small scale computers.

Flow: A general term to indicate a sequence of events.

Flow diagram: See *Flowchart*.

Flowchart: A graphical representation for the solution of a problem. It is used primarily to help in the development of a computer program by illustrating how a computer program's logic is laid out, and to provide documentation for the program.

Flowchart symbol: A symbol used to represent operations, data, equipment, or flow on a flowchart.

Flowchart template: A plastic guide containing cutouts of the flowchart symbols that are used in drawing a flowchart.

Foreground processing: The automatic execution of the computer programs that have been designed to preempt the use of the computing facilities.

Format: The general makeup of items, including arrangement and location of all information.

FORTRAN: FORmula TRANslation. A higher-level programming language designed for programming scientific-type problems.

Functional units of a computer: The organization of digital computers into five functional units: arithmetic unit, storage unit, control unit, input unit, and output unit.

Gang punch: To punch identical or constant information into all of a group of punch cards.

Garbage: A term often used to describe incorrect answers from a computer program; often a result of an equipment malfunction or a mistake in a computer program.

Gate: An electronic device that combines electrical impulses or the lack of such pulses in circuits to produce other impulses. Used in computers to perform logic operations.

General-purpose computer: A computer that is designed to solve a wide class of problems. The majority of digital computers are of this type.

Generator: A translating program which permits a computer to write other programs, automatically. Generators are of two types: (a) The character-controlled generator, which operates like a compiler in that it takes entries from a library tape. It is unlike a simple compiler in that it examines control characters associated with each entry, and alters instructions found in the library according to the directions contained in the control characters. (b) The pure generator which is a program that writes another program. When associated with an assembler, a pure generator is usually a section of program which is called into storage by the assembler from a library tape and which then writes one or more entries in another program.

GIGO: Garbage In-Garbage Out. A term used to describe the data into and out of a computer system—that is, if the input data is bad (Garbage In), then the output data will also be bad (Garbage Out).

Gram: A metric unit of mass or weight equal to 1/1000 kilogram.

Group printing: An operation during which information is printed from only the first card of each group passing through the accounting machine.

Grouping: Arranging data into related groups, each having common characteristics.

Hard copy: A printed copy of computer output—for example, printed reports, listings, or documents.

Hardware: The physical equipment in a computer system—e.g., mechanical, electrical, or magnetic devices. Contrasted with *Software.*

Hash: A term for unnecessary data.

Hexadecimal: A number system based on a radix of sixteen.

Hexadecimal point: The point that separates the fractional part of a hexadecimal number from the integer part.

High order: The most significant (leftmost) digit in a number.

High order column: The leftmost column of a punch card field.

Higher-level language: A computer programming language which is intended to be independent of a particular computer.

Hollerith code: A punched-card code based on a code developed by Dr. Herman Hollerith for tabulating census data for the U.S. Census Bureau.

Hollerith, Herman (1860–1929): As a statistician and employee of the Census Bureau he proposed using punched cards in conjunction with electromechanical relays to accomplish simple additions and sortings needed in the 1890 census. He set up a company to manufacture his punched card tabulator which later became one of the parents of International Business Machines Corporation.

Hollerith punched card: A punched card consisting of 80 columns, each of which is divided from top to bottom into 12 punching positions.

Housekeeping: The part of a program that is devoted to set-up operations: clearing storage areas, initializing or starting peripheral equipment, inserting constants, adjusting parameters, resetting addresses, and performing other initializing operations.

IBM card: See *Card*.

Idle time: The time that a computer system is available for use, but is not in actual operation.

IFIPS: International Federation of Information Processing Societies.

Illegal character: A character or combination of bits which is not accepted as a valid or known representation by the computer.

Illegal operation: A process which the computer cannot perform.

Immediate access storage: See *Internal storage*.

Indirect address: An address that specifies a storage location that contains either a direct address or another indirect address.

Information: Data that have been organized into a meaningful sequence.

Information processing: The totality of scientific and business operations performed by a computer; the handling of data according to rules of procedure for accomplishing operations such as classifying, sorting, calculating, and recording.

Information retrieval: A technique of classifying and indexing useful data in mass storage devices, in a format amenable to interaction with the user(s).

Input: The introduction of data from an external storage medium into a computer's internal storage unit.

Input unit: A device used to transmit data into a central processing unit—e.g., a card reader, a teletypewriter, a paper tape reader, a MICR reader, or an optical scanning reader.

Input-output: A general term for the peripheral devices used to communicate with a digital computer and the data involved in the communication.

Input-output control system: A set of routines for handling the many detailed aspects of input and output operations; commonly abbreviated IOCS.

Inquiry: A request for information from storage.

Instruction: A set of characters used to define a basic operation and tell the computer where to find the required data needed to carry out this operation.

Instruction format: The makeup and arrangement of a computer instruction.

Instruction word: A computer word which contains an instruction.

Integer: A whole number which may be positive, negative, or zero. It does not have a fractional part. Examples of integers are 26, -417, and 0.

Integrated circuit: A micro-miniature electronic circuit produced on a single crystal of silicon.

Intelligent Terminal: An input-output device in which a number of computer processing characteristics are physically built into, or attached to, the terminal unit.

Interface: A common boundary between two pieces of hardware or between two systems.

Interleave: To insert segments of one program into another program such that the two programs can be, in essence, executed simultaneously.

Internal storage: Addressible storage directly controlled by the central processing unit of a digital computer. It is an integral part of the central processing unit. The CPU uses internal storage to store programs while they are being executed. Also called primary storage, immediate-access storage, and main storage.

Interpreter: (a) A machine that is used to sense information recorded in a punch card and print that information on the face of the card. (b) A computer program that translates and executes each source language expression before translating and executing the next one.

Interrecord gap: Lengths of unrecorded magnetic tape inserted between records or groups of records. Such spacing facilitates tape start-stop operations.

Interrupt: To temporarily disrupt the normal execution of a program by a special signal from the computer.

Inventory management: A term applied to the daily and periodic bookkeeping commonly associated with inventory control and forecasting the future needs of items or groups of items.

I-O: An abbreviation for Input-Output.

IOCS: Input-Output Control System.

Job: A specified group of tasks prescribed as a unit of work for a computer.

Job Control Language (JCL): Commands used as a means of communication with the computer. Through the JCL statements, the computer operator or user can tell the computer what options are desired for a particular task.

K: When referring to storage capacity, 2^{10}; in decimal notation, 1 024.

Kelvin: The unit of temperature measurement of the SI, for normal use expressed in degrees Celsius.

Key: One or more characters within a data record used to identify the record or to control its use.

Keyboard: A group of marked levers operated manually for recording characters.

Keypunch: A keyboard-operated device which is used to punch holes in punch cards to represent data.

Keypunching: The process by which original, or source data is recorded in punch cards.

Kilo: Metric prefix, means 1 000 times, (10^3)

Kilogram: The base unit of mass in the SI.

Krypton 86: A colorless inert gaseous element. 1 650 763.73 wavelengths of the orange-red line produced by krypton 86 is the basis for defining the meter of the SI metric system. This length is precisely reproducible in a laboratory and therefore is a desirable way to define an international unit of measure.

Label: An identifier or name which is used in a computer program to identify or describe an instruction, a message, data values, a record, an item, or a file.

Language: A set of representations, conventions, and rules used to convey information.

Leading edge: The edge of a punched card which first enters the card reader.

Least significant: The character or bit in the rightmost position of a number.

Left-justified: The aligning of a group of characters according to the leftmost (most significant) characters.

Leibniz, Baron von (1646–1716): A German mathematician who invented a calculating machine called a "stepped reckoner" (in 1672) which could add, subtract, and multiply. The machine performed addition and subtraction in the same manner as Pascal's machine; however, additional gears were included in the machine which enabled it to multiply directly.

Library: A collection of standard, proven routines and subroutines which are accumulated and stored on magnetic tapes, magnetic discs, or magnetic drums for future use.

Library routine: A checked-out routine that is maintained in a program library.

Light pen: A stylus used with CRT display devices to add, modify, and delete information on the face of the CRT screen.

Line printer: An output unit used to record computer output in the form of printed characters.

Liter: A metric unit of liquid capacity equal to one cubic decimeter.

Location: See *Storage location*.

Logic: (a) The science dealing with the formal principles of reasoning and thought. (b) The basic principles and application of truth tables and the interconnection between logical elements which are both required for arithmetic computation in an automatic data processing system.

Logical decision: Generally a decision as to which one of two possible courses of action is to be followed.

Logical design: (a) The planning of a data processing system prior to its detailed engineering design. (b) The synthesizing of a network of logical elements to perform a specified function.

Logical record: A collection of fields independent of their physical environment.

Logical value: A value which may be either "true" or "false" depending on the result of a particular logical decision.

Loop: A sequence of program instructions which are repeated until a predetermined terminal condition is achieved.

Low order: The rightmost (least significant) digit in a number.

Low order column: The rightmost (highest numbered) column of a punch card field.

Low-level language: A computer programming language which is closely related to the internal binary language of a digital computer. Assembly language is an example of this type of language.

LPM: Lines Per Minute.

LSI: Large Scale Integration. Logic used in microprocessors and many newer computers.

Machine address: Same as *Absolute address*.

Machine independent: A term used to indicate that a program is developed in terms of the problem rather than in terms of the characteristics of the computer system.

Machine instruction: An instruction that a machine can recognize and execute.

Machine language: Basic language of a computer. Programs written in machine language require no further interpretation by a computer.

Macro instruction: An instruction in a source language that is equivalent to a specified sequence of machine instructions.

Magnetic core: A tiny doughnut-shaped piece of magnetizable material capable of storing one binary digit.

Magnetic core plane: A network of magnetic cores, each of which represents one core common to each storage location.

Magnetic core storage: A system of storage in which data is represented in binary form by means of the directional flow of magnetic fields in tiny doughnut-shaped arrays of magnetic cores.

Magnetic disk unit: A device used to read and write data on thin magnetic disks whose surfaces have been coated with a magnetizable material.

Magnetic drum unit: A device used to read and write data on a cylinder whose surface is covered with a magnetizable material.

Magnetic film storage: A storage device that uses 35mm magnetic film which is contained on a spool. The spool may be loaded onto a film handler unit.

Magnetic ink: An ink that can be magnetized. It is used for printing magnetic characters on forms such as checks, utility bills, invoices, and so forth. These magnetic characters are subsequently read by magnetic ink character-reading equipment.

Magnetic tape unit: A device used to read and write data in the form of magnetic spots on reels of tape coated with a magnetizable material.

Main frame: The part of the computer that contains the arithmetic unit, internal storage unit, and control functions. Same as the Central Processing Unit.

Main storage: See *Internal storage.*

Maintenance: Tests, adjustments repairs, or replacements that keep hardware and/or software in proper working order.

Malfunction: A failure in the operation of the hardware of a computer or computer peripheral.

Management information system: Abbreviated MIS. An all-inclusive system designed to provide instant data to management for effective and efficient business operation.

Manipulation: The actual work performed on source data processing.

Mark I: The first electromechanical digital computer. It was built in 1944 at Harvard University, under the direction of Howard Aiken. The Mark I was also called the Automatic Sequence Controlled Calculator.

Mark-sense card: A card designed to allow entering data on it with an electrographic pencil.

Mass storage: See *Direct access storage.*

Master file: A main reference file of data.

Matching: A data processing operation where two files are checked to determine if there is a corresponding card or group of cards in each file.

Mathematical model: A mathematical representation of a process, device, concept, or system.

Matrix printer: A high-speed printer that prints character-like configurations of dots.

Mauchly, John: Co-inventor of the ENIAC, the first electronic digital computer.

Medium: The physical substance upon which data is recorded—for example, magnetic tape, punch cards, and paper tape.

Memory: A term often used to refer to a computer's storage facility. See *Storage.*

Memory protection: See *Storage protection.*

Merge: To combine items into one sequenced file from two or more similarly sequenced files without changing the order of the items.

Meter: Base unit of length in the SI, approximately equal to 1.1 yards.

Metric System: Measurement system developed in France at the time of the French Revolution, based primarily on the meter, a length defined at that time as one ten millionth of the earth's circumference.

Length			*Mass (weight)*			*Capacity*		
kilometer	km	1 000 m	kilogram	kg	1 000 g	kiloliter	kl	1 000 l
hectometer	hm	100 m	hectogram	hg	100 g	hectoliter	hl	100 l
dekameter	dam	10 m	dekagram	dag	10 g	dekaliter	dal	10 l
meter	m	1 m	gram	g	1 g	liter	l	1 l
decimeter	dm	0.1 m	decigram	dg	0.1 g	deciliter	dl	0.1 l
centimeter	cm	0.01 m	centigram	cg	0.01 g	centiliter	cl	0.01 l
millimeter	mm	0.001 m	milligram	mg	0.001 g	milliliter	ml	0.001 l

Metric System, International (Systeme International d'Unites or SI): The modern version of the metric system currently in wide use in the world. It is based on 7 base units: meter, kilogram, second, ampere, kelvin (degree Celsius), candela, and mole.

Metric Ton: Measure of weight equal to 1 000 kilograms or about 2 200 pounds.

MICR: Magnetic Ink Character Recognition. A system of coding in which numeric and special characters are printed with magnetizable ink.

Microcomputer: A small computer consisting of a central processing unit with about 1 024 words of memory and costing about $1 000 or less. A microcomputer contains at least one microprocessor. It functions much the same way as a minicomputer.

Microelectronics: The field which deals with techniques for producing miniature circuits—for example, integrated circuits, thin film techniques, and solid logic modules.

Microfilm: A photocopy process of reproduction that is especially useful as a medium for the storage of permanent and semi-permanent data.

Microprocessor: Usually an LSI, MSI, or SSJ transistor logic circuits on boards. An example is the 8080 chip manufactured by Intel.

Microsecond: One millionth of a second. Abbreviated *us.*

Millisecond: One thousandth of a second. Abbreviated *ms.*

Minicomputer: Small, relatively inexpensive digital computers.

Mistake: A human failing—for example, faulty arithmetic, incorrect keypunching, incorrect formula, or incorrect computer instructions. Mistakes are sometimes called gross errors to distinguish from rounding and truncation errors. Thus, computers malfunction and people make mistakes. Computers do not make mistakes and people do not malfunction, in the strict senses of the words. Mistakes in a computer program are often referred to as "bugs."

Model: See *Mathematical model.*

Modem: A contraction of MOdulator DEModulator. Its function is to interface with data processing devices and convert data to a form compatible for sending and receiving on transmission facilities.

Monolithic integrated circuit: A class of integrated circuits wherein the substrate is an active material such as the semiconductor silicon.

MOS: Metal oxide semiconductor chip. Used in the memories of modern computers.

Most significant: The leftmost digit in a number.

MSI: Medium Scale Integration. Logic used in many newer computers.

Multilevel address: Same as *Indirect address.*

Multiplex: To interleave or simultaneously transmit two or more messages on a single channel.

Multiprocessing: Independent and simultaneous processing accomplished by a computer configuration consisting of more than one arithmetic and logic unit, each being capable of accessing a common memory.

Multiprogramming: Pertaining to the concurrent execution of two or more programs by a computer. The programs operate in an interleaved manner within one computer system.

Nanosecond: One billionth of a second. One thousandth of a millionth of a second. Abbreviated *ns.*

Napier, John (1550–1617): A Scottish aristocrat who made many contributions to mathematics and computing. He invented logarithms, created a calculating device known as Napier's bones, and improved the abacus.

Napier's bones: A set of numbering rods which are used to multiply, divide, and extract roots. The calculating rods were developed by John Napier in 1614, and were used by William Oughtred in 1630 in the invention of the slide rule.

NBS: National Bureau of Standards.

Network: The interconnection of a number of points by data communication facilities.

Nonvolatile storage: A storage media which retains its data in the absence of power.

Null: An absence of information, as contrasted with zero (a number) or blank (for the presence of no-information).

Number: The symbols used to represent a value in a numbering system.

Number base: See *Radix*.

Numeralization: Representation of alphabetic data through the use of digits.

Obey: The process whereby a computer carries out an operation as specified by one or more of the instructions forming the program currently in execution.

Object program: A computer program in the internal language of a particular computer; the machine language equivalent of a source program. Contrasted with *Source program.*

Octal: A numbering system based on a radix of eight.

Octal point: The point that separates the fractional part of an octal number from the integer part.

Off-line: Peripheral units which operate independently of the central processing unit; devices not under the control of the central processing unit.

On-line: Peripheral devices operating under the direct control of the central processing unit.

Open shop: A computer installation at which computer operation can be performed by a qualified person. Contrasted with *Closed shop.*

Operand: A unit of data to be operated upon.

Operating system: Software which controls the execution of computer programs and which may provide scheduling, input-output control, compilation, data management, debugging, storage assignment, accounting, and other similar functions.

Operation: Any defined action.

Operation code: The portion of an instruction which designates the operation to be performed by a computer—e.g., add, subtract, or move. Also called a "command."

Operator: See *Computer operator.*

Optical character reader: See *Character reader.*

Optical scanning: The translation of printed or handwritten characters into machine language.

Optimize: To rearrange instructions and/or data in storage to minimize time requirements.

Origination: Determining the type, nature, and origin of some documents.

Output: Data transferred from a computer's internal storage unit to storage or an output device.

Output unit: A device capable of recording data coming from a computer's internal storage unit—e.g., card punch, line printer, cathode ray tube display, magnetic disk, or teletypewriter.

Overflow: The result of some number exceeding the capacity of one of the storage registers in the central processing unit.

Packing density: The number of useful storage elements per unit of dimension—e.g., the number of bits per inch stored on a magnetic tape.

Paper tape: A continuous strip of paper into which data is recorded as a series of holes along its length. Data is read by a paper tape reader sensing the pattern of holes which represent coded data.

Paper tape code: The system of coding which is used to relate the patterns of holes in paper tape to the alphanumeric characters they represent.

Paper tape punch: An output unit used to encode data in paper tape.

Paper tape reader: An input unit used to sense information coded in paper tape.

Parallel reading: Row-by-row reading of a data card.

Parameter: A variable that is given a constant value for a specific purpose or process. Parameters are often used in computer programs to identify data values.

Parity bit: A binary digit added to a group of bits to make the count of all on-bits odd or even in order to conform with the design of the machine.

Parity check: A check which determines whether the number of ones in a character, byte, or word is odd or even. Also called "odd-even check."

Pascal, Blaise (1623–1662): A French mathematician who built the first desk-calculator type of adding machine in 1642. This device represented the numbers from zero to nine with teeth on gears. The machine could perform addition and subtraction. It was later modified by other scientists to perform multiplication by repeated addition. The principle of using repeated addition and subtraction is used in modern digital computers to perform multiplication and division operations.

Pass: A complete cycle of reading, processing, and writing—that is, a machine run.

Patch: A section of coding that is inserted into a program to correct a mistake or to alter the program.

Peripheral Equipment: The auxiliary machines which may be placed under the control of a central processing unit. Examples of this are card readers, card punches, magnetic tape transports, CRT display units, paper tape readers and punches, typewriters, and high-speed printers. Peripheral equipment may be used on-line or off-line depending upon computer design, job requirements, and economics. See *Input unit, Output unit,* and *Storage device.*

Picosecond: One trillionth of a second; one millionth of a millionth of a second. Abbreviated *ps.*

PL/I: A general-purpose programming language initially specified for the IBM System/360 computer, however it is now available on several machines. The language may be used for solving many types of problems: scientific, business, control, simulation, medical, educational, etc.

Plotter: See *Digital plotter.*

Plugboard: A removable patch panel containing an arrangement of plugs used to set up

Point-of-Sale (POS) Terminal: An intelligent input-output device that is used to capture data in retail stores; i.e., supermarkets or department stores. POS is a term used to indicate that data regarding a sale is entered directly into the computerized system without being converted to another form.

POL: Acronym for Procedure-Oriented Language and Problem-Oriented Language.

Powers code: A punched card code designed by James Powers for the 1910 census.

Precision: The degree of exactness with which a quantity is stated. The result of a calculation may have more precision than it has accuracy; for example, the true value of pi to six significant digits is 3.14159; the value 3.14162 is precise to six digits, given to six digits, but is accurate only to about five.

Preventive maintenance: The process used in a computer system which attempts to keep equipment in continuous operating condition by detecting, isolating, and correcting failures before occurrence. It involves cleaning and adjusting the equipment as well as testing the equipment under both normal and marginal conditions.

Primary storage: See *Internal storage.*

Prime shift: A working shift which coincides with the normal business hours of an organization.

Printer: See *Line printer.*

Problem definition: The formulation of the logic used to define a problem. A description of a task to be performed.

Problem-oriented language: A programming language designed for the convenient expression of a given class of problems—e.g., GPSS and COGO.

Procedure: A precise step-by-step method for effecting a solution to a problem.

Procedure-oriented language: A programming language designed for the convenient expression of procedures used in the solution of a wide class of problems—e.g., FORTRAN, COBOL, APL, and PL/I.

Process: A general term covering such terms as compile, compare, compute, assemble, and interpret.

Processor: (a) The program that translates a source program into object language—e.g., a compiler. (b) A computer.

Program: All of the instructions required to solve a specific problem on a computer.

Program card: A card which is punched with specific coding and is used to control the automatic operations of keypunches and verifiers.

Program control: A system in which a digital computer is used to direct the operation of the system.

Program flowchart: See *Flowchart.*

Program generator: See *Generator.*

Program language: A language which is used by computer users to write computer programs.

Program specifications: A document which identifies the data requirements of a system, files required, input-output specifications, and the processing details.

Programmer: See *Computer programmer.*

Programming: The process of translating a problem from its physical environment to a language that a computer can understand and obey. The process of planning the procedure for solving a problem. This may involve, among other things, an analysis of the problem, preparation of a flowchart, coding of the problem, establishing input-output formats, establishing testing and checkout procedures, allocation of storage, preparation of documentation, and supervision of the running of the program on a computer.

Programming analyst: See *Analyst.*

Programming language: A language used to prepare computer programs.

Pseudo-code: An arbitrary system of symbols used in programming languages to represent operators, operands, operations, index registers, and so forth.

Pseudo-instruction: (1) A symbolic representation in some assemblers or in a compiler or interpreter. (2) A group of characters which have the same general form as a computer instruction, but are never executed by the computer as an actual instruction.

Punch card code: A code used to represent data on cards. See *Hollerith code* and *Powers code.*

Punch tape code: See *Paper tape code.*
Punched card: See *Card.*
Punched paper tape: See *Paper tape.*
Punching station: The area on the card punch and the keypunch where a card is aligned
for the punching process.

Query: To ask for information.
Queue: A group of items waiting to be acted upon by the computer. The arrangement of
items determines the processing priority.

Radix: The quantity of characters or digit symbols required by a number system. Same
as base.

System	Radix
Binary	2
Octal	8
Decimal	10
Hexadecimal	16

Random-access storage: See *Direct-access storage.*
Rank: To arrange in an ascending or descending series according to importance.
Raw data: Data which has not been processed.
Read: To sense data from an input medium such as punched cards, magnetic tape,
punched paper tape, or MICR form.
Reader: Any device capable of transcribing data from an input medium.
Reader sorter: An input device used to sense MICR coded data.
Reading station: The part of a keypunch where a data card is aligned for reading by a
sensing mechanism.
Real-time system: A system where transactions are processed as they occur.
Record: A group of related items of data treated as a unit; e.g., the Inventory Master
Record. A complete set of such records form a file.
Record length: A measure of the size of a record, usually specified in units such as
words, bytes, or characters.
Recording: The process by which an input unit facilitates the presentation of source data
for processing.
Register: A temporary storage device used by the computer to store a specified amount
of data, such as one word.
Reliability: A measure of the ability to function without failure.
Relocate: To move a routine from one portion of storage to another and to adjust the
necessary address references so that the routine, in its new location, can be
executed.
Remote processing: The processing of computer programs through an input-output device that is remotely connected to a computer system.
Remote station: An input-output device that is located at a remote distance from a computer system. It is used to input programs and data to a computer and to
accept computed answers from a computer. Also called a "remote terminal."
Remote terminal: See *Remote station.*
Repertoire: The complete set of instructions that belongs to a specific computer or family of computers.

Report generator: A technique for producing complete data processing reports giving only a description of the desired content and format of the output records and certain information concerning the input file.

Reproduce: To copy information on a similar media—for example, to produce a duplicate card deck from a deck of punched cards.

Reproducer: See *Reproducing punch.*

Reproducing punch: A device that can be used to reproduce the punches in one card deck into another deck of cards. It can also be used to compare two decks of cards to insure that they are punched the same. Also called a *Reproducer.*

Rerun: To repeat all or part of a program on a computer.

Response time: The amount of time that elapses between the presentation of a transaction to the system and the completion of the processing of that transaction.

Rewind: To return a magnetic tape to its starting position on the tape.

Right justification: The aligning of a group of characters according to the rightmost (least significant) characters.

Routine: A set of functionally related instructions which directs the computer to carry out a desired operation. A subdivision of a program.

Row: (a) The horizontal members of one line of an array. (b) One of the horizontal lines of punching positions on a punched card.

RPG: Report Program Generator. A language designed with built-in logic to produce report-writing programs given input and output descriptions.

Run: A single, continuous performance of a computer program.

Sampling: Obtaining a value of a variable at regular or intermittent intervals.

Scatter read–Gather write: "Scatter read" refers to placing information from an input record into nonadjacent storage areas. "Gather write" refers to placing information from nonadjacent storage areas into a single physical record.

Scratchpad: A small, fast storage that is used in some computers in place of registers.

Second: Base unit of time in the SI, also used in our customary English system.

Second generation computers: A class of computers which utilized transistors in their electronic circuitry.

Secondary storage: Devices that are used to store large quantities of data and programs. To be processed, these data and programs must first be loaded into primary storage. Also called *Auxiliary storage.*

Selecting: Extracting certain cards from a deck for a specific purpose without disturbing the sequence in which they were originally filed.

Selection: Choosing between alternative choices.

Semantics: The meaning of a language.

Semiconductor Memory: A computer memory that uses silicon chips: bipolar and metal oxide.

Sense: (a) To examine, particularly according to some defined criterion. (b) To determine the present arrangement of some element of hardware. (c) To read holes punched on a card or tape.

Sequence: An arrangement of items according to a specified set of rules.

Sequence check: A check used to prove that a set of data is arranged in ascending or descending order.

Sequential: Pertaining to the occurrence of events in time sequence, with little or no overlap of events.

Sequential file: A file on which information is stored in the same order in which it is accessed by the central processing unit.

Serial: Pertaining to the sequential occurrence of two or more related activities in a single device.

Serial reading: Column-by-column reading of a punch card.

Service routines: See *Systems programs.*

SI: Standard abbreviation of the International Metric System, used around the world.

Simulate: To represent the functioning of one system by another; that is, to répresent a physical system by the execution of a computer program, or to represent a biological system by a mathematical model.

SLT: Solid Logic Technique. A term coined by IBM to refer to a microelectronic packaging technique for producing a circuit module. The module consists of a tiny chip transistor and diodes made from silicon which are assembled onto a ceramic base, connected by a printed circuit, and encased in plastic.

Software: The computer programs, procedures, and documentation concerned with the operation of a computer system—for example, assemblers, compilers, operating systems, diagnostic routines, program loaders, manuals, library routines, and circuit diagrams. Software is the name given to the programs that cause a computer to carry out particular operations. Contrasted with *Hardware.*

Solid state: The electronic components that convey or control electrons within solid materials—for example, transistors, germanium diodes, and magnetic cores.

Solid state circuit: Components in which all the required transistors, capacitors, etc., are an integral part of the circuitry.

Sort: To arrange numeric or alphabetic data in a given sequence.

Sorter: A machine used to sort punched cards either numerically or alphabetically.

Sort-Merge: To produce a single sequence of items, ordered according to some rule, from two or more previously unordered sequences, without changing the items in size, structure, or total number. Although more than one pass may be required for a complete sort, items are selected during each pass on the basis of the entire key.

Source computer: A computer used to translate a source program into an object program.

Source deck: A card deck comprising a computer program, in symbolic language.

Source document: An original document from which basic data is extracted—e.g., an invoice, sales slip, or inventory tag.

Source language: The original form in which a program is prepared prior to processing by the computer—e.g., FORTRAN or assembly language.

Source program: A computer program written in a symbolic programming language—e.g., assembly language program, FORTRAN program, COBOL program. A translator is used to convert the source program into an object program that can be executed on a computer. Contrasted with *Object program.*

Special character: A graphic character that is neither a letter nor a digit—e.g., the plus sign and the period.

Special-purpose computer: A computer designed to solve a specific class or narrow range of problems.

Spooling: The process by which various input-output devices appear to be operating simultaneously when actually the system is inputting or outputting data via buffers.

SSI: Small Scale Integration. Logic used in many newer computers.

Stacker: See *Card stacker.*

Standard: An accepted and approved criterion used for writing computer programs, drawing flowcharts, building computers, etc.

Standardize: To establish standards or to cause conformity with established standards.

Statement: The term used to refer to a particular instruction in a source language program.

Storage: The retention of data so that the data can be obtained at a later time.

Storage allocation: The process of reserving storage areas for instructions or data.

Storage capacity: The number of items of data which a storage device is capable of containing. Frequently defined in terms of computer words, or by a specific number of bytes or characters.

Storage device: A device used for storing data within a computer system—e.g., core storage, magnetic disk unit, magnetic tape unit, magnetic drum unit, etc.

Storage location: A position in storage where a character, byte, or word may be stored.

Storage map: An aid used by the programmer for estimating the proportion of storage capacity to be allocated to data and instructions.

Storage protection: A device which prevents a computer program from destroying or writing in computer storage beyond certain boundary limits.

Storage unit: The portion of the central processing unit which is used to store instructions and data.

Stored-program computer: A computer which utilizes an internal storage unit to store both the data being processed and the instructions for processing the data.

Structured programming: Techniques concerned with improving the programming process through better organization of programs and better programming notation to facilitate correct and clear description of data and control structures.

Stub card: A card containing a detachable stub to serve as a receipt for future reference.

Subprogram: A part of a larger program.

Subroutine: A set of instructions that directs the computer to carry out a well-defined mathematical, logical, or special operation. It may be used over and over in the same program and in different programs. There are two types of subroutines: open and closed. See *Closed subroutine, Open subroutine.*

Subscript: The notation used to refer to a particular element of an array in a programming language—e.g., in the array label TABLE(4), the subscript 4 is used to identify the fourth item in the array named TABLE.

Subscripted variable: A variable which is part of an array and is referred to by using subscript notation—e.g., AREA(4).

Subsystem: Systems subordinate to the main system.

Summarize: To condense a mass of data into a concise and meaningful form.

Summary punch: A card punch operating in conjunction with another machine, usually a tabulator, to punch into cards data which have been summarized or calculated by the other machine.

Symbolic address: An address expressed in symbols.

Symbolic assembly language: See *Assembly language.*

Symbolic coding: Coding in which the instructions are written in non-machine language —i.e., coding using symbolic notation for operators and operands.

System: An organized collection of machines, methods, and men required to accomplish a specific objective.

System/360–System/370: A family of compatible computer systems manufactured by the IBM Corporation.

System flowchart. A graphic representation of the system in which data provided by a source document are converted into final documents. Compare with *Program flowchart.*

Systems analysis: The examination of an activity, procedure, method, technique, or a business to determine what must be accomplished and how the necessary operations may best be accomplished by using data processing equipment.

Systems analyst: A person skilled in solving problems with a digital computer. He analyzes and develops information systems.

Systems programs: Computer programs provided by a computer manufacturer. Examples are operating systems, assemblers, compilers, debugging aids, input-output programs, etc.

Systems study: The detailed process of determining a set of procedures for using a computer for definite operations, and establishing specifications to be used as a basis for the selection of equipment suitable to the specific needs.

Systems synthesis: The planning of the procedures for solving a problem.

Table lookup: A method of searching a table to locate items of a certain type or value.

Tabulating equipment: Data processing machines which use punched cards for processing of data—e.g., sorter and collator.

Tabulator: A machine which reads information from one medium—for example, cards, paper tape, and magnetic tape—and produces lists, tables, and totals on separate forms or continuous paper.

Tape: A strip of material, which may be punched or coated with a magnetically sensitive substance, and is used for data input, storage, or output. The data are usually stored serially in several channels across the tape transversely to the reading or writing motion. See *Magnetic tape unit* and *Paper tape.*

Tape code: See *Paper tape code.*

Tape record: The data contained between two interrecord gaps.

Telecommunications: Pertaining to the transmission of data over long distances through telephone and telegraph facilities.

Teletypewriter: A keyboard printing unit that is often used to enter information into a computer and to accept output from a computer. The widest usage of the teletypewriter is as an input-output device in minicomputer systems, a remote terminal in a time-sharing system, and an operator console for computer systems.

Terminal: A point in a system or communications network at which data can either enter or leave.

Thin film: A high-speed storage device consisting of a molecular deposit of material on a substrate.

Third generation computers: A class of computers which utilized micro-miniaturized or integrated circuits.

Throughout: The total amount of useful processing carried out by a data processing system in a given time.

Time-sharing: A method of operation whereby a computer system automatically distributes processing time among many users simultaneously.

Trace: An interpretive diagnostic technique which provides an analysis of each executed instruction and writes it on an output device as each instruction is executed.

Track: The path along which data is recorded, as in magnetic disks and magnetic drums.

Trailer record: A record which follows a group of records and contains pertinent data related to the group of records.

Transaction file: A file containing relatively transient data to be processed in combination with a master file.

Transcribe: To copy from one external storage medium to another. The process may involve translation.

Transistor: A solid-state electronic device developed at Bell Telephone Laboratories in 1948.

Translate: To change data from one form of representation to another without significantly affecting the meaning.

Translator: A program which may be used to translate a source program into an object program. See *Compiler, Assembler,* and *Generator.*

Truth table: A Boolean operation table in which the values 0 and 1 given to the variables are interpreted as measuring "true" and "false."

Turing, A. M. (1912–1954): A famous English mathematician and logician who shortly before his death completed the design of one of the world's first modern high-speed digital computers. Turing's paper entitled *Computing Machinery and Intelligence* remains one of the most thorough discussions of the general question, "Can a machine think?"

Twelve-punch: A punch in the top row of a Hollerith punched card. Synonymous with Y-punch.

Typewriter: An input-output device which is capable of being connected to a digital computer and used for communication purposes.

Underpunch: A single punch in any position from row 1 through row 9 of an 80-column punch card.

Unit record: A separate record that is similar in form and content to other records.

UNIVAC: UNIVersal Automatic Computer.

UNIVAC I: The first commercial electronic digital computer. It was used by the Census Bureau for processing some of the data from the 1950 census. Forty-eight of these computers were built.

Update: To search a file, select an entry, perform an operation on the entry, and replace it in the file.

Utility system: A series of programs that perform basic data processing functions that are required by many different tasks placed upon the system.

Validity Check: A method of detecting unreasonable results produced by a computer.

Variable: A quantity that can assume any of a given set of values.

Variable field length: Pertaining to the property that fields within a machine may have a variable number of bits, bytes, or characters. Contrasted with *Fixed-word length.*

Variable word length: Having the property that a machine word may have a variable number of characters.

Variable-length record file: A file whose records are not uniform in length.

Venn Diagram: A topographical picture of logic, composed of the universal set with overlays of subsets.

Verifier: A machine which is used to check the correctness of manually recorded data.

Verify: (a) To determine whether a data processing operation has been accomplished accurately—e.g., to check the results of keypunching. (b) To check data validity.

Virtual Memory: A technique for managing a limited amount of high-speed memory and a (generally) much larger amount of lower-speed memory in such a way that the distinction is largely transparent to a computer user. The technique entails some means of swapping segments of program and data from the lower-speed memory (which would commonly be a drum or disk) into the high-speed memory, where it would be interpreted as instructions or operated upon as data. The unit of program or data swapped back and forth is called a *page*. The high-speed memory from which instructions are executed is *real memory*, while the lower-speed memory (drums or disks) is called virtual memory.

Volatile storage: A storage medium in which data cannot be retained without continuous power dissipation.

Von Neumann, John (1903–1957): One of the outstanding mathematicians of this century. He built one of the first electronic computers, contributed much to game theory, and introduced the stored program concept.

Wiener, Norbert (1894–1964): An American scientist who coined the term "cybernetics." The founder of a new branch of science, he believed that many thought processes in the human brain could be determined mathematically and adapted for computers. He was a pioneer in the theory of automata.

Word: An ordered set of characters which occupies one storage location and is treated by the computer circuits as a unit. Ordinarily, a word is treated by the control unit as a quantity. Word lengths may be fixed or variable depending on the particular computer.

Word length: The number of bits, bytes, or characters in a word.

Word mark: A bit used to define the length of a word in a variable word length computer.

Write: To transfer information, usually from internal storage to an output device.

X-punch: A punch in the eleventh punching position (row 11) of a Hollerith punched card. Synonymous with eleven-punch.

XY plotter: Same as *Plotter*.

Y-punch: A punch in the twelfth position (row 12) of a Hollerith card. Also called a high-punch. Synonymous with twelve-punch.

Zone punch: A punch in the O, X, or Y row on a Hollerith punched card.

Index